Strategic Intervention Teacher Guide

Grade 6

 Harcourt School Publishers

www.harcourtschool.com

Printed in the United States of America

ISBN 10: 0-15-365515-1
ISBN 13: 978-0-15-365515-9

4 5 6 7 8 9 10 0877 16 15 14 13 12 11 10

CONTENTS

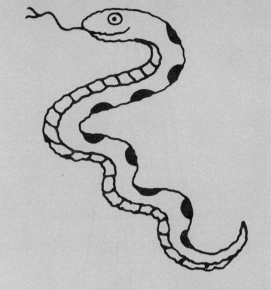

CONTENTS

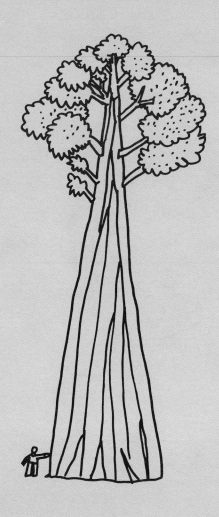

What Are Intervention Strategies?

Intervention strategies are designed to facilitate learning for those students who might experience some difficulty no matter how well we have planned our curriculum. These strategies offer support and guidance to the student who is struggling. The strategies themselves are no mystery. They are based on the same time-honored techniques that effective teachers have used for years—teaching students on their instructional reading level; modeling previewing and predicting; and directed instruction in strategic reading, vocabulary, phonics, fluency, and writing.

Intervention works best in conjunction with a strong core program. For an intervention program to be effective, instruction should focus on specific needs of students, as determined by systematic monitoring of progress.

Components of the Strategic Intervention Resource Kit

The goal of this *Strategic Intervention Resource Kit* is to provide the scaffolding, extra support, and extra reading practice that struggling readers need to succeed. Each kit in grades 2–6 includes the following components:

- *Teacher Guide* with lessons directly aligned with and correlated to the lessons in the *StoryTown* Teacher Edition.

- *Interactive Reader* that provides accessible reading material with built-in support for the student.

- *Skill Cards* to teach each lesson's Focus Skill.

- *Practice Book* with the following practice pages that accompany each lesson:

    - *Fluency Practice Page* with word lists and phrase-cued sentences that reinforce vocabulary and decoding skills and parallel the reading level of the *Interactive Student Edition* selection.

    - *Grammar Practice Page* that reinforces the lesson's grammar skill and can be used as a teacher-directed or independent activity.

    - *Writing Trait Practice Page* that reinforces the writing trait taught in the lesson.

    - *Decoding/Spelling Practice Page* that provides an additional opportunity to practice and apply the lesson's decoding/spelling skill.

- *Teacher Resource Book* with Copying Masters that include Vocabulary Word Cards and activities providing additional reinforcement of decoding/spelling, word attack, comprehension, grammar, and writing skills.

- *Assessment Book* to monitor progress and ensure success.

Using the Strategic Intervention Teacher Guide

The *Strategic Intervention Teacher Guide* gives support for struggling readers in key instructional strands, plus prerequisite phonics skills and oral-reading fluency. Each five-day lesson plan includes the following resources:

- *Vocabulary* lessons and Student-Friendly Explanations to preteach and reteach key vocabulary that appears in the *Interactive Reader* selection.

- *Robust Vocabulary* lessons to enrich students' listening and speaking vocabularies and help them master the language of school.

- *Decoding/Spelling* lessons to systematically preteach and reteach basic phonics skills and connect spelling and phonics.

- *Decoding/Word Attack* lessons to preteach and reteach phonics and word analysis skills.

- *Fluency* activities that reinforce key vocabulary, decoding/spelling, and word attack skills, while providing reading practice and promoting oral reading fluency.

- *Comprehension Focus Skill* lessons to ensure that struggling readers get the in-depth instruction they need to reach grade-level standards.

- *Directed Reading Lesson* for the *Interactive Reader* selection to reinforce basic comprehension skills, using questions and teacher modeling.

- *Interactive Writing Support* that reinforces key writing traits and forms.

- *Review Lessons* that provide cumulative reviews of skills.

Depending on your individual classroom and school schedules, you can tailor the instruction to suit your needs. The following pages show two options for pacing the instruction in this guide.

SUGGESTED LESSON PLANNERS

Grade 6: For Use with *StoryTown*

DAY 1

VOCABULARY

- Reteach the Vocabulary Words that were introduced on Day 1 in *StoryTown*.

COMPREHENSION

 Preteach the skill that will be introduced on Day 2 in *StoryTown*.

DECODING/SPELLING

- Reteach the skill that was introduced on Day 1 in *StoryTown*.

GRAMMAR/WRITING

- Preteach the aspect of the grammar skill that will be introduced on Day 2 in *StoryTown*.

FLUENCY

- Begin fluency practice for the current week.

DAY 2

VOCABULARY

- Provide guided practice of the week's Vocabulary Words.

COMPREHENSION

 Read the *Bold Moves* selection.

- Build Background
- Monitor Comprehension
- Have students answer the *Think Critically* questions

DECODING/SPELLING

- Reteach the decoding/spelling skill.

GRAMMAR/WRITING

- Preteach the aspect of the grammar skill that will be introduced on Day 3 in *StoryTown*.

FLUENCY

- Continue fluency practice for the current week.

Grade 6 OPTION: As a stand-alone program

DAY 1

VOCABULARY

- Reteach the Vocabulary Words.

COMPREHENSION

 Reteach the comprehension focus skill.

DECODING/SPELLING

- Reteach the decoding/spelling skill.

GRAMMAR/WRITING

- Teach another aspect of the grammar/writing skill.

FLUENCY

- Begin fluency practice for the current week.

DAY 2

VOCABULARY

- Provide guided practice of the Vocabulary Words.

COMPREHENSION

Read the *Bold Moves* selection.

- Build Background
- Monitor Comprehension
- Have students answer the *Think Critically* questions

DECODING/SPELLING

- Reteach the decoding/spelling skill.

GRAMMAR/WRITING

- Teach another aspect of the grammar/writing skill.

FLUENCY

- Continue fluency practice for the current week.

DAY 3

COMPREHENSION

- Preteach the skill that will be introduced on Day 4 in *StoryTown*.
- Reread and Summarize the *Bold Moves* selection.

DECODING/SPELLING

- Reteach the skill that is reviewed on Day 3 in *StoryTown*.

BUILD ROBUST VOCABULARY

- Teach additional vocabulary from the *Bold Moves* selection.

GRAMMAR/WRITING

- Reteach the writing trait that is taught this week in *StoryTown*.

FLUENCY

- Continue fluency practice for the current week.

DAY 4

COMPREHENSION

- Reteach the skill that was introduced on Day 4 in *StoryTown*.

DECODING/SPELLING

- Provide guided practice of the skill that is reviewed on Day 4 in *StoryTown*.

BUILD ROBUST VOCABULARY

- Review additional vocabulary from the *Bold Moves* selection.

GRAMMAR/WRITING

- Reteach the writing form that is taught this week in *StoryTown*.

FLUENCY

- Continue fluency practice for the current week.

DAY 5

for next week's *StoryTown* lesson

VOCABULARY

- Preteach the Vocabulary Words that will be introduced next week in *StoryTown*.

COMPREHENSION

- Preteach the skill that will be introduced on Day 2 next week in *StoryTown*.

DECODING/WORD ATTACK

- Preteach the skill that will be introduced on Day 1 next week in *StoryTown*.

DECODING/SPELLING

- Preteach the skill that will be introduced on Day 1 next week in *StoryTown*.

GRAMMAR/WRITING

- Preteach the aspect of the grammar skill that will be introduced on Day 1 next week in *StoryTown*.

FLUENCY

- Evaluate students' fluency performance for the current week.

DAY 3

COMPREHENSION

- Teach the comprehension skill.
- Reread and Summarize the *Bold Moves* selection.

DECODING/SPELLING

- Reteach the decoding/spelling skill.

BUILD ROBUST VOCABULARY

- Teach additional vocabulary from the *Bold Moves* selection.

GRAMMAR/WRITING

- Teach the writing trait. (This is labeled Reteach in our actual lessons.)

FLUENCY

- Continue fluency practice for the current week.

DAY 4

COMPREHENSION

- Reteach the comprehension skill.

DECODING/SPELLING

- Provide guided practice of the decoding/spelling skill.

BUILD ROBUST VOCABULARY

- Review additional vocabulary from the *Bold Moves* selection.

GRAMMAR/WRITING

- Teach the writing form. (This is reteach in our lessons.)

FLUENCY

- Continue fluency practice for the current week.

DAY 5

VOCABULARY

- Teach this week's Vocabulary Words.

COMPREHENSION

- Teach the comprehension focus skill.

DECODING/WORD ATTACK

- Teach the decoding/word attack skill.

GRAMMAR/WRITING

- Teach one aspect of the grammar/writing skill.

FLUENCY

- Evaluate students' fluency performance for the current week.

Fluency

"So that students will understand why rereading is done, we have involved them in a discussion of how athletes develop skill at their sports. This discussion brings out the fact that athletes spend considerable time practicing basic skills until they develop speed and smoothness at their activity. Repeated readings uses this same type of practice."

S. Jay Samuels
The Reading Teacher, February 1997
(originally published January 1979)

In the years since S. Jay Samuels pioneered the technique of repeated reading to improve fluency, continuing research has confirmed and expanded upon his observations. Ideally, oral reading mirrors the pacing, smoothness, and rhythms of normal speech. Fluency in reading can be defined as a combination of these key elements.

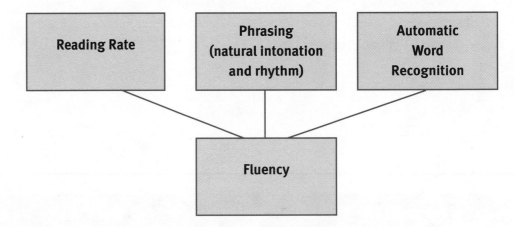

How Do Students Become More Fluent Readers?

Research and the experiences of classroom teachers make it clear that certain practices can and do lead to significant improvements in reading fluency. Techniques that have been shown to be successful include

- **Teacher modeling**
- **Repeated reading of short passages**
- **Daily monitoring of progress**

A program that incorporates these three elements will help struggling readers gain fluency and improve their comprehension.

Fluency Practice and Assessment

The plan for each lesson in the Strategic *Intervention Teacher Guide* includes daily fluency practice that incorporates the elements of teacher modeling, repeated reading, and self-monitoring.

The fluency portion of the lesson is designed to be completed in five minutes, though you may adjust the time according to students' needs and as your schedule allows.

About the *Strategic Intervention Practice Book* Fluency Page

The *Strategic Intervention Practice Book* Fluency page is designed to correlate with the phonics elements taught in the *Strategic Intervention Teacher Guide*, as well as with key vocabulary from the *Interactive Reader* selections. A total of twenty words that fall into these three categories are listed at the top of the Fluency page for each lesson.

On the bottom half of the page, you will find a set of numbered sentences that incorporate the words from the lists. Slashes are used to divide each sentence into phrases. To help students improve natural phrasing, model reading each phrase smoothly, as a unit, and encourage students to follow the same procedure in their repeated-reading practice.

This chart gives an overview of the fluency portion of the Intervention Program.

Day	Materials	Explanation
1	*Practice Book* Fluency page	Teacher models reading aloud word lists. Students then practice reading aloud the word lists with partners.
2	*Practice Book* Fluency page	Teacher models reading aloud the phrased fluency sentences. Students then practice repeated rereadings of the sentences with partners.
3	*Practice Book* Fluency page	Students read the fluency sentences to improve pacing and tone.
4	*Interactive Reader* selection	Students read aloud a selected short passage from the *Interactive Reader* selection three times, monitoring their progress after each reading.
5	*Interactive Reader* selection	Students read the same passage aloud to the teacher. Both teacher and student assess the student's progress.

Rhyming Activities

Rhyme-a-Day

Start each day by teaching students a short rhyme. Periodically throughout the day, repeat the rhyme with them. Say the rhyme together, have them say it alone, pause and leave out words for them to insert, or ask volunteers to say each line. Students will develop a repertoire of favorite rhymes that can serve as a storehouse for creating their own rhymes.

Rhyme Sort

Place on a tabletop pictures of items that rhyme. Have students sort the pictures into groups, according to names that rhyme. You also might want to try an "open sort" by having students create categories of their own to sort the picture cards.

Rhyme Pairs

To assess students' ability to recognize pairs of words that rhyme, say a list of twenty or more pairs of words. Half of the word pairs should rhyme. Students tell which word pairs rhyme and which do not. Have students indicate *yes* with a card marked *Y* or another symbol.

What Word Rhymes?

Use theme-related words from across the curriculum to focus on words that rhyme. For example, if you are studying animals, ask: **What rhymes with snake? bear? fox? deer? ant? frog? goat? hen? fish? whale?** If a special holiday is approaching, ask: **What rhymes with flag, year, or heart?** Use these word groups for sound-matching, sound-blending, or sound-segmenting activities.

Sound-Matching Activities

Odd Word Out

Form a group of four students. Say a different word for each group member to repeat. The student with the word that does not begin (or end) like the other words must step out of the group. For example, say *basket, bundle, cost,* and *bargain*. The student whose word is *cost* steps out of the group. The odd-word-out player then chooses three students to form a new group and the procedure continues.

Head or Toes, Finger or Nose?

Teach students the following rhyme. Be sure to say the sound, not the letter, at the beginning of each line. Recite the rhyme together several times while touching the body parts.

> **/h/ is for *head*.**
> **/t/ is for *toes*.**
> **/f/ is for *finger*.**
> **/n/ is for *nose*.**

Explain that you will say a list of words. Students are to touch the head when you say a word that begins with /h/, the toes for the words that begin with /t/, a finger for words that begin with /f/, and the nose for words that begin with /n/. Say words such as *fan, ten, horn, hat, feet, nut, ham, nest, toy, fish, note, tub, nail, time, fox,* and *house*.

Souvenir Sound-Off

Have students imagine that a friend has traveled to a special place and has brought them a gift. Recite the following verse, and ask a volunteer to complete it. The names of the traveler, the place, and the gift must begin with the same letter and sound.

- My friend [person]
- who went to [place]
- brought me back a [gift].

Example: *My friend Hannah*
who went to Hawaii
brought me back a hula skirt.

After repeating this activity a few times, ask partners to recite the missing words. As an alternative, you can focus on words with initial blends and digraphs. Students can focus on social studies and phonics skills by using a world map or globe to find names of places.

Match My Word

Have students match beginning or ending sounds in words. Seat students in pairs, sitting back to back. One student in each pair will say a word. His or her partner will repeat the word and say another word that begins with the same sound. Repeat the activity, reversing the roles of partners and focusing on ending sounds.

Sound Isolation Activities

What's Your N-N-N-Name?

Invite students to say their names by repeating the initial phoneme in the name, such as *M-M-M-M-Michael,* or by drawing out and exaggerating the initial sound, such as *Sssss-erena*. Have students say the names of others, such as friends or family members.

Singling Out the Sounds

Form groups of three students. Students can decide who will name the beginning, the middle, and the ending sounds in one-syllable picture names. Given a set of pictures, the group identifies a picture name, and then each group member isolates and says the sound he or she is responsible for. Group members can check one another's responses.

Chain Reaction

Have students form a circle. The student who begins will say a word, such as *bus*. The next student must isolate the ending sound in the word, /s/, and say a word that begins with that sound, such as *sun*. If the word is correct, the two students link arms, and the procedure continues with the next student isolating the final sound in *sun* and giving a word that begins with /n/. You will want all students to be able to link arms and complete the chain, so provide help when needed.

Sound-Addition, Deletion, or Substitution Activities

Add-a-Sound

Explain that the beginning sound is missing in each of the words you will say. Students must add the missing sound and say the new word. Some examples follow. Add:

/b/ to *at* (*bat*)	/f/ to *ox* (*fox*)
/k/ to *art* (*cart*)	/f/ to *ace* (*face*)
/p/ to *age* (*page*)	/h/ to *air* (*hair*)
/w/ to *all* (*wall*)	/j/ to *am* (*jam*)
/r/ to *an* (*ran*)	/b/ to *and* (*band*)
/d/ to *ark* (*dark*)	/f/ to *arm* (*farm*)
/d/ to *ash* (*dash*)	/s/ to *it* (*sit*)
/s/ to *oak* (*soak*)	/h/ to *eel* (*heel*)
/b/ to *end* (*bend*)	/m/ to *ice* (*mice*)
/n/ to *ear* (*near*)	/f/ to *east* (*feast*)
/b/ to *each* (*beach*)	/f/-/l/ to *at* (*flat*)
/sk/ to *ate* (*skate*)	/t/-/r/ to *eat* (*treat*)
/g/-/r/ to *ill* (*grill*)	/sh/ to *out* (*shout*)
/p/-/l/ to *ant* (*plant*)	

Remove-a-Sound

Reinforce rhyme while focusing on the deletion of initial sounds in words to form new words. Ask students to say:

hat without the /h/ (*at*)

fin without the /f/ (*in*)

tall without the /t/ (*all*)

box without the /b/ (*ox*)

will without the /w/ (*ill*)

peach without the /p/ (*each*)

nice without the /n/ (*ice*)

meat without the /m/ (*eat*)

band without the /b/ (*and*)

Continue with other words in the same manner.

Mixed-Up Tongue Twisters

Think of a simple tongue twister, such as *ten tired toads*. Say the tongue twister for students, but replace the initial letter in each word with another letter, such as *p*, to create nonsense words: *pen pired poads*. Explain to students that you need their help to make sense of the tongue twister by having them replace /p/ with /t/ and say the new tongue twister. Use the same procedure for other tongue twisters.

- *copper coffee cups*
- *nine new nails*
- *two ton tomatoes*
- *long lean legs*

Then ask partners to continue this activity together.

The Name Game

Occasionally when a new sound is introduced, students might enjoy substituting the first sound of their names for the name of a classmate. Students will have to stop and think when they call one another by name, including the teacher. For example, Paul would call Ms. Vega *Ms. Pega*; *Carmen* becomes *Parmen*; *Jason* becomes *Pason*; and *Kiyo* becomes *Piyo*. Just make certain beforehand that all names will be agreeable.

Take Away

New words can be formed by deleting an initial phoneme from a word. Have students say the new word that is formed.

flake without the /f/ (*lake*)
bring without the /b/ (*ring*)
swing without the /s/ (*wing*)
swell without the /s/ (*well*)
shrink without the /sh/ (*rink*)
shred without the /sh/ (*red*)
spread without the /s/-/p/ (*read*)
gloom without the /g/ (*loom*)
fright without the /f/ (*right*)
snout without the /s/-/n/ (*out*)
score without the /s/ (*core*)
slip without the /s/ (*lip*)
bride without the /b/ (*ride*)
block without the /b/ (*lock*)
spoke without the /s/ (*poke*)
snail without the /s/ (*nail*)

Sound Blending Activities

I'm Thinking of a Word

Play a guessing game with students. Tell students that you will give them clues to a word. Have them listen closely to blend the sounds to say the word.

- I'm thinking of something that has words—/b/-/oo/-/k/. (*book*)
- I'm thinking of something that comes in bunches—/g/-/r/-/ā/-/p/-/s/. (*grapes*)
- I'm thinking of something that shines in the night sky—/s/-/t/-/är/-/z/. (*stars*)
- I'm thinking of something that moves very slowly—/s/-/n/-/ā/-/l/. (*snail*)

What's in the Box?

Place various objects in a box or bag. Play a game with students by saying: **In this box is a /k/-/r/-/ā/-/o/-/n/. What do you think is in the box?** (crayon) Continue with the other objects in the box, segmenting the phonemes for students to blend and say the word.

Sound-Segmenting Activities

Sound Game

Have partners play a word-guessing game using a variety of pictures that represent different beginning sounds. One student says the name on the card, separating the beginning sound, as in *p-late*. The partner blends the sounds and guesses the word. After students are proficient with beginning sounds, you could have them segment all the sounds in a word when they give their clues, as in *d-o-g*.

Count the Sounds

Tell students that you are going to say a word. Have them listen and count the number of sounds they hear in that word. For example, say the word *task*. Have students repeat the word and tell how many sounds they hear. Students should reply *four*.

tone (3)	*four* (3)
great (4)	*peak* (3)
pinch (4)	*sunny* (4)
stick (4)	*clouds* (5)
flake (4)	*feel* (3)
rain (3)	*paint* (4)

The six activities on the following pages provide additional opportunities for vocabulary practice and application. Two activities are offered for individual students, two for pairs of students working together, and two for small groups of three or four students. All require a minimum of preparation and call for materials that are readily available in the classroom.

Personal Glossary

MATERIALS
- paper
- markers
- stapler or simple binding materials

INDIVIDUAL ACTIVITY As students progress through a theme, encourage them to identify new vocabulary that they find particularly interesting or that they think will be especially useful to them. Have individual students create a page for each of the special words they choose. Encourage them to check the spelling of the word and to include the definition and other information they might find helpful, such as the part of speech, how the word is divided into syllables, whether it has a prefix or a suffix, how it is pronounced, synonyms and antonyms, and how the word is related to other words they know. Students can also include example sentences or draw pictures with captions and labels where appropriate.

Upon completion of the theme, have students arrange their pages in alphabetical order and make a cover for their personal glossary. Staple the pages together, or help students use simple materials to bind them. Encourage students to share their personal glossaries with classmates and to use them as a resource for their writing.

Draw the Cat

MATERIALS

- list of Vocabulary Words from a complete theme
- either two sheets of paper and markers or chalk and chalkboard
- dictionary

PARTNER ACTIVITY Pairs of students can play this game on paper or on the board. Players should be designated Player 1 and Player 2. Player 1 begins by choosing a Vocabulary Word from the list for Player 2 to define. If Player 2 defines the word correctly, he or she gets to draw one part of a cat. If Player 2 cannot define the word correctly, he or she cannot draw on that turn. Players take turns choosing words for each other to define and adding parts to their cats each time they define a word correctly. Encourage students to use a dictionary to check definitions as necessary.

The first player to draw a complete cat wins the game. A completed cat drawing has ten parts, to be drawn in this order: (1) head, (2) body, (3) tail, (4) one ear, (5) the other ear, (6) one eye, (7) the other eye, (8) nose, (9) mouth, (10) whiskers.

Who Wants to Win 100?

MATERIALS

- list of Vocabulary Words from a theme
- scoreboard
- chalk
- dictionary

SMALL GROUP ACTIVITY Students play the roles of quizmaster, contestant, "lifeline," and judge. The quizmaster chooses Vocabulary Words from the list for the contestant to define. The contestant earns 25 points for each word he or she defines correctly. If the contestant is not sure about a word, he or she can ask the lifeline for help and still earn 25 points for a correct answer. The judge looks up each word in the dictionary and rules on whether or not the answer is correct, and the quizmaster adds up the points on the scoreboard. When the contestant has earned a total of 100 points, students exchange roles and play another game.

Tally-Ho!

MATERIALS

- list of Vocabulary Words from a theme
- pencil and paper
- dictionary

INDIVIDUAL ACTIVITY Make a list of eight to ten Vocabulary Words that may have given students some difficulty. Have students copy the words from the list and write a definition for each word from memory. Then have them use a dictionary to check their definitions. Tell them to make tally marks to show the number of words they defined correctly.

Then have students copy the words from the list in reverse order, beginning at the bottom. Have them again write a definition for each word from memory, check the definitions in a dictionary, and tally up the number they defined correctly. Tell students to compare this score to their first score to see how much they improved.

Show Time

MATERIALS

- list of Vocabulary Words from a theme
- paper
- pencil

SMALL GROUP ACTIVITY Have groups of students work cooperatively to write and dramatize brief scenes for TV shows that include Vocabulary Words from the theme. Explain that the scenes may be from comedy, drama, documentary, news, or other types of shows. Challenge students to use as many words as possible from the vocabulary list in their scenes. They can keep track of the words they use by checking them off on the list. Give students an opportunity to present their dramatizations for classmates.

Yes or No

MATERIALS

- list of Vocabulary Words from a theme
- scrap paper
- pencils

PARTNER ACTIVITY Display the list of Vocabulary Words where both players can see it. Students take turns choosing a word from the list for each other to guess. The student who is guessing may ask questions about the part of speech, meaning of the word, the number of syllables, whether it has a prefix or a suffix, or any other information they think may help them. However, every question can only be answered with yes or no.

Encourage students to jot down information that they find out about the word that can help narrow down the list. You may want to give examples of questions that players might ask and explain how they can use the information they obtain.

QUESTION: Is the word an adjective?

INFORMATION: If the answer is *yes,* you can rule out all the other words on the list and focus on the adjectives. If the answer is *no,* you can rule out the adjectives and ask questions that will help you narrow the list further.

QUESTION: Does the word have an *-ed* ending?

INFORMATION: If the answer is *no,* you can rule out all words with *-ed* endings. If the answer is *yes,* focus on the words with *-ed* endings. Ask more questions to figure out which of those words is the correct one.

Day 1

30+ Minutes

LESSON 1

The Comic

VOCABULARY

Reteach *hysterical, crestfallen, incapacitated, perishable, lamented, ricocheted, ecstatic, mirth*

COMPREHENSION

 Reteach Plot and Setting

DECODING/SPELLING

Reteach Words with Short Vowels and Vowel Digraphs

GRAMMAR/WRITING

Preteach Sentence Punctuation

FLUENCY

Fluency Practice

Materials Needed: *Bold Moves*

| Student Edition pp. 10–11 | Practice Book p. 3 | Skill Card 1 | Copying Master 2 |

RETEACH

Vocabulary

pp. 10–11

Lesson 1 Vocabulary Read aloud the Vocabulary Words and the Student-Friendly Explanations. Then have students turn to pages 10–11 in their books. Ask a volunteer to read the directions aloud. Point out that students need to choose a word to complete each blank. If students have difficulty choosing the correct word, refer to the Student-Friendly Explanations. After students have completed the pages, have volunteers take turns reading each article aloud. (Answers for pages 10–11: 2. *crestfallen*, 3. *ecstatic*, 4. *hysterical*, 5. *perishable*, 6. *incapacitated*, 7. *lamented*, 8. *ricocheted*)

RETEACH

Comprehension

Skill Card 1

Plot and Setting Have students look at side A of *Skill Card 1: Plot and Setting*. Invite volunteers to read aloud the information at the top. Then ask a volunteer to read the story as students read along. Direct students' attention to the chart. Ask students to identify the setting and the conflict in the story. Discuss how the setting affects the resolution of the conflict.

GUIDED PRACTICE Now have students look at side B of *Skill Card 1: Plot and Setting*. Have students take turns reading the passage. Have students work in pairs to complete the chart with information from the passage. Invite pairs to explain how the setting affects the resolution of the conflict. (Setting: by a pond in a park; Plot Events: Claire gets the ball out of the water, Riley squeezes out the water and moves away from the pond, Riley begins to juggle; Resolution: Riley is able to juggle, but if he drops a ball, it won't go in the water again.)

Decoding/Spelling

Copying Master 2

Words with Short Vowels and Vowel Digraphs   Write *depth* and *feather* on the board, and ask a volunteer to read each word aloud. Explain that both words have the short *e* sound. Underline the vowel and vowel digraph in each word. (e, ea) Point out that some words have a short vowel sound spelled with two vowels. Distribute *Copying Master 2*. Guide students as they read aloud the Spelling Words and identify those that contain a vowel digraph. (against, circuit, biscuit, feather)

Then have students work in pairs to complete the following activity based on the traditional Memory Game. Have pairs make two sets of game cards using the lesson's Spelling Words with the vowels missing; a dash appears in place of each vowel. After a student matches two cards, he or she must supply the correct missing letters to keep the game cards. If the wrong letter is supplied, the opponent gets the game cards and the next turn.

Grammar/Writing

Sentence Punctuation   Have students recall the four kinds of sentences. Write these sentences on the board:

> Help me fix this.   I am not sure.
> Do you know how?   You did it!

Guide students to identify each kind of sentence above. (imperative, declarative, interrogative, exclamatory) Then have them describe the end punctuation for each kind of sentence. Point out that some imperative sentences can also be exclamatory. Tell students that the first word in a sentence is always capitalized, regardless of the kind of sentence it is.

GUIDED PRACTICE   Write these sentences on the board:

> Where is your coat   that's a great idea
> It is red   watch out

Have volunteers identify the kind of sentence and write the correct end punctuation and capitalization. (interrogative, ?; declarative, That's, .; exclamatory, !; exclamatory/imperative, Watch, !]

Student-Friendly Explanations

hysterical A person who is hysterical is in a panic or very excited.

crestfallen Someone who is crestfallen is very disappointed and sad.

incapacitated Someone that is incapacitated is unable to work due to injury.

perishable Food that is perishable goes bad if it is not kept cold.

lamented If you lamented something, you expressed deep sadness because of it.

ricocheted When something ricocheted, it bounced around off other objects.

ecstatic If you are ecstatic, you are extremely happy.

mirth Mirth is a feeling of amusement that causes you to laugh out loud.

Fluency

Practice Book 3

Fluency Practice   Have students turn to *Practice Book* page 3. Read the words in the first column aloud. Invite students to track each word and repeat the words after you. Then have students work in pairs to read the words in the first column aloud to each other. Follow the same procedure with each of the remaining columns. After partners have practiced reading aloud the words in each of the columns, have them practice reading all of the words.

LESSON 1

DAY AT A GLANCE
Day 2

 30+ Minutes

VOCABULARY
Reteach hysterical, crestfallen, incapacitated, perishable, lamented, ricocheted, ecstatic, mirth

COMPREHENSION
"The Comic"
Build Background
Monitor Comprehension
Answers to *Think Critically* **Questions**

DECODING/SPELLING
Reteach Words with Short Vowels and Vowel Digraphs

GRAMMAR/WRITING
Preteach Interjections

FLUENCY
Fluency Practice

Materials Needed: *Bold Moves*

Student Edition pp. 12–19

Practice Book pp. 3, 4

Copying Masters 1, 2

Vocabulary

Lesson 1 Vocabulary Distribute a set of Vocabulary Word Cards to each pair of students. Hold up the card for the first word, and ask a volunteer to read it aloud. Have students repeat the word and hold up the matching card. Give the explanation for the word. Then ask students the questions below, and discuss their responses. Continue for each Vocabulary Word.

Copying Master 1

- Would you become **hysterical** in an emergency? How do you know?
- What would happen to a toy to make a child feel **crestfallen**?
- Does a cold leave you **incapacitated**? Explain.
- Where should you keep **perishable** foods? Why?
- When is a time you **lamented** a change in plans?
- What would happen if a rubber ball **ricocheted** off the walls of a room?
- What gift would make you **ecstatic**? Why?
- When is the last time a movie filled you with **mirth**?

Comprehension

Build Background: "The Comic"
Have students share their experiences watching or performing in talent shows or other student performances. What kinds of acts have they seen? Did everything go according to plan? If not, how did the audience and performers react?

Monitor Comprehension: "The Comic"
pp. 12–13
Read the title of the story aloud. Then have students read pages 12–13 to find out why June is feeling hysterical.

After reading the pages, ask: **Why is June hysterical?** (Possible response: She doesn't have an act, and she thinks she is too dull to be funny.) **DRAW CONCLUSIONS**

Discuss the Stop and Think question on page 12: **Why is Zeke surprised at June's plans?** (Possible response: Zeke is surprised because June is not usually very brave.) Guide students in writing the answer to this question. **CHARACTERS' TRAITS**

Discuss the Stop and Think question on page 13: **How does June see herself?** (Possible response: June sees herself as dull.) **How does Zeke see her?** (Possible response: Zeke sees June as timid but funny.) Guide students in writing the answer to this question. **MAKE COMPARISONS**

Tell students: **Madison tells June that the Take-Two Class Act will be a blast. What does she mean by this?** (She means that it will be a lot of fun.) **FIGURATIVE LANGUAGE**

pp. 14–15

Discuss the Stop and Think question on page 14: **Why does June tell Madison and Tom that her act is "topnotch"?** (Possible response: June says her act is "topnotch" because she doesn't want to admit to them that she still doesn't have an act.) Guide students in writing the answer to this question. **MAKE INFERENCES**

Remind students that this story is fiction. Model how to analyze a story to determine the type of fiction.

(THINK ALOUD) **I know this story is not about real people, but as I read, I realize that June and Zeke are similar to students I know. I can picture students acting and talking just like the students in this story. The events are all things that could happen in real life. The setting is a school. In many ways, this school is similar to ours. Because the details in this story are believable, I can figure out that this story is realistic fiction. FORMS OF FICTION**

Discuss the Stop and Think question on page 15: **How would you feel if you were June? Explain.** (Possible response: I would feel nervous because I didn't have an act.) Guide students in writing the answer to this question. **PERSONAL RESPONSE**

pp. 16–17

Ask: **How do you think Madison and Tom feel after their performance? Why?** (Possible response: I think they might feel embarrassed because they thought their act was good, but the audience clapped just a little.) **IDENTIFY WITH CHARACTERS**

Discuss the Stop and Think question on page 16: **What does June do on the stage?** (On the stage, June is so nervous she trips over a box and then knocks over the mike.) Guide students in writing the answer to this question. **PLOT AND SETTING**

Ask: **How does June feel when she first gets on stage?** (Possible response: She is nervous and afraid.) **How does she feel toward the end of her performance?** (Possible response: She is clowning around to make the audience laugh harder. She is confident her act is a hit.) **COMPARE AND CONTRAST**

Discuss the Stop and Think question on page 17: **What do you think will happen next?** (Possible response: I think June will win the contest.) Guide students in writing the answer to this question. **MAKE PREDICTIONS**

VOCABULARY

Student-Friendly Explanations

hysterical A person who is hysterical is in a panic or very excited.

crestfallen Someone who is crestfallen is very disappointed and sad.

incapacitated Someone that is incapacitated is unable to work due to injury.

perishable Food that is perishable goes bad if it is not kept cold.

lamented If you lamented something, you expressed deep sadness because of it.

ricocheted When something ricocheted, it bounced around off other objects.

ecstatic If you are ecstatic, you are extremely happy.

mirth Mirth is a feeling of amusement that causes you to laugh out loud.

Spelling Words: Lesson 1

1. absences	11. glimpse
2. against	12. nozzle
3. album	13. feather
4. circuit	14. plastic
5. bronze	15. publish
6. chess	16. pulse
7. biscuit	17. rapid
8. depth	18. snack
9. cabinet	19. solve
10. drenched	20. system

 Ask: **How do Madison and Tom surprise June?** (Possible response: They come up to her and admit she was really funny, even though they didn't think she could do it.) **Draw Conclusions**

Discuss the Stop and Think question on page 18: **What do you think Tom and Madison learn?** (Possible response: I think they learn that that you shouldn't play mean tricks on your friends.) Guide students in writing the answer to this question. **Make Judgments**

Ask: **Do you think it is true that June is the comic champ? Why or why not?** (Possible response: I think she is the comic champ because the audience laughed hardest at her act.) **Make Judgments**

 Answers to *Think Critically* Questions Help students read and answer the *Think Critically* questions on page 19. Then guide students in writing the answer to each question. Possible responses are provided.

1. I think that Zeke is a good friend because he is honest and tells her what Tom and Madison did. **Character**

2. [Resolution] June is so nervous, she makes funny mistakes. She wins the contest. **Plot**

3. I can learn that I can try new things even when I'm scared. **Author's Purpose**

RETEACH

Decoding/Spelling

 Words with Short Vowels and Vowel Digraphs Distribute *Copying Master 2*. Have students work in pairs. Have one partner secretly choose a word and give hints about the word. The hints can be about the word's meaning or its spelling. The partner tries to guess what the word is and to spell it correctly. Allow partners to give up to three hints. Then have partners switch roles.

Grammar/Writing

Practice Book 4

Interjections Tell students that an interjection is a word or group of words that express a strong feeling. Explain these rules for punctuating an interjection:

- Capitalize an interjection that stands alone.
- Use an exclamation point after an interjection that stands alone.
- Use a comma after an interjection if it begins a sentence.

Write *Yikes* and *Yikes that is cold* on the board. Model how to punctuate each by identifying the interjection that stands alone and the one that is part of a sentence. (Yikes! Yikes, that is cold!)

GUIDED PRACTICE Direct students to page 4 in their *Practice Books*. Ask a volunteer to read the directions aloud. Remind students that some sentences can be both exclamatory and imperative. Point out that an imperative sentence can end with exclamation mark or a period, depending on the strength of the feeling. Then have students complete the activity.

Fluency

Practice Book 3

Fluency Practice Invite students to look at the bottom half of *Practice Book* page 3. These sentences have been broken into natural phrases. Tell students to repeat each phrase after you, mirroring your expression, phrasing, and pace. After students have repeated each sentence, invite them to practice reading the sentences to a partner.

LESSON 1

30+ Minutes

DAY AT A GLANCE

Day 3

COMPREHENSION
Preteach Forms of Fiction
Reread and Summarize "The Comic"

DECODING/SPELLING
Reteach Memorize Spellings

BUILD ROBUST VOCABULARY
Teach Words from "The Comic"

GRAMMAR/WRITING
Reteach Writing Trait: Word Choice

FLUENCY
Fluency Practice

Materials Needed: *Bold Moves*

Student
Edition
pp. 12–18

Practice
Book
pp. 3, 5

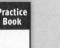

Copying
Master
3

PRETEACH

Comprehension

Copying Master 3

Forms of Fiction   Distribute *Copying Master 3*. Call on volunteers to read the information at the top of the page. Discuss and compare the characteristics of each form of fiction.

GUIDED PRACTICE   Working in pairs, have students read each description and identify the form of fiction it describes. Invite pairs to share their responses with the group.

Reread and Summarize

Have students reread and summarize "The Comic" in sections, as described below.

pp. 12–13   **Let's reread pages 12–13 to recall how June found herself signed up to perform in the Take-Two Class Act.**
Summary: Madison convinces June to perform in the Take-Two Class Act. However, June doesn't have an act. Zeke thinks she's brave to try, but also leads her to realize she's been tricked into performing.

pp. 14–15   **Now, let's reread pages 14–15 to find out what June's act will be and how she prepares for it.**
Summary: June watches TV to get ideas for her act. She pretends she has an act, but June doesn't know what she will do. As the performance draws near, many people don't think June will do well, including June herself.

pp. 16–18   **Last, let's reread pages 16–18 to recall how June's act goes and how it compares to Madison's and Tom's act.**
Summary: Madison's and Tom's act is a flop. June is so nervous that she knocks over the microphone and drops her notes. Thinking it is part of the act, the audience laughs. June keeps it up and is voted the comic champ.

RETEACH

Decoding/Spelling

Memorize Spellings   Write *depth* and *deapth* on the board. Have a volunteer circle the letters that stand for the /e/ in each. Ask if one of the words looks more "correct" than the other. Then ask another volunteer to underline the word that is spelled correctly.

Tell students that making mental pictures of words can help them remember how to spell them correctly. When proofreading, they should write different spellings of the words to decide which looks correct. If students are still unsure, they should check the dictionary.

TEACH

Build Robust Vocabulary

pp. 13–15

Words from "The Comic" Have students locate *misgiving* on page 13 of "The Comic." Ask a volunteer to read aloud the sentence in which this word appears. (Line 1: *"June," Zeke said June's name with some misgiving.*) Explain that this sentence means that Zeke said the name with a feeling of doubt or uncertainty. Continue by asking students to locate and read aloud the sentence in which *topnotch* appears on page 14. (Line 6: *"It's topnotch," bragged June.*) Explain that this sentence means that June bragged that her act was excellent. It was the best. Then ask students to locate and read aloud the sentence in which *frantic* appears on page 15. (Line 1: *As the date for the act came closer, June was frantic.*) Explain that this sentence means that June was very worried and scared about her act.

Write the words on separate cards. Make enough cards so there is one for each student. Put the cards in a large envelope. Have each student pull out a card and say the word. Then have the student call on a classmate to use the word in a sentence.

RETEACH

Grammar/Writing

Practice Book 5

Writing Trait: Word Choice Have students turn to page 5 in their *Practice Books.* Explain to students that using sensory, vivid, and precise words can help readers visualize details in their writing. Sensory words, such as *crumbling* or *shrill*, describe how things look, sound, feel, taste, and smell. Vivid words, such as *stomped* or *fluttered,* are strong and energetic. Precise words, such as *auditorium* or *cell phone*, describe objects exactly. Have students read the information. Guide students to identify how word choice helps them visualize the details in Part A.

GUIDED PRACTICE Have students work in pairs to discuss and complete Parts B and C. If time allows, have students share their sentences.

Fluency

Practice Book 3

Fluency Practice Tell students that today they will reread the sentences on the bottom of *Practice Book* page 3. Have students locate and point to the first sentence. Tell students that everyone is going to read the sentence together. This choral reading will give students an opportunity to hear others and listen to the natural phrasing of the sentences. Choral-read each of the sentences several times.

COMPREHENSION
Reteach Forms of Fiction

DECODING/SPELLING
Reteach Words with Short Vowels and Vowel Digraphs

BUILD ROBUST VOCABULARY
Reteach Words from "The Comic"

GRAMMAR/WRITING
Reteach Writing Form: Narrative

FLUENCY
Fluency Practice

Materials Needed: *Bold Moves*

| Student Edition pp. 12–18 | Practice Book p. 6 | Copying Master 4 |

Spelling Words: Lesson 1

1. absences	11. glimpse
2. against	12. nozzle
3. album	13. feather
4. circuit	14. plastic
5. bronze	15. publish
6. chess	16. pulse
7. biscuit	17. rapid
8. depth	18. snack
9. cabinet	19. solve
10. drenched	20. system

30+ Minutes

Comprehension

Forms of Fiction Have students recall the forms of fiction they have learned. Ask:

- **How is realistic fiction different from historical fiction?** (Realistic fiction has characters and a setting in modern times. It could happen today. Historical fiction is set in the past in a particular time period.)

- **How would the characters in a fable be different from those in a tall tale?** (The characters in a fable would most likely be animals that act like humans. The characters in a tall tale would be human but would have qualities that are exaggerated.)

Guide students to identify "The Comic" as realistic fiction. Ask students to name details about the characters, setting, or plot events that are clues that the story is realistic. Then invite students to speculate how the story might be different if it were a science fiction selection or a fantasy.

Decoding/Spelling

 Words with Short Vowels and Vowel Digraphs Have students number a sheet of paper 1–18. Write the Spelling Word *against* on the board, and circle the vowel digraph. Tell students that the first three words you will dictate are spelled with a vowel digraph. After students write each word, display it so they can proofread their work. Repeat this activity using the word *depth*. Circle the *e* and explain that this vowel has a short vowel sound. Tell students the remaining words you dictate have a short vowel sound spelled with one vowel.

1. circuit	2. biscuit	3. feather	4. absences
5. album	6. bronze	7. chess	8. cabinet
9. drenched	10. glimpse	11. nozzle	12. plastic
13. publish	14. pulse	15. rapid	16. snack
17. solve	18. system		

Have students turn to page 6 in their *Practice Books*. Ask a volunteer to read the directions aloud. Once students have completed the page, invite them to identify the Spelling Words in the sentences.

Build Robust Vocabulary

Words from "The Comic"   Review the meanings of the words *misgiving*, *topnotch*, and *frantic*. Then say these sentences and ask which word describes each sentence. Have students explain why.

- **Don had an uncertain feeling about whether he could finish his project on time.** (misgiving)

- **"Mom, this soup is the best!" Cal exclaimed.** (topnotch)

- **Matt was very worried and upset when he couldn't find his cat.** (frantic)

Grammar/Writing

Copying
Master
4

Writing Form: Narrative   Distribute *Copying Master 4*. Have a volunteer read aloud the information at the top of the page. Read the passage aloud as students follow along, pausing to discuss the steps in the margin. Point out how the writer's word choice helps readers visualize the setting, the conflict, and the resolution of the conflict.

GUIDED PRACTICE   Guide students in completing the activities. Allow time for students to share their responses.

Fluency

pp. 12–18

Fluency Practice   Have each student work with a partner to read passages from "The Comic" aloud to each other. Students may select a passage that they enjoyed or choose one of the following options:

- Read page 16. (Total: 121 words)

- Read page 17. (Total: 68 words)

Encourage students to read the selected passage aloud to their partner three times. Have the student rate his or her reading on the 1–4 scale.

1	Need more practice
2	Pretty good
3	Good
4	Great!

DAY AT A GLANCE

Day 5

VOCABULARY
Preteach *survey, inquire, tormented, meandering, emerged, hovered, subtle, frolicked*

COMPREHENSION
 Preteach Plot and Setting

DECODING/WORD ATTACK
Preteach Decode Longer Words

DECODING/SPELLING
Preteach Words with Long Vowels and Vowel Digraphs

GRAMMAR/WRITING
Preteach Complete and Simple Subjects

FLUENCY
Fluency Performance

Materials Needed: *Bold Moves*

 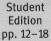

Student Edition pp. 12–18

Copying Master 5

PRETEACH
Vocabulary

Copying Master 5

Lesson 2 Vocabulary Distribute a set of Vocabulary Word Cards to each pair of students. Hold up the first word card, and ask a volunteer to read the word aloud. Have students repeat the word and hold up the matching card. Give the explanation for the word. Ask students the first question below and discuss their responses. Continue for each of the Vocabulary Words.

- If you watched a sleeping pet make a **subtle** movement, what could have happened?
- If I were to **inquire** how your day has been, what would you tell me?
- What kind of **survey** have you made of your classmates?
- What do people do when they are **meandering** through a forest?
- When was the last time something or someone **hovered** over you?
- How can an animal's look **torment** you?
- What kinds of places could a person **emerge** from?
- If dolphins **frolicked**, what would they be doing?

PRETEACH
Comprehension

pp. 12–18

Focus Skill

Plot and Setting Explain that the setting is where and when a story takes place. Point out that most story plots follow a pattern with a beginning, a rising action, a climax, a falling action, and a resolution. Have students recall "The Comic." Then ask:

- **What conflict does the main character have?** (June doesn't have a winning act for the Take-Two Class Act.)
- **What is the setting at the most exciting part of the story?** (the stage)
- **Why is the setting important to the resolution?** (Possible response: The setting provides the solution; June knocks over the props and creates a comic hit.)

Help students identify the rising and falling action in "The Comic." Ask:

- **What events happen as June tries to solve her problem?** (Madison and Tom trick June into entering the Take-Two Class Act; June cannot think of an act; Tom and Madison's skit falls flat.) Tell students that these events make up the rising action.
- **What events happen after the most exciting moment in the story?** (June is voted the comic champ; Madison and Tom become her top fans.) Point out that these events make up the falling action.

GUIDED PRACTICE Create a plot diagram. Work with students to identify what happens during these parts of "The Comic": conflict, rising action, climax, falling action, resolution.

Decoding/Word Attack

Decode Longer Words   Write *alive* on the board, and ask a volunteer to read it aloud. Ask students how many syllables are in *alive* and where the word should be divided. (2 syllables; a-live) Point out the CVCe pattern in the second syllable. Remind students that words with this pattern are usually pronounced with a long vowel sound. Then write *relax* on the board. Ask students how many syllables are in *relax* and where the word should be divided. (2 syllables; re-lax) Point out the open syllable pattern in the first syllable. Explain that when a syllable breaks before a consonant, the syllable is usually pronounced with a long vowel sound.

Decoding/Spelling

Words with Long Vowels and Vowel Digraphs

ā can be spelled *a-e, ai, ay*	
ē can be spelled *ee, ea, ie, ei*	
ī can be spelled *i-e*	
ō can be spelled *o-e, oa, ow*	
ū can be spelled *u, u-e, eu, uu*	

Copy the chart on the board. Write *sneeze, stride, aglow, essay,* and *vacuum* below the chart. As students echo-read each word, have them identify the long vowel sound and determine where each should be placed on the chart. (*ee; i-e; ow; ay; uu*) Explain to students that these are some of next lesson's Spelling Words.

Grammar/Writing

Complete and Simple Subjects   Write *The smiling, silly baby rubbed oatmeal in his hair* on the board. Read the sentence aloud. Underline *The smiling, silly baby*. Explain that a complete subject includes all the words that tell who or what the sentence is about. Then have a volunteer underline *baby* one more time. Tell students that *baby* is the simple subject—the main word in the complete subject.

Student-Friendly Explanations

survey When you survey a place, you look at and consider it carefully.

inquire If you inquire about something, you ask for more information about it.

tormented Someone who is tormented about something is extremely troubled by it.

meandering If you are moving slowly with a lot of bends or curves in your path, you are meandering.

emerged When something has emerged from somewhere, it has come out from behind, under, or inside somewhere.

hovered When something has hovered, it has been in the same place in the air without moving in any direction.

subtle When people or things are subtle, they are not immediately obvious.

frolicked If you have frolicked, you have played in a happy, lively way.

Fluency

Fluency Performance
pp. 12-18
Invite students to read aloud the passages from "The Comic" that they selected and practiced earlier. Note the number of words each student reads correctly and incorrectly. Have students rate their own oral reading on the 1–4 scale. Give students the opportunity to continue practicing and then to read the passage to you again.

LESSON 2

Song of the Sea

VOCABULARY
Reteach *survey, inquire, tormented, meandering, emerged, hovered, subtle, frolicked*

COMPREHENSION
 Reteach Plot and Setting

DECODING/SPELLING
Reteach Words with Long Vowels and Vowel Digraphs

GRAMMAR/WRITING
Preteach Complete and Simple Predicates

FLUENCY
Fluency Practice

Materials Needed: *Bold Moves*

| Student Edition pp. 20–21 | Practice Book p. 7 | Skill Card 2 | Copying Master 6 |

RETEACH

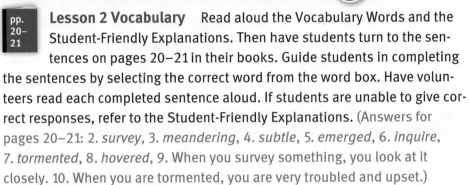

Vocabulary

pp. 20–21

Lesson 2 Vocabulary Read aloud the Vocabulary Words and the Student-Friendly Explanations. Then have students turn to the sentences on pages 20–21 in their books. Guide students in completing the sentences by selecting the correct word from the word box. Have volunteers read each completed sentence aloud. If students are unable to give correct responses, refer to the Student-Friendly Explanations. (Answers for pages 20–21: 2. *survey*, 3. *meandering*, 4. *subtle*, 5. *emerged*, 6. *inquire*, 7. *tormented*, 8. *hovered*, 9. When you survey something, you look at it closely. 10. When you are tormented, you are very troubled and upset.)

RETEACH

Comprehension

Skill Card 2

Focus Skill

Plot and Setting Have students look at side A of *Skill Card 2: Plot and Setting*. Read the definitions at the top of the card. Then have students look at the pictures. Ask:

- **What is the setting of this story?** (a rainy morning at a school bus stop)
- **What is the conflict?** (One boy is getting wet as he waits for the bus.)
- **How does the setting affect the conflict?** (The rain creates a problem for one of the boys because he is outside without an umbrella.)

Have students look at the diagram. Read the parts of the plot aloud as students follow along. Ask:

- **What are the different parts, or stages, of the plot called?** (conflict, rising action, climax, falling action, resolution)

GUIDED PRACTICE Have students look at side B of *Skill Card 2: Plot and Setting*. Read the Skill Reminder aloud. Then read the passage aloud while students read along. Guide students as they copy the diagram and complete it with the plot elements of the story. (CONFLICT: Sam and Ann both want to clean the board, but there's only one eraser; RISING ACTION: They argue over who gets to do it; CLIMAX: Mr. Boswell takes the eraser and talks about being polite; FALLING ACTION: Mr. Boswell asks Terry to clean the board; RESOLUTION: Ann and Sam learn a lesson.)

VOCABULARY

RETEACH

Decoding/Spelling

Copying Master 6

Words with Long Vowels and Vowel Digraphs   Distribute *Copying Master 6*. Model reading the words and have students repeat them. Write the Spelling Words with the long *a* and long *o* sounds on the board.

arcade	entertain	quaint	proclaim
essay	saying	globe	
aglow	tomorrow	approach	

Invite volunteers to circle the letters in each word that make the long *a* or long *o* sound. (*a-e; ai; ai; o, ai; ay; ay; o; ow; ow; o*)

PRETEACH

Grammar/Writing

Complete and Simple Predicates   Write the following sentence on the board:

> The baby rubbed icky, cold oatmeal in his hair.

Read the sentence aloud. Tell students that the predicate of a sentence tells what the subject is or does. Have a volunteer underline *rubbed*. Explain that *rubbed* is the simple predicate—the main word in the complete predicate. Point out that a complete predicate includes all the words that tell what the subject is or does. Have a volunteer underline *rubbed icky, cold oatmeal in his hair*. Ask: **What is the complete predicate in this sentence?** (rubbed icky cold oatmeal in his hair) **How do you know?** (Those are all the words that tell what the baby does.) Tell students that sometimes the simple and complete predicates are the same; for example, in a sentence such as *The baby cried*.

GUIDED PRACTICE   Write the following sentence on the board:

> A steaming bowl of vegetable soup tastes good on a cold day.

Have students work in pairs to identify the simple predicate (tastes) and complete predicate. (tastes good on a cold day) Ask volunteers to explain their responses.

VOCABULARY

Student-Friendly Explanations

survey   When you survey a place, you look at and consider it carefully.

inquire   If you inquire about something, you ask for more information about it.

tormented   Someone who is tormented about something is extremely troubled by it.

meandering   If you are moving slowly with a lot of bends or curves in your path, you are meandering.

emerged   When something has emerged from somewhere, it has come out from behind, under, or inside somewhere.

hovered   When something has hovered, it has been in the same place in the air without moving in any direction.

subtle   When people or things are subtle, they are not immediately obvious.

frolicked   If you have frolicked, you have played in a happy, lively way.

Fluency Builder

Practice Book 7

Fluency Practice   Have students turn to *Practice Book* page 7. Read the words in the first column aloud. Invite students to track each word and repeat the words after you. Then have students work in pairs to read the words in the first column aloud to each other. Follow the same procedure with each of the remaining columns. After partners have practiced reading aloud the words in each column, have them practice reading all of the words.

DAY AT A GLANCE
Day 2

VOCABULARY
Reteach *survey, inquire, tormented, meandering, emerged, hovered, subtle, frolicked*

COMPREHENSION
"Song of the Sea"

Build Background

Monitor Comprehension

Answers to *Think Critically* **Questions**

DECODING/SPELLING
Reteach Words with Long Vowels and Vowel Digraphs

GRAMMAR/WRITING
Preteach Simple and Complete Subjects and Predicates

FLUENCY
Fluency Practice

Materials Needed: *Bold Moves*

Student Edition pp. 22–29

Practice Book pp. 7, 8

Copying Masters 5, 6

Vocabulary

Lesson 2 Vocabulary Distribute a set of Vocabulary Word Cards to each small group of students. Have students print the words on index cards, spacing out each word into chunks. For example, write *subtle* as *sub t le*. Tell students to cut the "chunks" apart and then mix them in a box. Using the original word cards as a reference, have students pick out the letter cards and reconstruct each word. When students complete a word, ask them to use it in a sentence.

Copying Master 5

Comprehension

Build Background: "Song of the Sea"
Ask students to share experiences they may have had dealing with an emergency. Were they able to find others to help? Did they surprise themselves by thinking and acting quickly?

Monitor Comprehension: "Song of the Sea"
Read the title aloud. Tell students that a boy named Tomás is telling this story. Then have students read pages 22–23 to find out what information Tomás gives about the setting.

pp. 22–23

After reading the pages, discuss the Stop and Think question on page 22: **What do you learn about the setting?** (Possible response: Tomás tells me that the setting is a beach where people come to see whales.) Guide students in writing the answer to this question. **PLOT AND SETTING**

Discuss the Stop and Think question on page 23: **Why doesn't the narrator want anyone to hear his songs?** (Possible response: Tomás doesn't want people to hear his songs because he is shy or embarrassed about sharing his songs.) Guide students in writing the answer to this question. **CHARACTERS' EMOTIONS**

Discuss the Stop and Think question on page 24: **What is the problem in the story?** (Possible response: The problem is that a whale is beached and needs help.) Guide students in writing the answer to this question. **CONFLICT/RESOLUTION**

pp. 24–25

Ask: **How do you think Tomás and Rosa feel as they splash the whale while their parents run for help?** (Possible responses: worried, nervous, scared) **CHARACTERS' EMOTIONS**

Discuss the Stop and Think question on page 25: **What do you think will happen next?** (Possible responses: I think Tomás' parents will find other people to help keep the whale wet; the whale's condition will get worse; the tide will come in, and the whale will drift back out to sea.) Guide students in writing the answer to this question. **MAKE PREDICTIONS**

pp. 26–27 Read the first paragraph on page 26 aloud. Model using the strategy of creating visual images.

THINK ALOUD **As I read, I create a picture in my mind to help me understand how Tomás feels. I close my eyes and visualize his face as he looked first at the beached whale, then at the whales in the sea. I see his expression change from worried to hopeful as he remembered that whales like his songs.** CREATE VISUAL IMAGES

Discuss the Stop and Think question on page 26: **What seems to make the whale relax?** (Possible response: The whale seems to relax when Tomás sings.) Guide students in writing the answer to this question. MAKE INFERENCES

Ask: **Why does Rosa look puzzled when Tomás says that he will sing to the whale?** (Rosa doesn't know that Tomás can sing because he doesn't sing in front of other people.) NOTE DETAILS

Have students reread the first paragraph on page 27 and look at the picture. Ask: **In the falling action, how does the author develop the theme of helping others?** (In the falling action, many people come together to save the whale.) STORY STRUCTURE/THEME

Ask: **Do you think that the singing helps the whale? Why or why not?** (Possible response: Yes. The whale relaxes when Tomás begins singing and grows calmer when Tomás makes his song softer.) EXPRESS PERSONAL OPINIONS

Discuss the Stop and Think question on page 27: **Think about what Tomás does. What can you tell about him?** (Possible response: I can tell that Tomás is a kind-hearted person. He lets go of his reluctance to sing in front of other people in order to help the whale feel calm and safe.) Guide students in writing the answer to this question. MAKE INFERENCES

page 28 Discuss the Stop and Think question on page 28: **How do you think Tomás's life will be different now?** (Possible response: I think that Tomás will now be confident sharing his talent with others. He may spend less time at the beach and more time with other people.) Guide students in writing the answer to this question. MAKE PREDICTIONS

VOCABULARY

Student-Friendly Explanations

survey When you survey a place, you look at and consider it carefully.

inquire If you inquire about something, you ask for more information about it.

tormented Someone who is tormented about something is extremely troubled by it.

meandering If you are moving slowly with a lot of bends or curves in your path, you are meandering.

emerged When something has emerged from somewhere, it has come out from behind, under, or inside somewhere.

hovered When something has hovered, it has been in the same place in the air without moving in any direction.

subtle When people or things are subtle, they are not immediately obvious.

frolicked If you have frolicked, you have played in a happy, lively way.

Spelling Words: Lesson 2

1. sneeze	11. essay
2. arcade	12. tomorrow
3. vacuum	13. coffee
4. breathe	14. stride
5. belief	15. easel
6. proclaim	16. approach
7. entertain	17. globe
8. quaint	18. polite
9. aglow	19. duty
10. saying	20. grief

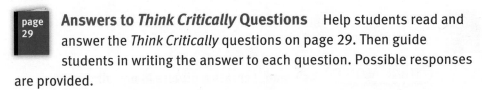

Answers to *Think Critically* Questions   Help students read and answer the *Think Critically* questions on page 29. Then guide students in writing the answer to each question. Possible responses are provided.

1. [Resolution] Tomás sings to the whale while everyone keeps it wet. The tide comes in and the whale drifts back out to sea. **PLOT**

2. The whale survives because Tomás keeps it relaxed with his singing, while his family and other people from the village keep it wet. **CAUSE AND EFFECT**

3. The story tells me that sharing your talents is important/good. **AUTHOR'S PURPOSE**

RETEACH

Decoding/Spelling

Copying Master 6

Words with Long Vowels and Vowel Digraphs   Distribute *Copying Master 6*. Model reading the words and have students repeat them. Then write the Spelling Words with the long *e* sound on the board. Call attention to the letters that make the long *e* sound.

sneeze	coffee	belief
grief	breathe	easel

On a sheet of paper, have students write the words, then circle the letters in each word that make the long *e* sound. Allow time for students to share their responses. (*ee; ee; ie; ie; ea; ea*)

Grammar/Writing

 Practice Book 8

Simple and Complete Subjects and Predicates   Write the following on the board:

> The hungry, little mouse ate half a sandwich.

Tell students the subject of a sentence tells who or what the sentence is about. The predicate tells what the subject is or does. Ask a volunteer to identify the subject and the predicate. (mouse; ate) Explain to students the following points:

- A complete subject includes all the words that tell who or what the sentence is about. A simple subject is the main word or words in the complete subject.

- A complete predicate includes all the words that tell what the subject is or does. A simple predicate is the main word or words in the complete predicate.

Have students identify the complete subject and the complete predicate in the sentence. (The hungry, little mouse; ate half a sandwich)

GUIDED PRACTICE   Guide students in completing the activity on page 8 in their *Practice Books*. Allow time for students to share their responses.

Fluency

Practice Book 7

Fluency Practice   Invite students to look at the bottom half of *Practice Book* page 7. These sentences have been broken into natural phrases. Tell students to repeat each phrase after you, mirroring your expression, phrasing, and pace. After students have repeated each sentence, invite them to practice reading the sentences to a partner.

COMPREHENSION
Preteach Poetic Devices
Reread and Summarize "Song of the Sea"

DECODING/SPELLING
Reteach Words with Long Vowels and Vowel Digraphs

BUILD ROBUST VOCABULARY
Teach Words from "Song of the Sea"

GRAMMAR/WRITING
Reteach Writing Trait: Word Choice

FLUENCY
Fluency Practice

Materials Needed: *Bold Moves*

Student Edition pp. 22–28

Practice Book pp. 7, 9

Copying Masters 6, 7

PRETEACH

Comprehension

Copying Master 7

Poetic Devices   Tell students that poets choose from a variety of tools, or poetic devices, to convey a certain tone to their work. Discuss the following points:

- The rhythm of a poem is like the rhythm of a song. Rhythm gives a poem a certain feeling.
- Rhyming words may appear in the same line, in consecutive lines, or at the end of every other line.

Distribute *Copying Master 7* and have a volunteer read the information at the top of the page aloud. Then have students follow along as you point out the poetic devices and their definitions.

GUIDED PRACTICE   Ask a volunteer to read the poem aloud. Then guide students in completing the activity.

Reread and Summarize   Have students reread and summarize "Song of the Sea" in sections, as described below.

pp. 22-23

Let's reread pages 22–23 to recall what Tomás's life is like at the beginning of the story.
Tomás spends as much time on the beach as the people who visit his town to see whales. He sits on the beach because he likes to sing— but not where people will hear.

pp. 24-25

Now let's reread p. 24–25 to remember what happens when Tomás finds a whale on the beach.
Summary: Knowing that a whale on the beach is a bad thing, Tomás calls to his sister, Rosa, for help. Tomás stays with the whale, while Rosa gets help. Tomás and Rosa keep the whale wet while their parents get more help.

pp. 26 - 28

Last, let's reread pages 26–28 to find out how the whale is saved.
Summary: Tomás surprises Rosa by singing, which calms the whale. Their parents and many others come to help. Tomás keeps singing. When the whale drifts back to sea, everyone claps—for the whale and for Tomás.

RETEACH

Decoding/Spelling

Copying Master 6

Words with Long Vowels and Vowel Digraphs   Distribute *Copying Master 6*. Model reading the words and have students repeat them. Then write *vacuum, cubicle, stride,* and *polite* on the board. Have students identify the letters that make the long *u* or long *i* sound. (*uu; u; i; i-e*) Next, have pairs of students make two sets of game cards using the lesson's Spelling Words with the vowels missing; a dash appears in place of each vowel. Based on the traditional Memory Game, after a student matches two cards, he or she must supply the correct missing letters to keep the game cards. If the wrong letter is supplied, the opponent gets the game cards and the next turn.

TEACH

Build Robust Vocabulary

pp. 22-28

Words from "Song of the Sea" Have students locate *cove* on page 22 of "Song of the Sea." Ask a volunteer to read aloud the sentence in which this word appears. (First sentence: *Every year, the whales stopped in our cove on their 6,000-mile trip to the Bering Sea*.) Explain that this sentence means that the whales stopped in a small body of water with land around it. Then ask students to locate and read aloud the sentence in which *astonished* appears on page 28. (Line 8: *I described how I spent my time alone on the beach, and they were astonished*.) Explain that this sentence means that the people that listened to the boy were very surprised or amazed at what he said.

Ask each student to choose one word and make up a sentence using the word. Have students say their sentences to the class.

RETEACH

Grammar/Writing

Practice Book 9

Writing Trait: Word Choice Have students turn to page 9 in their *Practice Books*. Explain that when poets write a poem, they use sensory words to help readers share their experience. Point out that, in addition to sensory words, the author of "Orca Island" uses repeated and rhyming words to create rhythm in the poem.

GUIDED PRACTICE Complete the page together. Discuss the word choices the students make.

Fluency

Practice Book 7

Fluency Practice Tell students that today they will reread the sentences on the bottom of *Practice Book* page 7. Have students locate and point to the first sentence. Tell students that everyone is going to read the sentence together. This choral reading will give students an opportunity to hear others and to listen to the natural phrasing of the sentences. Choral-read each sentence several times.

30+ Minutes

DAY AT A GLANCE

Day 4

COMPREHENSION
Reteach Poetic Devices

DECODING/SPELLING
Reteach Words with Long Vowel
Vowels and Vowel Digraphs

BUILD ROBUST VOCABULARY
Reteach Words from "Song of the Sea"

GRAMMAR/WRITING
Reteach Writing Form: Lyric Poem

FLUENCY
Fluency Practice

Materials Needed: *Bold Moves*

| Student Edition pp. 22–28 | Practice Book p. 10 | Copying Master 8 |

Spelling Words: Lesson 2

1. sneeze	11. essay
2. arcade	12. tomorrow
3. vacuum	13. coffee
4. breathe	14. stride
5. belief	15. easel
6. proclaim	16. approach
7. entertain	17. globe
8. quaint	18. polite
9. aglow	19. duty
10. saying	20. grief

Comprehension

Poetic Devices Remind students that a poet uses poetic devices to create a tone. Have students recall the poetic devices they learned: rhythm, rhyming words, alliteration, and onomatopoeia.

Write following examples on the board:

> Star tonight, Star so bright.
>
> Six seals sunned themselves side by side on the shore.
>
> Whisk, boom, bang! And off we went.
>
> Here you are next to me waiting so patiently

GUIDED PRACTICE Ask students to describe the tone that each example might give to a poem.

Decoding/Spelling

Practice Book 10

Words With Long Vowels and Vowel Digraphs Have students number a sheet of paper 1–15. Write the Spelling Word *sneeze* on the board, and point to the letters *ee*, which make the long *e* sound. Tell students that the first five words you will dictate have the long *e* sound. Remind students that each long vowel sound can be spelled in different ways. After students write each word, display it so they can proofread their work. Repeat this activity for the other long vowel sounds using these examples: *duty, globe, stride, saying*.

1. breathe	2. belief	3. coffee	4. easel
5. grief	6. vacuum	7. approach	8. tomorrow
9. aglow	10. polite	11. arcade	12. proclaim
13. entertain	14. quaint	15. essay	

Have students turn to page 10 in their *Practice Books*. Read the instructions aloud as students follow along. Then have students look at the picture and sentence choices for the first item. Ask students to circle the letter of the sentence that best describes the picture. (C) Then have students complete the page independently.

Build Robust Vocabulary

Words from "Song of the Sea" Review the meanings of the words *cove* and *astonished*. Then say these sentences and ask which word describes each sentence. Have students explain why.

- **We rowed our boat to a small body of water with land around it and had lunch.** (cove)

- **I was very surprised that my little brother ate such a huge piece of pie.** (astonished)

Grammar/Writing

| Copying |
| Master |
| 8 |

Writing Form: Lyric Poem Explain that a lyric poem conveys what a writer observes (through the senses) and feels. When you write a lyric poem, it is important to use sensory words to describe your observations. Using repeated words and words that rhyme can also help your readers more fully experience your poem. Distribute *Copying Master 8*. Have a volunteer read the description of a lyric poem aloud. Read the Student Model together.

GUIDED PRACTICE Guide students in completing the activity. Ask volunteers to share their responses to items 1 and 2. Challenge students to improve the last stanza of the model by revising the third line. Allow time for students to share their revised stanzas with the group.

Fluency

| pp. 22-28 |

Fluency Practice Have each student work with a partner to read passages from "Song of the Sea" aloud to each other. Students may select a passage that they enjoyed or choose one of the following options:

- Read page 23. (Total: 99 words)
- Read page 28. (Total: 94 words)

Encourage students to read the selected passage aloud to their partner three times. Have the student rate his or her reading on the 1–4 scale.

1	Need more practice
2	Pretty good
3	Good
4	Great!

30+ Minutes

VOCABULARY
Preteach *schemes, exerts, rigged, astounding, replica, stabilize, disbanded*

COMPREHENSION
 Preteach Text Structure: Chronological Order

DECODING/WORD ATTACK
Preteach Decode Longer Words

DECODING/SPELLING
Preteach Words with Variant Vowels and Diphthongs

GRAMMAR/WRITING
Preteach Compound Subjects

FLUENCY
Fluency Performance

Materials Needed: *Bold Moves*

| Student Edition pp. 22–28 | Skill Card 3 | Copying Master 9 |

PRETEACH

Vocabulary

Copying Master 9

Lesson 3 Vocabulary   Distribute a set of Vocabulary Word Cards to each pair of students. Hold up the card for the first word and ask a volunteer to read it aloud. Have students repeat the word and hold up the matching card. Give the explanation for the word. Then ask students the first question below and discuss their responses. Continue for each Vocabulary Word.

- What **schemes** for avoiding a punishment have you tried?
- Who or what **exerts** a force strong enough to awaken you when you are sleeping soundly?
- Have you ever **rigged** up a costume? What did it look like?
- Of all the true stories you've heard, which one was the most **astounding**?
- Have you seen a **replica** at a museum? What was it?
- Why is it important to **stabilize** an empty boat by anchoring it?
- Why would a neighborhood soccer team be **disbanded** if seven players were to move out of town?

PRETEACH

Comprehension

 Skill Card 3 *Focus Skill*

Text Structure: Chronological Order   Have students look at side A of *Skill Card 3: Text Structure: Chronological Order*. Have a volunteer read aloud the introductory paragraph. Then have students silently read the passage. Ask:

- **In what order are events told?** (Events are told in chronological order.)
- **What dates does the author include to help you tell the sequence of events in Owens' life?** (1913, 1936, 1955, 1976, 1980)

Point to the diagram. Ask:

- **What clue words help you tell the sequence in which the events took place?** (as a high school senior; Then, as a college student)

GUIDED PRACTICE   Have students identify two more events that could be added to the diagram. (Possible responses: Owens was awarded the Presidential Medal of Freedom in 1976; Owens died in 1980.)

Decoding/Word Attack

Decode Longer Words   Write the word *teapot* on the board, and ask a volunteer to read it aloud. Ask students how many syllables are in *teapot* and where the word should be divided. (2 syllables, tea/pot) Point out that the vowel pair *ea* is a vowel digraph and makes one sound, /ē/. Explain the following:

- Some vowel digraphs are classified as variant—they stand for a special sound that is not long or short, such as the letters *au* in *applaud* and the letters *oo* in *booklet*.

- Vowel diphthongs are pairs of either vowels or a vowel and a consonant that are blended together to make a combined sound, such as the letters *ew* in the word *shrewd*.

Decoding/Spelling

Words with Variant Vowels and Diphthongs   Tell students that one sound, such as /oy/, might be made by different combinations of vowels. Write the following words on the board:

corduroy	turquoise

Read each word aloud and have students repeat. Have students copy the words and circle the vowels in each word that make the /oy/ vowel sound. (oy; oi) Repeat this activity using *soothing, curfew, applaud,* and *withdrawn.* Help students understand that the same sound can be spelled in different ways.

Grammar/Writing

Compound Subjects   Explain that some sentences have two or more subjects with the same predicate. The subjects are connected with the word *and*. Write this example on the board and read it with students: *Tenecia and Alan play softball* on the board. Underline the subject once and the predicate twice. Circle *and*. Tell students that *Tenecia and Alan* is the compound subject. Then write *Tenecia, Karen, and Alan play softball* on the board. Ask: **What is the compound subject?** (Tenecia, Karen, and Alan) Explain that commas separate the subjects and use an *and* before the last subject.

Student-Friendly Explanations

schemes When you try various schemes, you try different plans.

exerts When something exerts pressure, it has created pressure through a sustained action.

rigged If you have rigged up an object, you have constructed it using materials that were available.

astounding When you find something astounding, it overwhelms you with surprise.

replica A replica is an exact model or copy of an object.

stabilize When you stabilize something, you make it less likely to move in response to outside forces such as wind.

disbanded When an organization is disbanded, its members stop working together as a group.

Fluency

Fluency Performance
pp. 22–28   Invite students to read aloud the passages from "Song of the Sea" that they selected and practiced earlier. Note the number of words each student reads correctly and incorrectly. Have students rate their own oral reading on the 1–4 scale. Give students the opportunity to continue practicing and then to read the passage to you again.

DAY AT A GLANCE

Day 1

30+ Minutes

LESSON 3

VOCABULARY
Reteach *schemes, exerts, rigged, astounding, replica, stabilize, disbanded*

COMPREHENSION
 Reteach Text Structure: Chronological Order

DECODING/SPELLING
Reteach Words with Variant Vowels and Diphthongs

GRAMMAR/WRITING
Preteach Compound Predicates

FLUENCY
Fluency Practice

Materials Needed: *Bold Moves*

| Student Edition pp. 30–31 | Practice Book p. 11 | Skill Card 3 | Copying Master 10 |

RETEACH

Vocabulary

pp. 30–31

Lesson 3 Vocabulary Read aloud the Vocabulary Words and the Student-Friendly Explanations. Then have students read the selection on page 30. Guide them in answering the questions on page 31. If students are unable to give reasonable responses, refer to the Student-Friendly Explanations. (Possible responses for page 31: 2. Schemes are plans. If you come up with the right scheme, it could make you money. 3. Adams needed the tire to keep its shape, even under pressure. 4. Yes. If someone gathered the correct materials, they could create a replica of Adams's tire. 5. When you find something astounding, it fills you with surprise. I think space exploration is astounding.)

RETEACH

Comprehension

Skill Card 3

Focus Skill

Text Structure: Chronological Order Have students look at side B of *Skill Card 3: Text Structure: Chronological Order*. Tell students to read the Skill Reminder and the paragraph. Ask:

- **How are events in this paragraph presented?** (in chronological order)

Direct students' attention to the chart. Ask:

- **What dates and clue words show the sequence of events in Matt's life?** (1998, When I was six, Two years ago, Last year)

GUIDED PRACTICE Ask students to relate details about a recent school event, such as an assembly. Record their sentences on the board. Guide students to identify any words or phrases that indicate time order. Have students suggest additional time order words to clarify the sequence of events.

RETEACH

Decoding/Spelling

Copying Master 10

Words with Variant Vowels and Diphthongs Distribute *Copying Master 10*. Write on the board the Spelling Words shown below.

> curfew   soothing
> pound   drowsy

Say each word and guide students to identify the letters that make the /ew/ or /ow/ sound. Then have students write each word and circle the letters that make the /ew/ or /ow/ sound. (*ew; oo; ou; ow*)

PRETEACH

Grammar/Writing

Compound Predicates Remind students that a predicate tells what the subject of a sentence does or is. Write the following sentence on the board:

> Raymond got out of bed, washed his face, and got dressed.

Model identifying the subject (Raymond) and underline it once. Then ask: **What did Raymond do?** (got out of bed, washed his face, got dressed) Draw two lines under the predicates. Note that there is one subject and three predicates. Point out the use of commas and *and* to separate the predicates. Tell students that they can create sentences with compound predicates by combining two or more short sentences. Write these sentences on the board:

> Irene did her homework.
> Irene practiced the drums.
> Irene fed the dog.

Have students identify the subject and predicates. (Irene; did her homework, practiced the drums, fed the dog) Help students combine the three sentences into one with a compound predicate. Remind them to use commas and the word *and*. (Irene did her homework, practiced the drums, and fed the dog.)

Student-Friendly Explanations

schemes When you try various schemes, you try different plans.

exerts When something exerts pressure, it has created pressure through a sustained action.

rigged If you have rigged up an object, you have constructed it using materials that were available.

astounding When you find something astounding, it overwhelms you with surprise.

replica A replica is an exact model or copy of an object.

stabilize When you stabilize something, you make it less likely to move in response to outside forces such as wind.

disbanded When an organization is disbanded, its members stop working together as a group.

Fluency

Practice Book 11

Fluency Practice Have students turn to *Practice Book* page 11. Read the words in the first column aloud. Invite students to track each word and repeat the words after you. Then have students work in pairs to read the words in the first column aloud to each other. Follow the same procedure with each of the remaining columns. After partners have practiced reading aloud the words in each of the columns, have them practice reading all of the words.

LESSON 3

DAY AT A GLANCE

Day 2

30+ Minutes

VOCABULARY
Reteach *schemes, exerts, rigged, astounding, replica, stabilize, disbanded*

COMPREHENSION
"Tom Adams and Santa Anna"

Build Background
Monitor Comprehension:
Answers to *Think Critically* Questions

DECODING/SPELLING
Reteach Words with Variant Vowels and Diphthongs

GRAMMAR/WRITING
Preteach Compound Subjects and Predicates

FLUENCY
Fluency Practice

Materials Needed: *Bold Moves*

Student Edition pp. 32–39

Practice Book pp. 11, 12

Copying Masters 9, 10

RETEACH

Vocabulary

Copying Master 9

Lesson 3 Vocabulary Distribute a set of word cards to each student. Read each sentence below and ask students to hold up the appropriate card.

1. **The miner had several ___ for reaching California during the Gold Rush.** (schemes)

2. **Jerri held the bicycle to ___ it while her little sister climbed aboard.** (stabilize)

3. **Jon bought a ___ of the Empire State Building when he visited New York.** (replica)

4. **The lasting popularity of barbecue potato chips is ___.** (astounding)

5. **Rex ___ up a splint for the injured bird's wing.** (rigged)

6. **A balloon bursts when the air inside it ___ too much pressure.** (exerts)

7. **Jana was sad when her Girl Scout troop ___.** (disbanded)

Comprehension

Build Background: "Tom Adams and Santa Anna"
Ask students to share experiences they may have had with a scheme that did not turn out as they expected. What was the scheme? Was the end result better or worse than they imagined? In what way?

 Monitor Comprehension: "Tom Adams and Santa Anna"
Read the title of the story aloud. Then have students read pages 32–33 to find out how an unknown American inventor comes to know the former president of Mexico.

After reading the pages, ask: **How does Tom Adams come to know Santa Anna?** (Adams is in New York when Santa Anna arrives. Santa Anna hires Adams as his assistant.) NOTE DETAILS

Discuss the Stop and Think question on page 32: **What do you want to learn from this selection?** (Possible response: I want to learn about the small event that affected many lives.) Guide students in writing the answer to this question. PERSONAL RESPONSE

Discuss the Stop and Think question on page 33: **How are Tom Adams and Santa Anna alike? How are they different?** (Possible responses: Here is how they are alike: they both want to make money. Here is how they are different: Adams is American and Santa Anna is Mexican. Tom is an inventor and Santa Anna is an ex-president.) Guide students in writing the answer to this question. COMPARE AND CONTRAST

pp. 34–35 Read aloud with students the first paragraph on page 34. Model the strategy of using context clues to understand the meaning of a word.

(THINK ALOUD) **It says that Santa Anna "had taken some *chicle* with him to the United States, after he was exiled . . ." So I can tell he was somewhere else, and then he traveled to the United States. And I know from the previous page that he was asked to leave Mexico. I think *exiled* must refer to being sent away from his homeland. CONTEXT CLUES**

Discuss the Stop and Think question on page 34: **What do you think will happen next?** (Possible response: Adams will use the *chicle* in his tire mix.) Guide students in writing the answer to this question. **MAKE PREDICTIONS**

Discuss the Stop and Think question on page 35: **Why doesn't the *chicle* work?** (Possible response: It doesn't work because *chicle* does not keep its shape, so objects made with it collapse.) Guide students in writing the answer to this question. **CAUSE AND EFFECT**

pp. 36–37 Discuss the Stop and Think question on page 36: **What happens after Adams decides to dump the *chicle*?** (After he decides to dump the *chicle,* he realizes that he can use the *chicle* to make chewing gum.) Guide students in writing the answer to this question. **SEQUENCE**

Discuss the Stop and Think question on page 37: **What does the time line show?** (The time line shows the history of gum.) Guide students in writing the answer to this question. **GRAPHIC AIDS**

pp. 38 Have students read page 38. Ask: **What time words or phrases help you understand how long it took for Adams to make his fortune selling gum?** (ten years later) **CHRONOLOGICAL ORDER**

Discuss the Stop and Think question on page 38: **Why do you think people like the new gum?** (Possible response: People like the new gum because it can stretch better than the old gum, which was made from wax.) Guide students in writing the answer to this question. **DRAW CONCLUSIONS**

VOCABULARY

Student-Friendly Explanations

schemes When you try various schemes, you try different plans.

exerts When something exerts pressure, it has created pressure through a sustained action.

rigged If you have rigged up an object, you have constructed it using materials that were available.

astounding When you find something astounding, it overwhelms you with surprise.

replica A replica is an exact model or copy of an object.

stabilize When you stabilize something, you make it less likely to move in response to outside forces such as wind.

disbanded When an organization is disbanded, its members stop working together as a group.

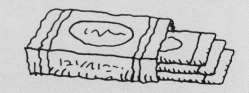

Spelling Words: Lesson 3

1. authentic		11. pound	
2. launch		12. awesome	
3. boycott		13. corduroy	
4. turquoise		14. shrewd	
5. withdrawn		15. soothing	
6. awkward		16. booklet	
7. faulty		17. drowsy	
8. applaud		18. moisture	
9. jigsaw		19. flaunt	
10. curfew		20. enough	

page 39

Answers to *Think Critically* Questions

Help students read and answer the *Think Critically* questions on page 39. Then guide students in writing the answer to each question. Possible responses are provided.

1. Next, Adams tried using *chicle* to make galoshes, masks, and balls. Finally, Adams made gum. **SEQUENCE**

2. Santa Anna helped Tom Adams by selling him *chicle*. **MAIN IDEA AND DETAILS**

3. Tom Adams was determined, hard working, and persistent. **CHARACTER**

RETEACH

Decoding/Spelling

Copying Master 10

Words with Variant Vowels and Diphthongs   Distribute *Copying Master 10*. Write on the board the following Spelling Words with the /aw/ sound.

authentic	launch	withdrawn	awkward
faulty	jigsaw	applaud	awesome

Model reading the words and have students repeat them. Guide students to discover the vowels that make the /aw/ sound. Then have students write each word on a separate sheet of paper and circle the letters that make the /aw/ sound. Invite volunteers to share their responses. (*au; au; aw; aw; au; aw; au; aw*)

Then have pairs of students write the Spelling Words on index cards. One student draws a card and reads the word aloud as the other student writes the word. Then partners switch roles. When a student spells a word correctly, he or she initials the card and returns it to the pile. Students should work through the pile twice or until each student has had the opportunity to spell each of the words. Have students write down each word they do not spell correctly to study later.

Grammar/Writing

 Compound Subjects and Predicates Tell students that a subject
Practice Book 12 tells who or what a sentence is about. A predicate tells what the
subject of the sentence is or does. Write the following on the board:

> Michael and Holly moved to
> Houston.

Ask students to identify the subjects and the predicate. (Michael; Holly;
moved) Explain to students that a compound subject is two or more subjects
with the same predicate and uses *and* to link the two subjects. Ask a
volunteer to identify the compound subject. (Michael and Holly) Then write
Holly moved to Houston and bought a house on the board. Have students
identify the subject and the predicates. (Holly; moved; bought) Explain to
students that a compound predicate is two or more predicates with the
same subject and uses *and* or *but* to link the two predicates. Now write this
sentence on the board:

> Michael, Holly, and baby Jack
> moved to Houston.

Explain to students that when using three or more subjects or predicates,
commas are used to separate them and to use *and* before the last subject or
predicate.

GUIDED PRACTICE　Direct students' attention to page 12 of their *Practice
Books.* Guide them in completing the activity. Allow time for students to
share their responses.

Fluency

 Fluency Practice Invite
Practice Book 11 students to look at the
bottom half of *Practice
Book* page 11. These sentences
have been broken into natural
phrases. Tell students to repeat
each phrase after you, mirroring
your expression, phrasing, and
pace. After students have repeated
each sentence, invite them to
practice reading the sentences to
a partner.

30+ Minutes

COMPREHENSION
Preteach Reference Sources

Reread and Summarize "Tom Adams and Santa Anna"

DECODING/SPELLING
Reteach Words with Variant Vowels and Diphthongs

BUILD ROBUST VOCABULARY
Teach Words from "Tom Adams and Santa Anna"

GRAMMAR/WRITING
Reteach Writing Trait: Voice

FLUENCY
Fluency Practice

Materials Needed: *Bold Moves*

Student Edition pp. 32–38

Practice Book pp. 11, 13

Copying Master 11

PRETEACH

Comprehension

Copying Master 11

Reference Sources Distribute *Copying Master 11*, and read aloud with students the introduction at the top of the page. Have volunteers read the descriptions of each reference source.

GUIDED PRACTICE Ask students to identify the best reference source for each piece of information listed. After all students have finished, call on volunteers to share their responses.

Reread and Summarize Have students reread and summarize "Tom Adams and Santa Anna" in sections, as described below.

pp. 32–33

Let's reread pages 32–33 to find out who Tom Adams and Santa Anna are, how they meet, and how they are alike.
Summary: Tom Adams is an inventor. Santa Anna is the former president of Mexico. They meet when Santa Anna comes to New York and hires Adams as his assistant. Both Santa Anna and Adams want to become rich.

pp. 34–35

Now let's reread pages 34–35 to remember what Santa Anna suggests to Adams and what happens when Adams takes the suggestion.
Summary: Santa Anna suggests that Adams add *chicle* to his tire mix. If *chicle* gets the tires to hold their shape, both men can make a lot of money. The suggestion doesn't work. *Chicle* is too flexible.

pp. 36–37

Let's reread pages 36–37 to recall the solution that Adams finds to his *chicle* problem.
Summary: When a kid buys a stick of gum, Adams remembers that in Mexico *chicle* is used in chewing gum. Now Adams knows what he can do with all his *chicle*!

page 38

Last, let's reread page 38 to find out how Adams makes his fortune.
Adams and his son begin selling sticks of gum made with *chicle*. It stretches much better than gum made with wax. Eventually, Adams makes his gum in bulk. It becomes a bestseller.

RETEACH
Decoding/Spelling

Words with Variant Vowels and Diphthongs   Write on the board the following Spelling Words with the /oy/ sound.

| boycott | turquoise | corduroy | moisture |

Read aloud the words and have students repeat them. Help students find the vowels that make the /oy/ sound. (*oy; oi; oy; oi*)

TEACH
Build Robust Vocabulary

pp. 33–35

Words from "Tom Adams and Santa Anna"   Have students locate *proposed* on page 33 of "Tom Adams and Santa Anna." Ask a volunteer to read aloud the sentence in which this word appears. (Last sentence: *Santa Anna proposed a better plan that involved something from his homeland.*) Explain that this sentence means that Santa Anna suggested a plan for Tom Adams to think about. Then ask students to locate and read aloud the sentence in which the word *flexible* appears on page 35. (Last sentence: *The chicle was just too flexible.*) Explain that this sentence means that the chicle easily bent without breaking.

Ask each student to make up a sentence using one of the words. Have them say their sentences without the words and ask the class to tell what word is missing.

RETEACH
Grammar/Writing

Practice Book 13

Writing Trait: Voice   Have students turn to page 13 in their *Practice Books*. Explain that in writing, as in speaking, it is important to let your personal voice come through. Tell students to look at the graphic organizer to find out what voice is and how it is reflected in a text.

GUIDED PRACTICE   Complete the page together. Have volunteers share their answers. Discuss other ways writers can let their personal voice come through in their writing.

Fluency

Practice Book 11

Fluency Practice   Tell students that today they will reread the sentences on the bottom of *Practice Book* page 11. Have students locate and point to the first sentence. Tell students that everyone is going to read the sentence together. This choral reading will give students an opportunity to hear others and listen to the natural phrasing of the sentences. Choral-read each of the sentences several times.

LESSON 3

COMPREHENSION
Reteach Reference Sources

DECODING/SPELLING
Reteach Words with Variant Vowels and Diphthongs

BUILD ROBUST VOCABULARY
Reteach Words from "Tom Adams and Santa Anna"

GRAMMAR/WRITING
Reteach Writing Form: Personal Letter

FLUENCY
Fluency Practice

Materials Needed: *Bold Moves*

| Student Edition pp. 32–38 | Practice Book p. 14 | Copying Master 12 |

Spelling Words: Lesson 3

1. authentic	11. pound
2. launch	12. awesome
3. boycott	13. corduroy
4. turquoise	14. shrewd
5. withdrawn	15. soothing
6. awkward	16. booklet
7. faulty	17. drowsy
8. applaud	18. moisture
9. jigsaw	19. flaunt
10. curfew	20. enough

RETEACH

Comprehension

Reference Sources Remind students that authors use different kinds of reference sources depending on what they are writing and what information they need. Have students identify a reference source where the following information can be found.

- where Mexico is in relation to New York (an atlas)
- the meaning of *galoshes* (a dictionary)
- a synonym for *stabilize* (a thesaurus)
- who Tom Adams was (a biography or encyclopedia)

GUIDED PRACTICE Have students identify two reference sources that they could use if they wanted to find the years in which Santa Anna was born and died. (Possible responses: an almanac, an encyclopedia, or the Internet)

RETEACH

Decoding/Spelling

Practice Book 14 **Words with Variant Vowels and Diphthongs** Have students number a sheet of paper 1–16. Write *authentic* on the board. Point to the letters that make the sound /aw/. Tell students that the first eight words you will dictate have the /aw/ sound. Remind them that the sound can be spelled different ways. Repeat this activity using these examples: *turquoise* /oy/, *curfew* /ew/, and *pound* /ow/. Then, tell students that you will dictate two Spelling Words that contain variant vowel sounds.

1. launch	2. withdrawn	3. awkward	4. faulty
5. applaud	6. awesome	7. jigsaw	8. flaunt
9. boycott	10. corduroy	11. moisture	12. soothing
13. shrewd	14. drowsy	15. booklet	16. enough

Have students turn to page 14 in their *Practice Book*s. Read the directions aloud. Remind students that each of the sounds they are asked to identify can be spelled in different ways. Have them complete the page independently and share their answers with the group.

RETEACH

Build Robust Vocabulary

Words from "Tom Adams and Santa Anna"   Review the meanings of the words *proposed* and *flexible*. Then say these sentences and ask which word describes each sentence. Have students explain why.

- **Dad suggested that we go to the beach for our family trip.** (proposed)

- **We were able to bend the cooked spaghetti without breaking it.**
  (flexible)

RETEACH

Grammar/Writing

| Copying |
| Master |
| 12 |

Writing Form: Personal Letter   Tell students that a personal letter uses the writer's voice to express feelings and views on just about any topic. Explain that when you compose a personal letter, it is important to write like you speak. The reader should be able to tell that the writer is you. Distribute *Copying Master 12*. Read the Student Model together. Then write the phrase "Oh, well," from the Student Model, on the board. Have students identify additional words and phrases that reflect the writer's personal voice. (smile, yuk)

GUIDED PRACTICE   Have students respond to the numbered questions at the bottom of the page. Allow time for students to share their revised paragraph with the group.

Fluency

| pp. 32–38 |

Fluency Practice   Have each student work with a partner to read passages from "Tom Adams and Santa Anna" aloud to each other. Students may select a passage that they enjoyed or choose one of the following options:

- Read page 34. (Total: 109 words)

- Read page 36. (Total: 97 words)

Encourage students to read the selected passage aloud to their partner three times. Have the student rate his or her reading on the 1–4 scale.

1	Need more practice
2	Pretty good
3	Good
4	Great!

VOCABULARY

Preteach *remedies, luxury, triumphant, propel, astonishment, intense, lunged, fumble*

COMPREHENSION

 Preteach Text Structure: Chronological Order

DECODING/WORD ATTACK

Preteach Decode Longer Words

DECODING/SPELLING

Preteach Words with Inflections *-ed, -ing*

GRAMMAR/WRITING

Preteach Simple Sentences

FLUENCY

Fluency Performance

Materials Needed: *Bold Moves*

Student Edition pp. 32–38

Copying Master 13

30+ Minutes

PRETEACH

Vocabulary

Copying Master 13

Lesson 4 Vocabulary   Distribute a set of Vocabulary Word Cards to each pair of students. Hold up the card for the first word, and ask a volunteer to read it aloud. Have students repeat the word and hold up the matching card. Give the explanation for the word. Then ask students the first question below and discuss their responses. Continue for each of the Vocabulary Words.

- What **remedies** do you use when you get a headache?
- What big **luxury** would you like to experience someday?
- What does a winning team do to show that they feel **triumphant**?
- What might make you **propel** yourself onto a sofa after school?
- What circus act might you watch in **astonishment**?
- How do people show an **intense** desire to learn?
- Why might you **lunge** for a piece of cake?
- How do you think a player feels when he **fumbles** a ball?

PRETEACH

Comprehension

pp. 32–38

Text Structure: Chronological Order   Ask students to recall what they read in "Tom Adams and Santa Anna." Then ask:

- **What are the key events in the story?** (Santa Anna hires Adams as his assistant; Adams experiments with *chicle*, which proves too flexible for his purposes; Adams makes gum with *chicle* and strikes it rich.)

Write on the board the time-order words and phrases *during, while, as, at the same time,* and *simultaneously.* Explain that authors use words and phrases like those to describe events that happen at the same time. Write this example on the board: *Adams added chicle to his tires while he was working for Santa Anna.* Read aloud the sentence. Then ask:

- **What two events took place at the same time?** (Adams added *chicle* to his tires; Adams worked for Santa Anna.)

- **What time-order word tells you that the two events occurred at the same time?** (while)

PRETEACH
Decoding/Word Attack

Decode Longer Words Write *color, colored,* and *coloring* on the board. Circle the base word *color* in all three words. Then explain these guidelines for adding *-ed* or *-ing*:

- If a word ends with a long vowel sound or two consonants, add *-ed* or *-ing*. Examples: *crush, crushed, crushing*

- If a word ends with a consonant that comes after a short vowel sound, double the final consonant before adding *-ed* or *-ing*. Examples: *stop, stopped, stopping*

- If a word ends with a consonant and silent *e*, drop the *e* and add the *-ed* or *-ing* ending. Examples: *cope, coped, coping*

- If a word ends with a *y*, change the *y* to *i* before adding *-ed*, but leave the *y* when adding *-ing*. Examples: *pry, pried, prying*

PRETEACH
Decoding/Spelling

Words with Inflections *-ed, -ing* Write the word *preparing* on the board and underline the base word. Ask whether the base word changed when *-ing* was added. (Yes, the letter *e* was dropped.) Then write *studying*. Ask whether the base word changed when *-ing* was added. (no) Continue with these words: envy (*envied, yes*); decorate (*decorating, yes*); frighten (*frightened, no*); plan (*planning, yes*); multiply (*multiplied, yes*); employ (*employed, no*).

PRETEACH
Grammar/Writing

Simple Sentences Write the following sentences on the board:

> Dad had peach cobbler for dessert.
> Dad and Mom went to a diner and had peach cobbler for dessert.

Tell students that both sentences are simple sentences because each expresses only one complete thought. Underline the subjects once (Dad; Dad and Mom) and predicates twice (had peach cobbler for dessert; went to a diner and had peach cobbler for dessert.). Explain that a simple sentence might have a compound subject, a compound predicate, or both.

VOCABULARY
Student-Friendly Explanations

remedies Remedies are used to fix a problem.

luxury A luxury is something good that costs a lot of money.

triumphant You feel triumphant when you have achieved a goal or a victory.

propel When you propel a body or object, you have caused it to move in a certain direction.

astonishment When you feel astonishment, you are greatly surprised or are experiencing a sense of wonder.

intense An intense feeling is a strong feeling.

lunged When you have lunged at something, you have moved suddenly toward it.

fumble If you fumble an object, you handle it clumsily, or perhaps even drop it.

Fluency

pp. 32–38 **Fluency Performance** Invite students to read aloud the passages from "Tom Adams and Santa Anna" that they selected and practiced earlier. Note the number of words each student reads correctly and incorrectly. Have students rate their own oral reading on the 1–4 scale. Give students the opportunity to continue practicing and then to read the passage to you again.

LESSON 4

VOCABULARY
Reteach *remedies, luxury, triumphant, propel, astonishment, intense, lunged, fumble*

COMPREHENSION
 Reteach Text Structure: Chronological Order

DECODING/SPELLING
Reteach Words with Inflections *-ed, -ing*

GRAMMAR/WRITING
Preteach Compound Sentences

FLUENCY
Fluency Practice

Materials Needed: *Bold Moves*

| Student Edition pp. 40–41 | Practice Book p. 15 | Skill Card 4 | Copying Master 14 |

Vocabulary

pp. 40–41

Lesson 4 Vocabulary Read aloud the Vocabulary Words and the Student-Friendly Explanations. Have students read the two ads on page 40 of their books. Guide them in completing the sentences in the ads by choosing the correct words from the box. Have students read the completed ads along with you. Repeat the activity using the two ads on page 41. If students are unable to give reasonable responses, refer to the Student-Friendly Explanations. (Answers for pages 40–41: 2. *astonishment*, 3. *luxury*, 4. *lunged*, 5. *triumphant*, 6. *fumble*, 7. *propel*, 8. *intense*.)

Comprehension

Skill Card 4

Text Structure: Chronological Order Have students look at side A of *Skill Card 4: Text Structure: Chronological Order*. Read the introductory paragraph with students. Have students silently read the story and examine the sequence chart. Ask:

- **What text structure did the author use? How can you tell?** (Chronological order. The events are told in the order in which they took place.)

- **What time-order words and phrases help you tell the sequence of events?** (early yesterday morning, while Evan got dressed, by the time, as)

Point out that authors use some time-order words, such as the ones in this story, to describe events that occur at the same time.

GUIDED PRACTICE Now have students look at side B of *Skill Card 4: Text Structure: Chronological Order*. Call on a volunteer to read aloud the information in the box. Then read the paragraph aloud with students. Guide students in copying the chart and completing it by sequencing events from the paragraph. (BOX 1: At age fourteen, Althea Gibson found her life's work. BOX 2: From 1956-1958, she won the French Open, Italian Open, and U.S. Open; became the first African American to win at Wimbledon; and became the first African American woman to be named athlete of the year. BOX 3: After winning her second U.S. Open, Gibson turned pro. BOX 4: Later, she joined the pro golf tour.)

RETEACH

Decoding/Spelling

Copying Master 14

Words with Inflections -ed, -ing Distribute *Copying Master 14.* Model reading the Spelling Words and have students repeat them. Review the instructions for adding the inflections *-ed* and *-ing* to base words, and then have students complete the following activity. Have students work in pairs. Each student writes a sentence for each Spelling Word but leaves a blank for the actual word. The partners then switch papers and fill in the blanks in each other's sentences. Students should give themselves one point for each correctly spelled word.

PRETEACH

Grammar/Writing

Compound Sentences Explain that a compound sentence is made up of two or more simple sentences joined by a comma and a coordinating conjunction. Write this example on the board:

> Emily and Sasha bicycle to school, but Natalie rides the bus.

Underline the two simple sentences in the compound sentence. Circle the coordinating conjunction. (but) Then revise the sentence to read as follows:

> Emily and Sasha bicycle to school; Natalie rides the bus.

Circle the semicolon and explain that a semicolon is sometimes used, instead of a comma and conjunction, to join simple sentences.

GUIDED PRACTICE Write the following sentences on the board.

> Reid grooms the cat, and Alexandra feeds her.
>
> Kevin needs to set his alarm, or he will oversleep.

Have volunteers underline the simple sentences and circle the coordinating conjunctions in each compound sentence.

VOCABULARY

Student-Friendly Explanations

remedies Remedies are used to fix a problem.

luxury A luxury is something good that costs a lot of money.

triumphant You feel triumphant when you have achieved a goal or a victory.

propel When you propel a body or object, you have caused it to move in a certain direction.

astonishment When you feel astonishment, you are greatly surprised or are experiencing a sense of wonder.

intense An intense feeling is a strong feeling.

lunged When you have lunged at something, you have moved suddenly toward it.

fumble If you fumble an object, you handle it clumsily, or perhaps even drop it.

Fluency

Practice Book 15

Fluency Practice Have students turn to *Practice Book* page 15. Read the words in the first column aloud. Invite students to track each word and repeat the words after you. Then have students work in pairs to read the words in the first column aloud to each other. Follow the same procedure with each of the remaining columns. After partners have practiced reading aloud the words in each of the columns, have them practice reading all of the words.

30+ Minutes

VOCABULARY

Reteach *remedies, luxury, triumphant, propel, astonishment, intense, lunged, fumble*

COMPREHENSION

"Babe in the Hall of Fame"

Build Background

Monitor Comprehension

Answers to *Think Critically* Questions

DECODING/SPELLING

Reteach Words with Inflections *-ed, -ing*

GRAMMAR/WRITING

Preteach Combining Simple Sentences into Compound Sentences

FLUENCY

Fluency Practice

Materials Needed: *Bold Moves*

Student Edition pp. 42–49

Practice Book pp. 15, 16

Copying Master 13

Vocabulary

Copying Master 13

Lesson 4 Vocabulary   Distribute a Vocabulary Word Card to each student. Students can work in pairs. One student can ask yes or no questions to try to guess his or her partner's word. Urge students to keep track of how many questions it takes to guess the Vocabulary Word. When one partner has guessed correctly, the other partner can take a turn.

Comprehension

Build Background: "Babe in the Hall of Fame"

Ask students to share experiences they may have had overcoming obstacles to achieve a goal. Did they have to convince themselves or others that they could do it? If so, what reasons did they give to help themselves succeed?

Monitor Comprehension: "Babe in the Hall of Fame"

pp. 42–43

Read the title of the story aloud. Then have students read pages 42–43 to find out what sports Babe Didrickson played well.

After reading the pages, ask: **What sports did Babe Didrickson play well?** (Babe was good at every sport that she tried: baseball, softball, tennis, and basketball.) **NOTE DETAILS**

Discuss the Stop and Think question on page 42: **What do you think you will learn in this selection?** (Posssible response: I think I will learn how Babe Didrickson became one of the greatest athletes of all time.) Guide students in writing the answer to this question. **MAKE PREDICTIONS**

Have a volunteer read aloud the third sentence on page 43. Ask: **How can you use the information in this sentence to figure out what *lunged* means?** (Possible response: I know that in softball, runners have to reach home plate before getting tagged. I think that when Babe lunged, she moved so suddenly and quickly so she could tag out the runners on the other team.) **CONTEXT CLUES**

Discuss the Stop and Think question on page 43: **What made the team owner start a track team?** (The team owner started a track team because he saw Babe's talent in track.) Guide students in writing the answer to this question. **CAUSE AND EFFECT**

pp. 44–45

Discuss the Stop and Think question on page 44: **How were women athletes treated in the 1930s?** (In the 1930s, women athletes were treated like they were odd ducks. Unlike men, they didn't earn money from competing in sports.) Guide students in writing the answer to this question. **SYNTHESIZE**

Explain that we can understand what happens in a selection better if we stop occasionally to summarize what we've read. Model using a summarizing strategy.

THINK ALOUD **I want to make sure that I know what's going on in the selection, so I'm going to take a moment to summarize what's happened so far: Babe was a baseball whiz as a kid. She was also terrific in basketball and track. In Babe's day, women athletes could not compete in most sports. Golf was an exception, so Babe learned to play golf. SUMMARIZE**

Discuss the Stop and Think question on page 45: **Think about Babe's actions. What can you tell about her?** (Possible response: I can tell that Babe was determined, confident, and focused. She didn't let critics stop her from earning money through sports and she learned to play golf because it offered women greater opportunity.) Guide students in writing the answer to this question. **MAKE INFERENCES**

pp. 46–47

Write this sentence from page 46 on the board, and read it with students: *When she smacked the ball, it went off like a rocket.* Ask: **What two things is the author comparing? What does the comparison help you visualize?** (Possible response: The author is comparing a golf ball set in motion by Babe and a rocket being launched. The comparison helps you visualize how hard and far Babe propelled the ball.) **AUTHOR'S CRAFT**

Discuss the Stop and Think question on page 46: **Think about the problems Babe faced. How would you feel if you were Babe? Explain your answer.** (Possible response: I would feel angry because I wasn't getting paid for competing, like the men were.) Guide students in writing the answer to this question. **PERSONAL RESPONSE**

Discuss the Stop and Think question on page 47: **What happened to Babe in 1953?** (In 1953, Babe got sick.) Guide students in writing the answer to this question. **CHRONOLOGICAL ORDER**

pp. 48

Discuss the Stop and Think question on page 48: **How did Babe help women today?** (Babe helped women today by modeling how women can be great athletes and get paid for competing in sports.) Guide students in writing the answer to this question. **DRAW CONCLUSIONS**

Spelling Words: Lesson 4

1. decorating	11. frightened
2. applying	12. panicked
3. delaying	13. relayed
4. employed	14. preparing
5. studying	15. replied
6. supposed	16. invited
7. exciting	17. multiplied
8. married	18. planning
9. envied	19. lying
10. studied	20. served

page 49

Answers to *Think Critically* Questions   Help students read and answer the *Think Critically* questions on page 49. Then guide students in writing the answer to each question. Possible responses are provided.

1. Next, Babe played basketball; Then Babe competed in track; Finally, Babe played golf. **SEQUENCE**

2. Babe solved the problems by not giving up; instead, she started a golf club in which women could compete for money. **MAIN IDEA AND DETAILS**

3. It's important because her story is inspiring. She was a world-class athlete who believed in herself and made her dreams come true. **AUTHOR'S PURPOSE**

RETEACH

Decoding/Spelling

Words with Inflections *-ed*, *-ing*   Remind students that when they add the inflection *-ed* or *-ing*, they may have to make a spelling change to the base word. Write the following on the board:

> frighten + ed = frightened
>
> prepare + ing = preparing

Help students see that no spelling change was needed to add the inflection *-ed* to *frighten*. Ask: **What spelling change was needed to add the inflection *-ing* to *prepare*?** (Drop the final *e* from *prepare*.)

Grammar/Writing

Practice Book 16

Combining Simple Sentences into Compound Sentences

Remind students the following about simple and compound sentences:

- A simple sentence expresses one complete thought.
- Two or more simple sentences can join to form a compound sentence.
- The subject, predicate, or both may be simple or compound.

Write the following sentences on the board:

> Jan ate a burrito for lunch.
>
> Julie chose salad.

Tell students simple sentences are joined by a comma and a coordinating conjunction such as *but, or, and,* or *for*. Ask students to combine the two sentences into a compound sentence. (Jan ate a burrito for lunch, but Julie chose salad.) Write *Jan ate a burrito for lunch; Julie chose salad* on the board. Explain to students that sometimes, simple sentences are joined by a semicolon.

GUIDED PRACTICE   Direct students' attention to their *Practice Books* page 16. Guide them in completing the activities. Allow time for students to share their responses.

Fluency

Practice Book 15

Fluency Practice   Invite students to look at the bottom half of *Practice Book* page 15. These sentences have been broken into natural phrases. Tell students to repeat each phrase after you, imitating your expression, phrasing, and pace. After students have repeated each sentence, invite them to practice reading the sentences to a partner.

30+ Minutes

COMPREHENSION
Preteach Reference Sources

Reread and Summarize "Babe in the Hall of Fame"

DECODING/SPELLING
Reteach Words with Inflections *-ed, -ing*

BUILD ROBUST VOCABULARY
Teach Words from "Babe in the Hall of Fame"

GRAMMAR/WRITING
Reteach Writing Trait: Voice

FLUENCY
Fluency Practice

Materials Needed: *Bold Moves*

| Student Edition pp. 42–48 | Practice Book pp. 15, 17 | Copying Master 15 |

PRETEACH

Comprehsion

Copying Master 15

Reference Sources Distribute *Copying Master 15.* Call on volunteers to read the information at the top of the page and the description of each reference source in the chart.

GUIDED PRACTICE Working in pairs, have students identify the best reference source for each piece of information listed. After students have finished, call on volunteers to give the correct responses.

Reread and Summarize Have students reread and summarize "Babe in the Hall of Fame" in sections, as described below.

pp. 42–43

Let's reread pages 42–43 to recall how Babe Didrickson got her nickname and what sports she played as a youth.
Summary: Mildred Didrickson was nicknamed "Babe" after the great baseball player, Babe Ruth. As a child and teenager, she excelled at baseball, basketball, softball, tennis, and track.

pp. 44–45

Now let's reread pages 44–45 to find out what challenge Babe faced as a woman athlete.
Summary: Babe won many medals. Babe didn't let the critics stop her. She encouraged people to attend women's sporting events. She learned to play golf, which offered greater opportunity for women.

pp. 46–48

Last, let's reread pages 46–48 to remember the battle that Babe lost and her lifetime achievements.
Summary: Babe became a champion golfer and founded a club in which women could compete for money. She became ill and ultimately died from her illness. Some people consider her one of the best athletes of all time.

RETEACH

Decoding/Spelling

Words with Inflections *-ed, -ing* Write *studied* and *studyed* on the board. Remind students that if a word ends with *y,* you change the *y* to *i* before adding *-ed,* but you leave the *y* when adding *-ing.* Circle *studied* and discuss again why this is the correct spelling of the word. Do the same with *decorating* and *decorateing,* having students apply the rule about changing the spelling of words ending in *e.*

Tell students that when they are proofreading, if a word with *-ed* or *-ing* doesn't look right, they should use the rule to correct the spelling.

TEACH

Build Robust Vocabulary

pp. 44–48 **Words from "Babe in the Hall of Fame"**   Have students locate *javelin* on page 44 in their books. Ask a volunteer to read aloud the sentence in which this word appears. (Line 3: *Her arm was so strong that she could propel a javelin for what seemed like miles.*) Describe a "javelin" as a long, thin piece of wood or metal that people throw in contests. Continue by asking students to locate and read aloud the sentence in which *press* appears on page 48. (First sentence: *The press named Babe Didrickson a top athlete of the 1900s.*) Explain that this sentence means that newspapers and magazines said she was one of the best athletes. Then ask students to locate and read aloud the sentence in which *inducted* appears on page 48. (Line 2: *She was inducted into the halls of fame for both track and golf.*) Explain that this sentence means that people honored Babe by making her a member of special groups of great athletes. "Induct" means to make someone a member of a special group.

Ask each student to scramble the letters for one of the words. Then have partners exchange their scrambled words, figure out what the word is, and tell its meaning.

RETEACH

Grammar/Writing

Practice Book 17 **Writing Trait: Voice**   Have students turn to page 17 in their *Practice Books*. Explain that when you write a story, it is important to use your own personal voice to convey your feelings about characters and events. Direct students' attention to the graphic organizer. Ask: **How does a writer's personal voice come through in his or her writing?** (in words and phrases that show the writer's feelings)

GUIDED PRACTICE   Complete Part B together. Have students complete Part C independently. Invite students to share their responses with the group.

Fluency

Practice Book 15 **Fluency Practice**   Tell students that today they will reread the sentences on the bottom of *Practice Book* page 15. Have students locate and point to the first sentence. Tell students that everyone is going to read the sentence together. This choral reading will give students an opportunity to hear others and listen to the natural phrasing of the sentences. Choral-read each of the sentences several times.

30+ Minutes

COMPREHENSION
Reteach Reference Sources

DECODING/SPELLING
Reteach Words with Inflections *-ed, -ing*

BUILD ROBUST VOCABULARY
Reteach Words from "Babe in the Hall of Fame"

GRAMMAR/WRITING
Reteach Writing Form: Short Story

FLUENCY
Fluency Practice

Materials Needed: *Bold Moves*

Student Edition pp. 42–48	Practice Book p. 18	Copying Master 16

Spelling Words: Lesson 4

1. decorating	11. frightened
2. applying	12. panicked
3. delaying	13. relayed
4. employed	14. preparing
5. studying	15. replied
6. supposed	16. invited
7. exciting	17. multiplied
8. married	18. planning
9. envied	19. lying
10. studied	20. served

Comprehension

Reference Sources   Remind students that there are many types of reference sources. Each type contains different kinds of information. Model how a writer decides which reference source would be best to use:

I want to compare the records of three top golfers. I might find information by reading books or articles about each golfer and comparing their records, but that would take a lot of time. I could look for a chart in an almanac to see how each golfer performed compared to the others. An almanac would be the best reference source for the information I need.

GUIDED PRACTICE   Invite volunteers to write questions that they have about athletes and sports on the board. Then ask students to write the name of the reference source that they would use to find the answer to each question. Discuss the list.

- Where an athlete's home town is located (atlas)
- When an athlete was born and died (encyclopedia article or the Internet)
- How to pronounce the word *javelin* (dictionary)

Decoding/Spelling

Practice Book 18   **Words with Inflections *-ed, -ing*** Have students number a sheet of paper 1–18. Write the Spelling Word *decorating* on the board. Tell students that in the first seven words you will dictate, the inflection *-ing* is found at the end of each word. After students write each word, display it so they can proofread their work. Repeat this activity for the inflection *-ed* using the example *supposed*.

1. applying	2. delaying	3. studying	4. exciting
5. preparing	6. planning	7. lying	8. employed
9. married	10. envied	11. studied	12. frightened
13. panicked	14. relayed	15. replied	16. invited
17. multiplied	18. served		

Have students turn to page 18 in their *Practice Books*. Read aloud the first set of instructions. Read aloud the second set of instructions. Have students complete the page independently, first adding to the drawing and then circling the words that have spelling changes when *-ed* or *-ing* is added at the end.

RETEACH

Build Robust Vocabulary

Words from "Babe in the Hall of Fame" Review the meanings of the vocabulary words *javelin*, *press*, and *inducted*. Then say these sentences and ask which word describes each sentence. Have students explain why.

- **A person has to have a strong arm to compete in throwing long, thin rods.** (javelin)
- **Magazines and newspapers help us know what is happening in the world.** (press)
- **The best baseball players become members of the Baseball Hall of Fame.** (inducted)

RETEACH

Grammar/Writing

Copying Master 16

Writing Form: Short Story Remind students that a short story has a main character who has a conflict. Explain that when authors write a story, they use vivid words and phrases to convey feelings about the characters and events. In this way, the voice sounds natural, and a personal voice comes through in the writing. Distribute *Copying Master 16*. Read the Student Model together. Have students circle a sentence that shows the main character and her conflict.

GUIDED PRACTICE Complete the activity by having students revise a sentence in the story and underline words and phrases that show how the writer feels about the main character and events. Allow time for students to share their revised sentences with the group.

Student-Friendly Explanations

remedies Remedies are used to fix a problem.

luxury A luxury is something good that costs a lot of money.

triumphant You feel triumphant when you have achieved a goal or a victory.

propel When you propel a body or object, you have caused it to move in a certain direction.

astonishment When you feel astonishment, you are greatly surprised or are experiencing a sense of wonder.

intense An intense feeling is a strong feeling.

lunged When you have lunged at something, you have moved suddenly toward it.

fumble If you fumble an object, you handle it clumsily, or perhaps even drop it.

Fluency

pp. 42–48

Fluency Practice Have each student work with a partner to read passages from "Babe in the Hall of Fame" aloud to each other. Students may select a passage that they enjoyed or choose one of the following options:

- Read page 44. (Total: 90 words)
- Read page 47. (Total: 71 words)

Encourage students to read the selected passage aloud to their partner three times. Have the student rate his or her reading on the 1–4 scale.

1	Need more practice
2	Pretty good
3	Good
4	Great!

DAY AT A GLANCE
Day 5

VOCABULARY
Preteach *intimidating, calamity, invaluable, quandary, composure, hindrance, steadfast, surpassed, sage, trepidation*

COMPREHENSION
 Preteach Plot and Setting

DECODING/WORD ATTACK
Preteach Decode Longer Words

DECODING/SPELLING
Preteach Words with Short Vowels and Vowel Digraphs

GRAMMAR/WRITING
Preteach Sentences, Subjects, and Predicates

FLUENCY
Fluency Performance

Materials Needed: *Bold Moves*

Student Edition pp. 42–48

Skill Card 5

Copying Master 17

PRETEACH
Vocabulary

Copying Master 17 **Lesson 5 Vocabulary** Distribute a set of Vocabulary Word Cards for each pair of students. Hold up the card for the first word, and ask a volunteer to read it aloud. Have students repeat the word and hold up the matching card. Give the explanation for the word. Then ask students the first question below and discuss their responses. Continue for each Vocabulary Word.

- How would you feel if you had to meet an **intimidating** person?
- What's a **calamity** that could take place in a kitchen?
- What **quandary** might you face at school?
- What knowledge is **invaluable** to you?
- How is keeping your **composure** different from losing your temper?
- How can losing a library card be a **hindrance**?
- How would a **steadfast** person handle homework?
- When has your knowledge **surpassed** someone else's?
- Is it a good idea to follow **sage** advice? Why?
- Why do some students feel **trepidation** about taking tests?

PRETEACH
Comprehension

 Skill Card 5 **Plot and Setting** Have students look at side A of *Skill Card 5: Review: Plot and Setting.* Ask a volunteer to read the introductory paragraph. Have other students take turns reading the story aloud. Ask:

- **What do you think is the most important event in the plot? Explain.** (Possible response: The narrator's finding the flower is an important event, because it gives her an idea to solve her problem.)

- **What is the setting of the story?** (Possible responses: the mall, a gift shop, a florist's shop, the narrator's house, a party)

Point out that the setting changes as the plot unfolds.

GUIDED PRACTICE Guide students in copying the story map on a separate sheet of paper. Have students use the story information as they fill in the map. (Characters : narrator, Grandmom, Granddad; Setting: mall, gift shop, florist's shop, narrator's house, anniversary party; Conflict: The narrator can't find an anniversary gift, and time is running out; Resolution: The narrator spends all her money on a flower and makes a card; her grandparents love the gift.)

PRETEACH

Decoding/Word Attack

Decode Longer Words Remind students that when they see a two-syllable word with two consonants next to each other in the middle, they often divide the word between those consonants. Write the words *candid* and *circuit* on the board. Have students identify the two syllables in each word. (can-did; cir-cuit) Review that:

- A syllable with the CVC pattern is usually pronounced with a short vowel sound. /can·did/
- If a vowel digraph is followed by a consonant, the syllable is sometimes pronounced with a short vowel sound. /cir·cuit/

PRETEACH

Decoding/Spelling

Words with Short Vowels and Vowel Digraphs Remind students that two vowels can sometimes stand for one short vowel sound. Write the following words on the board: *feather, headband, biscuit, against.* Have students identify the vowel digraph in each word. (ea, ea, ui, ai)

PRETEACH

Grammar/Writing

Sentences, Subjects, and Predicates Review the types of sentences and the correct punctuation that matches each type. Then have students recall that a sentence needs to have a subject and a predicate. Review that a subject is what the sentence is about, and a predicate tells what the subject did. Write these sentences on the board, leaving off the end punctuation:

> What did you do this weekend
>
> We saw a funny movie about a boy genius
>
> My family has never laughed so hard
>
> Please see it

Guide students to add the correct punctuation to each sentence. (?, ., !, .) Then have them identify the simple subjects and simple predicates. (you, did do; We, saw; family, has laughed; (you), see) Remind students that imperative sentences have an implied subject, *you*.

Student-Friendly Explanations

intimidating If something is intimidating to you, it makes you feel fearful or threatened.

calamity A calamity is an event that causes damage or distress.

quandary If you are in a quandary, you are uncertain about what to do.

invaluable If something is invaluable, you feel that you can't do without it.

composure When you maintain your composure, you remain calm.

hindrance A hindrance is someone or something that gets in the way of accomplishing a task.

steadfast When you are steadfast, you are firm and unwavering about what needs to be done.

surpassed Something that has surpassed something else has become stronger than the other thing.

sage Someone who is sage is wise and knowledgeable.

trepidation You feel trepidation when you are fearful or anxious about something that is going to happen.

Fluency

pp. 42–48

Fluency Performance Invite students to read aloud the passages from "Babe in the Hall of Fame" that they selected and practiced earlier. Note the number of words each student reads correctly and incorrectly. Have students rate their own oral reading on the 1–4 scale. Give students the opportunity to continue practicing and then to read the passage to you again.

DAY AT A GLANCE

Day 1

 30+ Minutes

LESSON 5

VOCABULARY
Reteach *intimidating, calamity, invaluable, quandary, composure, hindrance, steadfast, surpassed, sage, trepidation*

COMPREHENSION
 Preteach Text Structure: Chronological Order

DECODING/WORD ATTACK
Preteach Decode Longer Words

DECODING/SPELLING
Preteach Words with Long Vowels and Vowel Digraphs

GRAMMAR/WRITING
Preteach Sentences, Subjects, and Predicates

FLUENCY
Fluency Practice

Materials Needed: *Bold Moves*

Student Edition pp. 50–51	Practice Book pp. 19, 20	Skill Card 5	Copying Master 18

RETEACH

Vocabulary

pp. 50–51

Lesson 5 Vocabulary Read aloud the Vocabulary Words and the Student-Friendly Explanations. Then have students turn to pages 50–51 in their books. Ask a volunteer to read the directions aloud. Remind students that they should read each sentence to themselves with the word they choose to be sure it makes sense. If students have difficulty choosing the correct word, refer to the Student-Friendly Explanations. After students complete the pages, have volunteers take turns reading aloud each sentence. (Answers for pages 50–51: 2. *trepidation,* 3. *surpassed,* 4. *calamity,* 5. *quandary,* 6. *hindrance,* 7. *sage,* 8. *invaluable,* 9. *steadfast,* 10. *composure,* 11. Answers will vary. 12. Answers will vary.)

PRETEACH

Comprehension

Skill Card 5

Text Structure: Chronological Order Have students look at side B of *Skill Card 5: Review: Chronological Order.* Ask a volunteer to read the Skill Reminder. Then have volunteers take turns reading the story. Ask students the following questions to help guide what they might want to enter in their sequence charts:

- **In what three ways does Buddy get in trouble?** (First, Buddy chews Pete's slippers; then, Buddy slobbers on Sally's curtains; and last, Buddy barks.)

- **What happens after the landlord tells them they have to move?** (Sally thinks of hiring Mrs. Kaiser to walk Buddy. The walks make Buddy too tired to bark.)

GUIDED PRACTICE Have students copy and complete the sequence chart. When all students have finished, review their responses together. (Box 1: The Hetzlers get a dog; Box 2: Buddy gets in trouble, first by chewing, next by slobbering, and finally by barking. Box 3: The Hetzlers hire Mrs. Kaiser to walk Buddy, which tires him out and solves the problem.)

Student-Friendly Explanations

intimidating If something is intimidating to you, it makes you feel fearful or threatened.

calamity A calamity is an event that causes damage or distress.

quandary If you are in a quandary, you are uncertain about what to do.

invaluable If something is invaluable, you feel that you can't do without it.

composure When you maintain your composure, you remain calm.

hindrance A hindrance is someone or something that gets in the way of accomplishing a task.

steadfast When you are steadfast, you are firm and unwavering about what needs to be done.

surpassed Something that has surpassed something else has become stronger than the other thing.

sage Someone who is sage is wise and knowledgeable.

trepidation You feel trepidation when you are fearful or anxious about something that is going to happen.

PRETEACH

Decoding/Word Attack

Decode Longer Words Write the word *compose* on the board and point out the CVCe pattern in the second syllable. Review with students that words with this syllable pattern are usually pronounced with the long vowel sound. Then write the word *trader* on the board. Point out the open first syllable. Explain that words with open syllables are also usually pronounced with the long vowel sound.

PRETEACH

Decoding/Spelling

Copying Master 18

Words with Long Vowels and Vowel Digraphs Remind students that two or more letters—usually vowels—can combine to stand for one long vowel sound. Distribute *Copying Master 18*. Echo-read the Spelling Words with students. Then ask students to identify the words with long vowel sounds and the letters that stand for those sounds in each word.

RETEACH

Grammar/Writing

Practice Book 20

Sentences, Subjects, and Predicates Review the types of sentences, and remind students that each type has a subject and predicate. Write these examples on the board:

> Where are you going, Jason
>
> Wow, what an amazing story

Have students supply the end marks and explain why each is correct. (?, !)

GUIDED PRACTICE Have students turn to *Practice Book* page 20. Complete the first item together, discussing how the errors should be corrected. Have students work in pairs to complete the page. Allow time for pairs to share their responses.

Fluency

Practice Book 19

Fluency Practice Have students turn to *Practice Book* page 19. Read the words in the first column aloud. Invite students to track each word and repeat the words after you. Then have students work in pairs to read the words in the first column aloud to each other. Follow the same procedure with each of the remaining columns.

Day 2

30+ Minutes

VOCABULARY

Reteach *intimidating, calamity, invaluable, quandary, composure, hindrance, steadfast, surpassed, sage, trepidation*

COMPREHENSION

"My Song"
Build Background
Monitor Comprehension
Answers to *Think Critically* Questions

DECODING/WORD ATTACK

Preteach Decode Longer Words

DECODING/SPELLING

Preteach Words with Variant Vowels and Diphthongs

GRAMMAR/WRITING

Preteach Compound Subjects and Predicates and Simple and Compound Sentences

FLUENCY

Fluency Practice

Materials Needed: *Bold Moves*

Student Edition pp. 52–59

Practice Book p. 19

Copying Master 17

Vocabulary

Copying Master 17

Lesson 5 Vocabulary Distribute a set of Vocabulary Word Cards for each student. Read aloud the Student-Friendly Explanation for one of the Vocabulary Words. Have students display and read the matching word card. Invite students to give a synonym for the word. Continue until students have matched and given synonyms for all the words.

Comprehension

Build Background: "My Song"
Ask students to share experiences they may have had with stage fright. **What did they need to do in front of an audience? How did they overcome their nervousness?**

Monitor Comprehension: "My Song"
pp. 52–53
Read the title of the story aloud. Then have students read pages 52–53 to find out why Chris and Kendall look afraid and tense.

After reading the pages, ask: **Why do Chris and Kendall look afraid and tense?** (Chris and Kendall look afraid and tense because they have a big responsibility. They are going to greet a big pop star on stage, in front of the whole sixth grade.) **CONFLICT/RESOLUTION**

Discuss the Stop and Think question on page 52: **How do Chris and Kendall feel? How do their classmates feel?** (Chris and Kendall feel afraid and nervous. Their classmates feel excited.) Guide students in writing the answer to this question. **COMPARE AND CONTRAST**

Discuss the Stop and Think question on page 53: **What challenge do Chris and Kendall face?** (Their challenge is to calm down, relax, and put aside their fears so they can conduct the interview with Kara Clark.) Guide students in writing the answer to this question.
 PLOT AND SETTING

pp. 54–55
Discuss the Stop and Think question on page 54: **Would you be nervous if you were Chris? Explain.** (Possible response: I would not be nervous, because I like performing on stage.) Guide students in writing the answer to this question. **IDENTIFY WITH CHARACTERS**

Ask: **How is the story conflict developing?** (The interview that Chris and Kendall were so nervous about is going well.) If students have difficulty, model using the story structure strategy.

(THINK ALOUD) **I know that the story conflict is the problem that the main characters face. In "My Song," Chris and Kendall's conflict is inside themselves. They need to overcome their fear of interviewing a big star. I see the conflict developing in a way that suggests Chris and Kendall will overcome their fear. The interview that they were so nervous about is going well.** USE STORY STRUCTURE

Discuss the Stop and Think question on page 55: **What happens after Kara Clark walks on stage?** (After Kara walks on stage, she smiles and waves; then she sits down and looks at the hosts.) Guide students in writing the answer to this question. TEXT STRUCTURE: CHRONOLOGICAL ORDER

pp. 56–57 Discuss the Stop and Think question on page 56: **What problem did Kara face when she first started singing?** (Kara was afraid when she went on stage to sing.) Guide students in writing the answer to this question. CONFLICT/RESOLUTION

Point out that all the stories in students' books were written, in part, to teach. Ask: **What new vocabulary words can you learn on pages 56–57?** (Possible response: I can learn the lesson Vocabulary Words *trepidation, hindrance, sage, invaluable,* and *frantic* and *inspiring*.) AUTHOR'S PURPOSE/VOCABULARY

Discuss the Stop and Think question on page 57: **What tips do you think Kara might share?** (Possible response: Kara might share tips such as "Never give up, even if there are hindrances to your success.") Guide students in writing the answer to this question. MAKE PREDICTIONS

page 58 Discuss the Stop and Think question on page 58: **What do the hosts learn about overcoming fears?** (Possible response: They learn that it takes persistence, steadfastness, and determination to overcome fears.) Guide students in writing the answer to this question. THEME

Ask: **What imagery does the author use to describe how the class responds to Kara's song?** (The "thrilled fans jump up and begin clapping, singing, and swaying.") FIGURATIVE LANGUAGE

Ask: **What words at the end of the story state the theme?** ("Trust in yourself and you can go a long way.") THEME

VOCABULARY

Student-Friendly Explanations

intimidating If something is intimidating to you, it makes you feel fearful or threatened.

calamity A calamity is an event that causes damage or distress.

quandary If you are in a quandary, you are uncertain about what to do.

invaluable If something is invaluable, you feel that you can't do without it.

composure When you maintain your composure, you remain calm.

hindrance A hindrance is someone or something that gets in the way of accomplishing a task.

steadfast When you are steadfast, you are firm and unwavering about what needs to be done.

surpassed Something that has surpassed something else has become stronger than the other thing.

sage Someone who is sage is wise and knowledgeable.

trepidation You feel trepidation when you are fearful or anxious about something that is going to happen.

Spelling Words: Lesson 5

1. circuit	11. aglow
2. against	12. breathe
3. cabinet	13. pound
4. feather	14. applaud
5. system	15. turquoise
6. sneeze	16. awkward
7. proclaimed	17. delaying
8. grief	18. employed
9. approach	19. replied
10. arcade	20. preparing

 page 59

Answers to *Think Critically* Questions   Help students read and answer the *Think Critically* questions on page 59. Then guide students in writing the answer to each question. Possible responses are provided.

1. I think that Chris and Kendall were good hosts because they overcame their fears, conducted a good interview, and entertained the audience. **CONFLICT/RESOLUTION**

2. I think they felt happy, relieved that the interview went well, and proud of themselves for overcoming their stage fright and doing a good job. **CHARACTERS**

3. Kara, Chris, and Kendall all felt scared about going on stage, but they put aside their fear to achieve their goals. **COMPARE AND CONTRAST**

PRETEACH

Decoding/Word Attack

Decode Longer Words   Write the word *contain* on the board and ask students to read it aloud. Ask students how many syllables are in *contain* and where it should be divided. (2; con/tain) Point out that the vowel pair *ai* is a digraph because the two vowels stand for one sound.

Write the following words on the board and ask students to read them aloud

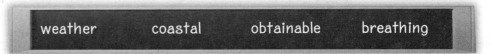

weather	coastal	obtainable	breathing

Ask students to identify the number of syllables in each word and where each word should be divided. (2, weath/er; 2, coast/al; 3, ob/tain/able; 2, breath/ing) Then have students identify the diagraph in each word. (*ea; oa; ai; ea*)

PRETEACH

Decoding/Spelling

Words with Variant Vowels and Diphthongs   Write *law* and *laud* on the board, and read them with students. Point out that the sound /aw/ is spelled *aw* in *law* and *au* in *laud* (which means "praise"). Remind students that the sounds /ow/, /oo/, and /oy/ can also be spelled in different ways. Write the following sentence on the board:

The *awdience/audience* *applauded/applawded* the ballet star in the *turqoyse/turquoise* costume; she had been *emploied/employed* as a teacher in the high *school/schewl*.

Have students select the correct word for each choice. (audience; applauded; turquoise; employed; school)

PRETEACH

Grammar/Writing

Compound Subjects and Predicates and Simple and Compound Sentences Remind students that compound subjects have the same predicate, and compound predicates have the same subject. Have students recall that simple sentences—which contain only one thought—can be combined into compound sentences by using the coordinating conjunctions *and, but, or,* or *for.* Then write these simple sentences on the board:

> Joanna and Polly play basketball.
>
> Only Joanna made the team.

Have students identify the compound subject and linking word in the first sentence. (Joanna, Polly; and) Guide students to combine the simple sentences to make a compound sentence. (Joanna and Polly play basketball, but only Joanna made the team.)

GUIDED PRACTICE Write the following sentences on the board:

> After school, Marla and I will eat a snack.
>
> After school, Marla and I will do our homework.
>
> After school, Marla and I will practice the guitar.

Have students work in pairs. Ask them to combine the sentences to make a sentence with a compound subject and a compound predicate. (After school, Marla and I will eat a snack, do our homework, and practice the guitar.)

Fluency

Practice Book 19 **Fluency Practice** Invite students to look at the bottom half of *Practice Book* page 19. These sentences have been broken into natural phrases. Tell students to repeat each phrase after you, mirroring your expression, phrasing, and pace. After students have repeated each sentence, invite them to practice reading the sentences to a partner.

30+ Minutes

COMPREHENSION
Preteach Forms of Fiction
Reread and Summarize "My Song"

DECODING/WORD ATTACK
Preteach Decode Longer Words

DECODING/SPELLING
Preteach Words with Inflections
-ed, -ing

BUILD ROBUST VOCABULARY
Teach Words from "My Song"

GRAMMAR/WRITING
Reteach Compound Subjects and
Predicates and Simple and Compound
Sentences

FLUENCY
Fluency Practice

Materials Needed: *Bold Moves*

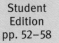

Student
Edition
pp. 52–58

Practice
Book
pp. 19, 21

Copying
Master
18

PRETEACH
Comprehension

Forms of Fiction   Remind students that there are different forms of fiction, each with particular characteristics. Then ask:

- **What kind of fiction is set in a particular time in history and has realistic characters and events?** (historical fiction)

- **How are fables, myths, legends, and folk tales alike?** (None is realistic.)

- **Is science fiction realistic?** (not in the world we know today—but it could be in the future)

GUIDED PRACTICE   Check students' understanding of forms of fiction by asking: **"My Song" is a play. Is it realistic or a fantasy? Explain.** (It is realistic because the characters and events seem real.)

Reread and Summarize   Have students reread and summarize "My Song" in sections, as described below.

 Let's reread pages 52–53 to find out what treat is in store for the sixth grade and why Chris and Kendall are nervous about it.
Summary: Kara Clark, a pop singing star, is performing for the sixth grade. Chris and Kendall are nervous because they will be on stage to greet and interview Kara.

 Now let's reread pages 54–55 to remember what happens as the presentation begins.
Summary: When the big moment arrives, Chris and Kendall do fine. Both students seem confident and comfortable as they interview Kara.

 Last, let's reread pages 56–58 to find out what Kara shares in words and song with the sixth grade.
Summary: Kara confesses that she was afraid to sing in public when she started out, explains how she overcame her fear, and urges students who want to be performers to stick with their goal. She performs her hit song. The class, clapping and swaying, sings along.

PRETEACH
Decoding/Word Attack

Decode Longer Words   Review with students that many verbs can take the endings *-ed* and *-ing*. Remind students that:

- When a verb ends in a short vowel followed by a consonant, you double the last letter of the verb before adding the ending. (*hop, hopped; split, splitting*)

- When a verb ends in *e* and contains a long vowel as its last or only syllable, you drop the last letter of the verb before adding the ending. (*cope, coped; care, caring*)

Write the following words on the board: *kidding, circling, underlined, roller skating.* Guide students to identify each verb and its inflectional ending.

Decoding/Spelling

Copying Master 18

Words with Inflections *-ed, -ing*   Distribute *Copying Master 18.* Remind students that a root verb sometimes—but not always—changes its spelling when the ending *-ed* or *-ing* is added. Have students identify the Spelling Words with *-ed* and *-ing* endings and name the root verb from which it was made. Then have them work with a partner to complete the activity.

Build Robust Vocabulary

pp. 52–55

Words from "My Song"   Have students locate the word *glee* on page 52 of "My Song." Ask a volunteer to read aloud the sentence in which this word appears. (Line 2: *The class is buzzing with glee as the students wait for her to arrive.*) Explain that this sentence means that the class is feeling very excited. Then ask students to locate and read aloud the sentence in which the word *buffs* appears on page 55. (Line 6: *Speaking of Kara buffs, do they send much fan mail?*) Explain that *buffs* are people who are excited and knowledgeable about a certain topic.

Ask each student to make up a sentence for each word. Have individuals tell the class their sentences but substitute the word *beep* for the real word. Have the class tell what *beep* stands for.

Grammar/Writing

Practice Book 21

Compound Subjects and Predicates and Simple and Compound Sentences   Review with students what they have learned about combining subjects, predicates, and sentences. Discuss when commas need to be added to compound parts.

GUIDED PRACTICE   Have students turn to *Practice Book* page 21. Have a student read the directions aloud. Point out that students will be combining subjects, predicates, or sentences, and they should correct punctuation when needed. Allow time to review and discuss students' responses.

Fluency

Practice Book 19

Fluency Practice   Tell students that today they will reread the sentences on the bottom of *Practice Book* page 19. Have students locate and point to the first sentence. Tell students that everyone is going to read the sentence together. This choral reading will give students an opportunity to hear others and listen to the natural phrasing of the sentences. Choral-read each of the sentences several times.

DAY AT A GLANCE

Day 4

COMPREHENSION
Preteach Reference Sources

DECODING/SPELLING
Cumulative Review

BUILD ROBUST VOCABULARY
Reteach Words from "My Song"

GRAMMAR/WRITING
Cumulative Review

FLUENCY
Fluency Practice

Materials Needed: *Bold Moves*

| Student Edition pp. 52–58 | Practice Book p. 22 | Copying Masters 19, 20 |

Spelling Words: Lesson 5

1. circuit	11. aglow
2. against	12. breathe
3. cabinet	13. pound
4. feather	14. applaud
5. system	15. turquoise
6. sneeze	16. awkward
7. proclaimed	17. delaying
8. grief	18. employed
9. approach	19. replied
10. arcade	20. preparing

Comprehension

Reference Sources   Remind students that there are many types of reference sources containing different types of information presented in various ways. Distribute *Copying Master* 19. Have volunteers read aloud the information at the top of the page. Suggest that students refer to the bulleted descriptions as they do the activity.

> *Copying Master 19*

GUIDED PRACTICE   Ask students to complete the page with a partner. Invite students to share and explain their responses.

Decoding/Spelling

Cumulative Review   Have students number a sheet of paper 1–16. Write the Spelling Word *circuit* on the board, read it aloud, and point to the digraph. (ui) Tell students that the first four words you will dictate have a short vowel sound made either by a single vowel or a vowel digraph. After students write each word, display it so they can proofread their work. Repeat this activity using the word *grief* for long vowel sounds made by a single vowel or a vowel digraph. Use the word *approach* for variant vowels and diphthongs. Use *proclaimed* for words with inflection *-ed, -ing*.

> *Practice Book 22*

1. against	2. cabinet	3. feather	4. system
5. arcade	6. aglow	7. sneeze	8. breathe
9. pound	10. applaud	11. turquoise	12. awkward
13. employed	14. delaying	15. replied	16. preparing

Have students turn to page 22 in their *Practice Books*. Ask a volunteer to read aloud the first set of instructions. Have students read and mark the text as instructed. Have a volunteer read aloud the second set of instructions. Complete the page together.

Build Robust Vocabulary

Words from "My Song"   Review the meanings of the words *glee* and *buffs*. Then say these sentences and ask which word describes each sentence. Have students explain why.

- **Bounce got very excited and delighted when he saw me get out the dog treats.** (glee)
- **Sarah and her brother are experts on birds. They go bird watching every weekend.** (buffs)

RETEACH
Grammar/Writing

Copying Master 20

Cumulative Review   Have students recall the grammar skills they reviewed in this lesson:

- kinds of sentences
- subjects and predicates
- compound subjects and predicates
- simple and compound sentences

Have students give examples of a declarative, interrogative, imperative, and exclamatory sentence and discuss the correct end punctuation for each.

GUIDED PRACTICE   Distribute *Copying Master 20*. Ask volunteers to read the directions. Have students complete the page independently. Allow time to review students' responses with the group.

Fluency

pp. 52–58   **Fluency Practice**   Have each student work with a partner to read passages from "My Song" aloud to each other. Remind students to:

- focus on accuracy to pronounce words correctly.
- use accuracy to better understand the text.

Encourage partners to read the selected passage aloud three times. Have the students rate their own reading on the 1–4 scale.

1	Need more practice
2	Pretty good
3	Good
4	Great!

DAY AT A GLANCE

Day 5

VOCABULARY
Preteach *jest, haywire, sinuous, immobile, supple, fused, intonation*

COMPREHENSION
 Preteach Plot and Characters

DECODING/WORD ATTACK
Preteach Decode Longer Words

DECODING/SPELLING
Preteach Words with Syllable Pattern Consonant Plus -*le*

GRAMMAR/WRITING
Preteach Prepositions

FLUENCY
Fluency Performance

Materials Needed: *Bold Moves*

Student
Edition
pp. 52–58

Copying
Master
21

30+ Minutes

PRETEACH

Vocabulary

Copying
Master
21

Lesson 6 Vocabulary   Distribute a set of Vocabulary Word Cards to each pair of students. Hold up the first word, and ask a volunteer to read it aloud. Have students repeat the word and hold up the matching card. Give the explanation for the word. Ask students the first question below and discuss their responses. Continue for each Vocabulary Word.

- **When did you tell a story in jest?**
- **What happened when one of your toys went haywire?**
- **Have you ever followed a sinuous trail?**
- **When was a time you were so scared you were immobile?**
- **Did you ever a have a ball that was supple? Was it rubber?**
- **What food have you eaten that became fused to the roof of your mouth?**
- **When you listen to someone speak without intonation in his or her voice, how does it make you feel?**

PRETEACH

Comprehension

pp. 52–58

Plot and Characters   Explain that the plot of a story consists of a conflict and the resolution of that conflict. Point out that characters' personality traits have an impact on what happens in a story. Ask students to recall "My Song." Then ask:

- **What challenge did Chris and Kendall face?** (They had to do a show, but they were nervous.)
- **What was the music teacher's advice?** (to have faith in yourself)
- **Were Chris and Kendall able to follow the advice? Explain.** (Yes, they believed they could do it and were able to perform in the show.)
- **What challenge did Kara share in the story?** (She had been afraid to sing in public.)
- **What might have happened if Kara were a different kind of person? What if she had not gotten past her fear?** (Her dream might not have come true; she wouldn't have become a famous singer.)

GUIDED PRACTICE   Have students work in small groups as they discuss changing the characters for "My Song." Tell students that Chris and Kendall could not get over being nervous. Have groups discuss how the plot would be different. (The show might not have gone on; the music teacher may have had to do the interview.) Have students discuss what other advice the music teacher might have had for these new characters.

PRETEACH

Decoding/Word Attack

Decode Longer Words Tell students that when a word ends in consonant-plus -*le*, you divide the word into syllables in front of the consonant. Explain that if there are two consonants before the -*le*, the previous syllable is usually pronounced with a short vowel sound. If there is one consonant before the -*le*, the previous syllable is usually pronounced with a long vowel sound. Write *wobble* and *maple* on the board. Draw a line between the syllables to show where each word should be divided. (wob/ble, ma/ple) Circle the consonant that ends the first syllable in *wobble* and the vowel that ends the first syllable in *maple*. (b, a) Then say the vowel sound in each word. Continue this exercise using *feeble* and *frazzle* (fee/ble, long *e*; fraz/zle, short *a*)

PRETEACH

Decoding/Spelling

Words with Syllable Pattern Consonant Plus -*le* Tell students to listen carefully for the ending sounds as you say the words *mantle* and *jumble*. Write the words on the board and show how the letters -*le* make the sound /əl/. Then write these words on the board: *mangle, muzzle, crinkle, brittle*. Explain that these are some of the next lesson's Spelling Words. Help students understand that when they hear /əl/ at the end of a word, it is often spelled -*le*.

PRETEACH

Grammar/Writing

Prepositions Tell students that prepositions usually tell about relationships of time or place. Write this sentence on the board:

> The tests are on the table.

Ask students which words in the sentence tell where the tests are. (on the table) Point out that *on* is the preposition. It connects the noun *tests* with another word in the sentence, *table*. Now, write this sentence on the board:

> Jamal eats lunch after fourth period.

Read the sentence aloud. Have students identify the preposition by asking them when Jamal eats lunch. Have a volunteer underline *after*. Ask students what nouns are connected by the preposition *after*. (lunch and period)

Fluency

pp. 102–108 **Fluency Performance** Invite students to read aloud the passages from "My Song" that they selected and practiced earlier. Have students rate their own oral reading on the 1–4 scale. Give students the opportunity to continue practicing and then to read the passage to you again.

DAY AT A GLANCE

Day 1

VOCABULARY
Reteach *jest, haywire, sinuous, immobile, supple, fused, intonation*

COMPREHENSION
 Reteach Plot and Characters

DECODING/SPELLING
Reteach Words with Syllable Pattern Consonant Plus *-le*

GRAMMAR/WRITING
Preteach Prepositional Phrases

FLUENCY
Fluency Practice

Materials Needed: *Bold Moves*

Student Edition pp. 60–61   Practice Book p. 23   Skill Card 6   Copying Master 22

LESSON 6

30+ Minutes

RETEACH

Vocabulary

Lesson 6 Vocabulary Read aloud the Vocabulary Words and the Student-Friendly Explanations. Read aloud the entries in Carla's diary on pages 60–61 as students follow along in their books. As you read each sentence, have students think about the Vocabulary Words they have learned. Guide students to choose the word that best completes each sentence. If students are unable to give reasonable responses, refer to the Student-Friendly Explanations. (Answers for pages 60–61: 2. *jest*, 3. *fused*, 4. *immobile*, 5. *intonation*, 6. *supple*, 7. *sinuous*)

pp. 60–61

RETEACH

Comprehension

Skill Card 6

Plot and Characters Have students look at side A of *Skill Card 6: Plot and Characters*. Have a volunteer read the information at the top of the card. Then ask a student to read the story aloud. Ask:

- **Who are the characters in this story?** (two groups of children ready to play soccer)
- **What is the conflict?** (There is only one soccer ball and one field.)
- **How is the conflict resolved?** (The children share the ball and play soccer together.)

Remind students that a character's qualities can affect what happens in the plot. Discuss how the plot would be different if the group of children with the ball had not shared.

GUIDED PRACTICE Now have students look at side B of *Skill Card 6: Plot and Characters*. Have a volunteer read the Skill Reminder aloud. Then read aloud the story while students read along. Guide students as they copy the chart and complete it. Then ask students how the story might be different if the characters' qualities were different. Invite them to explain how this would affect the plot. (If either of the girls were selfish, they may not share the money or the ice cream.)

Decoding/Spelling

Copying Master 22

Words with Syllable Pattern Consonant Plus -le Distribute *Copying Master 22*. Model reading the Spelling Words and have students repeat them. Review the instruction for consonant plus -le. Have pairs of students write the Spelling Words on index cards. Have one student draw a card and read the word aloud. The other student writes the word. When a student spells a word correctly, he or she initials the card and returns it to the pile. Then have partners switch roles. Students should work through the pile twice or until each student has had the opportunity to spell each of the words. Have students write down each word they do not spell correctly to study later.

Grammar/Writing

Prepositional Phrases Remind students that a preposition shows the relationship of a noun or pronoun to another word in the sentence. Prepositions often tell about time or place. Write the following sentence on the board:

> The boat is in the water.

Ask a volunteer to read the sentence aloud. Underline the word *in*, and explain that it is a preposition; it gives information about place. Tell students that a prepositional phrase is made up of the preposition, its object (the noun or pronoun that comes after the preposition), and any words in between. Using the same sentence, point out that *in the water* is the prepositional phrase.

GUIDED PRACTICE Write the following sentences on the board:

> We camped beside the roaring river.
>
> I hurried among the busy shoppers.

Ask students to identify the prepositional phrase in each sentence. (beside the roaring river; among the busy shoppers)

VOCABULARY

Student-Friendly Explanations

jest Something said in jest is said in a playful or joking manner.

haywire When something has gone haywire, it is not functioning well.

sinuous Something that is sinuous is long and curving like a snake.

immobile If something is immobile, it cannot be moved.

supple A supple object can move and bend easily without breaking or cracking.

fused When two or more things are fused together, they are joined to become one object.

intonation Intonation is the rise and fall in pitch of any sound.

Fluency

Practice Book 23

Fluency Practice Have students turn to *Practice Book* page 23. Read the words in the first column aloud. Invite students to track each word and repeat the words after you. Then have students work in pairs to read the words in the first column aloud to each other. Follow the same procedure with each of the remaining columns. After partners have practiced reading aloud the words in each of the columns, have them practice reading all of the words.

DAY AT A GLANCE

Day 2

VOCABULARY

Reteach *jest, haywire, sinuous, immobile, supple, fused, intonation*

COMPREHENSION

"It Takes Two!"

Build Background

Monitor Comprehension

Answers to *Think Critically* Questions

DECODING/SPELLING

Reteach Words with Syllable Pattern Consonant Plus *-le*

GRAMMAR/WRITING

Preteach Choosing the Correct Preposition

FLUENCY

Fluency Practice

Materials Needed: *Bold Moves*

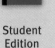

| Student Edition pp. 62–69 | Practice Book pp. 23, 24 | Copying Masters 21, 22 |

Vocabulary

Copying Master 21

Lesson 6 Vocabulary   Distribute a set of Word Cards to each pair of students. Read aloud the meaning of one of the Vocabulary Words and have students display and read the matching card. Challenge students to use the word in a sentence. Continue until all words have been used.

Comprehension

Build Background: "It Takes Two!"

Ask students to share experiences they may have had with meeting new friends. **Were they shy or bashful? Were they afraid to meet someone they didn't know?** Ask how they handled those situations or how they wish they had handled those situations.

pp. 62–63

Monitor Comprehension: "It Takes Two!"

Read the title of the story aloud. Then have students read to find out what happened to Ben on the way to school.

After reading the page, ask: **What happened to Ben on the way to school?** (Ben got splashed by a big truck. He is soaking wet.) NOTE DETAILS

Discuss the Stop and Think question on page 62: **Do you think Ben is upset? Why do you think so?** (Possible response: I think Ben is a bit upset. He is all wet from the passing truck.) Guide students in writing the answer to this question. DRAW CONCLUSIONS

Ask: **Why did Carla sit immobile as she listened for her name?** (She wasn't able to pick Ben herself, so she was hoping she wouldn't get someone else.) MAKE INFERENCES

Discuss the Stop and Think question on page 63: **What problem does Carla face?** (Carla's problem is that she is paired with someone she doesn't know.) Guide students in writing the answer to the question. CONFLICT/RESOLUTION

pp. 64–65 Ask students to describe the characters in the illustrations on pages 64 and 65. Then discuss the Stop and Think question on page 64: **Do you think Wendell will be a good teammate? Explain.** (Possible response: I think that Wendell might be a good teammate because he has a lab. He knows how to make things.) Guide students in writing the answer to this question. **MAKE PREDICTIONS**

Read aloud the third and fourth paragraphs on page 65. Model the strategy of identifying characters' traits, or qualities:

THINK ALOUD **I see that Carla is unsure about her ability to build a model. But Wendell is confident that Carla can add to the project and that they can make a good team. By looking at the illustration and the words, I can see that Wendell is organized and knows how to make models. By encouraging Carla, Wendell seems to be helpful and friendly. CHARACTERS' TRAITS**

Discuss the Stop and Think question on page 65: **What can you tell about Carla?** (Possible response: I can tell that Carla is uncertain, but willing to try working with Wendell.) Guide students in writing the answer to this question. **PLOT AND CHARACTERS**

pp. 66–67 Discuss the Stop and Think question on page 66: **Do you think the boats will sink? Explain your answer.** (Possible response: I think the boats will float because they used foam trays and set them on foam balls.) Guide students in writing the answer to this question. **NOTE DETAILS**

Ask: **What was Carla's plan to make the project complete?** (Her plan was to make a tape recording of water bubbling and running, like a stream.) **NOTE DETAILS**

Discuss the Stop and Think question on page 67: **How does Carla feel about having Wendell as a teammate now?** (Possible response: Carla feels proud and thankful that she has Wendell as a teammate.) Guide students in writing the answer to this question. **CHARACTERS' EMOTIONS**

page 68 Discuss the Stop and Think question on page 68: **How do Carla and Wendell use different talents to work together?** (Carla came up with the plan and Wendell made the plan work.) Guide students in writing the answer to this question. **MAKE COMPARISONS**

VOCABULARY

Student-Friendly Explanations

jest Something said in jest is said in a playful or joking manner.

haywire When something has gone haywire, it is not functioning well.

sinuous Something that is sinuous is long and curving like a snake.

immobile If something is immobile, it cannot be moved.

supple A supple object can move and bend easily without breaking or cracking.

fused When two or more things are fused together, they are joined to become one object.

intonation Intonation is the rise and fall in pitch of any sound.

Spelling Words: Lesson 6

1. nestle	11. jumble
2. mangle	12. kindle
3. feeble	13. dwindle
4. crinkle	14. swindle
5. wobble	15. assemble
6. frazzle	16. mantle
7. obstacle	17. brittle
8. tickle	18. freckle
9. hustle	19. muzzle
10. bridle	20. cuticle

page 69

Answers to *Think Critically* Questions

Help students read and answer the *Think Critically* questions on page 69. Guide students in writing the answer to each question. Possible responses are provided.

1. [Resolution:] Carla and Wendell work together to make a great project. **Conflict/Resolution**

2. Here is how they are alike: they are both talented and good team-mates. Here is how they are different: Carla has not had a lot of practice building models, but Wendell has. Carla's talent is planning. Wendell's talent is building. **Compare and Contrast**

3. I think the author wants us to learn how to work well on a team. **Author's Purpose**

RETEACH

Decoding/Spelling

Copying Master 22

Words with Syllable Pattern Consonant Plus *-le* Distribute *Copying Master 22* and remind students that a word ending with *-le* makes the /əl/ sound. Have students echo-read the words, noting if each has a long or short vowel sound in the syllable that preceeds the consonant plus *-le*.

Then divide the group into two teams. Have each team write questions that can be answered with Spelling Words. Ask them to write the question on the front of an index card and the answer on the back. Have teams take turns. Ask them to continue play until each student has had a turn to ask or answer a question.

PRETEACH

Grammar/Writing

Practice Book 24

Choosing the Correct Preposition   Remind students of the following:

- A preposition shows the relationship of a noun or a pronoun to another word in the sentence.

- Prepositions tell about time or place.

- A prepositional phrase is made up of a preposition, its object (the noun or pronoun that follows it), and any words in between.

Write *A raft floats _____the water* (*before, on, among*) on the board. Ask students to choose the correct preposition to complete this sentence. (on) Have them explain why they chose their response

GUIDED PRACTICE   Direct students' attention to their *Practice Books* page 24. Guide them in completing the activities. Allow time for students to share their responses.

Fluency

Practice Book 23   **Fluency Practice**   Invite students to look at the bottom half of *Practice Book* page 23. These sentences have been broken into natural phrases. Tell students to repeat each phrase after you, mirroring your expression, phrasing, and pace. After students have repeated each sentence, invite them to practice reading the sentences to a partner.

COMPREHENSION
Preteach Vocabulary Strategies, Poetic Devices

Reread and Summarize "It Takes Two!"

DECODING/SPELLING
Reteach Words with Syllable Pattern Consonant Plus *-le*

BUILD ROBUST VOCABULARY
Teach Words from "It Takes Two!"

GRAMMAR/WRITING
Reteach Writing Trait: Ideas

FLUENCY
Fluency Practice

Materials Needed: *Bold Moves*

Student Edition pp. 62–68

Practice Book p. 25

Copying Master 23

Comprehension

 Vocabulary Strategies Distribute *Copying Master 23* and have students listen as you read the information at the top of the page. Then have a volunteer read the passage. Ask a volunteer to read the first sentence aloud. Model how to identify the context clues that help readers know that this *bat* is a metal or wooden stick-like device used when playing baseball.

GUIDED PRACTICE Extend the activity by having students think of other multiple-meaning words and using them in sentences. Challenge classmates to identify the context clues.

Poetic Devices Tell students that poetic devices are tools poets use when they write poems. Write *word choice, alliteration, onomatopoeia, rhythm, repetition,* and *rhyme* on the board. Discuss the musical quality each adds to the tone or style of a poem.

Reread and Summarize Have students reread and summarize "It Takes Two!" in sections, as described below.

 Let's reread pages 62–63 to recall how Carla felt about Ben and Wendell.
Summary: Carla felt Ben was her pal. She felt they would make a good team for Teamwork Week. Carla did not know Wendell and wasn't happy about being his partner.

 Now let's reread pages 64–65 to remember what happens when Carla goes to Wendell's house.
Summary: Carla is worried when she learns that Wendell is in his "lab." Wendell, it turns out, has everything needed to make a model. He encourages Carla, who admits that she's good at planning things.

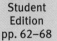 **Last, let's reread pages 66–68 to find out what happened with Carla and Wendell's project.**
Summary: Carla and Wendell made their model amusement park ride out of clay, water, and foam. A tape of running water adds to their presentation. Carla and Wendell realize that it took two to get the job done.

Decoding/Spelling

Words with Syllable Pattern Consonant Plus *-le* Say *jumble,* and ask students to listen carefully to the last syllable. Name the letters that make up this last syllable. (ble) Write the word on the board. Remind students that the /əl/ sound is spelled *le*. Then write the following words on the board:

crinkle	wobble	kindle
swindle	dwindle	mantle

Guide students as they divide each word into syllables. Suggest to students that when they are not sure how to spell a word that ends with /əl/, they should divide it into syllables, write the last syllable with consonant-plus *le,* and then check in a dictionary to verify that the spelling is correct. (crin/kle; wob/ble; kin/dle; swin/dle; dwin/dle; man/tle)

TEACH

Build Robust Vocabulary

pp. 65–68

Words from "It Takes Two!" Have students locate the word *coaxed* on page 65 of "It Takes Two!" Ask a volunteer to read aloud the sentence in which this word appears. (Line 6: *"Come on, Carla!" coaxed Wendell.*) Explain that this sentence means that Wendell gently tried to urge or talk Carla into working with him. Continue by asking students to locate and read aloud the sentence in which the word *moat* appears on page 66. (Line 7: T*hey put the model in a pan filled with water to make a moat around the tree grove.*) Explain that a moat is a deep ditch filled with water around a castle, fort, or town. Then ask students to locate and read aloud the sentence in which the word *insisted* appears on page 68. (Line 9: *"Well, Wendell made the plan work," Carla insisted.*) Explain that this sentence means that Carla made her comment in a strong way as if she were sure it was true.

Write the words on separate cards. Turn the cards face down. Have each student select a card, read the word, and use it in a sentence.

RETEACH

Grammar/Writing

Practice Book 25

Writing Trait: Ideas Have students turn to page 25 in their *Practice Books.* Help students understand that realistic details help create the characters, setting, conflict, and resolution in a realistic story. Ask a volunteer to read the first part of the page. Remind students that the setting is where a story takes place. Note that the details help readers "see" the basement. Have a student read Part B. Point out that some details might describe both the setting and the character. For example, *Jason snapped his gum* helps us both "see" Jason and "hear" the setting.

GUIDED PRACTICE Have pairs of students complete the page. Allow time for students to share their responses.

Fluency

Practice Book 23

Fluency Practice Tell students that today they will reread the sentences on the bottom of *Practice Book* page 23. Have students locate and point to the first sentence. Tell students that everyone is going to read the sentence together. This choral reading will give students an opportunity to hear others and to listen to the natural phrasing of the sentences. Choral-read each of the sentences several times.

30+ Minutes

COMPREHENSION
Reteach Vocabulary Strategies, Poetic Devices

DECODING/SPELLING
Reteach Words with Syllable Pattern Consonant Plus -*le*

BUILD ROBUST VOCABULARY
Reteach Words from "It Takes Two!"

GRAMMAR/WRITING
Reteach Writing Form: Realistic Story

FLUENCY
Fluency Practice

Materials Needed: *Bold Moves*

Student Edition pp. 62–68

Practice Book p. 26

Copying Master 24

Spelling Words: Lesson 6

1. nestle	11. jumble
2. mangle	12. kindle
3. feeble	13. dwindle
4. crinkle	14. swindle
5. wobble	15. assemble
6. frazzle	16. mantle
7. obstacle	17. brittle
8. tickle	18. freckle
9. hustle	19. muzzle
10. bridle	20. cuticle

Comprehension

Vocabulary Strategies Remind students that the following information can help them use context to determine a word's meaning:

- Many words have more than one meaning.
- Multiple-meaning words may be a verb in one context and a noun in another.
- To determine a word's meaning, look at context clues, or the words.

Poetic Devices Have students recall that imagery, figurative language, rhythm, repetition, and rhyme are poetic devices found in poetry. Write this poem on the board:

> Splish, splash, splosh!
> Like a racing rocket, a fish shot up,
> Over my head, it seemed to float,
> Landed in my rickety boat,
> Then flip, flop, kerplunk!
> Back into the stream it went.

Have students find examples in the poem to match the poetic devices.

Decoding/Spelling

Practice Book 26

Words with Syllable Pattern Consonant Plus -*le* Have students number a sheet of paper 1–18. Write the Spelling Word *nestle* on the board and point to the last syllable. Tell students that the first fifteen words you will dictate have two consonants before the -*le* and a short vowel sound in the first syllable. After students write each word, display it so they can proofread their work. Repeat this activity for one consonant before the -*le* and a long vowel sound in the first syllable using *bridle*.

1. mangle	2. crinkle	3. wobble	4. frazzle
5. tickle	6. hustle	7. jumble	8. kindle
9. dwindle	10. swindle	11. mantle	12. brittle
13. freckle	14. muzzle	15. assemble	16. feeble
17. cuticle	18. obstacle		

Have students turn to page 26 in their *Practice Books*. Ask students to read the story and circle the words that end with consonant plus -*le*. Guide students in completing the second activity. Allow time for students to share their responses.

RETEACH
Build Robust Vocabulary

Words from "It Takes Two!"   Review the meanings of the words *coaxed, moat,* and *insisted*. Then say these sentences, and ask which word describes each sentence. Have students explain why.

- **Alice gently urged her baby brother to eat his breakfast.** (coaxed)

- **Don scooped out sand to make a deep ditch filled with water around his sandcastle.** (moat)

- **Indy said very firmly that she was sure her dog was smarter than her friend's hamster.** (insisted)

RETEACH
Grammar/Writing

| Copying Master 24 |

Writing Form: Realistic Story   Distribute *Copying Master 24*. Have a volunteer read the information about a realistic story aloud. Then ask volunteers to read the passage aloud. Point out the margin notes explaining the steps in writing a realistic story. Write *He got a piece of cardboard and lined up the dogs* on the board. Point out that it is a perfectly good sentence. Note, however, that it is not very descriptive. Write the actual sentence from the passage: *He got a piece of stiff cardboard and lined up the poodle and some of the other little dogs.* Discuss how details help create pictures in readers' minds.

GUIDED PRACTICE   Guide students in completing the activity. Invite students to share their responses with the group.

Fluency

| pp. 62– 68 |

Fluency Practice   Have each student work with a partner to read passages from "It Takes Two!" aloud to each other. Students may select a passage that they enjoyed or choose one of the following options:

- Read page 66. (Total: 89 words)

- Read page 67. (Total: 85 words)

Encourage students to read the selected passage aloud to their partner three times. Have the student rate his or her reading on the 1–4 scale.

1	Need more practice
2	Pretty good
3	Good
4	Great!

DAY AT A GLANCE

Day 5

30+ Minutes

VOCABULARY
Preteach *disown, convince, treason, ordinary, suit, defeatist, rejected*

COMPREHENSION
 Preteach Plot and Characters

DECODING/WORD ATTACK
Preteach Decode Longer Words

DECODING/SPELLING
Preteach Words with VCCV and VCCCV

GRAMMAR/WRITING
Preteach Independent and Dependent Clauses; Phrases

FLUENCY
Fluency Performance

Materials Needed: *Bold Moves*

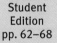

Student
Edition
pp. 62–68

Copying
Master
25

PRETEACH

Vocabulary

Copying
Master
25

Lesson 7 Vocabulary Distribute a set of Vocabulary Word Cards to each pair of students. Hold up the card for the first word, and ask a volunteer to read it aloud. Have students repeat the word and hold up the matching card. Give the explanation for the word. Then ask students the first question below and discuss their responses. Continue for each Vocabulary Word.

- **Would you disown a friend if he or she didn't tell you the truth?**
- **How would you convince someone to go ice-skating with you?**
- **Why is it treason if a soldier leaves the battlefield without permission?**
- **What would be an ordinary day for you?**
- **Would it suit a bird if it couldn't fly? Why or why not?**
- **What sorts of things might a defeatist say before competing in a race?**
- **How would you feel if your project for the Science Fair was rejected?**

PRETEACH

Comprehension

pp. 62–68
Focus Skill

Plot and Characters Tell students that a character's qualities and what the character thinks, says, and does affect the plot of a story. Remind students that the plot is a series of events, usually involving a problem, or conflict, and how the characters solve that problem. Refer students to "It Takes Two!" and talk briefly about the main characters, Carla and Wendell. Ask:

- **Would you describe Wendell as rude or helpful?** (helpful)
- **If Carla had refused to work with Wendell, how might the story have been different?** (Possible response: Neither student would have done as well on the project.)

GUIDED PRACTICE Now look at some specific passages in "It Takes Two!" Have students think about the characters' qualities and how they affect the plot by answering these questions:

- **Read the third and fourth paragraphs on page 65. What do Wendell's comments to Carla tell you about him?** (Possible response: Wendell seems confident and polite.)
- **Read page 68. How have Wendell's qualities affected the outcome of the story?** (Possible response: Wendell's encouragement gave Carla confidence. Wendell contributed his talents, Carla contributed hers, and they turned out to be a good team.)

PRETEACH

Decoding/Word Attack

Decode Longer Words Write *wander* on the board, and read it aloud. Tell students that when they see a word with two consonants together in the middle of the word, the syllables are usually divided between the two consonants. Ask students to identify the letters in *wander* that stand for the /wan/ sound. (wan) Then have them identify the letters that stand for the /dər/ sound. (der) Point out that when a syllable breaks after a consonant, the syllable is usually pronounced with a short vowel sound. Then write *complaint* on the board, and read it aloud. Have students note that there are three consonants together in the middle of the word. Point out that words with three consonants are often divided between the first two consonants. (com/plaint) Explain to students that the second syllable usually starts with a blend.

PRETEACH

Decoding/Spelling

Words with VCCV and VCCCV Write these Spelling Words on the board:

pattern	collapse	exclude	instance

Read the first word aloud and ask students to identify where to divide the syllables. (pat/tern) Have students divide the remaining words. Explain that these are some of the next lesson's Spelling Words.

PRETEACH

Grammar/Writing

Independent and Dependent Clauses; Phrases Write the following sentence on the board: *We got a new flag.* Read the sentence aloud. Tell students that an **independent clause** can stand alone. It makes sense by itself. Then write this phrase on the board: *because ours was torn.* Read it aloud. Tell students that a **dependent clause** is a phrase, or incomplete sentence. It cannot stand alone. Point out that a clause or phrase can give more information about a sentence. Write the two clauses together to form one sentence. Read the sentence aloud. Discuss with students how putting the two clauses or phrases together gives more information about why we got a new flag.

VOCABULARY

Student-Friendly Explanations

disown If you disown someone or something, you break your connection with them.

convince When you convince others of something, you persuade them that what you are saying is true.

treason Someone who betrays his or her country is committing the crime of treason.

ordinary If something is ordinary, it is not special, or different in any aspect.

suit For something to suit you, it must be appropriate for you.

defeatist Someone who expects, accepts, or is resigned to failure is a defeatist.

rejected When something has been turned down or not accepted, it has been rejected.

Fluency

pp. 62–68 **Fluency Performance** Invite students to read aloud the passages from "It Takes Two!" that they selected and practiced earlier. Note the number of words each student reads correctly and incorrectly. Give students the opportunity to continue practicing and then to read the passage to you again.

DAY AT A GLANCE
Day 1

VOCABULARY
Reteach *disown, convince, treason, ordinary, suit, defeatist, rejected*

COMPREHENSION
 Reteach Plot and Characters

DECODING/SPELLING
Reteach Words with VCCV and VCCCV

GRAMMAR/WRITING
Preteach Complex Sentences

FLUENCY
Fluency Practice

Materials Needed: *Bold Moves*

		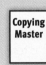	
Student Edition pp. 70–71	Practice Book p. 27	Skill Card 7	Copying Master 26

RETEACH

Vocabulary

pp. 70–71

Lesson 7 Vocabulary Read aloud the Vocabulary Words and the Student-Friendly Explanations. Then have students open their books to pages 70–71. Have volunteers read the paragraphs aloud. Guide students in completing the sentences by selecting the correct Vocabulary Word. Have a volunteer read each completed sentence aloud. Then guide students to discover the missing word in the word web. (Answers for pages 70–71: 2. treason, 3. rejected, 4. suit, 5. defeatist, 6. disown, 7. ordinary, [WEB:] ordinary)

RETEACH

Comprehension

Skill Card 7

 Plot and Characters Have students look at side A of *Skill Card 7: Plot and Characters*. Ask a student to read the information at the top of the card. Have students read the passage. Then direct students' attention to the chart and ask these guiding questions to help them understand the statements in the chart:

- **What conflict does Teresa face?**
- **What qualities do you think Teresa has?**
- **What is the resolution?**

Remind students that a character's qualities affect the outcome of a story's plot.

GUIDED PRACTICE Now have students look at side B of *Skill Card 7: Plot and Characters*. Ask volunteers to read aloud the Skill Reminder, and then the passage. Guide students to complete the graphic organizer by identifying the conflict, the character's qualities, and the resolution. (Conflict: It takes practice to get into the all-state singing group; Character's Qualities: He practices daily. He is able to sing even though he's scared. Resolution: The boy performs well for the judge and receives praise.)

RETEACH

Decoding/Spelling

Copying Master 26

Words with VCCV and VCCCV   Distribute *Copying Master 26*. Model reading the Spelling Words as students repeat them. Review the instruction for syllable patterns VCCV and VCCCV. Then have pairs of students write the Spelling Words on index cards. One student draws a card and reads its word aloud; the other student writes the word. Then partners switch roles. When a student spells a word correctly, he or she initials the card and returns it to the pile. Students should work through the pile twice or until each student has had the opportunity to spell each word. Have students write down each word they do not spell correctly to study later.

PRETEACH

Grammar/Writing

Complex Sentences   Remind students that an independent clause can stand alone and still make sense. A dependent clause cannot stand alone. Write the following sentence on the board:

> We got a new flag because ours was torn.

Tell students a complex sentence is made up of an independent clause and a dependent clause. Draw a line between *flag* and *because*. Have students identify which clause is independent and which is dependent. Note that the clauses in such a sentence are joined by a subordinating conjunction. (because) Then, write this sentence below the first:

> Because our flag was torn, we got a new one.

Tell students that when a sentence begins with a dependent clause, it is separated from the independent clause by a comma.

GUIDED PRACTICE   Write the following sentences on the board:

> My dog ate his food as soon as I put it in the bowl.
> Because my dog was hungry he ate his food immediately.

Ask volunteers to underline the subordinating conjunctions and to add a comma where needed. (underline: as soon as, because; comma after hungry)

VOCABULARY

Student-Friendly Explanations

disown If you disown someone or something, you break your connection with them.

convince When you convince others of something, you persuade them that what you are saying is true.

treason Someone who betrays his or her country is committing the crime of treason.

ordinary If something is ordinary, it is not special, or different in any aspect.

suit   For something to suit you, it must be appropriate for you.

defeatist Someone who expects, accepts, or is resigned to failure is a defeatist.

rejected When something has been turned down or not accepted, it has been rejected.

Fluency

Practice Book 27

Fluency Practice   Have students turn to *Practice Book* page 27. Read the words in the first column aloud. Invite students to track each word and repeat the words after you. Then have students work in pairs to read the words in the first column aloud to each other. Follow the same procedure with each of the remaining columns. After partners have practiced reading aloud the words in each column, have them practice reading all of the words.

LESSON 7

VOCABULARY
Reteach *disown, convince, treason, ordinary, suit, defeatist, rejected*

COMPREHENSION
"The Mixed-Up All-Stars"
Build Background
Monitor Comprehension
Answers to *Think Critically* Questions

DECODING/SPELLING
Reteach Words with VCCV and VCCCV

GRAMMAR/WRITING
Preteach Combining Sentences into Complex Sentences

FLUENCY
Fluency Practice

Materials Needed: *Bold Moves*

Practice Book

Copying Master

Student Edition pp. 72–79

Practice Book pp. 27, 28

Copying Masters 25, 26

Vocabulary

Copying Master 25

Lesson 7 Vocabulary Distribute a set of Vocabulary Word Cards to each student or pair of students. Read aloud the following sentences, leaving out the Vocabulary Word. Have students hold up the card that completes each sentence. Reread the sentence with the correct word.

1. **The team might** (disown) **me if I don't play well.**
2. **I tried to** (convince) **my friends that I DID get an A on the test.**
3. **Selling military secrets to another country would be an act of** (treason).
4. **My dog is no** (ordinary) **dog because he can dive under water.**
5. **That new outfit** (suits) **you.**
6. **I am not a** (defeatist) **because I do not accept failure.**
7. **I may get** (rejected) **if I don't fill out this form correctly.**

Comprehension

Build Background: "The Mixed-Up All-Stars"
Ask students to share experiences they have had making decisions they weren't sure about. Did they talk with family members or friends to help make up their minds? If so, what decisions were made and why?

pp. 72–73

Monitor Comprehension: "The Mixed-Up All-Stars"
Read the title of the story aloud. Then have students read pages 72–73 to find out who is telling the story and what seems to be the problem.

After reading the pages, ask: **Who is telling the story and what seems to be the problem?** (Gail; she's been asked to sing with the all-male Harlem Stars Glee Club and she doesn't think her voice will blend with theirs.) **POINT OF VIEW/SUMMARIZE**

Discuss the Stop and Think question on page 72: **What does Gail mean when she says she'll "sleep on it"?** (Possible response: Gail means that she won't make a decision until tomorrow.) Guide students in writing the answer to this question. **FIGURATIVE LANGUAGE**

Ask: **What word does Gail use to describe her singing to her Mom?** (crowing) **FIGURATIVE LANGUAGE**

Discuss the Stop and Think question on page 73: **What is the conflict in this story?** (Possible response: The conflict is that Gail does not think her singing style matches that of the Harlem Stars Glee Club, which she has been invited to join.) Guide students in writing the answer to this question. **PLOT AND CHARACTERS**

pp. 74–75 Discuss the Stop and Think question on page 74: **Why does Mr. Willow change the name of the club?** (Possible response: He changes the name because he wants to indicate that the group is changing.) Guide students in writing the answer to this question. **DRAW CONCLUSIONS**

Reread page 74 and model the strategy of identifying Characters' Traits by reading how Gail handles her opportunity to join the club.

(THINK ALOUD) **I reread this page because I wanted to make sure that I understand what happened. Gail woke up and saw small green buds growing on the trees and decided it was time for her to grow, too. She told her mom she at least needed to see if joining the club would work. This tells me that Gail is thoughtful and that she is willing to try new things, even if she has doubts. CHARACTERS' TRAITS**

Discuss the Stop and Think question on page 75: **Do you think Gail will give up? Explain your answer.** (Possible response: I think she'll find a way to make it work because she's a good singer.) Guide students in writing the answer to this question. **MAKE PREDICTIONS**

 pp. 76–77 Discuss the Stop and Think question on page 76: **What is happening in Gail's dream?** (Possible response: In Gail's dream, the voices of the Harlem All-Stars are blending.) Guide students in writing the answer to this question. **SUMMARIZE**

Ask: **What does Gail do as a result of her dream?** (Possible response: She shares her singing idea with her friends, then with Mr. Willow and the club.) **CAUSE AND EFFECT**

Discuss the Stop and Think question on page 77: **How do you think the girls feel now? Why do you think so?** (Possible response: I think the girls feel excited because their plan worked.) Guide students in writing the answer to this question. **CHARACTERS' EMOTIONS**

page 78 Discuss the Stop and Think question on page 78: **What do you learn about sharing talents?** (Possible response: I learn that you should share your talents with others.) Guide students in writing the answer to this question. **THEME**

Ask: **How did Gail's qualities affect the plot of the story?** (Gail was strong, confident and inventive. She was willing to work out a plan so that the girls and the boys could sing together.) **PLOT AND CHARACTERS**

VOCABULARY

Student-Friendly Explanations

disown If you disown someone or something, you break your connection with them.

convince When you convince others of something, you persuade them that what you are saying is true.

treason Someone who betrays his or her country is committing the crime of treason.

ordinary If something is ordinary, it is not special, or different in any aspect.

suit (v.) For something to suit you, it must be appropriate for you.

defeatist Someone who expects, accepts, or is resigned to failure is a defeatist.

rejected When something has been turned down or not accepted, it has been rejected.

Spelling Words: Lesson 7

1. pattern	11. emphasize
2. associate	12. exclude
3. exhale	13. disturb
4. bulletin	14. mammoth
5. collapse	15. necessary
6. complaint	16. impact
7. instance	17. splendid
8. dessert	18. stampede
9. difficulty	19. survival
10. franchise	20. wander

 Answers to _Think Critically_ Questions   Help students read and answer the _Think Critically_ questions on page 79. Guide students in writing the answer to each question. Possible responses are provided.

1. [Event 2:] Gail decides to give it a try. [Event 3:] Gail finds a way to blend the voices. [Event 4:] The Harlem All-Stars perform their first show. **PLOT**

2. The author describes Gail's dream because she wants to show readers how she comes up with her idea. **AUTHOR'S PURPOSE**

3. Gail decides to try out because she doesn't want to give up; she wants to show her parents that she can do it. **CHARACTER**

RETEACH

Decoding/Spelling

 Words with VCCV and VCCCV   Divide the group into two or three teams. On the board, create a grid for a bar graph; each team's points will be recorded with a bar. Have students write each Spelling Word on an index card. Shuffle the Spelling Word Cards. Have a volunteer from Team A pick a card. The team then reads aloud the Spelling Word and states whether it is a VCCV word or a VCCCV word. Then the team tells where to divide the syllables. Add to the team's bar graph for each word identified and divided correctly. Team B then takes a turn with a new word. If a team does not identify or divide a word correctly, give another team the chance to do so. If that team handles the word correctly, they win the point. After the cards have been completed, the team with the tallest bar on the graph wins!

PRETEACH

Grammar/Writing

 Practice Book 28

Combining Sentences Into Complex Sentences   Remind students of the following:

- An independent clause is a sentence that can stand alone. It makes sense.

- A dependent clause is an incomplete sentence. It does not make sense alone.

- A complex sentence has both an independent and a dependent clause.

Write this sentence on the board:

> Susan forgot her book although her mom reminded her.

Ask students to identify the dependent clause and the independent clause. (dependent: although her mom reminded her; independent: Susan forgot her book) Then underline *although* and point out to students that when combining clauses, a subordinate conjunction is needed. Tell students words such as *before, because, if, after, and which* are subordinating conjunctions. Now, write these sentences on the board:

> Although her mom reminded her, Susan forgot her book.
>
> Susan, because she forgot her book, wasn't prepared for class.

Point to the first example, and tell students when a dependent clause begins the sentence, it is separated from the independent clause by a comma. Point to the second example, and explain when a dependent clause is in the middle of a sentence, two commas separate it.

GUIDED PRACTICE   Direct students' attention to page 28 in their *Practice Books*. Guide them in completing the activities. Allow time for students to share their responses.

Fluency

Practice Book 27   **Fluency Practice**   Invite students to look at the bottom half of *Practice Book* page 27. These sentences have been broken into natural phrases. Tell students to repeat each phrase after you, mirroring your expression, phrasing, and pace. After students have repeated each sentence, invite them to practice reading the sentences to a partner.

DAY AT A GLANCE

Day 3

COMPREHENSION
Preteach Shades of Meaning

Reread and Summarize "Mixed-Up All-Stars"

DECODING/SPELLING
Reteach Words with VCCV and VCCCV

BUILD ROBUST VOCABULARY
Teach Words from "The Mixed-Up All-Stars"

GRAMMAR/WRITING
Reteach Writing Trait: Ideas

FLUENCY
Fluency Practice

Materials Needed: *Bold Moves*

Student Edition pp. 72–78

Practice Book pp. 27, 29

Copying Master 27

30+ Minutes

PRETEACH

Comprehension

Shades of Meaning Distribute *Copying Master 27* and have students listen as you read the instruction at the top of the page.

GUIDED PRACTICE Have students look at the chart of synonyms for *walk* and discuss the shades of meaning. Use the following sentence to explore the shades of meaning: **I (walked) across the room to greet my best friend.**

Reread and Summarize Have students reread and summarize "The Mixed-Up All-Stars" in sections, as described below.

pp. 72–73 **Let's reread pages 72–73 to recall how Gail felt about being asked to join the Harlem Stars Glee Club.**
Summary: Gail doesn't want to join the club. With encouragement from her mother, Gail agrees to think about it overnight.

pp. 74–75 **Now let's reread pages 74–75 to remember what Gail's first day with the Harlem Stars is like.**
Summary: Gail decides to give the group a try. The first practice is disappointing. She doesn't feel that the girls blend with the boys. Gail's dad encourages her to make it work.

pp. 76–78 **Last, let's reread pages 76–78 to find out what happens in Gail's dream and if her dream comes true.**
Summary: Gail dreams that the girls add their high notes to the boys' low notes in a new and pleasing way. The girls sing for Mr. Willow and he agrees. The first Harlem All-Stars show is a success.

RETEACH

Decoding/Spelling

Words with VCCV and VCCCV Tell students that all the Spelling Words follow one of two patterns: VCCV or VCCCV. Remind students that words with the VCCV pattern usually have syllables divided between the two middle consonants (VC/CV). Words with the VCCCV pattern usually have syllables divided between the first and second consonant (VC/CCV). Write the following words on the board:

| exhale | collapse | franchise | disturb |

Have a volunteer recite the first word, spell it, and identify where to divide the syllables. Show students how each syllable contains a vowel sound. Repeat with each word. (ex/hale; col/lapse; fran/chise; dis/turb)

TEACH

Build Robust Vocabulary

pp. 72–77

Words from "The Mixed-Up All-Stars" Have students locate *gazed* on page 72 of "The Mixed-Up All-Stars." Ask a volunteer to read aloud the sentence in which this word appears. (Line 2: *I gazed out the window to hide my feelings.)* Explain that this sentence means that Gail stared out the window for a long time. Continue by asking students to locate and read aloud the sentence in which the word *mellow* appears on page 75. (Line 5: *They were all low, slow, and mellow.)* Explain that this sentence means that the songs the group sang were low, slow, and soft and calming. Then ask students to locate and read aloud the sentence in which the word *demonstrated* appears on page 77. (Line 8: *When we demonstrated our plan, Mr. Willow and the Harlem All-Stars stopped and smiled.)* Explain that this sentence means that the girls gave an example of how they thought the group should sing.

Play a guessing game with students by giving clues such as: *I am thinking of a word that describes something I can do with my eyes.* What is the word? Encourage students to make up clues for the other words.

RETEACH

Grammar/Writing

Practice Book 29

Writing Trait: Ideas Have students turn to page 29 in their *Practice Books*. Help students understand that they can use a chart like this to organize their thoughts and feelings about something they read. Ask a volunteer to read aloud the chart entries in section A. Guide students to recall additional details from "The Mixed-Up All-Stars" and enter them in the chart.

GUIDED PRACTICE Complete the page together. Discuss with students how focusing their ideas will make them better writers. Have students share their responses with the group.

Fluency

Practice Book 27

Fluency Practice Tell students that today they will reread the sentences on the bottom of *Practice Book* page 27. Have students locate and point to the first sentence. Tell students that everyone is going to read the sentence together. This choral reading will give students an opportunity to hear others and to listen to the natural phrasing of the sentences. Choral-read each of the sentences several times.

30+ Minutes

COMPREHENSION
Reteach Shades of Meaning

DECODING/SPELLING
Reteach Words with VCCV and VCCCV

BUILD ROBUST VOCABULARY
Reteach Words from "The Mixed-Up All-Stars"

GRAMMAR/WRITING
Reteach Writing Form: Response to Literature

FLUENCY BUILDER
Fluency Practice

Materials Needed: *Bold Moves*

Practice Book

Copying Master

Student Edition pp. 72–78

Practice Book p. 30

Copying Masters 27, 28

Spelling Words: Lesson 7

1. pattern	11. emphasize
2. associate	12. exclude
3. exhale	13. disturb
4. bulletin	14. mammoth
5. collapse	15. necessary
6. complaint	16. impact
7. instance	17. splendid
8. dessert	18. stampede
9. difficulty	19. survival
10. franchise	20. wander

Comprehension

Copying Master 27

Shades of Meaning Have students review *Copying Master 27*. Explain to students that context can help identify the shades of meaning of related words. Help students come up with more words related to *eat* and talk about the shades of meaning of each. Some possibilities are *snack, nibble, wolf, chomp,* and *devour*. Point out that by identifying shades of meaning in related words, students can write and speak more effectively.

GUIDED PRACTICE Have students work in pairs. Tell pairs to come up with words related to *talk*. Ask them to write sentences using some of the words from their list. Invite pairs to share their sentences with the class. Discuss how the words give different shades of meaning to each sentence.

Decoding/Spelling

Practice Book 30

Words with VCCV and VCCCV Have students number a sheet of paper 1–18. Write the Spelling Word *pattern* on the board. Tell students that the first fourteen words you dictate have the VCCV pattern. After students write each word, display it so they can proofread their work. Repeat this activity with the VCCCV words (words 15–18), using *complaint* as the model.

1. wander	2. bulletin	3. exhale	4. collapse
5. difficulty	6. stampede	7. impact	8. necessary
9. associate	10. dessert	11. splendid	12. mammoth
13. disturb	14. survival	15. exclude	16. instance
17. emphasize	18. franchise		

Have students turn to page 30 in their *Practice Books*. Have volunteers read portions of the story aloud. Then have a volunteer read the first question. Have students circle their answer. Check by having a volunteer reread the question with the answer. Repeat for the remaining questions.

Build Robust Vocabulary

Words from "The Mixed-Up All-Stars"   Review the meanings of the words *gazed, mellow,* and *demonstrated*. Then say these sentences and ask which word describes each sentence. Have students explain their answers.

- **The boy stared out over the water until the sun set.** (gazed)
- **Dad played a soft, calming CD to help the baby sleep.** (mellow)
- **Mom showed Kayla how to fold the paper into an airplane.**
  (demonstrated)

Grammar/Writing

Copying Master 28

Writing Form: Response to Literature   Remind students that when writing a response to literature, they should organize their thoughts to help them focus on the most important details they want to recall. Distribute *Copying Master 28*. Have a volunteer read the instruction at the top of the page. Then read the student model together. Discuss the margin notes that emphasize the key points in writing a response to literature.

GUIDED PRACTICE   Complete the activity by having students follow the directions at the bottom of the page. Review students' responses as a group.

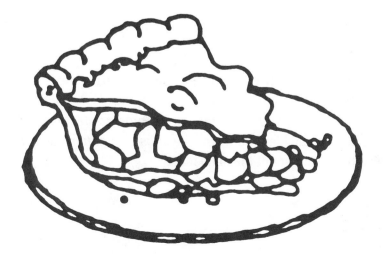

Fluency

pp. 72–78

Fluency Practice   Have each student work with a partner to read passages from "The Mixed-Up All-Stars" aloud to each other. Students may select a passage that they enjoyed or choose one of the following options:

- Read page 74. (Total: 132 words)
- Read page 77. (Total: 132 words)

Encourage students to read the selected passage aloud to their partner three times. Have the student rate his or her reading on the 1–4 scale.

1	Need more practice
2	Pretty good
3	Good
4	Great!

DAY AT A GLANCE

Day 5

VOCABULARY
Preteach *plea, intercept, seeped, diagnosed, rendezvous, devoured, lethal*

COMPREHENSION
 Preteach Main Idea and Details

DECODING/WORD ATTACK
Preteach Decode Longer Words

DECODING/SPELLING
Preteach Words with VCV Syllable Pattern

GRAMMAR/WRITING
Preteach Review Clauses

FLUENCY
Fluency Performance

Materials Needed: *Bold Moves*

| Student Edition pp. 72–78 | Skill Card 8 | Copying Master 29 |

30+ Minutes

PRETEACH

Vocabulary

Copying Master 29

Lesson 8 Vocabulary Distribute a set of Vocabulary Word Cards to each pair of students. Hold up the card for the first word and ask a volunteer to read it aloud. Have students repeat the word and hold up the matching card. Give the explanation for the word. Then ask students the first question below and discuss their responses. Continue for each Vocabulary Word.

- Have you ever had to make a **plea** for something? What did you do?
- When might you want to **intercept** someone?
- If water **seeped** from the faucet, how fast would it go?
- If a plumber **diagnosed** a problem, what or where might it be?
- Have your ever set up a **rendezvous** with a friend? Where?
- Have you ever **devoured** food? When?
- When could contact with a wild animal be **lethal**?

PRETEACH

Comprehension

Skill Card 8

Main Idea and Details Have students look at side A of *Skill Card 8: Main Idea and Details*. Ask a student to read the definitions in the first paragraph aloud. Then have a volunteer read the passage aloud as students follow along. Point to the chart, and have students locate the following information on it:

- **What are some of the details in this passage**?
- **What is the main idea?**
- **How do the details connect to lead readers to the main idea?** (The details give evidence for how and why the storm was the worst that had ever been recorded.)

Point out to students that readers can use details in a passage to figure out the main idea.

GUIDED PRACTICE Write this main idea on the board: *Some types of weather can cause great damage*. Then list these words: *hurricanes, autumn, tornadoes, hail, clouds,* and *heavy rain*. Have students identify the details that would fit the main idea. Guide them to cross out *autumn* and *clouds* as the details that would not fit the main idea.

PRETEACH
Decoding/Word Attack

Decode Longer Words   Write *robot* on the board. As you say it, draw a line to divide the syllables. (ro/bot) Note that the first syllable ends with a vowel that has a long vowel sound. Tell students that this is called an open syllable. Now, write *lemon* on the board. Repeat the process. (lem/on) Lead students to understand that a closed syllable has a vowel with a short sound and ends in a consonant.

PRETEACH
Decoding/Spelling

Words with VCV Syllable Pattern   Write the following words on the board: *vital, ego, robot, minor.* Say *vital,* elongating the first syllable. Underline the *i* and say: **I can hear that the *i* is long because it says its own name.** Have volunteers say each of the other words and underline the vowel that is long. Then write these words on the board: *linen, panel, valid, lemon.* Point out that some words have a short vowel sound in the first syllable. Say *linen,* elongating the first syllable. Have volunteers say each of the other words and underline the vowel in the first syllable that is short.

PRETEACH
Grammar/Writing

Review Clauses   Remind students that there are two kinds of clauses: independent and dependent. Both kinds of clauses have a subject and a predicate. An independent clause can stand alone. A dependent clause cannot. Write these clauses, and read them aloud:

> **Many people died from the disease**
> **Because there was no cure**

Tell students that the first item is an independent clause. It could be a sentence all by itself. The second item is a dependent clause. It cannot stand alone as a sentence. Next, combine the clauses, and have a volunteer read the sentence aloud:

> **Many people died from the disease because there was no cure.**

Tell students this is a complex sentence. It combines an independent clause and a dependent clause. Have volunteers identify the two clauses. Point out that *because* is a subordinating conjunction. Dependent clauses always begin with subordinating conjunctions.

VOCABULARY
Student-Friendly Explanations

plea   When you ask for something in an emotional or intense way, you are making a plea.

intercept   When you intercept someone en route, you meet them before they reach their destination.

seeped   When a liquid or gas has seeped into a place, it has leaked there slowly.

diagnosed   When an illness or problem has been identified, it has been diagnosed.

rendezvous   When you have a rendezvous with someone, you meet that person at an arranged place.

devoured   You have devoured something when you have eaten it quickly and enthusiastically.

lethal   When something is capable of killing, it is lethal.

Fluency

pp. 72–78   **Fluency Performance** Invite students to read aloud the passages from "The Mixed-Up All-Stars" that they selected and practiced earlier. Note the number of words each student reads correctly and incorrectly. Have students rate their own oral reading on the 1–4 scale. Give students the opportunity to continue practicing and then to read the passage to you again.

Day 1

30+ Minutes

LESSON 8

VOCABULARY

Reteach *plea, intercept, seeped, diagnosed, rendezvous, devoured, lethal*

COMPREHENSION

 Reteach Main Idea and Details

DECODING/SPELLING

Reteach Words with VCV Syllable Pattern

GRAMMAR/WRITING

Preteach Identify Compound-Complex Sentences

FLUENCY

Fluency Practice

Materials Needed: *Bold Moves*

| Student Edition pp. 80–81 | Practice Book p. 31 | Skill Card 8 | Copying Master 30 |

RETEACH

Vocabulary

pp. 80–81

Lesson 8 Vocabulary Read aloud the Vocabulary Words and the Student-Friendly Explanations. Then have students read the passage on page 80 of their books. Guide them in answering the questions on page 81 by recalling what they read. (Possible responses for page 81: 2. I can tell the disease was lethal, because it claimed 12,000 lives. 3. A disease must be diagnosed so that doctors can find a cure. 4. Dr. Vaugh intercepted a plea for help from doctors in Boston. 5. The disease was probably passed at rendezvous points along the railroad because that is where people come together and mix with others. 6. Some organisms are so small that they can pass through the holes in a mask and get people sick.)

RETEACH

Comprehension

Skill Card 8

Focus Skill

Main Idea and Details Have students look at side B of *Skill Card 8: Main Idea and Details*. Have a volunteer read the Skill Reminder. Then read the passage as students follow along. Discuss details in the passage with students. Have students underline sentences that give details you've discussed. Based on the details, have students identify the main idea in the passage.

GUIDED PRACTICE Guide students in copying the chart. From your discussion about the passage, have students identify three details and enter them in the chart. Ask students whether the main idea is stated or implied. Have students write the main idea in the chart. (Details: Being active helps students sit still. Being outside calms students. Fresh air and the color green soothe students' nerves. Main Idea: Recent studies about how to get students to pay attention in school have had some suprising findings.)

RETEACH

Decoding/Spelling

Copying Master 30

Words with VCV Syllable Pattern Distribute *Copying Master 30*. Model reading the Spelling Words, and have students repeat them. Remind students that some words have a long vowel sound in the first syllable and some have a short vowel sound. Have pairs of students write the Spelling Words on index cards. Have one student draw a card and read the word aloud. The partner should write the word. Then have partners switch roles. When a student spells a word correctly, he or she initials the card and returns it to the pile. Students should work through the pile twice or until each student has had the opportunity to spell each of the words. Have students write down each word they do not spell correctly to study later.

PRETEACH

Grammar/Writing

Identify Compound-Complex Sentences Tell students that when a sentence has two or more independent clauses and one or more dependent clauses, it is a compound-complex sentence. Write the following sentence on the board:

> Because it was raining, we had to
> stay inside, but we had fun anyway.

Read the sentence aloud. Underline the first clause, and ask a volunteer to identify the type of clause. Repeat for each clause. (dependent, independent, independent) Circle the comma after the first clause. Note that when a dependent clause begins a sentence, a comma must follow it. Circle the word *but* and show students how it joins the two independent clauses.

GUIDED PRACTICE Write the following sentences on the board:

> Jay will bring the food and Mark will pick you up,
> unless it rains.
> When we woke up, the sun was shining and the
> birds were singing.

Guide students to identify each clause as dependent or independent. (1st sentence: independent, independent, dependent; 2nd sentence: dependent, independent, independent) Note subordinating and coordinating conjunctions and the use of commas. Help students conclude that each sentence is a compound-complex sentence.

VOCABULARY

Student-Friendly Explanations

plea When you ask for something in an emotional or intense way, you are making a plea.

intercept When you intercept someone en route, you meet them before they reach their destination.

seeped When a liquid or gas has seeped into a place, it has leaked there slowly.

diagnosed When an illness or problem has been identified, it has been diagnosed.

rendezvous When you have a rendezvous with someone, you meet that person at an arranged place.

devoured You have devoured something when you have eaten it quickly and enthusiastically.

lethal When something is capable of killing, it is lethal.

Fluency

Practice Book 31

Fluency Practice Have students turn to *Practice Book* page 31. Read the words in the first column aloud. Invite students to track each word and repeat it after you. Then have students work in pairs to read the words in the first column aloud to each other. Follow the same procedure with each of the remaining columns. After partners have practiced reading aloud the words in each column, have them practice reading all of the words.

LESSON 8

DAY AT A GLANCE

Day 2

VOCABULARY
Reteach *plea, intercept, seeped, diagnosed, rendezvous, devoured, lethal*

COMPREHENSION
"The 1918 Epidemic"

Build Background

Monitor Comprehension

Answers to *Think Critically* Questions

DECODING/SPELLING
Reteach Words with VCV Syllable Pattern

GRAMMAR/WRITING
Preteach Combine Sentences into Compound-Complex Sentences

FLUENCY
Fluency Practice

Materials Needed: *Bold Moves*

Student Edition pp. 82–89

Practice Book pp. 31, 32

Copying Master 29

30+ Minutes

RETEACH

Vocabulary

Copying Master 29

Lesson 8 Vocabulary Distribute a set of Vocabulary Word Cards to each student. Review the Student-Friendly Explanations. Then say a word, and have students hold up the matching card. Then choose a volunteer to use the word in a sentence. Continue until all words have been used.

Comprehension

Build Background: "The 1918 Epidemic"
Ask students if they know of other illnesses or diseases, such as AIDS or cancer, that have affected people all over the world. Elicit what they know about the illness and what they would do to help, if they could.

pp. 82–83

Monitor Comprehension: "The 1918 Epidemic"
Read the title of the story aloud. Then have students read pages 82–83 to find out where the epidemic started and how it spread.

After reading the pages, ask: **Where did the epidemic start?** (at a fort in Kansas) **How did it spread?** (Some soldiers from that fort went across the sea and spread it to other soldiers.) **NOTE DETAILS**

Discuss the Stop and Think question on page 82: **How can you tell that the illness is easy to catch?** (Possible response: I can tell that it's easy to catch because so many people got sick in a short time.) Guide students in writing the answer to this question. **MAKE INFERENCES**

Ask: **How many men were sick in the first week of the illness?** (500) **NOTE DETAILS**

Discuss the Stop and Think question on page 83: **What happens when the illness passes from man to man?** (As the illness passes from man to man, it gets stronger.) Guide students in writing the answer to this question. **CAUSE AND EFFECT**

pp. 84–85

Discuss the Stop and Think question on page 84: **What happens after the illness comes back to the United States?** (Possible responses: After it comes back, doctors begin to study the illness. Doctors diagnose the illness and call it the Spanish Flu.) Guide students in writing the answer to this question. **GENERALIZE**

Read aloud the second paragraph on page 84. Model the strategy of collecting details to determine the main idea.

THINK ALOUD **When I read the paragraph, I find details about the disease. Hundreds of people were sick just at one camp. Sixty-three men died in one night. Doctors had never seen this kind of disease before. I think the main idea is not stated. These details tell me that the main idea is that the disease was very dangerous and that doctors did not know about it or understand it.** **MAIN IDEA AND DETAILS**

Discuss the Stop and Think question on page 85: **What do you think will happen next?** (Possible response: I think that the doctors will continue to study the disease.) Guide students in writing the answer to this question. **MAKE PREDICTIONS**

pp. 86–87

Ask: **How did the new disease differ from a normal case of the flu?** (Possible response: A normal case would go away after rest, but the new disease would not.) **MAKE COMPARISONS**

Discuss the Stop and Think question on page 86: **Why does the disease seem to follow the railroads?** (Possible response: It seems to follow the railroads because sick people ride on the trains and spread the disease.) Guide students in writing the answer to this question. **MAKE INFERENCES**

Ask: **If you were a mayor, would you inform people of the disease? Why or why not?** (Possible responses: Yes, so people could start to protect themselves from the disease. No, so people would not panic.) **PERSONAL RESPONSE**

Discuss the Stop and Think question on page 87: **Why do the shops and factories close?** (Possible response: The shops and factories close because people don't want to spread the illness or to catch it from their co-workers.) Guide students in writing the answer to this question. **DRAW CONCLUSIONS**

page 88

Discuss the Stop and Think question on page 88: **How is the epidemic like a storm?** (Possible response: It is like a storm because it is scary while it is happening, but then it is over.) Guide students in writing the answer to this question. **FIGURATIVE LANGUAGE**

Ask: **What does *immune* mean?** (Possible response: *Immune* means "unable to get the disease.") **CONTEXT CLUES**

Ask: **Do you think an epidemic such as this could take doctors by surprise now?** (Possible responses: No; doctors know more now than they did. Yes; diseases are changing all the time.) **PERSONAL RESPONSE**

Spelling Words: Lesson 8

1. report	11. lemon
2. climate	12. limit
3. crusade	13. linen
4. ego	14. major
5. retail	15. minor
6. future	16. panel
7. robot	17. sequel
8. humane	18. valid
9. tiger	19. veto
10. laser	20. vital

 page 89

Answers to *Think Critically* Questions

Help students read and answer the *Think Critically* questions on page 89. Possible responses are provided.

1. [Main Idea] In 1918, the United States faced a deadly flu epidemic. **MAIN IDEA AND DETAILS**

2. After the epidemic was over, doctors studied the organism that caused the illness. **CAUSE AND EFFECT**

3. It's important to remember these events because we might be able to prevent them from happening again. **AUTHOR'S PURPOSE**

RETEACH

Decoding/Spelling

Words with VCV Syllable Pattern Arrange students in two groups. Give one student from each group an index card with a Spelling Word on it. The student from Group A states the meaning of the word, or gives a clue about the word, without saying the word. Members of Group A then have one chance to guess the word. If they guess correctly, another group member spells the word. Group A gets one point for a correct guess and one point for a correct spelling. Repeat the process with Group B. Continue with other Spelling Words, as time allows.

PRETEACH

Grammar/Writing

Practice Book 32 **Combine Sentences Into Compound-Complex Sentences**
Explain that a compound-complex sentence has two or more independent clauses and one or more dependent clauses. Write the following sentence on the board:

> Although I was scared, I rode that roller coaster, and I grinned all day.

Underline *Although I was scared* and identify it as a dependent clause. Point out that dependent clauses cannot stand alone. Circle *Although* and remind students that dependent clauses always begin with subordinating conjunctions. Then draw two lines beneath *I rode that roller coaster* and *I grinned all day*. Explain that both clauses are independent because they can stand alone.

Remind students to use correct punctuation and conjunctions when combining short sentences into a compound-complex sentence. Point out the commas and the word *and* in the sentence on the board. Then direct students to complete the activity on page 32 in their *Practice Books*.

GUIDED PRACTICE Read aloud the directions for the activity. Do the first exercise as a group. Guide students to come up with a workable conjunction as they build the compound-complex sentence. Guide students in forming the remaining compound-complex sentences. Have volunteers read their sentences aloud.

Fluency

Practice Book 31 **Fluency Practice** Invite students to look at the bottom half of *Practice Book* page 31. These sentences have been broken into natural phrases. Tell students to repeat each phrase after you, mirroring your expression, phrasing, and pace. After students have repeated each sentence, invite them to practice reading the sentences to a partner.

COMPREHENSION
Preteach Shades of Meaning
Reread and Summarize "The 1918 Epidemic"

DECODING/SPELLING
Reteach Words with VCV Syllable Pattern

BUILD ROBUST VOCABULARY
Teach Words from "The 1918 Epidemic"

GRAMMAR/WRITING
Reteach Writing Trait: Conventions

FLUENCY
Fluency Practice

Materials Needed: *Bold Moves*

| Student Edition pp. 82–88 | Practice Book pp. 31, 33 | Copying Master 31 |

Comprehension

 Shades of Meaning Distribute *Copying Master 31* and have a student read the information at the top of the page aloud as students follow along.

GUIDED PRACTICE Have students read each item and choose the word that best fits the situation. If students have trouble choosing a word, talk about the shades of meaning that the words have. Extend the activity by having students explain the shades of meaning of both the words in each item.

Reread and Summarize Have students reread and summarize "The 1918 Epidemic" in sections, as described below.

 Let's reread pages 82–83 to recall how the illness starts and spreads from man to man.
Summary: The illness starts at a fort in Kansas and spreads when men go across the sea. When the illness returns, it is stronger, even lethal.

 Now let's reread pages 84–85 to remember how the disease is diagnosed and whether the doctors can explain the illness.
Summary: The disease is diagnosed as the Spanish Flu, and even though records make it seem like the sniffles, this disease baffles them.

Last, let's reread pages 86–88 to find out how the disease spreads and what happens in the end.
Summary: The disease spreads from the forts to the towns and infects hundreds of people. Shops and factories closed. The disease killed 195,000 people in October, 1918. By May 1st, the epidemic was over.

Decoding/Spelling

Words with VCV Syllable Pattern Write the following words on the board:

| report | climate | crusade | sequel |
| panel | linen | lemon | valid |

Point out that breaking a word into smaller parts, or chunks, can make it easier to spell. Read a word slowly, sounding out each syllable. Have students repeat it, also sounding out each syllable. Then have a volunteer spell the word. Repeat for each word.

TEACH

Build Robust Vocabulary

pp. 82–88 **Words from "The 1918 Epidemic"** Have students locate *epidemic* on page 82 of "The 1918 Epidemic." Ask a volunteer to read aloud the sentence in which this word appears. (Line 2: *An epidemic swept across the land.*) Explain that an epidemic is an illness that spreads very quickly and makes lots of people sick. Continue by asking students to locate and read aloud the sentence in which *baffled* appears on page 85. (Line 6: *But this disease baffled them.*) Explain that this sentence means that people were so confused about how this illness worked that they couldn't understand it. Then ask students to locate and read aloud the sentence in which *ensure* appears on page 88. (Line 12: *They hope their hard work will ensure that an epidemic like the one in 1918 will never happen again.*) Explain that this sentence means that people want to be sure that an epidemic will never happen again.

Ask yes/no questions, such as the following, and have students explain their answers.

- **Would it be a good idea to wash your hands a lot during an epidemic?**
- **Would you enjoy reading a book that baffled you?**
- **Will saving money ensure that you will be rich?**

RETEACH

Grammar/Writing

Practice Book 33 **Writing Trait: Conventions** Have students turn to page 33 in their *Practice Books.* Ask a volunteer to read the instruction aloud. Talk about the information in the chart. Then read the directions to Part A and have a volunteer read the first sentence. Guide students to understand the responses. Have students complete Part A.

GUIDED PRACTICE Guide students to complete Parts B and C together.

Fluency

Practice Book 31 **Fluency Practice** Tell students that today they will reread the sentences on the bottom of *Practice Book* page 31. Have students locate and point to the first sentence. Tell students that everyone is going to read the sentence together. This choral reading will give students an opportunity to hear others and to listen to the natural phrasing of the sentences. Choral-read each sentence several times.

30+ Minutes

COMPREHENSION
Reteach Shades of Meaning

DECODING/SPELLING
Reteach Words with VCV Syllable Patterns

BUILD ROBUST VOCABULARY
Reteach Words from "The 1918 Epidemic"

GRAMMAR/WRITING
Reteach Writing Form: Skit

FLUENCY
Fluency Practice

Materials Needed: *Bold Moves*

Student Edition pp. 82–88

Practice Book p. 34

Copying Master 32

Spelling Words: Lesson 8

1. report		11. lemon	
2. climate		12. limit	
3. crusade		13. linen	
4. ego		14. major	
5. retail		15. minor	
6. future		16. panel	
7. robot		17. sequel	
8. humane		18. valid	
9. tiger		19. veto	
10. laser		20. vital	

Comprehension

Shades of Meaning Remind students that words with similar meanings are used in slightly different ways. These words are said to have different shades of meaning. Write these sentences on the board:

> I asked my boss for a raise.
>
> I made a plea to my boss for a raise.
>
> I demanded a raise from my boss.

Ask these questions: **What are the three words or phrases that have similar meanings in these sentences?** (*asked, made a plea, demanded*) **Which sentence describes a polite request?** (the first) **Which sentence describes a forceful statement?** (the third) **Which sentence describes a strong emotional statement?** (the second)

GUIDED PRACTICE Pose the following questions to students. Discuss their word choices and the shades of meaning.

An illness causes people to die. Is it *dangerous* or is it *lethal*? (lethal)

Kim did her math. Did she *solve* the problems or *diagnose* the problems? (solve)

Two spies get together. Do they have an *appointment* or a *rendezvous*? (rendezvous)

Decoding/Spelling

Practice Book 34 **Words with VCV Syllable Pattern** Have students number a sheet of paper 1–18. Write the Spelling Word *lemon* on the board. Remind students that some words have a short vowel sound in the first syllable and that separating a word into chunks can help them spell it correctly. Tell students that the first four words you will dictate have a short vowel sound in the first syllable. Repeat, using *future* for words that have a long vowel sound in the first syllable.

1. limit	2. linen	3. panel	4. valid
5. sequel	6. minor	7. major	8. laser
9. tiger	10. humane	11. robot	12. retail
13. ego	14. crusade	15. climate	16. report
17. vital	18. veto		

Have students turn to page 34 in their *Practice Books*. Read the instructions aloud. Have a volunteer describe the first picture for the group. Guide students to select the sentence that best describes the picture. Repeat for each picture.

RETEACH
Build Robust Vocabulary

Words from "The 1918 Epidemic" Review the meanings of the words *epidemic, baffled,* and *ensure.* Then say these sentences and ask which word describes each sentence. Have students explain why.

- **The school closed because so many people got sick from a flu that spread very quickly.** (epidemic)
- **The directions for putting together the toy were so hard to understand that Jake was confused.** (baffled)
- **Study hard to make sure that you will do well on the test.** (ensure)

RETEACH
Grammar/Writing

Copying Master 32

Writing Form: Skit Remind students that one way to keep writing interesting is to use a variety of punctuation. Distribute *Copying Master 32.* Have a volunteer read the paragraph at the top of the page aloud. Read the Student Model together and discuss the boxed text. Then, write the following sentences on the board:

> Maybe we can find a cure. Then we can stop the disease.

Model for students how the writing can be made more interesting:

> If we can find a cure, then we can stop the disease!

GUIDED PRACTICE Have students complete the activity. Allow them to share their revised stage directions and dialogue with the group.

Fluency

Fluency Practice Have each student work with a partner to read passages from "The 1918 Epidemic" aloud to each other. Students may select a passage that they enjoyed or choose one of the following options:

- Read page 83. (Total: 69 words)
- Read page 88. (Total: 107 words)

Encourage students to read the selected passage aloud to their partner three times. Have the student rate his or her reading on the 1–4 scale.

1	Need more practice
2	Pretty good
3	Good
4	Great!

DAY AT A GLANCE

Day 5

VOCABULARY
Preteach *equipped, reserve, rely, altitude, extent, hampered, overshadowed*

COMPREHENSION
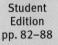 **Preteach** Main Idea and Details

DECODING/WORD ATTACK
Preteach Decode Longer Words

DECODING/SPELLING
Preteach Easily Confused Words

GRAMMAR/WRITING
Preteach Common Nouns

FLUENCY
Fluency Performance

Materials Needed: *Bold Moves*

Student Edition pp. 82–88

Copying Master 33

PRETEACH

Vocabulary

Copying Master 33

Lesson 9 Vocabulary   Distribute a set of Vocabulary Word Cards to each pair of students. Hold up the card for the first word, and ask a volunteer to read it aloud. Have students repeat the word and hold up the matching card. Give the explanation for the word. Then ask students the first question below and discuss their responses. Continue for each Vocabulary Word.

- **How is your classroom equipped for you to learn?**
- **Why would it be good to have a reserve supply of water in the desert?**
- **Could you rely on your bicycle to get you to school every day? Explain.**
- **What could you climb to reach a higher altitude?**
- **To what extent would you go to help a friend?**
- **How would playing outside be hampered if it were raining?**
- **When has a friend's accomplishments overshadowed your own?**

PRETEACH

Comprehension

pp. 82–88

Main Idea and Details   Tell students that the main idea of a selection, whether it is a paragraph or an entire book, is the most important thing the writer has to say. Discuss the following points about Main Idea and Details:

- The main idea may be stated in a sentence, or it may be suggested.
- Details support the main idea by telling more about it. The reader can use the details to establish the main idea.
- A piece of writing with many paragraphs has an overall main idea. Readers can identify the main idea of each paragraph and combine them to determine an overall main idea.
- Good readers keep the main ideas in mind as they read. When they read other selections on the same subject, they can understand the topic better.

Have students recall what they read in "The 1918 Epidemic." Ask a volunteer to read the last two paragraphs on page 88 aloud. Ask:

- **Which sentence gives the main idea?** (The first sentence; The epidemic was over; doctors were left with a need to find out more.)
- **What details support this statement?** (Student responses should support this main idea.)

PRETEACH

Decoding/Word Attack

Decode Longer Words   Write the word *illusion* on the board and ask a volunteer to read the word aloud. Model how to identify that there are three syllables in the word. Show students where the word should be divided. (il/lu/sion) Point out that the first syllable breaks between the consonants. Then tell students:

- **When a word has two consonants in the medial position, divide the word between the consonants.** (il/lu)
- **Closed syllables are usually pronounced with a short vowel sound.** (/il/)
- **Open syllables are usually pronounced with a long vowel sound.** (/lu/)
- **Longer words may contain syllables with long vowel sounds and syllables with short vowel sounds.**

PRETEACH

Decoding/Spelling

Easily Confused Words   Tell students that the spelling of some words can be easily confused. Some words have similar letters, but have different meanings. Write the words below on the board and have a student read them aloud. Ask students to underline the letters that are different.

> affect - effect   adapt - adopt

Explain that these are some of next lesson's Spelling Words. Tell students a clue to spelling easily confused words is to know their meaning.

PRETEACH

Grammar/Writing

Common Nouns   Tell students a common noun names a person, place, or thing. Write the following sentence on the board:

> The firefighters jumped into action when told of the blaze at the landfill.

Have a volunteer read the sentence aloud. Underline *firefighter*. Tell students that *firefighter* is a common noun that names a person. Then underline *action,* and explain that it names an idea or concept. Underline *blaze,* and tell students that the word names a thing. Then underline *landfill,* and point out that it names a place.

Student-Friendly Explanations

equipped When you have been equipped with something, it has been provided to you.

reserve When you keep something in reserve, it is available when you need it.

rely When you rely on something, you trust that it will be there when you need it.

altitude The altitude of a land mass is its height above sea level.

extent Something's extent is the size of the area it covers.

hampered If you have been hampered, something has made it difficult for you to accomplish what you had wanted to.

overshadowed If something is overshadowed by another, it is viewed as less successful, important, or impressive than what it is being compared to.

Fluency

pp. 82–88 **Fluency Performance** Invite students to read aloud the passages from "The 1918 Epidemic" that they selected and practiced earlier. Note the number of words each student reads correctly and incorrectly. Have students rate their own oral reading on the 1–4 scale. Give students the opportunity to continue practicing and then to read the passage to you again.

LESSON 9

DAY AT A GLANCE

Day 1

VOCABULARY
Reteach *equipped, reserve, rely, altitude, extent, hampered, overshadowed*

COMPREHENSION
 Reteach Main Idea and Details

DECODING/SPELLING
Reteach Easily Confused Words

GRAMMAR/WRITING
Preteach Proper Nouns

FLUENCY
Fluency Practice

Materials Needed: *Bold Moves*

Student Edition pp. 90–91	Practice Book p. 35	Skill Card 9	Copying Master 34

RETEACH

Vocabulary

pp. 90–91 **Lesson 9 Vocabulary** Read aloud the Vocabulary Words and the Student-Friendly Explanantions. Then have students read the news articles on pages 90–91 of their books. Have a volunteer read each article aloud as the other students follow along. Guide them in completing the sentences within each article by selecting the correct Vocabulary Word. Have a volunteer read each completed sentence aloud. If students are unable to give reasonable responses, refer to the Student-Friendly Explanations. (Answers to pages 90–91: 2. *equipped*, 3. *altitude*, 4. *hampered*, 5. *extent*, 6. *reserve*, 7. *overshadowed*)

RETEACH

Comprehension

Skill Card 9 **Main Idea and Details** Have students look at side A of *Skill Card 9: Main Idea and Details*. Have a volunteer read aloud the information. Have students read the passage. Then have a volunteer read the instruction aloud. Model with students how the chart shows details that lead to a main idea. As you discuss the chart, remind students to underline the sentences or words that make up the details and the main idea.

GUIDED PRACTICE Have students look at side B of *Skill Card 9: Main Idea and Details*. Have a volunteer read the Skill Reminder. Then have students read the passage. Guide students as they copy the chart and complete it with details from the passage. Then have students write a short sentence stating the main idea. (Details: Brenda Gowen helps put children in a better situation; She started a Back-to-School program; She gets children backpacks filled with school supplies; Main Idea: Some volunteers work to help children.)

Decoding/Spelling

Easily Confused Words Distribute *Copying Master 34*. Model reading the Spelling Words as students repeat them. Have a volunteer read aloud the instruction for spelling easily confused words. Then have students work in pairs to complete the following activity: A student writes a sentence for each Spelling Word but leaves a blank for the actual word. The partners then switch papers and fill in the blanks in each other's sentences. Students should give themselves one point for each correctly spelled word.

Copying Master 34

PRETEACH

Grammar/Writing

Proper Nouns Tell students that a proper noun names a particular person, place, or thing. Write this sentence on the board:

> Captain Jefferson lives in the town of Frankfort.

Have students identify the nouns. Underline *Captain Jefferson* and *Frankfort*. Tell students these are proper nouns, because they name a particular person and place. Now, underline the word *town*. Ask students to identify this noun as common or proper. (common) Now, write this sentence on the board:

> Mr. and Mrs. Smith went to a show.

Tell students that a person's name may be used with a title of respect. Underline *Mr.* and *Mrs. Smith*. Point out that *Mr.* and *Mrs.* are titles of respect. Other titles can be used, such as *Dr., Sgt., Ms.,* and *Capt.* Titles are usually capitalized and have a period after them.

GUIDED PRACTICE Write the following sentences on the board:

> Capt. McMahon is in charge of the Clayton Fire Department.
>
> My favorite teacher at Center Middle School is Mrs. Marvin.

Guide students to identify the abbreviated titles and proper nouns in each sentence. (titles: Capt. Mrs.; proper nouns: Capt. McMahon, Clayton Fire Department, Center Middle School, Mrs. Marvin)

VOCABULARY

Student-Friendly Explanations

equipped When you have been equipped with something, it has been provided to you.

reserve When you keep something in reserve, it is available when you need it.

rely When you rely on something, you trust that it will be there when you need it.

altitude The altitude of a land mass is its height above sea level.

extent Something's extent is the size of the area it covers.

hampered If you have been hampered, something has made it difficult for you to accomplish what you had wanted to.

overshadowed If something is overshadowed by another, it is viewed as less successful, important, or impressive than what it is being compared to.

Fluency

Fluency Practice Have students turn to *Practice Book* page 35. Read the words in the first column aloud. Invite students to track each word and repeat the words after you. Then have students work in pairs to read the words in the first column aloud to each other. Follow the same procedure with each of the remaining columns. After partners have practiced reading aloud the words in each of the columns, have them practice reading all of the words.

Practice Book 35

LESSON 9

DAY AT A GLANCE

Day 2

30+ Minutes

VOCABULARY

Reteach *equipped, reserve, rely, altitude, extent, hampered, overshadowed*

COMPREHENSION
"The Volunteers"
Build Background
Monitor Comprehension
Answers to *Think Critically* **Questions**

DECODING/SPELLING
Reteach Easily Confused Words

GRAMMAR/WRITING
Preteach Abbreviations

FLUENCY
Fluency Practice

Materials Needed: *Bold Moves*

| Student Edition pp. 92–99 | Practice Book pp. 35, 36 | Copying Masters 33, 34 |

Vocabulary

Copying Master 33

Lesson 9 Vocabulary   Distribute a set of Vocabulary Word Cards to each student or pair of students. Read aloud the meaning of one of the Vocabulary Words, and have students hold up the matching card. Have a volunteer say a sentence that uses the matching word. Continue until students have matched all the words.

Comprehension

Build Background: "The Volunteers"
Ask students if they have visited a fire station, or have talked with a firefighter. Discuss what they learned. Then ask students if they have ever volunteered to help someone. What kind of work did they do? How did it make them feel to help someone else?

Monitor Comprehension: "The Volunteers"
pp. 92–93
Read the title of the story aloud. Then have students read pages 92–93 to find out if volunteer firefighters have other jobs.

After reading the pages, ask: **What other jobs do volunteer firefighters have?** (Volunteers work in stores, as teachers, as carpenters, or as farmers.) **NOTE DETAILS**

Discuss the Stop and Think question on page 92: **What facts do you learn about volunteer firefighters?** (I learn that volunteer firefighters work at other jobs, don't get paid, and put out fires at any time.) Guide students in writing the answer to this question. **NOTE DETAILS**

Ask: **If we didn't have volunteer firefighters, what do you think could happen?** (Possible response: If we didn't have volunteer firefighters, a fire might get out of control, or people might be injured.) **CAUSE AND EFFECT**

Ask: **If you wanted to volunteer, what would you like to do?** (Answers will vary.) **PERSONAL RESPONSE**

Discuss the Stop and Think question on page 93: **Do you think it would be difficult to be a volunteer firefighter? Explain.** (Possible response: I think that it would be difficult because you would have to stop what you were doing and face danger.) **DRAW CONCLUSIONS**

pp. 94–95 Read aloud the first paragraph on page 94. Model how you go about identifying the main idea and details of a passage.

(THINK ALOUD) **As I read the paragraph, I see many details about the fire departments in the United States. The big departments have paid workers and overshadow the volunteer departments. But the main idea of the paragraph is that most fire departments are made up of volunteers.** MAIN IDEA AND DETAILS

Discuss the Stop and Think question on page 94: **How are volunteer firefighters like paid firefighters?** (Both are trained, equipped, and willing to put their lives on the line.) Guide students in writing the answer to this question. MAKE COMPARISONS

Discuss the Stop and Think question on page 95: **How does a Fire Board plan a fire department?** (A Fire Board determines what areas the fire department will protect, how to get and store equipment, and how many volunteers they'll need to staff the department.) Guide students in writing the answer to this question. SEQUENCE

 pp. 96–97 Ask: **Why types of equipment do you think a fire department needs to help fight fires?** (fire trucks, hoses, clothing, ladders, pumps) USE PRIOR KNOWLEDGE

Ask: **How do volunteer fire departments get money for equipment and training?** (Some have reserve funds, some seek grants, or they may get equipment from other fire departments.) NOTE DETAILS

Discuss the Stop and Think question on page 96: **What does a community need to form a volunteer fire department?** (A community needs money, equipment and volunteers.) Guide students in writing the answer to this question. GENERALIZE

Discuss the Stop and Think question on page 97: **What do you think the volunteers do next?** (Possible response: I think the volunteers will wait for the smoke to escape, then spray water on the fire.) Guide students in writing the answer to this question. MAKE PREDICTIONS

 page 98 Discuss the Stop and Think question on page 98: **Do you think you would like to be a volunteer firefighter? Explain.** (Possible response: I think I would like to be a volunteer firefighter because I'd like to save lives.) Guide students in writing the answer to this question. PERSONAL RESPONSE

Ask: **Why do you think the author wanted to tell you about volunteer firefighters?** (Possible response: I think the author wanted to tell us how valuable volunteer firefighters are, and how they risk their lives to help us.) AUTHOR'S PURPOSE

VOCABULARY

Student-Friendly Explanations

equipped When you have been equipped with something, it has been provided to you.

reserve When you keep something in reserve, it is available when you need it.

rely When you rely on something, you trust that it will be there when you need it.

altitude The altitude of a land mass is its height above sea level.

extent Something's extent is the size of the area it covers.

hampered If you have been hampered, something has made it difficult for you to accomplish what you had wanted to.

overshadowed If something is overshadowed by another, it is viewed as less successful, important, or impressive than what it is being compared to.

Spelling Words: Lesson 9

1. accept	11. except
2. adapt	12. formally
3. adopt	13. formerly
4. affect	14. illusion
5. allusion	15. incite
6. complement	16. insight
7. compliment	17. principal
8. device	18. principle
9. devise	19. precede
10. effect	20. proceed

Answers to *Think Critically* Questions Help students read and answer the *Think Critically* questions on page 99. Possible responses are provided.

1. Many small communities rely on volunteer fire departments.
   MAIN IDEA AND DETAILS

2. The community might have a fire that could not be controlled; the community might ask for money or equipment to start a department. **CAUSE AND EFFECT**

3. I think the author feels proud; admiring; thankful. **AUTHOR'S PURPOSE**

RETEACH

Decoding/Spelling

Easily Confused Words Distribute *Copying Master 34*. Have students work in pairs. Have one partner select a Spelling Word and use it in a sentence. The other partner can use the list of Spelling Words to identify the word. Ask the student to name the letters that spell the word. Then have the student repeat the spelling a second time without looking at the list. Have partners alternate roles, selecting Spelling Words and spelling the correct words.

Copying Master 34

Grammar/Writing

Practice Book 36

Abbreviations   Remind students that abbreviations are shortened forms of words. Titles of respect such as Mr., Mrs., and Dr. are capitalized and may be abbreviated with a period after them. Tell students that abbreviations for weights and measures are not capitalized, but many have a period at the end. Write the following sentence on the board:

> The scale showed 80 lbs. when
> Mr. Smith weighed his dog Carson.

Point out the abbreviation for pounds and the title of respect. (lbs., Mr.) Then explain that measurements in the metric system, such as kilometer (km) do not use periods. Guide students to understand that days of the week, months, street names, and states are other words that can be abbreviated.

Then remind students that a common noun names a person, place, thing, idea, or concept, and that a proper noun names a particular person, place or thing.

GUIDED PRACTICE   Have students turn to page 36 in their *Practice Books*. Ask volunteers to read the directions aloud. Model for students how to complete the first sentence in each activity. Then have students complete the remaining sentences on their own.

Fluency

Practice Book 35

Fluency Practice   Invite students to look at the bottom half of *Practice Book* page 35. These sentences have been broken into natural phrases. Tell students to repeat each phrase after you, mirroring your expression, phrasing, and pace. After students have repeated each sentence, invite them to practice reading the sentences to a partner.

30+ Minutes

COMPREHENSION

Preteach Text Structure: Cause and Effect

Reread and Summarize "The Volunteers"

DECODING/SPELLING

Reteach Easily Confused Words

BUILD ROBUST VOCABULARY

Teach Words from "The Volunteers"

GRAMMAR/WRITING

Reteach Writing Trait: Conventions

FLUENCY

Fluency Practice

Materials Needed: *Bold Moves*

Student Edition pp. 92–98

Practice Book pp. 35, 37

Copying Master 35

PRETEACH

Comprehension

Copying Master 35

Text Structure: Cause and Effect Distribute *Copying Master 35*, and have a volunteer read the information about cause and effect aloud. Tell students about words that alert readers to cause and effect, such as *because, due to, since,* and *therefore.*

GUIDED PRACTICE Have volunteers read paragraphs from the passage on *Copying Master 35*. Guide students to look at the chart, and model how each cause creates an effect. Point out how one effect leads to another.

Reread and Summarize Have students reread and summarize "The Volunteers" in sections, as described below.

pp. 92–93

Let's reread pages 92–93 to find out what the volunteers do for their regular jobs.
Summary: Volunteers donate their time to help others. They have other paying jobs as teachers, sales clerks, carpenters, and farmers.

pp. 94–95

Now let's reread pages 94–95 to remember how a town creates a Fire Board and what the Fire Board does.
Summary: A town picks volunteers for a Fire Board. The Board creates a plan for the Volunteer Fire Department. It determines what areas will be protected, how they'll get equipment, and how many volunteers they'll need.

pp. 96–98

Last, let's reread pages 96–98 to find out how the job of a volunteer firefighting team is the same as other firefighting teams.
Summary: Just like paid firefighting teams, a volunteer team first checks to see who must be saved. Then they put out the fire. Finally, they look over the area to determine how the fire may have started.

RETEACH

Decoding/Spelling

Easily Confused Words Write the words *complement* and *compliment* on the board. Have a volunteer read the first word and correctly use it in a sentence. Then have another volunteer read the second word and correctly use it in a sentence. Ask students to identify the letters that make the words different. (i and e) Explain to students that the meanings and the pronunciations of easily confused words are clues to their spelling. Write these word pairs on the board:

precede	principal
proceed	principle

Repeat the exercise. Tell students that when proofreading their writing, they should be sure to use the correct spelling. If they are unsure, remind them to check the word and its meaning in a dictionary.

Build Robust Vocabulary

Words from "The Volunteers"   Have students locate *soar* on page 92 of "The Volunteers." Ask a volunteer to read aloud the sentence in which this word appears. (Line 5: *Hundreds of sparks soar up and float away like little stars.*) Explain that this sentence means that the sparks rise into the air. Next, ask students to locate and read aloud the sentence in which *remote* appears on page 95. (First sentence: *Most towns that form volunteer fire departments are in remote areas, such as the mountains.*) Explain that this sentence means that the places that form volunteer departments are far away from where other people live. Then ask students to locate and read aloud the sentence in which *grants* appears on page 96. (Line 8: *Volunteer fire departments sometimes seek grants to help pay for what they need.*) Explain that a grant is money given by the government or another group to pay for certain things.

Make up silly sentences that use the words incorrectly. Have students explain what is wrong with each sentence. Example: *The elephants soar into the air.*

Grammar/Writing

Practice Book 37

Writing Trait: Conventions   Have students turn to page 37 of their *Practice Books*. Have a volunteer read the instruction aloud as the other students follow along. Review the chart, and have volunteers read the punctuation and usage in each row. Then, read the directions for Part A. Help students complete the activity. Next, have volunteers read the passage in Part B and answer the questions.

GUIDED PRACTICE   Have a volunteer read the directions for Part C on page 37 of their *Practice Books*. Allow students time to share their responses and explain the conventions they used in their sentences.

Fluency

Practice Book 35

Fluency Practice   Tell students that today they will reread the sentences on the bottom of *Practice Book* page 35. Have students locate and point to the first sentence. Tell students that everyone is going to read the sentence together. This choral reading will give students an opportunity to hear others and listen to the natural phrasing of the sentences. Choral-read each of the sentences several times.

DAY AT A GLANCE
Day 4

COMPREHENSION
Reteach Text Structure: Cause and Effect

DECODING/SPELLING
Reteach Easily Confused Words

BUILD ROBUST VOCABULARY
Reteach Words from "The Volunteers"

GRAMMAR/WRITING
Reteach Writing Form: News Story

FLUENCY
Fluency Practice

Materials Needed: *Bold Moves*

| Student Edition pp. 92–98 | Practice Book p. 38 | Copying Master 36 |

Spelling Words: Lesson 9

1. accept	11. except
2. adapt	12. formally
3. adopt	13. formerly
4. affect	14. illusion
5. allusion	15. incite
6. complement	16. insight
7. compliment	17. principal
8. device	18. principle
9. devise	19. precede
10. effect	20. proceed

30+ Minutes

Comprehension

Text Structure: Cause and Effect Remind students that a cause-and-effect text structure explains why something happened. Then have them recall that sometimes a cause or an effect is unstated. Use the example of the classroom door slamming shut as the effect. Have students speculate on possible causes, such as the wind blowing the door, a student pushing the door, or the doorstop coming undone. Then explain that the door slamming shut might be the cause of something else. Invite volunteers to name new effects, such as students being startled, or the slamming door blowing a stack of papers off the teacher's desk.

GUIDED PRACTICE Tell students to imagine there is a big puddle of water on the floor under the classroom window. Explain that this is the effect of something. Invite pairs to speculate what the cause might be. Ask students to share their ideas. Then tell students that the puddle of water will cause something else to happen. Invite volunteers to predict what might happen next.

Decoding/Spelling

Practice Book **38**

Easily Confused Words Have students number a sheet of paper 1–20. Write *allusion* the board, and have students write it on their papers. Remind students that *allusion* can be easily confused with another Spelling Word. Ask students to name the word and spell it. (illusion) Repeat the process for all of the words. Remind students to listen to the pronunciation carefully to help them spell the words correctly. When necessary, use the word in a sentence to guide students. After dictating each word, write it on the board so students can proofread their work.

1. allusion	2. illusion	3. adapt	4. adopt
5. affect	6. effect	7. complement	8. compliment
9. device	10. devise	11. accept	12. except
13. formally	14. formerly	15. incite	16. insight
17. principal	18. principle	19. precede	20. proceed

Have students turn to page 38 in their *Practice Books*. Have a volunteer read the instruction aloud and ask students to complete the page.

Build Robust Vocabulary

Words from "The Volunteers" Review the meanings of the words *soar,* *remote,* and *grants.* Then say these sentences, and ask which word describes each sentence. Have students explain why.

- **A strong wind makes a kite go high up in the air.** (soar)
- **The Brown family camped in a place that was far from a city.** (remote)
- **Our school received money from the government to buy more books for our library.** (grant)

Grammar/Writing

Copying Master 36

Writing Form: News Story Distribute *Copying Master 36.* Invite a volunteer to read the information about a news story at the top of the page aloud. Then have other volunteers read the student model aloud. Discuss with students the four steps used to organize a news story. Have students identify the *who, what, where, why, when,* and *how* of the selection. Remind students that correct writing conventions can help the reader better understand a news story. Then write the following sentence on the board:

> When a gust of wind blew on State Highway 50 at 4:30 P.M., a blinding duststorm was kicked up!

Show students how the comma creates a pause and separates the dependent clause from the independent clause. Ask students to identify what the exclamation point does to the sentence. (creates excitement) Then ask students to point out the abbreviation that indicates the time of day. (P.M.) Ask what part of the day it signifies. (afternoon) Show students the abbreviation for morning. (A.M.)

GUIDED PRACTICE Read the directions for the activity on *Copying Master 36.* Have students work independently to complete the questions. Allow time for volunteers to share their responses.

Fluency

pp. 92–98

Fluency Practice Have each student work with a partner to read passages from "The Volunteers" aloud to each other. Students may select a passage that they enjoyed or choose one of the following options:

- Read page 92. (Total: 84 words)
- Read page 97. (Total: 107 words)

Encourage students to read the selected passage aloud to their partner three times. Have the student rate his or her reading on the 1–4 scale.

1	Need more practice
2	Pretty good
3	Good
4	Great!

DAY AT A GLANCE

Day 5

VOCABULARY
Preteach *concede, confidential, justification, unearthed, alibi, culprit, confront, scandal, sheepishly, vying*

COMPREHENSION
 Preteach Plot and Characters

DECODING/WORD ATTACK
Preteach Decode Longer Words

DECODING/SPELLING
Preteach Consonant-*le* Words

GRAMMAR/WRITING
Preteach Prepositional Phrases, Common and Proper Nouns

FLUENCY
Fluency Performance

Materials Needed: *Bold Moves*

Student Edition pp. 92–98

Copying Master 37

Skill Card 10

PRETEACH

Vocabulary

Copying Master 37

Lesson 10 Vocabulary Distribute a set of Vocabulary Word Cards for each student. Hold up the card for the first word, and ask a volunteer to read it aloud. Have students repeat the word and hold up the matching card. Give the explanation for the word. Then ask students the first question below and discuss their responses. Continue for each of the Vocabulary Words.

- When would you **concede** to a decision made by your family?
- Would the President tell you **confidential** information? Explain.
- What would be a **justification** for you sleeping late into the morning?
- What would you do if you **unearthed** a small box in your backyard?
- Why would you need an **alibi** if someone accused you of stealing?
- What does it mean if you are considered to be the **culprit**?
- Would you **confront** someone if they were teasing another person?
- Why would the arrest of a city's mayor cause a **scandal**?
- What would cause you to act **sheepishly**? Why?
- What happens when two people are **vying** for the same spot?

PRETEACH

Comprehension

Skill Card 10   **Plot and Characters** Have students look at side A of *Skill Card 10: Review: Plot and Characters*. Discuss how characters' traits can affect the plot of a story. Ask a volunteer to read aloud the Skill Reminder. Review with students that the resolution is affected by how the characters interact and react to the conflict. Have a volunteer read the story aloud.

GUIDED PRACTICE Ask students to copy the chart on a separate sheet of paper. Guide them as they complete the chart by identifying the conflict, the characters' qualities, and the resolution. Discuss how each character's traits leads to the resolution. (Conflict: Mom and Megan lose the trail; Characters' Traits: Megan is nervous and unsure, Mom is calm and prepared for emergencies; Resolution: Mom tells Megan how to use the compass to find their way back.)

PRETEACH

Decoding/Word Attack

Decode Longer Words Write *snuggle* on the board, and have students read it aloud. Have a volunteer divide it into syllables and identify the consonant plus *-le* pattern. (snug/gle) Point out that the first syllable has a short vowel sound because it ends with a consonant. Repeat with *bridle*. (bri/dle) Explain that since the first syllable ends with a vowel, it has a long vowel sound. Remind students that longer words may have syllables with long vowel sounds and short vowel sounds, such as *untamable*. Write *tumble, able, eagle,* and *combustible* on the board, and have students identify the pattern. Then have them blend the syllables to read each word.

PRETEACH

Decoding/Spelling

Consonant *-le* Words Remind students that in words ending in a consonant plus *-le*, the pattern forms a syllable. Write *muzzle* on the board. Explain that if two consonants appear before *-le*, the first syllable usually has a short vowel sound. Then write *bridle*. Show students when only one consonant appears before the *-le*, the first syllable usually has a long vowel sound. Have students find the pattern in *swindle, mangle,* and *tickle*, and divide each into syllables. (swin/dle, man/gle, tick/le) Explain that *-ck* stays together in *tickle*.

PRETEACH

Grammar/Writing

Prepositional Phrases, Common and Proper Nouns Review prepositions, prepositional phrases, common nouns, and proper nouns with students. Have students brainstorm prepositions. Remind students that proper nouns are capitalized. Then write this sentence on the board:

> The Great Chicago Fire burned most of the city in little time.

Guide students to identify the proper noun. (Great Chicago Fire) Then have them identify the prepositional phrases. (of the city, in little time)

Student-Friendly Explanations

concede When you concede to something, you acknowledge or admit it to be true.

confidential If something is confidential, it is meant to be secret.

justification When you provide a reason or explanation for a certain action, you provide justification.

unearthed Something that has been unearthed has been discovered.

alibi When you have an alibi, you can offer an explanation as to where you were when an event occurred.

culprit The culprit in a crime is the person who committed the crime.

confront When you challenge someone face-to-face, you confront them.

scandal An event that causes public outrage is known as a scandal.

sheepishly If you feel embarrassed or foolish, you sometimes act sheepishly.

vying If two competitors are vying for something, they are competing for the same goal.

Fluency

pp. 92–98

Fluency Performance Invite students to read aloud the passages from "The Volunteers" that they selected and practiced earlier. Note the number of words each student reads correctly and incorrectly. Have students rate their own oral reading on the 1–4 scale.

LESSON 10

VOCABULARY
Reteach *concede, confidential, justification, unearthed, alibi, culprit, confront, scandal, sheepishly, vying*

COMPREHENSION
Preteach Main Idea and Details

DECODING/WORD ATTACK
Preteach Decode Longer Words

DECODING/SPELLING
Preteach VCCV Words and VCCCV Words

GRAMMAR/WRITING
Reteach Prepositional Phrases, Common and Proper Nouns

FLUENCY
Fluency Practice

Materials Needed: *Bold Moves*

| Student Edition pp. 100–101 | Practice Book pp. 39, 40 | Skill Card 10 | Copying Masters 38 |

RETEACH

Vocabulary

pp. 100–101

Lesson 10 Vocabulary Have students turn to pages 100–101 in their books. Ask a volunteer to read the first sentence aloud and choose the correct word to complete the sentence. Then have another student read aloud the completed sentence. Repeat with each sentence. If students are unable to give reasonable responses, refer to the Student-Friendly Explanations. (Answers for pages 100–101: 2. *concede*, 3. *sheepishly*, 4. *culprit*, 5. *alibi*, 6. *justification*, 7. *confidential*, 8. *scandal*, 9. *unearthed*, 10. *vying*, 11. If I confront someone, I am challenging them face-to-face. 12. Possible response: An alibi can help him because it offers an explanation as to where he was when the event occurred.)

PRETEACH

Comprehension

Skill Card 10
Focus Skill

Main Idea and Details Have students look at side B of *Skill Card 10: Review: Main Idea and Details*. Ask a volunteer to read the Skill Reminder. Remind students that not all passages state the main idea. They will need to identify details to figure it out. Then read the passage aloud as students read along.

GUIDED PRACTICE Guide students to copy the chart on a separate piece of paper. Discuss if the main idea is stated or not. Then discuss a possible main idea for the passage. (Garter snakes are very common. It is not stated.) Have students complete the chart by identifying the details that support this main idea. (Detail: most widely found snakes in North America; Detail: even spotted in Alaska; Detail: easily adapt to many locations; Detail: make their homes in wet and dry places, near and far from water, in marshes, and on hillsides)

PRETEACH

Decoding/Word Attack

Decode Longer Words Write *banker* and *brother* on the board. Have a volunteer divide *banker* into syllables and identify the VCCV pattern of letters. (ban/ker, anke) Repeat with *brother*. (broth/er, othe) Explain that

- words with this pattern are usually divided between the consonants.
- if the words form a cluster or digraph, such as *ck*, *th*, *sh*, and *ch*, then they are divided after the consonants.

PRETEACH

Decoding/Spelling

Copying Master 38

VCCV Words and VCCCV Words Distribute *Copying Master 38*, and echo-read the Spelling Words with students. Then guide them to identify the words with the VCCV/VCCCV spelling pattern and divide them into syllables. (bul/le/tin, dif/fi/cul/ty, ex/clude, sur/viv/al, fran/chise) Remind students that words with the VCCV pattern are divided between the consonants (VC/CV) and words with the VCCCV pattern are usually divided between the first and second consonant. (VC/CCV).

RETEACH

Grammar/Writing

Practice Book 40

Prepositional Phrases, Common and Proper Nouns Remind students that as they proofread, they should make sure that

- **prepositions are used correctly to show the relationship of one noun to another in the same sentence.**
- **proper nouns are capitalized.**

GUIDED PRACTICE Have students turn to page 40 of their *Practice Books*. Ask a volunteer to read the directions. Guide students as they complete the activity.

VOCABULARY

Student-Friendly Explanations

concede When you concede to something, you acknowledge or admit it to be true.

confidential If something is confidential, it is meant to be secret.

justification When you provide a reason or explanation for a certain action, you provide justification.

unearthed Something that has been unearthed has been discovered.

alibi When you have an alibi, you can offer an explanation as to where you were when an event occurred.

culprit The culprit in a crime is the person who committed the crime.

confront When you challenge someone face-to-face, you confront them.

scandal An event that causes public outrage is known as a scandal.

sheepishly If you feel embarrassed or foolish, you sometimes act sheepishly.

vying If two competitors are vying for something, they are competing for the same goal.

Fluency

Practice Book 39

Fluency Practice Have students turn to *Practice Book* page 39. Read the words in the first column aloud. Invite students to track each word and repeat the words after you. Then have students work in pairs to read the words in each of the columns.

30+ Minutes

VOCABULARY
Reteach *concede, confidential, justification, unearthed, alibi, culprit, confront, scandal, sheepishly, vying*

COMPREHENSION
"The Case of the Missing Garter Snake"
Build Background
Monitor Comprehension
Answers to *Think Critically* Questions

DECODING/WORD ATTACK
Preteach Decode Longer Words

DECODING/SPELLING
Preteach Open and Closed Syllable Patterns

GRAMMAR/WRITING
Preteach Clauses and Sentences

FLUENCY
Fluency Practice

Materials Needed: *Bold Moves*

| Student Edition pp. 102–109 | Practice Book p. 39 | Copying Masters 37, 38 |

Vocabulary

Copying Master 37

Lesson 10 Vocabulary Distribute a set of Vocabulary Word Cards for each student. Divide the group into two teams. Read aloud the Student-Friendly Explanation for one of the words, leaving out the word. Have each team choose the correct word to match the explanation. If both teams are correct, have the group read the word aloud, and mark a point for each team. Continue until students have matched all the words. The team with the most points wins.

Comprehension

Build Background: "The Case of the Missing Garter Snake"
Ask students to share experiences they have had taking care of pets. What kinds of strange pets have they had to care for? What are the challenges of taking care of exotic pets like birds, insects, or reptiles?

pp. 102–103

Monitor Comprehension: "The Case of the Missing Garter Snake"
Read the title of the story aloud. Then have students read pages 102–103 to find out where the snake may have hidden.

After reading the pages, ask: **Where do you think the snake may have hidden?** (Possible response: I think the snake may have hidden under the desk, in the sink, under the counter, or in the box.) MAKE PREDICTIONS

Discuss the Stop and Think question on page 102: **Why is Mr. Burnside upset?** (Mr. Burnside is upset because he discovered that the garter snake is missing from its tank in the lab.) Guide students in writing the answer to this question. PLOT AND CHARACTERS

Ask: **Do you think someone left the screen off the tank or did the snake move it by itself?** (Possible response: I think someone did it because the snake wouldn't be strong enough; if the screen was loose, the snake could have slipped out.) MAKE INFERENCES

Discuss the Stop and Think question on page 103: **How do you think Ann feels about snakes? How do you know?** (Possible response: I think Ann feels afraid because she stands up on her desk.) Guide students in writing the answer to this question. CHARACTERS' EMOTIONS

Ask: **What would you do next?** (Possible response: I would find the snake.) PERSONAL RESPONSE

pp. 104–105 Read Marcus's lines in the middle of page 104. Model identifying how a character's qualities can affect the plot of a story.

(THINK ALOUD) **When I read Marcus's lines, I see that he has the quality of keeping things under control. The plot of the snake escaping could start a panic, but Marcus's character trait helps the class to focus and find a resolution to the conflict.** PLOT AND CHARACTERS

Discuss the Stop and Think question on page 104: **Do you think Mr. Burnside is a fair teacher? Why do you think so?** (Possible response: Mr. Burnside is fair because he realizes he could have left the screen off the tank. He didn't just blame the students.) Guide students in writing the answer to this question. CHARACTERS' TRAITS

Discuss the Stop and Think question on page 105: **How do the kids view the problem of the escaped snake? How can you tell?** (Possible response: The kids view the problem as funny and comical because they keep trying to imagine tomorrow's headlines and plots.) Guide students in writing the answer to this question. MAKE INFERENCES

pp. 106–107 Ask: **Why do you think it's good to search for the snake in teams?** (Possible response: I think it's good because one person may miss a spot and they can check each other because the snake moves around.) MAKE INFERENCES

Discuss the Stop and Think question on page 106: **Does Mr. Burnside think they will find the snake? How can you tell?** (Possible response: Mr. Burnside thinks they will find the snake because he tells Ann that he'll return it to the tank *when* they find it, not if they find it.) Guide students in writing the answer to this question. DRAW CONCLUSIONS

Discuss the Stop and Think question on page 107: **What do you think Mr. Burnside and the kids see?** (Possible response: I think they see the snake on the shelf.) Guide students in writing the answer to this question. MAKE PREDICTIONS

page 108 Discuss the Stop and Think question on page 108: **What does Mr. Burnside want the kids to learn from this?** (Mr. Burnside wants them to learn to put the screen on the cage, so the snake can't escape like it did when he forgot.) Guide students in writing the answer to this question. MAIN IDEA AND DETAILS

Ask: **Where do you think the author got the idea for this story?** (Possible response: I think the author got the idea from personal experience.) AUTHOR'S PERSPECTIVE

Spelling Words: Lesson 10

1.	mangle	11.	ego
2.	tickle	12.	linen
3.	bridle	13.	minor
4.	swindle	14.	veto
5.	muzzle	15.	vital
6.	bulletin	16.	complement
7.	difficulty	17.	compliment
8.	exclude	18.	formally
9.	survival	19.	formerly
10.	franchise	20.	precede

 page 109

Answers to *Think Critically* Questions

Help students read and answer the *Think Critically* questions on page 109. Guide students in writing the answer to each question. Possible responses are provided.

1. The snake escaped because someone had forgotten to put the screen back on the tank. **CAUSE AND EFFECT**

2. If the snake hadn't been found, then the kids would have had to tell the rest of the school that a snake was loose; they would have to search the rest of the school. **PLOT**

3. I think that this story could really happen because some science classes have animals, and they could get out. **AUTHOR'S CRAFT**

PRETEACH

Decoding/Word Attack

Decode Longer Words Write *fever* and *travel* on the board. Say the words aloud, divide them into syllables, and identify the first vowel as long or short. (fe/ver, long; trav/el, short) Review that in two-syllable words with a single consonant between vowels, they should divide syllables before the consonant if the first vowel is long. They should divide syllables after the consonant if the first vowel is short. Have students practice identifying each pattern and the vowel sound with *savor, silent, clever,* and *hotel.* (sa/vor, long; si/lent, long; clev/er, short; ho/tel, long)

PRETEACH

Decoding/Spelling

Copying Master 38

Open and Closed Syllable Patterns Have students identify the words with the VCV pattern on *Copying Master 38*. Write the words on the board. (ego, linen, minor, veto, vital, precede) Have a volunteer pronounce *ego* and show how to divide it. (e/go) Remind students that many words with a VCV pattern and a long first vowel sound are divided before the consonant. VCV words with a short first vowel sound are divided after the consonant. Repeat with the remaining words. (lin/en, mi/nor, ve/to, vi/tal)

PRETEACH

Grammar/Writing

Clauses and Sentences Write these sentences on the board:

> Because you like reptiles, you might like a gecko for a pet.

Invite students to identify the subordinating conjunction in the sentence on the board. (Because) Show students how it makes the first clause depend on the independent clause for completeness. Point out the comma after an introductory subordinating clause. Then ask students if the sentence is compound, complex, or compound-complex. (complex)

> Sheri does not like snakes, so she wouldn't touch it.
> He was concerned when the lizard escaped.

GUIDED PRACTICE Have students work in pairs to identify the clauses in each sentence by finding the conjunction. (so, when) Then ask them to identify each sentence as compound, complex, or compound-complex. (compound, complex)

Fluency

Practice Book 39

Fluency Practice Invite students to look at the bottom half of *Practice Book* page 39. These sentences have been broken into natural phrases. Tell students to repeat each phrase after you, mirroring your expression, phrasing, and pace. After students have repeated each sentence, invite them to practice reading the sentences to a partner.

COMPREHENSION
Preteach Shades of Meaning

Reread and Summarize "The Case of the Missing Garter Snake"

DECODING/WORD ATTACK
Preteach Decode Longer Words

DECODING/SPELLING
Preteach Easily Confused Words

BUILD ROBUST VOCABULARY
Teach Words from "The Case of the Missing Garter Snake"

GRAMMAR/WRITING
Reteach Clauses and Sentences

FLUENCY
Fluency Practice

Materials Needed: *Bold Moves*

Student Edition
pp. 102–108

Practice Book
pp. 39, 41

Copying Master
38

PRETEACH

Comprehension

Shades of Meaning   Review with students how related words have similar meanings. Demonstrate how the meanings are slightly different. Write this sentence on the board:

> The horse trotted off into the field.

Ask students to describe how the horse behaves as he goes into the field. (happy, relaxed) Invite students to replace *trotted* with *thundered* or *stumbled*. Discuss how each word changes how we picture the horse moving.

Reread and Summarize   Have students reread and summarize "The Case of the Missing Garter Snake" in sections, as described below.

 pp. 102–103 **Let's reread pages 102–103 to recall the dilemma in Mr. Burnside's class.**
Summary: When the students get to class, they discover that the garter snake has escaped from its tank and can't be found.

 pp. 104–105 **Now let's reread pages 104–105 to remember the student's reactions about the lost garter snake.**
Summary: No one knows who left the screen top off, but they don't want word to get out to the rest of the school. If it did, they can just imagine the stories that might be made up about the snake's escape.

 pp. 106–108 **Last, let's reread pages 106–108 to recall how the play ends.**
Summary: The students split into teams to look for the snake, but they can't find it. Finally, Ann spots the snake on the top shelf. Mr. Burnside hopes the students learn from his mistake.

PRETEACH

Decoding/Word Attack

Decode Longer Words   Remind students of the ways they can decode long words syllable by syllable.

- Look for familiar letter patterns, such as digraphs *-sh, -th*
- Look for familiar spelling patterns, such as VCCV words.
- Look for structural patterns, such as prefix-root words.
- Look to see if the word is a compound word.
- Look for context clues.

Write *otherwise, handicap, atmosphere,* and *subway* on the board. For each word, have students identify the strategy they use to decode the word.

Decoding/Spelling

Copying Master 38

Easily Confused Words   Write *adapt* and *adopt* on the board. Have a volunteer circle the letter that is different in each word. Review with students that some word pairs are easily confused because they have similar spellings, even though the pronunciations and meanings are different. Repeat with *principle* and *principal*. Distribute *Copying Master 38* and have pairs of students complete the following activity. Have students write the Spelling Words on index cards. One student draws a card and reads the word aloud, and the other student writes the word. Then have partners switch roles. When a student spells a word correctly, he or she initials the card and returns it to the pile. Students should work through the pile until each student has had the opportunity to spell each of the words. Have students write down each word they do not spell correctly to study later.

Build Robust Vocabulary

pp. 104–106

Words from "The Case of the Missing Garter Snake"   Have students locate *roaming* on page 104 in their books. Ask a volunteer to read aloud the sentence in which this word appears. (Line 11: *If it gets out that our snake is roaming around free, it could start a panic.*) Explain that "roaming" means wandering all over a large area. Then ask students to locate and read aloud the sentence in which the word *fret* appears on page 106. (Line 12: *There's no need for you to fret, Ann.*) Explain that this sentence means that there is no need for Ann to worry or be troubled.

Have students act out both words. Ask the class to tell how each performance fits the word.

Grammar/Writing

Practice Book 41

Clauses and Sentences   Write on the board *Andy said that the jar was empty, but it had plenty.*

Guide students to identify the conjunction, dependent clause, and independent clause in the sentence. (but, that the jar was empty, Andy said) Underline the clause that follows the conjunction. Point out that since the sentence has all of these features, it is a compound-complex sentence.

GUIDED PRACTICE   Have students turn to page 41 of their *Practice Book* and complete the page.

Fluency

Practice Book 39

Fluency Practice   Tell students that today they will reread the sentences on the bottom of *Practice Book* page 39. Have students locate and point to the first sentence. Tell students that everyone is going to read the sentence together. This choral reading will give students an opportunity to hear others and listen to the natural phrasing of the sentences. Choral-read each of the sentences several times.

LESSON 10

DAY AT A GLANCE

Day 4

COMPREHENSION
Preteach Vocabulary Strategies

DECODING/SPELLING
Cumulative Review

BUILD ROBUST VOCABULARY
Reteach Words from "The Case of the Missing Garter Snake"

GRAMMAR/WRITING
Cumulative Review

FLUENCY
Fluency Practice

Materials Needed: *Bold Moves*

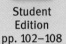

Student Edition pp. 102–108

Practice Book p. 42

Copying Masters 39, 40

Spelling Words: Lesson 10

1. mangle		11. ego	
2. tickle		12. linen	
3. bridle		13. minor	
4. swindle		14. veto	
5. muzzle		15. vital	
6. bulletin		16. complement	
7. difficulty		17. compliment	
8. exclude		18. formally	
9. survival		19. formerly	
10. franchise		20. precede	

30+ Minutes

PRETEACH

Comprehension

Vocabulary Strategies   Remind students that they can use words and sentences around a word for clues about its specific meaning. Write *pool* on the board. Guide students to come up with possible meanings. (pond, swimming place, game of billiards, to combine) Then write *We decided to pool our money* on the board, and model for students how the context of the sentence helps you determine which meaning is correct. (to combine)

Copying Master 39

GUIDED PRACTICE   Have a volunteer read aloud the instruction on *Copying Master 39*. Then read the passage aloud as students follow along. Discuss the word web and guide students as they answer the questions.

RETEACH

Decoding/Spelling

Cumulative Review   Have students number a sheet of paper 1–16. Write *mangle* on the board, and point to the consonant *-le* ending. Tell students that the first four words you will dictate have this ending. After students write each word, display it so they can proofread their work. Repeat this activity for the other word strategies using these examples: *bulletin, ego,* and *complement.*

Practice Book 42

1. tickle	2. bridle	3. swindle	4. muzzle
5. difficulty	6. exclude	7. survival	8. franchise
9. linen	10. minor	11. veto	12. vital
13. compliment	14. formally	15. formerly	16. precede

Have students turn to page 42 in their *Practice Books*. Explain that they will complete the activity by choosing the correct sentence that describes each picture.

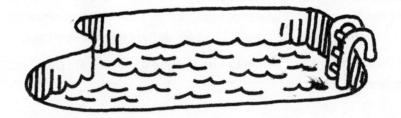

Build Robust Vocabulary

Words from "The Case of the Missing Garter Snake" Review the meanings of the words *roaming* and *fret*. Then say these sentences and ask which word describes each sentence. Have students explain why.

- On weekends, I wander around my neighborhood to see if any of my friends are out playing. (roam)

- Mom was worried that there wouldn't be enough stew for the guests who stopped by. (fretted)

Grammar/Writing

Copying Master 40

Cumulative Review Have students recall the grammar skills they learned in this lesson. Discuss examples for each skill:

- prepositions and prepositional phrases
- common and proper nouns
- subordinate and independent clauses
- compound, complex, and compound-complex sentences

GUIDED PRACTICE Distribute *Copying Master 40*. Guide students to proofread each sentence and circle the mistakes. Then have them write each sentence correctly. Allow time for students to share the errors they found in the sentences.

Fluency

pp. 102–108

Fluency Practice Have each student work with a partner to read passages from "The Case of the Missing Garter Snake" aloud to each other. Remind students to:

- vary their tone of voice to reflect feelings and emotions appropriately when they read aloud.

- read aloud smoothly at a pace that is neither too fast nor too slow for listeners to understand.

Encourage students to read the selected passage aloud to their partner three times. Have the student rate his or her reading on the 1–4 scale.

1	Need more practice
2	Pretty good
3	Good
4	Great!

VOCABULARY
Preteach *thrive, illuminates, bearable, abundant, phenomenon, refuge*

COMPREHENSION
 Preteach Figurative Language

DECODING/WORD ATTACK
Preteach Decode Longer Words

DECODING/SPELLING
Preteach Words with Suffixes *-able, -ible*

GRAMMAR/WRITING
Preteach Singular and Plural Nouns

FLUENCY
Fluency Performance

Materials Needed: *Bold Moves*

| Student Edition pp. 102–108 | Copying Master 41 | Skill Card 11 |

PRETEACH

Vocabulary

Copying Master 41

Lesson 11 Vocabulary Distribute a set of Vocabulary Word Cards for each pair of students. Hold up the card for the first word, and ask a volunteer to read it aloud. Have students repeat the word and hold up the matching card. Give the explanation for the word. Then ask students the first question below and discuss their responses. Continue for each Vocabulary Word.

- **What does a green plant need to thrive?**
- **Why is it useful to explorers when a flashlight illuminates a cave?**
- **What things can make a really hot day bearable?**
- **If sunlight were not abundant, what might happen?**
- **If you discovered an extraordinary phenomenon, whom would you tell and why?**
- **Why might an endangered animal need a wildlife refuge?**

PRETEACH

Comprehension

Skill Card 11

Figurative Language Direct students' attention to side A of *Skill Card 11: Figurative Language*. Have a volunteer read the introduction aloud as students follow along. Ask:

- **How do writers use figurative language?** (to make their descriptions more lively and to help readers picture events)
- **What are three types of figurative language?** (simile, metaphor, and personification)

GUIDED PRACTICE Direct students' attention to the chart. Have them read the row about similes. Ask:

- **How was the thunder like the roar of an angry lion?** (Both can make a loud and frightening sound.)

Have students cover column 3. Read together the definition for metaphor in column 2 and the example metaphor in column 1. Ask:

- **What does the metaphor mean?** (Water on the road made cars and trucks spin dangerously.)

Have students' compare their responses with the answer in column 3. Repeat the procedure for *personification*.

Decoding/Word Attack

Decode Longer Words Write *passable* and *accessible* on the board, and read them with students. Tell students that these words contain suffixes— word parts added to the end of root words. Ask a volunteer to identify the root words. (pass; access) Explain to students that looking for suffixes can help break longer words into syllables. The suffixes *-able* and *-ible* are divided after the *a* or *i*. Then use other strategies to break the root or root word into syllables.(pass/a/ble; ac/ces/si/ble)

Decoding/Spelling

Words with Suffixes *-able, -ible* Write *excitable* and *sensible* on the board. Have a volunteer read the words aloud. Underline the suffixes *-able* and *-ible*, and point out that they have the same sound. Explain that they also add the same meaning to a root word—"capable or worthy of." Then ask students to name the root words, and write them on the board. (excite; sense) Point out that the silent e in a root word is often dropped with adding these suffixes.

Grammar/Writing

Singular and Plural Nouns Write *car* and *wind* on the board, and tell students that both words are singular nouns. Then add *-s* to the end of both words. Explain that you add *-s* to form the plural of most nouns. Use the the words *boss, coach, brush,* and *fox* to explain that you add *-es* to form the plural of nouns ending in *s, ch, sh,* or *x.* Use *city* and *story* to explain that you change the *y* to *i* and add *-es* to form the plural of nouns ending in a consonant and *y.*

Student-Friendly Explanations

thrive When a living thing is growing in a healthy manner, it is said to thrive.

illuminates When something illuminates an object, it shines a light on it to make it brighter or more visible.

bearable Something that you can usually put up with is bearable.

abundant When something is abundant, there are large quantities of it.

phenomenon Something that is out of the ordinary is called a phenomenon.

refuge A refuge is a place that provides shelter and protection.

Fluency

pp. 102– 108 **Fluency Performance** Invite students to read aloud the passages from "The Case of the Missing Garter Snake" that they selected and practiced earlier. Have students rate their own oral reading on the 1–4 scale. Give students the opportunity to continue practicing and then to read the passage to you again.

DAY AT A GLANCE

Day 1

 30+ Minutes

LESSON 11

STRANDED ON THE ICE

VOCABULARY
Reteach *thrive, illuminates, bearable, abundant, phenomenon, refuge*

COMPREHENSION
 Reteach Figurative Language

DECODING/SPELLING
Reteach Words with Suffixes *-able, -ible*

GRAMMAR/WRITING
Preteach Plural Nouns

FLUENCY
Fluency Practice

Materials Needed: *Bold Moves*

	Practice Book	Skill Card	Copying Master
Student Edition pp. 110–111	Practice Book p. 43	Skill Card 11	Copying Master 42

RETEACH

Vocabulary

pp. 110–111 **Lesson 11 Vocabulary** Read aloud the Vocabulary Words and the Student-Friendly Explanations. Then have students read the selection on pages 110–111 of their books. Guide them in completing the sentences by selecting the correct word from the box. Have a volunteer read each completed sentence aloud. Then have students read the completed selection along with you. If students are unable to give reasonable responses, refer to the Student-Friendly Explanations. (Answers for pages 110–111: 2. *illuminates*, 3. *bearable*, 4. *thrive*, 5. *phenomenon*, 6. *refuge*)

RETEACH

Comprehension

Skill Card 11 Focus Skill **Figurative Language** Have students look at side B of *Skill Card 11: Figurative Language*. Read together the Skill Reminder. Then call on a volunteer to read the passage.

Ask:

- **What is a simile in the second sentence?** (like blazes)
- **What is a metaphor in the third sentence?** (The middle ear is a pocket of air.)
- **What are personified in the fourth sentence?** (germs)
- **What is a simile in the last sentence?** (like a balloon that wants to pop)

GUIDED PRACTICE Guide students as they copy the chart and complete it by classifying and explaining the figurative language they find in the passage. (Row 1: simile. It can hurt really badly; Row 2: metaphor. The middle ear is an area filled with air; Row 3: personification. Germs can cause an infection in the ear; Row 4: simile. It can make your ear feel swollen and painful.)

Decoding/Spelling

Copying Master 42

Words with Suffixes -able, -ible   Distribute *Copying Master 42.* Model reading the Spelling Words as students repeat them. Read with students the instruction for adding the suffix *-able* or *-ible* to a word. Have pairs of students write the Spelling Words on index cards. Have one student draw a card and read the word aloud as the other student writes the word; then have partners switch roles. When a student spells a word correctly, he or she initials the card and returns it to the pile. Students should continue until each student has had the opportunity to spell each of the words. Have students write down each word they do not spell correctly to study later.

Grammar/Writing

Plural Nouns   Explain that to form the plural of many nouns ending in *f* or *fe*, you change the *f* to *v* and add *-es*. Use these examples to illustrate the rule and to review regular plural nouns:

> We read the fairy <u>tale</u> about the <u>elf</u>.
>
> The <u>carpenter</u> kept the sharp <u>knife</u> on the <u>workbench</u>.

Copy the sentences on the board. Have volunteers erase the underlined words and replace them with plural nouns. (*tales, elves, carpenters, knives, workbenches*)

GUIDED PRACTICE   Write the words *thief, life, wife,* and *hoax* on the board. Then write the sentence frame shown below. Make sure that students know the meaning of *hoax*. Then have them fill in the sentence frame using the plural form of a noun from the board. (*wives, hoaxes, lives, thieves*)

> The men's _____ saw through the _____. The women had known all their _____ how to spot crooks and _____.

Student-Friendly Explanations

thrive   When a living thing is growing in a healthy manner, it is said to thrive.

illuminates   When something illuminates an object, it shines a light on it to make it brighter or more visible.

bearable   Something that you can usually put up with is bearable.

abundant   When something is abundant, there are large quantities of it.

phenomenon   Something that is out of the ordinary is called a phenomenon.

refuge   A refuge is a place that provides shelter and protection.

Fluency

Practice Book 43

Fluency Practice   Have students turn to *Practice Book* page 43. Read the words in the first column aloud. Invite students to track each word and repeat the words after you. Then have students work in pairs to read the words in the first column aloud to each other. Follow the same procedure with each of the remaining columns. After partners have practiced reading aloud the words in each of the columns, have them practice reading all of the words.

VOCABULARY
Reteach *thrive, illuminates, bearable, abundant, phenomenon, refuge*

COMPREHENSION
"Stranded on the Ice"

Build Background

Monitor Comprehension

Answers to *Think Critically* Questions

DECODING/SPELLING
Reteach Words with Suffixes *-able, -ible*

GRAMMAR/WRITING
Preteach Irregular Plural Nouns

FLUENCY
Fluency Practice

Materials Needed: *Bold Moves*

Student Edition pp. 112–119

Practice Book pp. 43, 44

Copying Masters 41, 42

30+ Minutes

Vocabulary

Copying Master 41

Lesson 11 Vocabulary Distribute a set of Vocabulary Word Cards to each student. Call on a volunteer to read aloud the meaning of one of the Vocabulary Words, and have the other students display and read the matching card. Continue until students have matched all the words.

Comprehension

Build Background: "Stranded on the Ice"
Ask students to share experiences they may have had in very cold or very hot weather. What did they do to stay comfortable and safe?

Monitor Comprehension: "Stranded on the Ice"

pp. 112–113

Read the title of the selection aloud. Then have students read pages 112–113 to learn about two adventurous men who sail to Antarctica.

After reading the pages, ask: **What are the names of two adventurous men who sail to Antarctica?** (Ernest Shackleton and Frank Hurley) **What are their jobs?** (Shackleton is captain and pilots the ship; Hurley records the journey in pictures.) **Note Details**

Discuss the Stop and Think question on page 112: **What do you want to know about this trip?** (Possible response: I want to know what will happen on the trip.) Guide students in writing the answer to this question. **Main Idea and Details**

Ask: **What detail suggests that Hurley is an ideal picture-taker for the journey?** (Hurley is known for his images of barren landscapes.) **Note Details**

Ask: **How does Hurley use the glass plates?** (Hurley uses the glass plates like we use film today, to make pictures.) **Make Inferences**

Discuss the Stop and Think question on page 113: **What can you tell about Frank Hurley?** (Possible responses: I can tell that Frank Hurley is adventurous, strong, and determined; I can tell that he enjoys taking pictures.) Guide students in writing the answer to this question. **Make Inferences**

pp. 114–115 Discuss the Stop and Think question on page 114: **Why do you think the author describes Antarctica?** (Possible response: I think he describes Antarctica because he wants us to know how hard it is to survive there.) Guide students in writing the answer to this question. **Author's Purpose**

Direct students' attention to the simile "The ice crushed the ship like a tin can" on page 115.

> **THINK ALOUD** **When I read the comparison, I notice the word *like*, which tells me it's a simile. I don't quite understand what the simile means, but the verb *crushed* gives a clue. I know what a soda can looks like when it's crushed. I see that the ice crushed the ship as easily as a can can be crushed!** **Figurative Language**

Discuss the Stop and Think question on page 115: **What do you think the men will do next?** (Possible response: I think the men will look for a place to find shelter.) Guide students in writing the answer to this question. **Make Predictions**

 pp. 116–117 Discuss the Stop and Think question on page 116: **How is the ice like a frozen puzzle?** (The ice is like a frozen puzzle because the surface is cracked and the pieces fit together.) Guide students in writing the answer to this question. **Figurative Language**

Have students look at the pictures on pages 116–117. Ask: **How do the pictures help you understand the text?** (Possible response: The pictures show me how the men were able to prepare food and make shelters. They make the text come alive.) **Graphic Aids**

Discuss the Stop and Think question on page 117: **How do you think the men who were left behind felt?** (Possible response: I think the men felt scared that they would not be rescued.) Guide students in writing the answer to this question. **Identify with Characters**

page 118 Ask: **What causes the risk of snow blindness to increase as the days grow longer?** (As the days grow longer, the sun is higher in the sky and reflects off the snow more intensely.) **Cause and Effect**

Discuss the Stop and Think question on page 118: **How do you feel about this selection's ending?** (Possible response: I feel happy about the selection's ending because it shows Shackleton's loyalty to his men and how resourceful people can be.) Guide students in writing the answer to this question. **Personal Response**

VOCABULARY

Student-Friendly Explanations

thrive When a living thing is growing in a healthy manner, it is said to thrive.

illuminates When something illuminates an object, it shines a light on it to make it brighter or more visible.

bearable Something that you can usually put up with is bearable.

abundant When something is abundant, there are large quantities of it.

phenomenon Something that is out of the ordinary is called a phenomenon.

refuge A refuge is a place that provides shelter and protection.

Spelling Words: Lesson 11

1. noticeable	11. destructible
2. passable	12. excitable
3. convertible	13. invincible
4. wearable	14. sensible
5. avoidable	15. edible
6. capable	16. comprehensible
7. profitable	17. credible
8. applicable	18. returnable
9. accessible	19. permissible
10. breakable	20. reproducible

page 119

Answers to *Think Critically* Questions

Help students read and answer the *Think Critically* questions on page 119. Possible responses are provided.

1. [What I Learned] The men were stranded on the ice for two years, but they survived. Not a single man died. **MAIN IDEA AND DETAILS**

2. I learned that Ernest Shackleton was strong, loyal to his men, and a good leader. **CHARACTERS' TRAITS**

3. They gained endurance by learning how to survive in a very difficult place. **CAUSE AND EFFECT**

RETEACH

Decoding/Spelling

Copying Master 42

Words with Suffixes *-able, -ible* On the board, draw a two-column chart with the headings *-able* and *-ible*. Divide the group in two. Give a list of Spelling Words to Group A. Tell Group B to stand in front of the board. Have a member of Group A say one of the words and a member of Group B write it under the appropriate column. Guide students to correct any misspelled words and write them under the correct heading. After five words, have the groups change places. Continue until all the words have been used.

PRETEACH

Grammar/Writing

Practice Book 44

Irregular Plural Nouns Explain that some nouns do not follow set rules for forming plurals. These are called irregular plural nouns. Write these examples on the board:

> trout/trout   die/dice   species/species

Write the following sentence on the board:

> As we rolled the <u>die</u>, we noticed three <u>trout</u> of different <u>species</u> on the game board.

Help students write and spell irregular plural forms of the underlined nouns. (dice, trout, species)

GUIDED PRACTICE Read with students the instructions for the activity on page 44 in their *Practice Books*. Read and complete the first sentence together. Have students complete the page independently. When all students have finished, call on volunteers to give the correct responses to the group.

Fluency

Practice Book 43

Fluency Practice Invite students to look at the bottom half of *Practice Book* page 43. These sentences have been broken into natural phrases. Tell students to repeat each phrase after you, mirroring your expression, phrasing, and pace. After students have repeated each sentence, invite them to practice reading the sentences to a partner.

30+ Minutes

COMPREHENSION

Preteach Prefixes, Suffixes, and Roots

Reread and Summarize "Stranded on the Ice"

DECODING/SPELLING

Reteach Words with Suffixes *-able, -ible*

BUILD ROBUST VOCABULARY

Teach Words from "Stranded on the Ice"

GRAMMAR/WRITING

Reteach Writing Trait: Sentence Fluency

FLUENCY

Fluency Practice

Materials Needed: *Bold Moves*

Student Edition pp. 112–118

Practice Book pp. 43, 45

Copying Master 43

PRETEACH

Comprehension

Copying Master 43

Prefixes, Suffixes, and Roots   Tell students that knowing how words are put together can help them figure out the meanings of unfamiliar words as they read. Distribute *Copying Master 43,* and read the information at the top of the page with students.

GUIDED PRACTICE   Using the chart, have students analyze and form words using prefixes, suffixes, and roots. Complete the activity together.

Reread and Summarize   Have students reread and summarize "Stranded on the Ice" in sections, as described below.

pp. 112–113   **Let's reread pages 112–113 to recall when and why the *Endurance* set sail and the jobs of two important men on board.**
Summary: The *Endurance* set sail in the fall of 1914 to explore and take pictures of Antarctica. Ernest Shackleton, the captain, piloted the ship. Frank Hurley carried his camera to record the expedition on film.

pp. 114–115   **Now, let's reread pages 114–115 to find out what Antarctica is like and what happened to the *Endurance* there.**
Summary: Antarctica is freezing cold, yet some animals thrive in the harsh climate. The *Endurance* got trapped because the pack ice broke up late, let the ship in, and then froze solid again.

pp. 116–118   **Last, let's reread pages 116–118 to find out how the men coped with the disaster.**
Summary: The men used what they could salvage from the ship to survive. When spring came, Shackleton and two men sailed off for help. In the end, they returned and rescued their twenty-two crewmates.

RETEACH

Decoding/Spelling

Words with Suffixes *-able, -ible*   Write the word *wearable* on the board. Ask students what familiar word they see within the word. Cover the suffix *-able* and have students say the root word *wear*. Point out that many words ending in *-able* or *-ible* have roots that are whole words or parts of familiar words. Explain that looking closely at the root can make it easier to remember a word's spelling.

TEACH

Build Robust Vocabulary

pp. 113–116

Words from "Stranded on the Ice" Have students locate *bulky* on page 113 of "Stranded on the Ice." Ask a volunteer to read aloud the sentence in which this word appears. (First sentence: On the trip, Hurley carried his bulky cameras wherever he could get a good shot.) Explain that this sentence means that Hurley took his large and hard-to-carry cameras with him. Continue by asking students to locate and read aloud the sentence in which *fantastic* appears on page 114. (Line 8: Hurley made a film of this fantastic scene with his moving-picture camera.) Explain that this sentence means that Hurley made a film of a scene that was so amazing and unusual that it didn't seem real. Then ask students to locate and read aloud the sentence in which *suspended* appears on page 116. (Line 2: Suspended on the ice, the broken ship protected them from the winds.) Explain that this sentence means that the ship was hanging over the water, supported by the ice.

Write the words on the board. Under each word, help students list things that are bulky, fantastic, and things that are or could be suspended.

RETEACH

Grammar/Writing

Practice Book 45

Writing Trait: Sentence Fluency Have students turn to page 45 in their *Practice Books*. Read the information at the top of the page aloud as students read along. Ask a volunteer to read the descriptions of the sentence types. Then write on the board the following examples:

> I'm going home.
> What's for lunch?
> I'm starving!

Have students identify each sentence on the board by type. (declarative, interrogative, exclamatory) Elicit additional examples of each type.

GUIDED PRACTICE Complete the page together. Help students understand that using a variety of sentence types makes their writing more interesting.

Fluency

Practice Book 43

Fluency Practice Tell students that today they will reread the sentences on the bottom of *Practice Book* page 43. Have students locate and point to the first sentence. Tell students that everyone is going to read the sentence together. This choral reading will give students an opportunity to hear others and listen to the natural phrasing of the sentences. Choral-read each of the sentences several times.

LESSON 11

DAY AT A GLANCE

Day 4

30+ Minutes

COMPREHENSION
Reteach Prefixes, Suffixes, and Roots

DECODING/SPELLING
Reteach Words with Suffixes -able, -ible

BUILD ROBUST VOCABULARY
Reteach Words from "Stranded on the Ice"

GRAMMAR/WRITING
Reteach Writing Form: Descriptive Composition

FLUENCY
Fluency Practice

Materials Needed: *Bold Moves*

Student Edition pp. 112–118

Practice Book p. 46

Copying Master 44

Spelling Words: Lesson 11

1. noticeable	11. destructible
2. passable	12. excitable
3. convertible	13. invincible
4. wearable	14. sensible
5. avoidable	15. edible
6. capable	16. comprehensible
7. profitable	17. credible
8. applicable	18. returnable
9. accessible	19. permissible
10. breakable	20. reproducible

RETEACH

Comprehension

Prefixes, Suffixes, and Roots Review the definitions of *prefix, suffix,* and *root*. Point out that some prefixes, such as *dis-* and *un-,* have the same meaning. Ask:

- **How can you tell whether the prefix *dis-* or the prefix *un-* works best with a root word, such as *true*?** (You can use what you already know or a dictionary to help you select the better prefix—in this case, *un-*.)

Remind students that some words can take both a prefix and a suffix. Write the following words on the board: *happy, cycle, view.* Ask:

- **What word can you create by adding both a prefix and a suffix to a word on the board?** (Possible responses: *unhappily, bicyclist, previewing*)

GUIDED PRACTICE Have students skim "Stranded on the Ice" to find words with prefixes and suffixes. Call on volunteers to write their words on the board. Discuss how the affixes change the meanings of the root words.

RETEACH

Decoding/Spelling

Practice Book 46 **Words with Suffixes -able, -ible** Have students number a sheet of paper 1–18. Write the Spelling Word *noticeable* on the board, and underline the suffix. Tell students that in the first nine words you will dictate, the suffix *-able* is found at the end of each word. Remind students that the ending of some root words change when adding a suffix. After students write each word, display it so they can proofread their work. Repeat this activity for the suffix *-ible* using the example *convertible.*

1. passable	2. wearable	3. avoidable	4. capable
5. profitable	6. applicable	7. breakable	8. excitable
9. returnable	10. accessible	11. destructible	12. invincible
13. sensible	14. edible	15. comprehensible	16. credible
17. permissible	18. reproducible		

Have students turn to page 46 in their *Practice Books*. Ask a volunteer to read the directions. Have students complete the page independently. Call on volunteers to share their responses with the group.

RETEACH

Build Robust Vocabulary

Words from "Stranded on the Ice" Review the meanings of the words *bulky, fantastic,* and *suspended*. Then say these sentences, and ask which word describes each sentence. Have students explain why.

- **I helped Dad carry the large, hard-to-handle box to the basement.** (bulky)

- **The team's win, after being so far behind, was almost too amazing to believe.** (fantastic)

- **The lamp was hanging over the dining room table.** (suspended)

RETEACH

Grammar/Writing

Copying Master 44

Writing Form: Descriptive Composition Explain that writers use a variety of sentences in descriptive compositions. Remind students that different sentence types need the correct ending punctuation. Distribute *Copying Master 44.* Have a volunteer read the information at the top of the page aloud. Then read the Student Model aloud as students follow along. Point out the margin notes that show the steps to writing a descriptive composition.

GUIDED PRACTICE Guide students in completing the activities. Allow time for students to share their revisions with the group.

Fluency

pp. 112–118

Fluency Practice Have each student work with a partner to read passages from "Stranded on the Ice" aloud to each other. Students may select a passage that they enjoyed or choose one of the following options:

- Read page 112. (Total: 110 words)
- Read page 118. (Total: 112 words)

Encourage students to read the selected passage aloud to their partner three times. Have the student rate his or her reading on the 1–4 scale.

1	Need more practice
2	Pretty good
3	Good
4	Great!

DAY AT A GLANCE

Day 5

VOCABULARY
Preteach *ideal, perched, wedged, pelting, slunk, blurted, stranded*

COMPREHENSION
 Preteach Figurative Language

DECODING/WORD ATTACK
Preteach Decode Longer Words

DECODING/SPELLING
Preteach Words with Suffixes *-ous, -ious, -eous*

GRAMMAR/WRITING
Preteach Singular and Plural Possessive Nouns

FLUENCY
Fluency Performance

Materials Needed: *Bold Moves*

Student Edition pp. 112–118

Copying Master 45

PRETEACH

Vocabulary

Copying Master 45

Lesson 12 Vocabulary   Distribute a set of Vocabulary Word Cards to each pair of students. Hold up the card for the first word, and ask a volunteer to read it aloud. Have students repeat the word and hold up the matching card. Give the explanation for the word. Then ask students the first question below and discuss their responses. Continue for each Vocabulary Word.

- **What would be an ideal breakfast for you?**

- **Would a dog or a cat more likely be perched in a tree? Explain.**

- **If your foot got wedged in a door, what would you do as quickly as possible?**

- **Would you prefer pelting snow if you were inside or outside? Explain.**

- **If a friend had slunk out of the kitchen with a cookie in her hand, what would you think?**

- **Have you ever blurted out a secret or a surprise? Explain.**

- **What could cause a truck or car to get stranded?**

PRETEACH

Comprehension

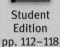 **Figurative Language**   Remind students that authors use figurative language to make their writing more interesting and lively. Give students an example of a simile, a metaphor, and personification. Then use the following points to summarize:

- A simile compares two unlike things, using the words *like* or *as*.

- A metaphor also compares two unlike things, but it does not use *like* or *as*.

- Personification is a kind of metaphor that gives human characteristics to something that is not human.

GUIDED PRACTICE   Work with students to revisit "Stranded on the Ice" to find examples of figurative language and explain their meanings. Ask:

- **The author writes that "ice crushed the ship like a tin can." What type of figurative language is that?** (a simile that compares two unlike things—the ship and a tin can—using the word *like*)

- **The author says that the "Antarctic winter is one long stretch of twilight." What type of figurative language is that?** (a metaphor that compares two unlike things—Antarctic winter and twilight—without using *like* or *as*)

Decoding/Word Attack

Decode Longer Words   Write the suffixes *-ous*, *-ious*, and *-eous* on the board. Explain that all three suffixes mean *full of* and that a word ending with any one of them is an adjective. Then write *grievous, injurious,* and *aqueous* on the board. Identify the root in each word: *grieve, injury, aqua.* Help students determine the meaning of each word, with and without the suffix.

Decoding/Spelling

Words with Suffixes *-ous, -ious, -eous*   Write each of the words below on the board, and read them with students. Make the changes necessary to form the words in parentheses. Point out that when a root word ends in y, drop the y and add *-ious*. Read the words aloud, and have students repeat them.

poison (poisonous)   **study** (studious)   **advantage** (advantageous)
glamor (glamorous)   **industry** (industrious)   **nausea** (nauseous)

Help students understand that since the three suffixes (*-ous, -ious,* and *-eous*) have the same meaning and the same sound, they may need to use a dictionary to tell which suffix to use with a specific word.

Grammar/Writing

Singular and Plural Possessive Nouns   Write the following phrase on the board, and read it aloud with students:

> Gary model airplane

Add *'s* to show possession. Explain that because *Gary's* is a singular possessive noun, you add the apostrophe before the *-s*. Then write the following phrase, and read it together:

> two owls' feathers

Underline *owls*, and circle the apostrophe. Explain that an apostrophe is added after the *-s* to show possession in a regular plural noun such as *owls*.

Student-Friendly Explanations

ideal   When something is perfectly suited for a particular purpose, it is ideal.

perched   If you are perched on an object, you are sitting on its edge.

wedged   Something that is wedged into a space is packed in tightly.

pelting   When you say that something is pelting down, you mean that it is falling hard and hitting with force.

slunk   Someone who has slunk away has left quietly and secretively.

blurted   When you have blurted out something, you have said it suddenly or impulsively.

stranded   When something is stranded, it has been left some place and cannot get back.

Fluency

pp. 112–118   **Fluency Performance**
Invite students to read aloud the passages from "Stranded on the Ice" that they selected and practiced earlier. Note the number of words each student reads correctly and incorrectly. Have students rate their own oral reading on the 1–4 scale. Give students the opportunity to continue practicing and then to read the passage to you again.

LESSON 12

DAY AT A GLANCE

Day 1

30+ Minutes

VOCABULARY
Reteach *ideal, perched, wedged, pelting, slunk, blurted, stranded*

COMPREHENSION
 Reteach Figurative Language

DECODING/SPELLING
Reteach Words with Suffixes *-ous, -ious, -eous*

GRAMMAR/WRITING
Preteach Irregular Plural Possessive Nouns

FLUENCY
Fluency Practice

Materials Needed: *Bold Moves*

Student Edition pp. 120–121	Practice Book p. 47	Skill Card 12	Copying Master 46

RETEACH

Vocabulary

pp. 120–121

Lesson 12 Vocabulary Read aloud the Vocabulary Words and the Student-Friendly Explanations. Then read aloud with students the story on pages 120–121 of their books. Pause when you come to an incomplete sentence, and have a volunteer say the Vocabulary Word that completes it. Next, guide students to complete the synonym web on page 121. If students are unable to give reasonable responses, refer to the Student-Friendly Explanations. (Answers for pages 120–121: 2. *perched*, 3. *blurted*, 4. *stranded*, 5. *pelting*, 6. *wedged*, 7. *slunk*, 8. *ideal*)

RETEACH

Comprehension

Figurative Language Have students look at side A of *Skill Card 12: Figurative Language*. Read the introductory paragraph together. Call on a volunteer to read the instructions. After students examine the picture, have them cover the second and third columns of the chart. Read the first example: *The wind was a swarm of bees*. Ask:

- **What type of figurative language is this?** (metaphor)
- **What does the metaphor mean?** (Have students check their responses against the answer in column 2.)

Repeat the procedure using the remaining examples in the chart.

GUIDED PRACTICE Have students look at side B of *Skill Card 12: Figurative Language*. Have students read the Skill Reminder. Ask a volunteer to read the paragraph. Guide students in copying the chart and recording the literal meaning and type of figurative language for each example. (Example #1: *When she gets mad, Muriel is like a tornado whipping around* is a <u>simile</u> that means Muriel darts angrily around the room. Example #2: *When she is tired, she is an innocent baby who purrs in your arms* is an example of <u>personification</u> that means the cat seems like an innocent baby when she is asleep. Example #3: *When she is hungry, cover your ears: Muriel is a car alarm!* is a <u>metaphor</u> that means the cat meows so loudly that it hurts your ears.)

RETEACH

Decoding/Spelling

Words with Suffixes -ous, -ious, -eous Distribute *Copying Master 46*. Model reading the Spelling Words as students repeat them. Go over the information about the suffixes *-ous*, *-ious*, and *-eous*. Then have students work in pairs to complete the following activity. Each student writes a sentence for each Spelling Word but leaves a blank for the actual word. The partners then switch papers and fill in the blanks in each other's sentences. Students should give themselves one point for each correctly spelled word.

PRETEACH

Grammar/Writing

Irregular Plural Possessive Nouns Have students recall that an irregular plural is a noun that does not add *-s* to make it plural. Tell students that for irregular plural nouns, the possessive has an apostrophe before the *-s*. Write these examples on the board:

| trout's | sheep's | geese's | children's |

Have students generate additional examples of irregular plural nouns. If students have difficulty, suggest that they think of plural nouns that name animals or people. Write students' examples on the board. Have them guide you to write the plural possessives.

GUIDED PRACTICE Write the following sentences on the board. Have students copy and complete the sentences with the possessive form of the nouns in parentheses. (mice's, people's)

All newborn (mice) skin is furless.

The (people) will was shown when the votes were counted.

Student-Friendly Explanations

ideal When something is perfectly suited for a particular purpose, it is ideal.

perched If you are perched on an object, you are sitting on its edge.

wedged Something that is wedged into a space is packed in tightly.

pelting When you say that something is pelting down, you mean that it is falling hard and hitting with force.

slunk Someone who has slunk away has left quietly and secretively.

blurted When you have blurted out something, you have said it suddenly or impulsively.

stranded When something is stranded, it has been left some place and cannot get back.

Fluency

Fluency Practice Have students turn to *Practice Book* page 47. Read the words in the first column aloud. Invite students to track each word and repeat the words after you. Then have students work in pairs to read the words in the first column aloud to each other. Follow the same procedure with each of the remaining columns. After partners have practiced reading aloud the words in each of the columns, have them practice reading all of the words.

30+ Minutes

DAY AT A GLANCE
Day 2

VOCABULARY
Reteach *ideal, perched, wedged, pelting, slunk, blurted, stranded*

COMPREHENSION
"The Long Hike"
Build Background
Monitor Comprehension
Answers to *Think Critically* Questions

DECODING/SPELLING
Reteach Words with Suffixes *-ous, -ious, -eous*

GRAMMAR/WRITING
Preteach Avoiding Common Errors

FLUENCY
Fluency Practice

Materials Needed: *Bold Moves*

  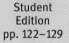

Student Edition pp. 122–129

Practice Book pp. 47, 48

Copying Masters 45, 46

Vocabulary

Lesson 12 Vocabulary Distribute a set of Vocabulary Word Cards to each pair of students. Have partners take turns using each Vocabulary Word in a sentence, continuing until both students have constructed a sentence with each word.

Copying Master 45

Comprehension

Build Background: "The Long Hike"
Ask students to share experiences they may have had in fixing something that they valued. What did they need to fix and why? What steps did they have to take in order to fix it?

Monitor Comprehension: "The Long Hike"
Read the title of the story aloud. Then have students read pages 122–123 to find out what is helping Robert get used to his new home.

pp. 122–123

After reading the pages, ask: **What is helping Robert get used to his new home?** (Possible response: Robert's new pals and his first hike up a mountain are helping him get used to his new home.) **MAKE INFERENCES**

Discuss the Stop and Think question on page 122: **What details do you learn about the narrator? Underline them in the story.**
(I learn that the narrator is Robert, a boy who just moved from a big city to a small town in the mountains. Students should underline *"Come on Robert, let's go!"* and *I had just moved from a big city to Stone Mount, a small town nestled in the mountains.*) Guide students in writing the answer to this question. **NOTE DETAILS**

Discuss the Stop and Think question on page 123: **Do you think the trees are really waving hello? How do you know?** (Possible responses: I think the trees are not really waving hello. Robert uses a simile to describe them this way.) Guide students in writing the answer to this question. **FIGURATIVE LANGUAGE**

Discuss the Stop and Think question on page 124: **Do you think Robert is scared?** (Possible response: I think that Robert is scared because the sky is darkening, and he hears an unfamiliar sound.) Guide students in writing the answer to this question. **CHARACTERS' EMOTIONS**

pp. 124–125

Have students reread the first two sentences on page 125. Model the strategy of using context to confirm the literal meaning of figurative language.

THINK ALOUD **If it weren't for the picture on page 124, I wouldn't know what the author means when he says that the kids found "a small brown ball of puff." If I keep reading, I find the answer in the very next sentence. The "small brown ball of puff" is a baby owl. The author is using figurative language to describe the owl.** USE CONTEXT TO CONFIRM MEANING/ FIGURATIVE LANGUAGE

Discuss the Stop and Think question on page 125: **What do you think the hikers will do?** (Possible response: I think the hikers will find a way to help the stranded and hurt baby owl.) Guide students in writing the answer to this question. MAKE PREDICTIONS

pp. 126–127 Discuss the Stop and Think question on page 126: **What can you tell about Robert?** (Possible response: I can tell that Robert is sensitive to animals' feelings, because he insists on not leaving the baby owl behind when he and his pals go for help.) Guide students in writing the answer to this question. CHARACTERS' TRAITS

Ask: **Why won't Mom listen to Robert's explanation for why he is late?** (Possible response: Mom is worried when Robert doesn't come home on time. She is relieved when she sees that he is safe, but she is also angry. She is also afraid that he will catch cold.) MAKE INFERENCES

Discuss the Stop and Think question on page 127: **Why are Robert's clothes messy?** (Robert's clothes are messy because he gets caught in a rainstorm and uses his jacket to protect the owl.) Guide students in writing the answer to this question. CAUSE AND EFFECT

page 128 Discuss the Stop and Think question on page 128: **Do you think that Robert's parents are still mad at him? Explain.** (Possible response: I think Robert's parents are not still mad at him because now they know that he was late for a good reason.) Guide students in writing the answer to this question. DRAW CONCLUSIONS

Ask: **How do two minor characters, Miss Garza and the vet, help illustrate the theme of helping others?** (Possible response: Miss Garza helps the kids by contacting the vet, her sister; the vet helps the injured baby owl.) THEME

Ask: **What imagery does the author use twice (with slightly different words) to describe the baby owl?** (At the end of the story, the baby owl is described as "a little brown ball of fluff." This repeats the earlier image of the owl as "a small brown ball of puff.") WRITER'S CRAFT

VOCABULARY

Student-Friendly Explanations

ideal When something is perfectly suited for a particular purpose, it is ideal.

perched If you are perched on an object, you are sitting on its edge.

wedged Something that is wedged into a space is packed in tightly.

pelting When you say that something is pelting down, you mean that it is falling hard and hitting with force.

slunk Someone who has slunk away has left quietly and secretively.

blurted When you have blurted out something, you have said it suddenly or impulsively.

stranded When something is stranded, it has been left some place and cannot get back.

Spelling Words: Lesson 12

1. poisonous	11. envious
2. glamorous	12. industrious
3. joyous	13. infectious
4. adventurous	14. mysterious
5. courageous	15. suspicious
6. disastrous	16. advantageous
7. generous	17. gorgeous
8. miraculous	18. nutritious
9. studious	19. nauseous
10. hilarious	20. outrageous

 page 129

Answers to *Think Critically* Questions

Help students read and answer the *Think Critically* questions on page 129. Possible responses are provided.

1. Robert's new home is in the mountains, and it has tall trees and wild animals, unlike his old home in the city. **COMPARE AND CONTRAST**

2. [Conflict] Robert is in trouble with his parents for being late and for being wet and messy. [Resolution] Robert's parents excuse his coming home late when they learn the reason. **PLOT**

3. I think the author feels that helping animals is important because several characters in the story work together to save a baby owl. **AUTHOR'S PURPOSE**

RETEACH

Decoding/Spelling

Copying Master 46

Words with Suffixes *-ous, -ious, -eous* Working in pairs, have students write the root words and suffixes of each Spelling Word except *gorgeous* on separate index cards. Tell players to shuffle the cards and spread them out, face down. Player A turns over two cards. If the two cards spell a word, that player keeps both cards and turns over two more. If the two cards do not spell a word, the cards are returned to their original positions. Player B follows the same procedure. Play continues until all cards have been collected. The player with more cards wins.

Grammar/Writing

Avoiding Common Errors   Write each example on the board as you review the following rules for forming singular and plural possessive nouns:

Practice Book **48**

- Possessive nouns show ownership or possession. In a regular singular noun, an apostrophe comes before the *-s* to show possession.
Lexi's skateboard

- In a regular plural noun, an apostrophe comes after the *-s* to show possession.
the three boys' mittens

- In an irregular plural noun, the possessive is formed by adding an apostrophe before the *-s*.
the sheep's wool

- An apostrophe is not ordinarily used to form a plural noun.
The McBrians like to make sandcastles on the beach.

Explain that sometimes mistakes are made in writing plural and plural possessive nouns. Point out that the word *McBrians*, in the last example sentence, is a plural noun. Since *McBrians* does not show possession, it does not get an apostrophe.

GUIDED PRACTICE   Refer students to page 48 in their *Practice Books*. Complete the page together. Have students read aloud their responses.

Fluency

Practice Book **47**

Fluency Practice   Invite students to look at the bottom half of *Practice Book* page 47. These sentences have been broken into natural phrases. Tell students to repeat each phrase after you, mirroring your expression, phrasing, and pace. After students have repeated each sentence, invite them to practice reading the sentences to a partner.

DAY AT A GLANCE

Day 3

30+ Minutes

COMPREHENSION
Preteach Poetic Devices

Reread and Summarize "The Long Hike"

DECODING/SPELLING
Reteach Words with Suffixes *-ous, -ious, -eous*

BUILD ROBUST VOCABULARY
Teach Words from "The Long Hike"

GRAMMAR/WRITING
Reteach Writing Trait: Sentence Fluency

FLUENCY
Fluency Practice

Materials Needed: *Bold Moves*

Student Edition pp. 122–128

Practice Book pp. 47, 49

Copying Master 47

Comprehension

 Poetic Devices Distribute *Copying Master 47*. Have a volunteer read the information at the top of the page aloud. Read the paragraphs together.

GUIDED PRACTICE Work with students to find examples of a metaphor, a simile, personification, and imagery in the paragraphs and record each on the chart.

Reread and Summarize Have students reread and summarize "The Long Hike" in sections, as described below.

 Let's reread pages 122–123 to recall who the narrator is and what change has happened in his life.
Summary: The narrator is a boy named Robert who has moved from a big city to a small mountain town.

 Now, let's reread pages 124–125 to remember what happens when Robert and his pals go on a "quick" hike up a mountain.
Summary: Robert climbs a tree, hears a strange noise, and scrambles down. He, Kiley, and Luis find an injured baby owl on the ground.

 Last, let's reread pages 126–128 to find out how the hikers get help and what happens after Robert arrives home late.
Summary: The children take the owl back to school. Their teacher agrees to take the owl to her sister, a vet. Robert arrives home late. His mom is mad, until she learns the reason: Robert and his pals saved a baby owl.

Decoding/Spelling

Words with Suffixes *-ous, -ious, -eous* Tell students that the spellings of words ending in *-ous, -ious,* and *-eous* do not follow a particular pattern. To be sure of the correct suffix, students must use a dictionary.

Have students work in pairs to practice adding the suffixes *-ous, -ious,* and *-eous* to the root of each Spelling Word. Tell them to use a dictionary, either to build the words or to check their work. Before students begin, point out that the word *gorgeous* does not have a root word.

TEACH

Build Robust Vocabulary

Words from "The Long Hike" Have students locate *nestled* on page 122 of "The Long Hike." Ask a volunteer to read aloud the sentence in which this word appears. (Line 5: *I had just moved from a big city to Stone Mount, a small town nestled in the mountains.*) Explain that this sentence means that the town was in a safe spot protected by the mountains. Then ask students to locate and read aloud the sentence in which *startled* and *scrambled* appear on page 124. (Line 3: *Just then, a sound startled me, and I scrambled from the branch to the ground as fast as a monkey in the zoo.*) Explain that *startled* means that Robert was surprised or upset by a sudden noise or movement. *Scrambled* means that he moved quickly to get away.

Ask groups to plan a short skit or role play related to one of the words. Have the class guess the word after each group performs.

RETEACH

Grammar/Writing

Writing Trait: Sentence Fluency Have students turn to page 49 in their *Practice Books*. Explain that it is important for students to use a variety of sentences in their writing to keep readers interested. Ask a volunteer to read the information in the box aloud. Then have students name three different sentence structures. (simple, compound, complex) Complete Parts A and B together.

GUIDED PRACTICE Have students complete Part C independently. Call on volunteers to share their responses.

Fluency

Fluency Practice Tell students that today they will reread the sentences on the bottom of *Practice Book* page 47. Have students locate and point to the first sentence. Tell students that everyone is going to read the sentence together. This choral reading will give students an opportunity to hear others and listen to the natural phrasing of the sentences. Choral-read each of the sentences several times.

LESSON 12

COMPREHENSION
Reteach Poetic Devices

DECODING/SPELLING
Reteach Words with Suffixes *-ous, -ious,
-eous*

BUILD ROBUST VOCABULARY
Reteach Words from "The Long Hike"

GRAMMAR/WRITING
Reteach Writing Form: Summary

FLUENCY
Fluency Practice

Materials Needed: *Bold Moves*

Student
Edition
pp. 122–128

Practice
Book
p. 50

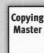

Copying
Master
48

Spelling Words: Lesson 12

1. poisonous	11. envious
2. glamorous	12. industrious
3. joyous	13. infectious
4. adventurous	14. mysterious
5. courageous	15. suspicious
6. disastrous	16. advantageous
7. generous	17. gorgeous
8. miraculous	18. nutritious
9. studious	19. nauseous
10. hilarious	20. outrageous

Comprehension

Poetic Devices   Review what students have learned about poetic devices. Use the following questions:

- **How does imagery help readers experience what an author is describing?** (By relating something to the senses, imagery helps readers experience the way something looks, sounds, smells, tastes, or feels.)

- **How are similes and metaphors the same and different?** (Both compare two unlike things; a simile—but not a metaphor—uses the word *like* or *as*.)

- **What is personification?** (Personification is a poetic device that gives human characteristics to something that is not human.)

GUIDED PRACTICE   Have the group read a poem together. On the board, make a chart with four columns labeled Imagery, Simile, Metaphor, and Personification. Have students guide you to list in the appropriate column the examples of poetic devices that they find.

Decoding/Spelling

Practice
Book
50

Words with Suffixes *-ous, -ious, -eous*   Have students number a sheet of paper 1–17. Write the Spelling Word *poisonous* on the board and point to the suffix. Tell students that in the first six words you will dictate, the suffix *-ous* is found at the end of each word. After students write each word, display it so they can proofread their work. Repeat this activity for the other suffixes using *studious,* and *advantageous*.

1. glamorous	2. joyous	3. adventurous	4. disastrous
5. generous	6. miraculous	7. hilarious	8. envious
9. industrious	10. infectious	11. mysterious	12. suspicious
13. nutritious	14. gorgeous	15. nauseous	16. outrageous
17. courageous			

Have students turn to page 50 in their *Practice Books*. Read the story and directions for the activity together. Have students complete the page independently. After all students have finished, call on volunteers to give the correct responses.

RETEACH

Build Robust Vocabulary

Words from "The Long Hike" Review the meanings of the words *nestled,* *startled,* and *scrambled.* Then say these sentences, and ask which word describes each sentence. Have students explain why.

- **The puppy was safely snuggled up to its mother, who protected him.** (nestled)

- **I was surprised when the balloon popped.** (startled)

- **When the cat heard barking, she quickly ran out of the room.** (scrambled)

RETEACH

Grammar/Writing

Copying
Master
48

Writing Form: Summary Tell students that a summary should include all of the main ideas and important details in a text. Distribute *Copying Master 48.* Have a volunteer read the description of a summary aloud. Then read the Student Model together. Discuss the margin notes to point out the steps in writing a summary.

GUIDED PRACTICE Have students complete items 1–4 independently. When all students have finished, review their responses together.

Fluency

pp.
122–
128

Fluency Practice Have each student work with a partner to read passages from "The Long Hike" aloud to each other. Students may select a passage that they enjoyed or choose one of the following options:

- Read page 122. (Total: 104 words)

- Read page 125. (Total: 96 words)

Encourage students to read the selected passage aloud to their partner three times. Have the student rate his or her reading on the 1–4 scale.

1	Need more practice
2	Pretty good
3	Good
4	Great!

DAY AT A GLANCE
Day 5

30+ Minutes

VOCABULARY
Preteach *imperative, disoriented, premonition, receded, haphazardly, remorse, optimistic*

COMPREHENSION
 Preteach Theme

DECODING/WORD ATTACK
Preteach Decode Longer Words

DECODING/SPELLING
Preteach Words with Endings /ən/, /əl/

GRAMMAR/WRITING
Preteach Subjective Case Pronouns

FLUENCY
Fluency Performance

Materials Needed: *Bold Moves*

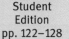

Student Edition pp. 122–128 | Skill Card 13 | Copying Master 49

PRETEACH
Vocabulary

Copying Master 49

Lesson 13 Vocabulary Distribute a set of Vocabulary Word Cards to each pair of students. Hold up the card for the first word, and ask a volunteer to read it aloud. Have students repeat the word and hold up the matching card. Give the explanation for the word. Then ask students the first question below and discuss their responses. Continue for each Vocabulary Word.

- **Why is it imperative for you to drink water?**
- **Would you feel disoriented if the room went completely dark? Why?**
- **What would you do if you had a premonition about a friend?**
- **When the wave receded, where did it go?**
- **Would you haphazardly pack your clothes to go on a long vacation?**
- **Have you ever felt remorse when you said something you didn't mean?**
- **Would you feel optimistic about a math test? Why or why not?**

PRETEACH
Comprehension

Skill Card 13

Theme Have students look at side A of *Skill Card 13: Theme*. Have a volunteer read the introduction aloud. Then have volunteers take turns reading the story aloud. Ask students:

- **What is the setting?** (small village with fields next to a river)
- **What character trait do we learn about Adeline at the beginning?** (She frightens easily.)
- **What are Adeline's actions in the story?** (She wants to run but realizes she has to help the children first.)

Read the theme on the chart aloud. Guide students to understand that the theme of the story is based on the details above and what Adeline learned.

PRETEACH
Decoding/Word Attack

Decode Longer Words Write the words *mitten* and *curtain* on the board. Divide each word into syllables and underline the second syllable. Tell students that the vowel sound is the schwa sound. Have students blend the syllables to read the words. Then repeat with *cattle* and *flannel*. Share the following:

- Many words end with a vowel, or a vowel combination, followed by the letter *n*. The vowel sound is usually the schwa sound.
- Many other words end with a vowel, or a vowel combination, followed by the letter *l*. The vowel sound is usually the schwa sound.
- Syllables with the schwa sound at the end of a word are unaccented.

Decoding/Spelling

Words with Endings /ən/, /əl/   Draw a two-column chart on the board. Title one side: *Words Ending in /ən/;* and the other: *Words Ending in /əl/.* Say the words *beckon* and *burden* aloud. Ask students if the words end with the same sound. Write the words in the correct column on the board, and circle the letters that stand for the /ən/ sound. Point out that the sound can be spelled *-on* or *-en.* Repeat for the words *peddle* and *medal.* Then write the following words on the board: *example, natural, veteran, sudden.* Have a volunteer read each word, identify its ending, and write it in the correct column on the chart. Tell students that these are some of the next lesson's Spelling Words.

Grammar/Writing

Subjective Case Pronouns   Tell students that subject pronouns can take the place of one or more nouns as the subject of a sentence. Write the following sentence on the board:

> Kathy likes to knit. She made me a sweater.

Have a volunteer read the sentence. Underline the word *She* and point out that it takes the place of the subject noun *Kathy.* Tell students that the noun that a pronoun replaces is called an antecedent. Then write the following sentence on the board:

> Kathy and Meg went for a walk.
> They enjoy the exercise.

Underline the pronoun *They.* Ask what subject nouns this pronoun replaces. Underline *Kathy and Meg* and tell students this is the antecedent. Write the following sentence pairs on the board:

> The bike is mine. It is brand new.
> Chip wants to help. He dried the dishes.

Guide students to identify the pronoun and the subject noun antecedent in each one. (It—The bike; He—Chip)

Student-Friendly Explanations

imperative If something is imperative, it must be done no matter what is keeping it from being completed.

disoriented If you feel lost or have lost your sense of direction, you are disoriented.

premonition A premonition is a feeling that something, usually unpleasant, is about to occur.

receded When water has receded, it has flowed away from where it was before.

haphazardly Something that is organized haphazardly is not well planned or arranged.

remorse If you feel remorse about an action, you feel guilt or regret about it.

optimistic You are optimistic when you feel positive about the future.

Fluency

pp. 122–128   **Fluency Performance** Invite students to read aloud the passages from "The Long Hike" that they selected and practiced earlier. Note the number of words each student reads correctly and incorrectly. Have students rate their own oral reading on the 1–4 scale. Allow students to continue practicing and then to read the passage to you again.

Day 1

LESSON 13

VOCABULARY
Reteach *imperative, disoriented, premonition, receded, haphazardly, remorse, optimistic*

COMPREHENSION
 Reteach Theme

DECODING/SPELLING
Reteach Words with Endings /ən/, /əl/

GRAMMAR/WRITING
Preteach Objective Case Pronouns

FLUENCY
Fluency Practice

Materials Needed: *Bold Moves*

| Student Edition pp. 130–131 | Practice Book p. 51 | Skill Card 13 | Copying Master 50 |

RETEACH

Vocabulary

pp. 130–131

Lesson 13 Vocabulary Read aloud the Vocabulary Words and the Student-Friendly Explanations. Then have volunteers read the paragraphs on pages 130–131 of their books. Guide students in completing the sentences in each paragraph by selecting the correct Vocabulary Words. Then have a volunteer read each completed sentence aloud. If students are unable to give reasonable responses, refer to the Student-Friendly Explanations. Then help students answer the questions on page 131 of their books. (Answers for pages 130–131: 2. *disoriented*, 3. *receded*, 4. *haphazardly*, 5. *premonition*, 6. *remorse*, 7. *optimistic*, 8. Possible responses: it must be done right away, 9. Possible responses: not helping when they should have helped.)

RETEACH

Comprehension

Skill Card 13

Theme Have students look at side B of *Skill Card 13: Theme*. Have a volunteer read the Skill Reminder aloud. Read the instruction aloud. Then ask a volunteer to read the passage aloud. Ask:

- **How would you describe Matt?** (greedy, wants as much as possible)

- **What actions does Matt make?** (He grabbed a big handful of marbles; He got his hand stuck.)

- **How does the setting affect the actions?** (Possible response: The jar was in the toy store. If something else was in the jar, Matt may not have wanted it.)

GUIDED PRACTICE Guide students as they use the information from the passage to complete the chart. Then discuss with students what the theme might be. (Character's Qualities: always wanted too much; Character's Actions: couldn't get hand out of jar; Setting: toy store; Theme: Possible responses: Do not grab (or attempt) too much at one time; Being greedy can get you in trouble.)

Decoding/Spelling

Copying Master 50

Words with Endings /ən/, /əl/ Distribute *Copying Master 50*. Model reading the Spelling Words as students repeat them. Have a volunteer read the instruction for words ending with /ən/, /əl/. Then have students complete the following activity: Based on the traditional Memory Game, have pairs of students each make game cards, using the lesson's Spelling Words, but with a dash in place of each ending. After a student matches two cards, he or she must supply the correct missing letters to keep the game cards. If the wrong letters are supplied, the opponent gets the game cards and the next turn.

Grammar/Writing

Objective Case Pronouns Tell students that object pronouns take the place of one or more nouns that come after an action verb or after a preposition. Write the following sentence on the board:

> This card is for my grandmother.

Underline the words *my grandmother*, and point out how it follows the preposition *for*. Tell students *my grandmother* can be replaced by the object pronoun *her*. Then reread the sentence with the object pronoun in place. Then write this sentence on the board:

> My dog played with Chris and Cheryl.

Help students to identify the object nouns *Chris and Cheryl* and the preposition *with*. Then have them name an object pronoun to replace the object nouns. (them)

GUIDED PRACTICE Write the words *me, you, him, her, it, us,* and *them* on the board. Tell students these are object pronouns. Write the sentences below on the board. Guide students to identify the object noun in each sentence and tell if it follows a verb or a preposition. (John, follows the action verb *challenged;* Jessie and me, follows the action verb *helps*) Then have them suggest an object pronoun to replace each noun. (him; us)

> Sam challenged John.
> My sister helps Jessie and me.

Student-Friendly Explanations

imperative If something is imperative, it must be done no matter what is keeping it from being completed.

disoriented If you feel lost or have lost your sense of direction, you are disoriented.

premonition A premonition is a feeling that something, usually unpleasant, is about to occur.

receded When water has receded, it has flowed away from where it was before.

haphazardly Something that is organized haphazardly is not well planned or arranged.

remorse If you feel remorse about an action, you feel guilt or regret about it.

optimistic You are optimistic when you feel positive about the future.

Fluency

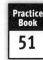

Practice Book 51

Fluency Practice Have students turn to *Practice Book* page 51. Read the words in the first column aloud. Invite students to track each word and repeat the words after you. Then have students work in pairs to read the words in the first column aloud to each other. Follow the same procedure with each of the remaining columns. After partners have practiced reading aloud the words in each of the columns, have them practice reading all of the words.

LESSON 13

DAY AT A GLANCE

Day 2

VOCABULARY
Reteach *imperative, disoriented, premonition, receded, haphazardly, remorse, optimistic*

COMPREHENSION
"Run for the Hills!"
Build Background
Monitor Comprehension
Answers to *Think Critically* Questions

DECODING/SPELLING
Reteach Words with Endings /ən/, /əl/

GRAMMAR/WRITING
Preteach Pronoun-Antecedent Agreement: Gender and Number

FLUENCY
Fluency Practice

Materials Needed: *Bold Moves*

| Student Edition pp. 132–139 | Practice Book pp. 51, 52 | Copying Master 50 |

 30+ Minutes

RETEACH

Vocabulary

Lesson 13 Vocabulary   Have students work in pairs. Have one partner read aloud a Student-Friendly Explanation, saying "blank" in place of the Vocabulary Word. The partner guesses the correct word and uses it in a sentence. Have partners take turns in each role until each student has named all of the words.

Comprehension

Build Background: "Run for the Hills!"
Ask students to share if they have ever had a premonition. Have they noticed their animals behaving oddly? Have they noticed, or felt, something that made them feel uneasy or frightened?

Monitor Comprehension: "Run for the Hills!"
pp. 132–133 Read the title of the story aloud. Then have students read pages 132–133 to find out who is telling the story and what other characters will be in the story.

After reading the pages, ask: **Who is the narrator? Who are the other characters in the story?** (A boy is the narrator; his Nani, and the two birds) **Note Details**

Discuss the Stop and Think question on page 132: **What do you learn about the characters and setting?** (I learn that the setting is a small town by the sea; that the boy is responsible for taking care of Nani, and the birds are behaving oddly.) Guide students in writing the answer to this question. **Characters' Traits/Context Clues**

Ask: **Why is the boy watching Nani?** (His parents are off at a town down the coast.) **Cause and Effect**

Ask: **When the birds are flying *haphazardly*, what do you think it means?** (They are flying without direction.) **Vocabulary**

Discuss the Stop and Think question on page 133: **Why do you think the birds are behaving so strangely?** (Possible response: I think the birds are behaving strangely because something about the weather is making them feel disoriented.) Guide students in writing the answer to this question. **Draw Conclusions**

 pp. 134–135 Discuss the Stop and Think question on page 134: **What do you learn about Nani?** (Possible response: I learn that Nani is wise and sensitive to people and animals.) Guide students in writing the answer to this question. **Characters' Traits**

148 Lesson 13 • Bold Moves

Read aloud the last paragraph on page 135. Model using character traits to determine the theme of a story.

(THINK ALOUD) **When I read the paragraph, I was not sure why the birds were acting strangely. Because Nani is wise, she senses what the birds feel, and has a premonition of something frightening that is about to happen. By what I've read so far, I think the theme might be that it is important to follow your feelings and instincts.**

 THEME

Discuss the Stop and Think question on page 135: **What do you think will happen next?** (Possible response: I think that Raj will warn everyone about the high wave.) **Guide students in writing the answer to this question. MAKE PREDICTIONS**

pp. 136–137

Tell students to recall how Raj warns the tourists about the danger. Then ask: **What character trait does this show that Raj has?** (Possible response: He is a responsible boy; He thinks about others before himself.) **CHARACTERS' TRAITS**

Discuss the Stop and Think question on page 136: **What problem does Raj have?** (Raj has a problem when some of the tourists don't believe a high wave will come.) **Guide students in writing the answer to this question. GENERALIZE**

Have students read the first two paragraphs on page 137. Then ask: **How would you feel if you needed to carry someone on your back up a hill?** (Possible response: I think I would feel tired, too.) **IDENTIFY WITH CHARACTERS**

Discuss the Stop and Think question on page 137: **How does Raj feel about his promise?** (Possible response: Raj feels that the promise is too hard for him to keep.) **Guide students in writing the answer to this question. CHARACTERS' EMOTIONS**

page 138

Discuss the Stop and Think question on page 138: **What lesson does Raj learn from his experience?** (Possible response: Raj learns that he is strong and that he can keep his promise.) **Guide students in writing the answer to this question.**  THEME

Ask: **How does the setting help you remember events in the story?** (Possible response: A big wave might not happen to a town far away from the sea.) **DRAW CONCLUSIONS**

Ask: **What did you learn from this story?** (Possible response: I learned it is important to trust your feelings and follow your instincts; with a little extra effort, you can accomplish many things.) **EXPRESS PERSONAL OPINION**

Day 2

Spelling Words: Lesson 13

1. actual	11. medal
2. beckon	12. peddle
3. burden	13. personal
4. captain	14. pigeon
5. comparison	15. several
6. example	16. special
7. foreign	17. sudden
8. people	18. natural
9. informal	19. veteran
10. label	20. usual

page 139 **Answers to *Think Critically* Questions** Help students read and answer the *Think Critically* questions on page 139. Possible responses are provided.

1. [Plot Events] 1. The birds sense danger and behave strangely. 2. Nani understands what the birds' behavior means. 3. Raj warns the people and carries Nani to safety. **PLOT**

2. The author includes Raj's thoughts because he wants to show what Raj is thinking and feeling. **AUTHOR'S PURPOSE**

3. Raj feels proud and happy to see his birds. **CHARACTER**

RETEACH

Decoding/Spelling

Copying Master 50 **Words with Endings /ən/, /əl/** Divide the group into two teams. Assign each team five Spelling Words from *Copying Master 50*. Have the members of the team work together to create an "uh-oh card" for each word. An "uh-oh card" has the Spelling Word spelled correctly up to the ending. The ending may be spelled correctly or incorrectly. Have teams take turns challenging one another by showing an "uh-oh card." If the word on the card is spelled correctly, the challenged team says "correct." If not, the challenged team says "uh-oh," and then must spell the word correctly. Teams receive one point for each correct answer. The team with the most points wins.

PRETEACH

Grammar/Writing

Practice Book 52 **Pronoun-Antecedent Agreement: Gender and Number**   Remind students that subject pronouns can take the place of one or more nouns as the subject of a sentence. The noun that a pronoun replaces is called an antecedent. Subject pronouns include *I, you, he, she, it, we, you,* and *they*. Then have students recall that object pronouns take the place of one or more nouns after an action verb or a preposition. Object pronouns include *me, you, him, her, it, us,* and *them*. Tell students a pronoun's gender tells whether it is masculine, feminine, or neuter (both). Write the following sentences on the board:

> They went to the movies.
>
> Give the pencil to her.
>
> This drink is for him.

Have students identify the pronoun in the first sentence. (they) Point out that *they* is a subject pronoun. Show students how the gender of *they* is neuter because they cannot tell if it refers to male or female subjects. Then ask students to identify the object pronouns in the other sentences. (her, him) Have them identify the gender of *her* and *him*. (feminine, masculine) Then show students that the pronoun *they* means more than one person. The pronoun's number is plural. Ask students to identify the number of the pronouns *her* and *him*. (singular)

GUIDED PRACTICE   Direct students' attention to *Practice Book* page 52. Have a volunteer read aloud the instruction. Then guide students through the activities.

Fluency

Practice Book 51 **Fluency Practice**   Invite students to look at the bottom half of *Practice Book* page 51. These sentences have been broken into natural phrases. Tell students to repeat each phrase after you, mirroring your expression, phrasing, and pace. After students have repeated each sentence, invite them to practice reading the sentences to a partner.

30+ Minutes

COMPREHENSION
Preteach Author's Purpose and Perspective

Reread and Summarize: "Run for the Hills!"

DECODING/SPELLING
Reteach Words with Endings /ən/, /əl/

BUILD ROBUST VOCABULARY
Teach Words from "Run for the Hills!"

GRAMMAR/WRITING
Reteach Writing Trait: Organization

FLUENCY
Fluency Practice

Materials Needed: *Bold Moves*

| Student Edition pp. 132–138 | Practice Book pp. 51, 53 | Copying Master 51 |

Comprehension

Copying Master 51

Author's Purpose and Perspective Distribute *Copying Master 51*. Have a volunteer read the information aloud at the top of the page. Then have volunteers take turns reading the passage aloud. Ask students the first question and help them identify the author's purpose. Ask a volunteer to read the second question on *Copying Master 51*. Guide students in identifying the author's perspective.

Reread and Summarize

Have students reread and summarize "Run for the Hills!" in sections, as described below.

pp. 132–133

Let's reread pages 132–133 to recall why Raj is taking care of Nani.
Summary: Raj was taking care of Nani because his mom and dad were at a faraway town selling their paintings and pottery. He notices that his birds seem to be acting strangely.

pp. 134–135

Now, let's reread pages 134–135 to remember why the birds were acting so odd.
Summary: The birds had a premonition something was wrong. They flew away the next morning. Nani thinks this means a big wave is coming, and people need to be warned.

pp. 136–138

Last, let's reread pages 136–138 to find out what happens after Raj warns the tourists to run for the hills.
Summary: Raj warns the tourists, and they head up into the hills. When Nani worries that she cannot make it, Raj carries Nani the rest of the way. The people and animals are safe.

Decoding/Spelling

Word with Endings /ən/, /əl/ Write these pairs of words on the board:

| becken | captain | peddle | lable |
| beckon | capten | peddel | label |

Have a volunteer come up and underline the letters that stand for the /ən/ sound in the first pair. Then ask another volunteer to come up and circle the correct spelling. Repeat with each pair of words. Tell students that when they are proofreading their writings, or someone else's, they should write out the possible spellings for a word's ending to see which one looks right. Remind students to always check the dictionary if they are unsure.

TEACH

Build Robust Vocabulary

pp. 132–138

Words from "Run for the Hills"   Have students locate *shuffled* on page 135 of "Run for the Hills." Ask a volunteer to read aloud the sentence in which this word appears. (Line 6: *"Raj, I believe the birds' behavior was indeed a premonition," Nani explained, as she shuffled to the door.*) Explain that this sentence means that Nani moved slowly to the door dragging her feet along rather than picking them up. Continue by asking students to locate and read aloud the sentence in which *engulf* appears on page 136. (Line 6: *"A high wave is coming, and it will engulf the town, so you must run for the hills!"*) Explain that this sentence means that the wave will wash over and cover up the town.

Ask yes/no questions and have students explain their answers.

- **If you always shuffled your feet, would it be good for your shoes?**
- **Would you want waves to engulf a sandcastle you had built?**

RETEACH

Grammar/Writing

Practice Book 53

Writing Trait: Organization   Tell students that writers need to organize their ideas in a logical way. One way is to show that each problem and solution leads to a conclusion. Have students look at page 53 in their *Practice Books*. Have a volunteer read the information aloud. Show students how the chart helps to organize a writer's ideas. Have a volunteer read the paragraph aloud for Part A. Assist students in following the activities. Repeat with Part B.

GUIDED PRACTICE   Tell students that as one problem leads to another, suspense and excitement builds in a story. As each problem is solved, the next one needs to be solved, and so on, until the story ends. Guide students to organize ideas by completing Part C on page 53 of their Practice Books.

Fluency

Practice Book 51

Fluency Practice   Tell students that today they will reread the sentences on the bottom of *Practice Book* page 51. Have students locate and point to the first sentence. Tell students that everyone is going to read the sentence together. This choral reading will give students an opportunity to hear others and listen to the natural phrasing of the sentences. Choral-read each of the sentences several times.

DAY AT A GLANCE

Day 4

COMPREHENSION
Reteach Author's Purpose and Perspective

DECODING/SPELLING
Reteach Words with Endings /ən/, /əl/

BUILD ROBUST VOCABULARY
Reteach Words from "Run for the Hills!"

GRAMMAR/WRITING
Reteach Writing Form: Problem-and-Solution Composition

FLUENCY
Fluency Practice

Materials Needed: *Bold Moves*

Student Edition pp. 132–138

Practice Book p. 54

Copying Master 52

Spelling Words: Lesson 13

1. actual	11. medal
2. beckon	12. peddle
3. burden	13. personal
4. captain	14. pigeon
5. comparison	15. several
6. example	16. special
7. foreign	17. sudden
8. people	18. natural
9. informal	19. veteran
10. label	20. usual

30+ Minutes

Comprehension

Author's Purpose and Perspective   Remind students that three main purposes for which authors write are to entertain, to inform, or to persuade. Give students the following selection ideas and ask them to identify the author's purpose and have them explain why. Give students other genres where they might find the same purpose.

- a folktale about a boy rescuing a baby bird (to entertain; realistic fiction, mysteries, science fiction)

- a recipe for a healthy meal (to inform; magazine articles, newspaper articles, encyclopedias)

- an advertisement for a product (to persuade; editorials)

Remind students that identifying the author's purpose will help them figure out the author's perspective, or viewpoint.

Decoding/Spelling

Practice Book 54

Words with Endings /ən/, /əl/   Have students number a sheet of paper 1–18. Write the Spelling Word *foreign* on the board and point to the /ən/ ending syllable. Tell students the first seven words you will dictate have the /ən/ syllable ending. After students write each word, display it so they can proofread their work. Repeat this process using the word *special* for the /əl/ ending syllable sound.

1. beckon	2. burden	3. comparison	4. sudden
5. veteran	6. captain	7. pigeon	8. medal
9. peddle	10. usual	11. example	12. people
13. actual	14. personal	15. natural	16. informal
17. label	18. several		

Have students turn to page 54 in their *Practice Books*. Guide students as they respond to the sentence that best describes each picture.

RETEACH

Build Robust Vocabulary

Words from "Run for the Hills" Review the meanings of the words *shuffled* and *engulf*. Then say these sentences, and ask which word describes each sentence. Have students explain why.

- **Ken did not want to take out the trash, so he moved slowly dragging his feet.** (shuffled)
- **Drivers should not go through flooded streets because the water could wash over and cover the car.** (engulf)

RETEACH

Grammar/Writing

Copying Master 52

Writing Form: Problem-and-Solution Composition Tell students when writers organize their ideas by showing a problem and a solution that leads to a conclusion, they are writing a problem-and-solution composition. Point out that when a writer uses smaller problems and solutions within the details of the main problem, it can make the story more exciting. Draw two boxes on the board, one above the other, with an arrow pointing from the top to the bottom box. Label the top box *Problem*, and the bottom box *Solution*. Show students that a problem-and-solution chart can help them plan their writing. Distribute *Copying Master 52* and have a volunteer read the information at the top of the page aloud.

GUIDED PRACTICE Have volunteers take turns reading the Student Model. Discuss the steps noted in the right margin. Then guide students as they respond to the questions and directions at the bottom of the page.

Fluency

pp. 132–138

Fluency Practice Have each student work with a partner to read passages from "Run for the Hills!" aloud to each other. Students may select a passage that they enjoyed or choose one of the following options:

- Read page 135. (Total: 115 words)
- Read page 137. (Total: 121 words)

Encourage students to read the selected passage aloud to their partner three times. Have the student rate his or her reading on the 1–4 scale.

1	Need more practice
2	Pretty good
3	Good
4	Great!

30+ Minutes

VOCABULARY
Preteach *cocky, gingerly, winced, terminal, acquaintance, stymied, retrieve, rank*

COMPREHENSION
 Preteach Theme

DECODING/WORD ATTACK
Preteach Decode Longer Words

DECODING/SPELLING
Preteach Words with Ending /ər/

GRAMMAR/WRITING
Preteach Possessive Pronouns

FLUENCY
Fluency Performance

Materials Needed: *Bold Moves*

Student Edition pp. 132–138

Copying Master 53

PRETEACH

Vocabulary

Copying Master 53

Lesson 14 Vocabulary Distribute a set of Vocabulary Word Cards for each student. Hold up the card for the first word, and ask a volunteer to read it aloud. Have students repeat the word and hold up the matching card. Give the explanation for the word. Then ask students the first question below and discuss their responses. Continue for each of the Vocabulary Words.

- Why would a team act **cocky** after winning every game?
- Why would you walk by **gingerly** if your dad was sleeping?
- Would you have **winced** if you saw a friend trip and fall? Why?
- What facial expression would show **terminal** happiness?
- How would meeting your mom's friend make her an **aquaintance**?
- When would you be **stymied** if you were asked a question?
- What happens when you **retrieve** a soccer ball that went out of bounds?
- Why do wet shoes and socks smell **rank**?

PRETEACH

Comprehension

pp. 132–138

 Focus Skill

Theme Tell students that the theme of a story is its underlying meaning or message. Many times, it is implied, or suggested, rather than stated directly. Tell students that these points will help them find the theme of a story:

- Ask yourself, "What point is the author trying to make?"
- Think about the characters' traits and actions. What do you think they learned?
- Think about the setting. What happens because of the setting?

Guide students in using the ideas stated above to analyze "Run for the Hills!" and determine its theme. (Some things may not be easy, and it takes effort to keep promises and succeed.)

Decoding/Word Attack

Decode Longer Words   Tell students that the vowel sound in unaccented syllables often has the *schwa* sound. Write *deeper* on the board, and ask a volunteer to read it aloud. Point out the letters that stand for the /ər/ sound. (er) Say the first syllable. (deep) Have students blend the word parts to say *deeper*. Repeat using the word *dreamer*. Tell students that /ər/ may be spelled *er, or, ar,* or *ir*.

Decoding/Spelling

Words with Ending /ər/   Write *pillar, vapor,* and *lumber* on the board, and read them aloud. Ask students to identify where the /ər/ sound appears. (at the end of each word) Circle the letters that stand for the sound in each word. (ar, or, er) Repeat with *beggar, consumer,* and *error*. Explain to students that these are some of the next lesson's Spelling Words.

Grammar/Writing

Possessive Pronouns   Write the following sentences on the board:

> My gloves fit well.
>
> Our class has twenty students.

Underline *My* and *Our*. Tell students that possessive pronouns take the place of the possessive nouns. They can come before nouns or they can be used by themselves. Point out that *My* and *Our* appear before a noun. Also, point out that *My* is singular and *Our* is plural. Now write this example on the board: *This pen is mine, but that one is theirs.* Underline *mine* and *theirs*, and explain that these possessive pronouns stand by themselves: *Mine* is singular, and *theirs* is plural. Tell students that other singular possessive pronouns include *my, her, hers, his, your, yours,* and *its*. Other plural possessive pronouns include *our, ours, your, yours,* and *their*.

Student-Friendly Explanations

cocky   Cocky people are very confident and sure of themselves.

gingerly   If you approach something cautiously and tentatively, you are approaching it gingerly.

winced   You have winced when you have moved away from something in anticipation of something unpleasant.

terminal   If a condition is terminal, you are unable to improve its present situation.

acquaintance   You have an acquaintance with someone you have met, but do not know very well.

stymied   You feel stymied when you feel like you are prevented from making progress on a task.

retrieve   To retrieve something, you go get it and bring it back to where you were before.

rank   Something that is rank tastes or smells foul.

Fluency

pp. 132–138   **Fluency Performance**   Invite students to read aloud the passages from "Run for the Hills!" that they selected and practiced earlier. Note the number of words each student reads correctly and incorrectly. Have students rate their own oral reading on the 1–4 scale. Give students the opportunity to continue practicing and then to read the passage to you again.

LESSON 14

DAY AT A GLANCE

Day 1

VOCABULARY
Reteach *cocky, gingerly, winced, terminal, acquaintance, stymied, retrieve, rank*

COMPREHENSION
 Reteach Theme

DECODING/SPELLING
Reteach Words with Ending /ər/

GRAMMAR/WRITING
Preteach Reflexive Pronouns

FLUENCY
Fluency Practice

Materials Needed: *Bold Moves*

Student Edition pp. 140–141

Practice Book p. 55

Skill Card 14

Copying Master 54

RETEACH

Vocabulary

pp. 140–141   **Lesson 14 Vocabulary**   Read aloud the Vocabulary Words and the Student-Friendly Explanations. Then have students read the diary on pages 140–141 of their books. Read the sentences aloud as students follow along. Guide them in completing the sentences by selecting the correct Vocabulary Word. Have a volunteer read each completed sentence aloud. If students are unable to give reasonable responses, refer to the Student-Friendly Explanations. (Answers for pages 140–141: 2. *winced*, 3. *cocky*, 4. *acquaintance*, 5. *gingerly*, 6. *rank*, 7. *retrieve*, 8. *stymied*)

RETEACH

Comprehension

Skill Card 14   **Theme**   Have students look at side A of *Skill Card 14: Theme*. Remind students that the theme of a story is its underlying meaning or message. Have a volunteer read aloud the definition for theme. Then read the passage as students follow along. Have volunteers read the details aloud and discuss how to identify the stated theme for the passage.

GUIDED PRACTICE   Now have students look at side B of *Skill Card 14: Theme*. Have a volunteer read aloud the Skill Reminder. Then have volunteers share reading aloud the passage. Guide students in completing the chart and have them write a short sentence identifying the theme. (Details: 1. Kevin and Mark damage the front steps riding their skateboards: 2. Kevin blames Mark for the damage; 3. Kevin admits he lied when he sees it will get Mark in trouble; Theme: Telling a lie can make things even worse.)

Decoding/Spelling

Words with Ending /ər/ Distribute *Copying Master 54*. Have a volunteer read the instruction for words ending with the /ər/ sound. Then have students complete the following activity. Ask students to work in pairs to write the Spelling Words on index cards. Have one student draw a card and read its word aloud and the other student write the word; then have partners switch roles. When a student spells a word correctly, he or she initials its card and returns it to the pile. Students should work through the pile twice or until each student has had the opportunity to spell each of the words. Have students write down each word they do not spell correctly to study later.

Copying Master 54

Grammar/Writing

Reflexive Pronouns Tell students that reflexive pronouns are formed by adding *-self* or *-selves* to some possessive and personal pronouns. Write the following sentence on the board: *Ray made himself dinner.* Circle *himself*, and tell students a reflexive pronoun refers back to a noun or pronoun earlier in the sentence. It shows that the same person or thing is involved. Then write this sentence on the board: *The children got themselves a treat.* Ask students to identify the reflexive pronoun and the word it refers to. (themselves, children)

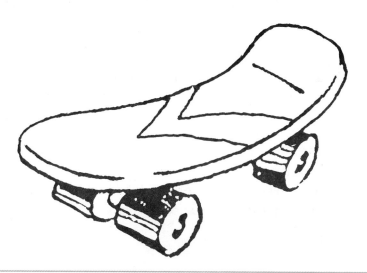

VOCABULARY

Student-Friendly Explanations

cocky Cocky people are very confident and sure of themselves.

gingerly If you approach something cautiously and tentatively, you are approaching it gingerly.

winced You have winced when you have moved away from something in anticipation of something unpleasant.

terminal If a condition is terminal, you are unable to improve its present situation.

acquaintance You have an acquaintance with someone you have met, but do not know very well.

stymied You feel stymied when you feel like you are prevented from making progress on a task.

retrieve To retrieve something, you go get it and bring it back to where you were before.

rank Something that is rank tastes or smells foul.

Fluency

Fluency Practice Have students turn to *Practice Book* page 55. Read the words in the first column aloud. Invite students to track each word and repeat the words after you. Then have students work in pairs to read the words in the first column aloud to each other. Follow the same procedure with each of the remaining columns. Then have them practice reading all of the words.

Practice Book 55

VOCABULARY
Reteach *cocky, gingerly, winced, terminal, acquaintance, stymied, retrieve, rank*

COMPREHENSION
"Hiking with Ace"
Build Background
Monitor Comprehension
Answers to *Think Critically* Questions

DECODING/SPELLING
Reteach Words with Ending /ər/

GRAMMAR/WRITING
Preteach Indefinite Pronouns

FLUENCY
Fluency Practice

Materials Needed: *Bold Moves*

Student Edition pp. 142–149

Practice Book pp. 55, 56

Copying Master 53

RETEACH

Vocabulary

Lesson 14 Vocabulary   Distribute a set of Vocabulary Word Cards for each student or pair of students. Say the meaning of one of the Vocabulary Words, and have student display and read the matching word card. Continue until students have matched all the words.

Comprehension

Build Background: "Hiking with Ace"
Ask students to share experiences they may have had hiking, or taking a nature walk. What did they see? Where did they go? Did they experience something they would not have seen or heard elsewhere?

Monitor Comprehension: "Hiking with Ace"
Read the title of the story aloud. Then have students read pages 142–143 to find out how Ace felt about taking Nancy along on the hike.

After reading the pages, ask: **How did Ace feel about taking Nancy along on the hike?** (Ace felt that Nancy would hold him back and slow him down.) **CHARACTERS' EMOTIONS**

Discuss the Stop and Think question on page 142: **What can you tell about the setting?** (I can tell that there are trees, mountains with a steep slope, and a trail.) Guide students in writing the answer to this question. **NOTE DETAILS**

Ask: **How does the setting affect the characters' actions?** (Possible response: The characters are able to do things they wouldn't be able to do at home.) **CONTEXT CLUES**

Ask: **What did Nancy do when Ace finally agreed to take her along?** (Nancy got ready in a hurry, and stuffed her gear in her pack.) **How did she keep up with Ace?** (She had to take twice as many steps.) **SEQUENCE/NOTE DETAILS**

Discuss the Stop and Think question on page 143: **Why can't Nancy go hiking by herself?** (Nancy can't go by herself because she is too little.) Guide students in writing the answer to this question. **CONTEXT CLUES**

Discuss the Stop and Think question on page 144: **How do you think Nancy feels?** (Possible response: I think Nancy feels worried about her brother and is scared to be alone.) Guide students in writing the answer to this question. **CHARACTERS' EMOTIONS**

Read aloud page 145. Model the strategy of using characters' traits to identify why Ace was acting cocky.

(THINK ALOUD) **When I read the page, I wondered why Ace acted like his sister was avoiding him. I know Ace didn't want Nancy to come with him, but now I think he is glad she did. I think he doesn't want to admit it. Ace's character trait seems to say he doesn't want to show his true feelings and that he is tough.** CHARACTERS' TRAITS

Discuss the Stop and Think question on page 145: **What do you think happened to Ace?** (Possible response: I think that Ace tripped, or fell, and hurt his leg.) Guide students in writing the answer to this question. DRAW CONCLUSIONS

pp. 146–147

Ask: **What steps did Nancy take to help Ace?** (Nancy had him move to lean against a tree, gave him water, put a cold pack on his leg, and gave him a power bar.) SEQUENCE

Discuss the Stop and Think question on page 146: **What does Ace discover about Nancy?** (Ace discovers that Nancy is organized, prepared and could help him.) Guide students in writing the answer to this question. CHARACTERS' TRAITS/THEME

Ask: **After reading all the things Nancy did to help Ace and set up a signal, how would you describe Nancy's character traits?** (Possible response: She is prepared, knows how to act in an emergency, and is calm and confident.) CHARACTERS' TRAITS

Discuss the Stop and Think question on page 147: **What do you think will happen next?** (Possible response: I think that they will be rescued.) Guide students in writing the answer to this question. MAKE PREDICTIONS

page 148

Discuss the Stop and Think question on page 148: **Why does Ace say he'll need some humble pie?** (Ace says this because he is feeling humble about not wanting Nancy to come along, but now is glad she did.) Guide students in writing the answer to this question. FIGURATIVE LANGUAGE

Ask: **What lesson do you think the author wants you to learn from this story?** (Possible response: Be prepared for the unknown.) THEME

Ask: **How does the setting affect the theme?** (Possible response: The setting gives a realistic example of where being unprepared can affect the characters' actions.) SETTING

Spelling Words: Lesson 14

1. beggar	11. monitor
2. burglar	12. partner
3. cedar	13. pillar
4. computer	14. prisoner
5. consumer	15. rumor
6. error	16. trader
7. calendar	17. traitor
8. grammar	18. vapor
9. hanger	19. vinegar
10. lumber	20. whimper

 page 149

Answers to *Think Critically* Questions

Help students read and answer the *Think Critically* questions on page 149. Then guide students in writing the answer to each question. Possible responses are provided.

1. [Resolution] Nancy brought supplies for emergencies, and she knows what to do when Ace is injured. **PLOT**

2. The author teaches me that you shouldn't judge people hastily. **AUTHOR'S PURPOSE**

3. At the beginning, Ace feels annoyed that Nancy is coming. At the end, Ace feels grateful and humble for Nancy's preparedness. **COMPARE AND CONTRAST**

RETEACH

Decoding/Spelling

Words with Ending /ər/   Remind students that words ending with the /ər/ sound can be spelled *ar, or, er,* or *ir.* Also remind students the syllable is pronounced /ər/. Divide students into two teams. Set up four chairs in front of the class, so that a student will face the student from their team, similar to the Password game. Using the Spelling Word index cards from the previous day, give Player 1 from each team the same word. The first team gives a clue to the word and the partner should try to guess the word. If the partner guesses the word, then have him or her spell the word correctly. If the first team cannot guess the word, then Team 2 has the turn. Have partners alternate roles for the next word. Continue using other students from each team until all the Spelling Words have been identified and spelled correctly.

Grammar/Writing

Practice Book 56 **Indefinite Pronouns** Tell students that indefinite pronouns refer to people, places, or things in a general way. Unlike reflexive pronouns, they do not have to refer to other nouns in the sentence. Write *anybody, everyone, none, somebody, each, nobody, some,* and *something* on the board. Have students read these indefinite pronouns aloud. Then write this example: *Did anyone finish their extra credit assignment?* Have a volunteer identify the indefinite pronoun. (anyone)

GUIDED PRACTICE Ask students to turn to page 56 of their *Practice Books.* Guide students as they complete the activities on the page.

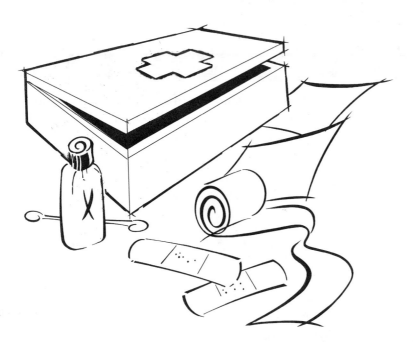

Fluency

Practice Book 55 **Fluency Practice** Invite students to look at the bottom half of *Practice Book* page 55. These sentences have been broken into natural phrases. Tell students to repeat each phrase after you, mirroring your expression, phrasing, and pace. After students have repeated each sentence, invite them to practice reading the sentences to a partner.

COMPREHENSION
Preteach Author's Purpose and Perspective

Reread and Summarize "Hiking with Ace"

DECODING/SPELLING
Reteach Words with Ending /ər/

BUILD ROBUST VOCABULARY
Teach Words from "Hiking with Ace"

GRAMMAR/WRITING
Reteach Writing Trait: Organization

FLUENCY
Fluency Practice

Materials Needed: *Bold Moves*

| Student Edition pp. 142–148 | Practice Book pp. 55, 57 | Copying Master 55 |

Comprehension

 Author's Purpose and Perspective Distribute *Copying Master 55*. Have a volunteer read the initial information aloud. Explain to students that an author's purpose is to inform, persuade, or entertain. Authors tell their ideas or themes from their own unique perspective. Have volunteers share reading the passage. Then guide students as they answer the questions.

Reread and Summarize

Have students reread and summarize "Hiking with Ace" in sections, as described below.

 Let's reread pages 142–143 to recall how Ace felt about Nancy going on the hike and how Nancy got ready to go.
Summary: Ace didn't want Nancy to go because it would slow him down. When Nancy convinced him to take her, she stuffed her gear in a pack, getting ready in a hurry.

 Now let's reread pages 144–145 to remember what happened when Nancy came up the path to a clearing.
Summary: When Nancy came up to the clearing, she couldn't find Ace. She looked around, and when she heard Ace call her name, found him clutching his leg in pain.

 Last, let's reread pages 146–148 to find out how Nancy cares for Ace and prepares for a rescue.
Summary: Nancy gets Ace to lean against a tree and puts a cold pack on his leg. She uses rocks to make an arrow for a signal and gives Ace a poncho to keep warm.

Decoding/Spelling

Words with Ending /ər/ Tell students that in spelling, one strategy to use is to compare spellings. Explain to students that if they are unsure of a spelling, they can first try writing the word with other possible spellings to see which one looks right. Write the following on the board:

err	er
vineg	or
trad	ar

Have volunteers draw a line to connect the syllables to spell the words correctly. Point out that if each word were matched with the ending straight across, then the spelling does not look right.

TEACH

Build Robust Vocabulary

Words from "Hiking with Ace"   Have students locate the word *lingered* on page 142 of "Hiking with Ace." Ask a volunteer to read the sentence in which this word appears aloud. (Line 3: *Ace was by now far in front of her and had not even noticed when she lingered behind*.) Explain that this sentence means that Nancy moved slowly as if she didn't want to keep up with Ace. Continue by asking students to locate and read the sentence in which *clutching* appears on page 145 aloud. (Line 4: *Nancy found Ace down a slope, clutching his leg*.) Explain that this sentence means that Ace was holding tightly onto his leg. Then ask students to locate and read the sentence in which *hobble* appears on page 146 aloud. (Line 3: *"Hobble over to that tree," she instructed*.) Explain that "hobble" means to have trouble walking or to limp.

Play a modified game of charades. Give each student a slip of paper with one of the words written on it. Have each student act out his or her word for the class to guess.

RETEACH

Grammar/Writing

Writing Trait: Organization   Tell students to turn to page 57 of their *Practice Books*. Have a volunteer read the instruction. Tell students that how-to texts often use key words to signal sequence. Write the following sentence on the board:

> First open the book, then read the introduction.

Show students how the words *first* and *then* signal a new step in the sequence. Help students complete Part A.

GUIDED PRACTICE   Guide students through Part B and Part C. Model for students how using a sequence chart can help them list the steps when completing Part C.

Fluency

Fluency Practice   Tell students that today they will reread the sentences on the bottom of *Practice Book* page 55. Have students locate and point to the first sentence. Tell students that everyone is going to read the sentence together. This choral reading will give students an opportunity to hear others and listen to the natural phrasing of the sentences. Choral-read each of the sentences several times.

30+ Minutes

COMPREHENSION
Reteach Author's Purpose and Perspective

DECODING/SPELLING
Reteach Words with Ending /ər/

BUILD ROBUST VOCABULARY
Reteach Words from "Hiking with Ace"

GRAMMAR/WRITING
Reteach Writing Form: How-to Essay

FLUENCY
Fluency Practice

Materials Needed: *Bold Moves*

Student Edition pp. 142–148

Practice Book p. 58

Copying Master 56

Spelling Words: Lesson 14

1. beggar	11. monitor
2. burglar	12. partner
3. cedar	13. pillar
4. computer	14. prisoner
5. consumer	15. rumor
6. error	16. trader
7. calendar	17. traitor
8. grammar	18. vapor
9. hanger	19. vinegar
10. lumber	20. whimper

Comprehension

Author's Purpose and Perspective   Remind students that an author's purpose is to inform, persuade, or entertain. Have a volunteer recall the author's purpose in "Hiking with Ace." (to entertain readers with a story about a hike in the mountains) Remind students that authors also share an idea, or theme from their own unique perspective. Discuss with students how the author's perspective influences the events of the story.

Decoding/Spelling

Practice Book 58

Words with Ending /ər/   Have students number a sheet of paper 1–17. Write *vinegar* on the board and circle the *-ar*. Tell students that the first six words you will dictate have the *-ar* ending. After students write each word, display it so they can proofread their work. Repeat with *consumer* for the *-er* ending and *traitor* for the *-or* ending.

1. beggar	2. burglar	3. cedar	4. calendar
5. grammar	6. pillar	7. computer	8. hanger
9. lumber	10. partner	11. prisoner	12. trader
13. whimper	14. error	15. monitor	16. rumor
17. vapor			

Have students turn to page 58 in their *Practice Books*. Have students look at the picture. Then read aloud the instructions. Have students complete the page on their own.

RETEACH

Build Robust Vocabulary

Words from "Hiking with Ace" Review the meanings of the words *lingered, clutching,* and *hobble*. Then say these sentences and ask which word describes each sentence. Have students explain why.

- **Maria had so much fun at the party that she moved slowly when her mom came to take her home.** (lingered)

- **The baby held tightly to her favorite teddy bear.** (clutched)

- **When Jon had a cast on his leg, he limped.** (hobbled)

RETEACH

Grammar/Writing

Copying Master 56

Writing Form: How-To Essay Remind students that when writers explain how to do or make something, they must organize their ideas in a logical order. Have students look at *Copying Master 56* and ask a volunteer to read the instruction aloud. Draw the following chart on the board:

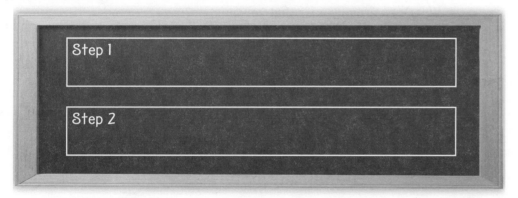

Step 1

Step 2

Tell students that using a sequence chart like the one on the board will help them list the steps in sequential order. Writers should check their charts to be sure all the steps and materials needed are listed, and that special terms are explained.

GUIDED PRACTICE Have volunteers read the Student Model on *Copying Master 56*. Discuss the margin notes. Then guide students to follow the directions.

Fluency

pp. 142–148

Fluency Practice Have each student work with a partner to read passages from "Hiking with Ace" aloud to each other. Students may select a passage that they enjoyed or choose one of the following options:

- Read page 144. (Total: 99 words)

- Read page 148. (Total: 108 words)

Encourage students to read the selected passage aloud to their partner three times. Have the student rate his or her reading on the 1–4 scale.

1	Need more practice
2	Pretty good
3	Good
4	Great!

DAY AT A GLANCE

Day 5

30+ Minutes

VOCABULARY

Preteach *communal, dissatisfied, demands, apparent, indebted, bliss, arduous, prudent, stationary, entwined*

COMPREHENSION

 Reteach Figurative Language

DECODING/WORD ATTACK

Reteach Decode Longer Words

DECODING/SPELLING

Reteach Words with Suffixes *-able, -ible*

GRAMMAR/WRITING

Reteach Nouns

FLUENCY

Fluency Performance

Materials Needed: *Bold Moves*

Student Edition pp. 142–148

Skill Card 15

Copying Master 57

PRETEACH

Vocabulary

Copying Master 57

Lesson 15 Vocabulary Distribute a set of Vocabulary Word Cards to each pair of students. Hold up the card for the first word, and ask a volunteer to read it aloud. Have students repeat the word and hold up the matching card. Give the explanation for the word. Then ask students the first question below and discuss their responses. Continue for each of the Vocabulary Words.

- How much food would you prepare for a **communal** breakfast? Why?

- Why would a tennis player be **dissatisfied** if his or her doubles partner missed the ball?

- What would happen if you made unreasonable **demands** on your mom or dad?

- If hikers came in from outside with their teeth chattering, what would be **apparent** about the weather?

- What could make you **indebted** to someone you don't know very well?

- What were you doing the last time you felt **bliss**?

- What's an **arduous** task that you must do?

- Would a **prudent** girl check the air pressure in her tires before going for a long bicycle ride? Why or why not?

- Why should you remain **stationary** when you are getting your hair cut?

- What would be an easy way to separate your **entwined** hands?

RETEACH

Comprehension

Skill Card 15

Figurative Language Invite students to look at side A of *Skill Card 15: Review: Figurative Language*. Have volunteers read the Skill Reminder aloud. Then read the passage aloud as students read along. Discuss how students can identify a simile, a metaphor, or personification.

GUIDED PRACTICE Guide students in copying the chart onto a separate sheet of paper. Invite students to share their examples of figurative language with the group. (Similes: my eyes widened like a slime mold in a petri dish, coming home is like wrapping yourself up in a comfortable old blanket; Metaphors: My mouth was an *O* the size of a baseball, the trip was a dream; Personification: our horses are often skittish and cranky, police horses are unfailingly calm and cooperative, a hotel that took in the view of Central Park)

Decoding/Word Attack

Decode Longer Words Write the words *passable* and *convertible* on the board, and read them aloud. Have students repeat the words and tell how many syllables they hear. Then have a volunteer tell the root and suffix of each word. (pass, *-able*; convert, *-ible*) Remind students that these suffixes have the same meaning and pronunciation. Give students examples of roots of words ending in *-ible* that are not complete words or may change in spelling. (*ed-* in *edible*; *apply* in *applicable*)

Decoding/Spelling

Words with Suffixes *-able, -ible* Write *breakable* and *credible* on the board. Draw a slash between the root and the suffix (break/able; cred/ible). Remind students that roots that stand alone as words usually take *-able* (as in breakable), while roots that are not words by themselves are more likely to take *-ible* (as in credible). Point out that the silent *e* in a root is often dropped when these suffixes are added. (excitable, reproducible)

Grammar/Writing

Nouns Remind students that singular nouns show one and that plural nouns show more than one. Review the rules for forming plural nouns. Have students recall that the singular and plural forms of some nouns are the same. On the other hand, the spelling of some nouns changes completely to form the plural. Write *city, treetop, calf, dress, half,* and *stitch* on the board. Help students use the rules they have learned to form the plurals. (cities, treetops, calves, dresses, halves, stitches)

Remind students that possessive nouns show ownership and need an apostrophe. Review the rules for forming possessive nouns. Then write *truck, princesses,* and *women* on the board. Guide students as they write the possessive form of each word. (truck's, princesses', women's)

Student-Friendly Explanations

communal Something that is shared by a group of people is communal.

dissatisfied When you are dissatisfied with something, you are unhappy about the way it has turned out.

demands If someone makes demands of you, you are expected to give your time, facilities, or resources.

apparent Something that is clear and obvious is apparent.

indebted You are indebted to a person if you are grateful or obliged for a favor or assistance given to you by that person.

bliss When you feel bliss, you feel happy and content.

arduous An arduous task requires you to work extremely hard to complete it.

prudent People who are prudent are sensible and practical in their actions.

stationary Objects that are stationary stay in one place and do not move.

entwined When things are entwined, they are twisted together and wound around one another.

Fluency

pp. 142–148 **Fluency Performance** Invite students to read aloud the passages from "Hiking With Ace" that they selected and practiced earlier. Note the number of words each student reads correctly and incorrectly. Have students rate their own oral reading on the 1–4 scale. Allow students to practice and then to read the passage to you again.

30+ Minutes

LESSON 15

VOCABULARY

Reteach *communal, dissatisfied, demands, apparent, indebted, bliss, arduous, prudent, stationary, entwined*

COMPREHENSION

 Reteach Theme

DECODING/WORD ATTACK

Reteach Decode Longer Words

DECODING/SPELLING

Reteach Words with Suffixes *-ous, -ious, -eous*

GRAMMAR/WRITING

Reteach Nouns

FLUENCY

Fluency Practice

Materials Needed: *Bold Moves*

| Student Edition pp. 150–151 | Practice Book pp. 59, 60 | Skill Card 15 | Copying Master 58 |

RETEACH

Vocabulary

Lesson 15 Vocabulary Read aloud the Vocabulary Words and the Student-Friendly Explanations. Have students turn to pages 150–151 in their books. Ask a volunteer to read the directions aloud. Remind students that they should read each sentence to themselves with the word they choose to be sure it makes sense. If students have difficulty choosing the correct word, refer to the Student-Friendly Explanations. After students complete the pages, have volunteers take turns reading each sentence aloud. (Answers for pages 150–151: 2. *bliss*, 3. *stationary*, 4. *dissatisfied*, 5. *arduous*, 6. *prudent*, 7. *apparent*, 8. *demands*, 9. *indebted*, 10. *entwined*, 11. A communal fire is one shared by a group of people; 12. Students' responses will vary. Students should describe a difficult, time-consuming task.)

RETEACH

Comprehension

Theme Have students look at side B of *Skill Card 15: Review: Theme*. Ask a volunteer to read the Skill Reminder aloud. Remind students that a theme is often implied rather than stated directly. Then read the story aloud as students read along. Ask students to think about the twins and their grandmother. Discuss what they are like and their actions in the story. Invite students to tell how the setting affects everyone's expectations of how they should act.

GUIDED PRACTICE Guide students in copying the chart and completing it by listing details from the story. Then discuss possible ideas for theme by asking students: **What message do you think the writer wants you to learn?** (Possible response: People aren't always what they seem.)

RETEACH

Decoding/Word Attack

Decode Longer Words   Remind students they have learned to decode words that end in *-ous, -ious*, or *-eous*. Write *poisonous, industrious*, and *piteous* on the board. Ask volunteers to identify the root of each word. (poison, industry, pity) Review how to divide each word into syllables. Point out that the suffixes *-ious* and *-eous* can be divided to be a part of two different syllables (in/dus/tri/ous, pit/e/ous).

RETEACH

Decoding/Spelling

Copying Master 58

Words with Suffixes *-ous, -ious, -eous*   Distribute *Copying Master 58*. Echo-read the Spelling Words with students. Have them identify the words with the suffixes *-ous, -ious*, or *-eous*. (glamorous, infectious, advantageous, gorgeous, joyous) Write those words on the board. Have a volunteer draw a slash between the root and suffix in each word. Remind students that since the three suffixes sound the same, they may need to use a dictionary to tell which suffix to add to a specific root.

RETEACH

Grammar/Writing

Practice Book 60

Nouns   Remind students that when they proofread, they should make sure that plurals are formed correctly and that an apostrophe is used to show possession. Write the following sentences on the board:

> The womens' jeweles sparkled in the sunlight.
>
> A mooses' antleer are shed and regrown each year.
>
> The seamstress mended an actors' costume with ten stitchs.

Have volunteers identify and correct the errors. (women's, jewels, moose's, antlers, actor's, stitches)

GUIDED PRACTICE   Direct students to *Practice Book* page 60. Have students work in pairs to do both sets of activities. Allow time for pairs to share their responses.

VOCABULARY

Student-Friendly Explanations

communal Something that is shared by a group of people is communal.

dissatisfied When you are dissatisfied with something, you are unhappy about the way it has turned out.

demands If someone makes demands of you, you are expected to give your time, facilities, or resources.

apparent Something that is clear and obvious is apparent.

indebted You are indebted to a person if you are grateful or obliged for a favor or assistance given to you by that person.

bliss When you feel bliss, you feel happy and content.

arduous An arduous task requires you to work extremely hard to complete it.

prudent People who are prudent are sensible and practical in their actions.

stationary Objects that are stationary stay in one place and do not move.

entwined When things are entwined, they are twisted together and wound around one another.

Fluency

Practice Book 59

Fluency Practice   Have students turn to *Practice Book* page 59. Read the words in the first column aloud. Invite students to track each word and repeat the words after you. Then have students work in pairs to read the words in the first column aloud to each other. Follow the same procedure with each of the remaining columns. Then have partners practice reading all of the words.

DAY AT A GLANCE

Day 2

VOCABULARY
Reteach *communal, dissatisfied, demands, apparent, indebted, bliss, arduous, prudent, stationary, entwined*

COMPREHENSION
"Raven and the Tides"
Build Background
Monitor Comprehension
Answers to *Think Critically* Questions

DECODING/WORD ATTACK
Reteach Decode Longer Words

DECODING/SPELLING
Reteach Words with Endings /ən/, /əl/

GRAMMAR/WRITING
Reteach Pronouns

FLUENCY
Fluency Practice

Materials Needed: *Bold Moves*

| Student Edition pp. 152–159 | Practice Book p. 59 | Copying Masters 57, 58 |

RETEACH

Vocabulary

Copying Master 57

Lesson 15 Vocabulary Distribute a set of Vocabulary Word Cards for each pair of students. Have students print the Vocabulary Words neatly on index cards. Tell them to cut the words apart into sections to make puzzle cards and mix the cards up. Using the original Word Cards as a reference, have students pick out the letters to reconstruct each word. Have them tell the meaning of each word after they have completed it.

Comprehension

Build Background: "Raven and the Tides"
Ask students to share other myths or legends that they have read. Discuss the characters in these stories. Have they ever known someone who was clever, sneaky, and good-hearted at the same time? How did he or she show these characteristics?

pp. 152–153

Monitor Comprehension: "Raven and the Tides"
Read the title of the story aloud. Then have students read pages 152–153 to find out who the storyteller is and to whom the story is being told.

After reading the pages, ask: **Who is telling the story?** (A storyteller wearing a raven mask is telling the story.) **Who is his audience?** (families who lived on the Northwest Coast ages ago) **POINT OF VIEW**

Discuss the Stop and Think question on page 152: **Why are the Ancestors dissatisfied?** (The Ancestors are dissatisfied because the sea has covered the beach, so they cannot gather crabs and clams.) Guide students in writing the answer to this question. **SUMMARIZE**

Ask: **How does the author show us that Raven is very hungry?** (Possible response: The author uses a simile, "my belly is rumbling like thunder," to show that Raven is so hungry his tummy is growling.)
 FIGURATIVE LANGUAGE

Discuss the Stop and Think question on page 153: **What do you think Mighty Spirit will tell Raven?** (Possible response: I think Mighty Spirit will tell Raven what he can do to help the hungry Ancestors.) Guide students in writing the answer to this question. **MAKE PREDICTIONS**

pp. 154–155

Have students read Mighty Spirit's first speech on page 154. Model how you answer questions to figure out what is happening in a passage.

THINK ALOUD **I don't understand how the Old One can hold the line and keep the tide from flowing out. So, I ask myself these questions about what puzzles me: *What is high tide? What happens if you hold a line between one thing and another?* I remember that, at high tide, the shore is covered with water; you can't even see the beach—much less gather clams and crabs. I also recall that you can hold something in by using a line, like a rope. The Old One is using a line to hold in the tide. ANSWER QUESTIONS**

Discuss the Stop and Think question on page 154: **What does Raven need to do?** (Possible response: Raven needs to get the Old One to let go of the tide line.) Guide students in writing the answer to this question. **GENERALIZE**

Discuss the Stop and Think question on page 155: **How is the Old One like a giant totem pole?** (Possible response: She is like a giant totem pole because she sits stone-faced and still as wood.) Guide students in writing the answer to this question. **FIGURATIVE LANGUAGE**

 pp. 156–157

Discuss the Stop and Think question on page 156: **Why does Raven pretend to find clams?** (Possible response: Raven pretends to find clams because he wants to distract the Old One so that she will drop the tide line.) Guide students in writing the answer to this question. **DRAW CONCLUSIONS**

Discuss the Stop and Think question on page 157: **What happens when Raven grabs the tide line?** (Possible response: When Raven grabs the line, the tide rushes out, leaving clams and crabs on the shore.) Guide students in writing the answer to this question. **CAUSE AND EFFECT**

page 158

Discuss the Stop and Think question on page 158: **What natural event does this legend try to explain?** (Possible response: This legend tries to explain why the tides come in and go out twice a day.) Guide students in writing the answer to this question. **THEME**

Ask: **Is being a trickster like Raven a good thing or a bad thing in this legend?** (Possible response: Being a trickster is a good thing. Raven tricks the Old One to get food not only for himself but also for the Ancestors.) **MAKE JUDGMENTS**

VOCABULARY

Student-Friendly Explanations

communal Something that is shared by a group of people is communal.

dissatisfied When you are dissatisfied with something, you are unhappy about the way it has turned out.

demands If someone makes demands of you, you are expected to give your time, facilities, or resources.

apparent Something that is clear and obvious is apparent.

indebted You are indebted to a person if you are grateful or obliged for a favor or assistance given to you by that person.

bliss When you feel bliss, you feel happy and content.

arduous An arduous task requires you to work extremely hard to complete it.

prudent People who are prudent are sensible and practical in their actions.

stationary Objects that are stationary stay in one place and do not move.

entwined When things are entwined, they are twisted together and wound around one another.

Spelling Words: Lesson 15

1. convertible	11. beckon
2. breakable	12. example
3. sensible	13. foreign
4. permissible	14. informal
5. profitable	15. sudden
6. glamorous	16. consumer
7. infectious	17. monitor
8. advantageous	18. rumor
9. gorgeous	19. vinegar
10. joyous	20. whimper

page 159

Answers to *Think Critically* Questions

Help students read and answer the *Think Critically* questions on page 159. Then guide students in writing the answer to each question. Possible responses are provided.

1. The main problem is that the Old One won't let go of the tide line, so the tide can go out, and the Ancestors can gather clams and crabs to eat. The problem is resolved when the Old One agrees to let go of the tide line twice a day. **PLOT**

2. I think Raven decides to help because he is hungry, too, and understands how the Ancestors feel. **CHARACTERS**

3. I think the author uses a storyteller because she wants to show how the legend was told long ago on the Northwest Coast. **AUTHOR'S PURPOSE**

RETEACH

Decoding/Word Attack

Decode Longer Words Write these words on the board: *dimple, actual, label, pedal, informal, veteran, sudden, captain,* and *pigeon.* Have students say the words after you. Point out that the final syllable is said more softly than the rest of the word. This final, unaccented syllable has the *schwa* sound.

RETEACH

Decoding/Spelling

Copying Master 58

Words with Endings /ən/, /əl/   Have students review *Copying Master 58* to identify those Spelling Words that end with a vowel followed by the letter *n* or *l*. (beckon, informal, sudden) Write the words on the board, and have students read them aloud as you circle the vowel. Point out that the vowel sound is pronounced /ə/. Write the word *sensible,* and have a volunteer read it aloud. Remind students that the syllable *-le* at the end of a word is pronounced /əl/. Have students find a Spelling Word with the *-le* ending. (example)

RETEACH

Grammar/Writing

Pronouns   Remind students that pronouns take the place of nouns and can be used as the subject or object in a sentence. Point out that

- a pronoun always has an antecedent, which is the word or words to which the pronoun refers.

- possessive pronouns show ownership and take the place of possessive nouns.

- apostrophes are not used in possessive pronouns.

- reflexive pronouns reflect the action back to the noun or pronoun just named.

- indefinite pronouns refer to a person or thing not named specifically.

Fluency

Practice Book 59

Fluency Practice   Invite students to look at the bottom half of *Practice Book* page 59. These sentences have been broken into natural phrases. Tell students to repeat each phrase after you, mirroring your expression, phrasing, and pace. After students have repeated each sentence, invite them to practice reading the sentences to a partner.

30+ Minutes

COMPREHENSION
Reteach Prefixes, Suffixes, and Roots

Reread and Summarize "Raven and the Tides"

DECODING/WORD ATTACK
Reteach Decode Longer Words

DECODING/SPELLING
Reteach Words with Ending /ər/

BUILD ROBUST VOCABULARY
Teach Words from "Raven and the Tides"

GRAMMAR/WRITING
Reteach Pronouns

FLUENCY
Fluency Practice

Materials Needed: *Bold Moves*

Student
Edition
pp. 152–158

Practice
Book
pp. 59, 61

Copying
Master
58

RETEACH

Comprehension

Prefixes, Suffixes, and Roots Remind students that a root is the basic word part that gives a word its meaning. Write *inexplicable* on the board. Have students identify the root, prefix, and suffix. (*in-, explic, -able*) Ask: **How can the prefix help you tell the meaning of the word?** (Possible response: Knowing that the prefix *in-* means "not," helps me tell that the word means "not able to be explained.")

GUIDED PRACTICE Write *remembering, amazement, wonderfully,* and *impossibly* on the board. Ask students to work in small groups to identify the prefixes and/or suffixes and roots. Have them identify one or more parts in each word that help them tell what the word means. (Possible responses: *re- /-ing / member; amaze /-ment; -ful / wonder; im- /-ly / possible*)

Reread and Summarize Have students reread and summarize "Raven and the Tides" in sections, as described below.

 pp. 152–153 **Let's reread pages 152–153 to recall the setting and the story problem.**
Summary: A storyteller tells about a time before there were tides. The sea rose high along the edge of land. The Ancestors could not gather things to eat. Raven wanted to help.

 pp. 154–155 **Now, let's reread pages 154–155 to recall what Mighty Spirit tells Raven and what Raven does.**
Summary: Mighty Spirit explains that the Old One holds the tide line in her lap, so the water is always high. Raven tricks the Old One to let go of the line by distracting her.

pp. 156–158 **Last, let's reread pages 156–158 to find out how Raven brings the tides.**
Summary: The Old One lets her grip on the tide line slip. Raven grabs the line. The tide goes out. The Old One agrees to let go of the tide line twice a day, so the Ancestors can get food.

RETEACH

Decoding/Word Attack

Decode Longer Words Remind students that when a word ends in a vowel and the letter *r* in an unaccented syllable, the vowel often has the *schwa* sound. Write *computer, beggar, trigger, scooter,* and *flavor* on the board. Point out that the final vowel and *r* stay together to form the last syllable.

Decoding/Spelling

Copying Master 58

Words with Ending /ər/   Have students review *Copying Master 58* and identify those Spelling Words that end in *ar, er,* or *or.* (consumer, monitor, rumor, vinegar, whimper) **Write the words on the board, and underline the endings. Challenge students to brainstorm to identify and spell additional words with the ending /ər/.**

Then have pairs of students play the Memory Game, as described on the bottom of *Copying Master 58.*

Build Robust Vocabulary

pp. 152–158

Words from "Raven and the Tides"   Have students locate *emerged* on page 152 of "Raven and the Tides." Ask a volunteer to read aloud the sentence in which this word appears. Explain that this sentence means that the storyteller came out of his lodge. Then ask students to locate and read aloud the sentence in which *long* appears on page 153. Explain that in this sentence "long" means to want something badly.

Write the words as column headings. Help students brainstorm synonyms to list under each heading.

Grammar/Writing

Practice Book 61

Pronouns   Tell students that when they proofread, they should make sure that pronouns are used correctly. Remind students that apostrophes are used in possessive nouns but not possessive pronouns. Write the following paragraph on the board:

> Mitchell was so bored by the end of he's summer vacation that him did not know what to do. Mom listened wide-mouthed as Mitchell hisself expressed a keen desire for seventh grade to begin.

Invite volunteers to underline the mistakes and make corrections. (Underline: he's, him, hisself; Write: his, he, himself)

GUIDED PRACTICE   Have students work in pairs to complete the activities on page 61 in their *Practice Books.*

Fluency

Practice Book 59

Fluency Practice   Tell students that today they will reread the sentences on the bottom of *Practice Book* page 59. Have students locate and point to the first sentence. Tell students that everyone is going to read the sentence together. This choral reading will give students an opportunity to hear others and listen to the natural phrasing of the sentences. Choral-read each of the sentences several times.

COMPREHENSION
Reteach Poetic Devices

DECODING/SPELLING
Cumulative Review

BUILD ROBUST VOCABULARY
Reteach Words from "Raven and the Tides"

GRAMMAR/WRITING
Cumulative Review

FLUENCY
Fluency Practice

Materials Needed: *Bold Moves*

Student Edition pp. 152–158

Practice Book p. 62

Copying Masters 59, 60

Spelling Words: Lesson 15

1. convertible	11. beckon
2. breakable	12. example
3. sensible	13. foreign
4. permissible	14. informal
5. profitable	15. sudden
6. glamorous	16. consumer
7. infectious	17. monitor
8. advantageous	18. rumor
9. gorgeous	19. vinegar
10. joyous	20. whimper

30+ Minutes

Comprehension

Copying Master 59

Poetic Devices Remind students that they have learned about a variety of poetic devices. Distribute *Copying Master 59*, and have volunteers read the information at the top of the page aloud. Remind students to look for poetic devices as they read the paragraphs.

GUIDED PRACTICE Ask students to complete the page with a partner. Invite students to share and discuss their responses with the class.

Decoding/Spelling

Practice Book 62

Cumulative Review Have students number a sheet of paper 1–16. Write *convertible* on the board. Tell students that the first four words you will dictate end with the suffix *-ible* or *-able*. After students write the word, display it so they can proofread their work. Repeat this activity using the word *glamorous* for suffixes *-ous, -ious*, and *-eous*. Use the word *example* for words ending with /ən/ or /əl/. Use *consumer* for words that end in *ar, er,* or *or*.

1. breakable	2. sensible	3. permissible	4. profitable
5. infectious	6. advantageous	7. gorgeous	8. joyous
9. beckon	10. foreign	11. informal	12. sudden
13. monitor	14. rumor	15. vinegar	16. whimper

Have students turn to page 62 in their *Practice Books*. Ask a volunteer to read the directions aloud. Point out that students should study the picture and identify the sentence that best matches the picture. Once students have completed the page, have them identify the Spelling Words in the sentences.

Build Robust Vocabulary

Words from "Raven and the Tides"   Review the meanings of the words *emerged* and *long*. Then say these sentences and ask which word describes each sentence. Have students explain why.

- **The turtle's head slowly came out of its shell.** (emerged)
- **Today is so hot that I very badly want a snow cone.** (long)

Grammar/Writing

Copying Master 60

Cumulative Review   Have students recall the grammar skills they learned in this lesson:

- singular and plural nouns
- subject and object pronouns and antecedents
- possessive, reflexive, and indefinite pronouns

Write the sentences below on the board:

> The swallowes nested in the cliffes.
>
> Three of the houses's shutters are painted dark green.
>
> Ms. Cocanour gave the book to myself.

Guide students to proofread the sentences. Have volunteers correct the errors. (swallows, cliffs; houses'; me)

GUIDED PRACTICE   Distribute *Copying Master 60*. Invite a student to read the directions aloud. Then have students work in pairs to complete the page. Allow time for students to share their responses.

Fluency

pp. 152–158

Fluency Practice   Have each student work with a partner to read passages from "Raven and the Tides" aloud to each other. Remind students to

- pay attention to punctuation while reading.
- use punctuation to read fluently and with expression.

Encourage students to read the selected passage aloud to their partner three times. Have the student rate his or her reading on the 1–4 scale.

1	Need more practice
2	Pretty good
3	Good
4	Great!

DAY AT A GLANCE

Day 5

30+ Minutes

VOCABULARY
Preteach *regulates, precise, compensate, trial, perfectionist, counteracted, meticulously, petition*

COMPREHENSION
 Preteach Point of View

DECODING/WORD ATTACK
Preteach Decode Longer Words

DECODING/SPELLING
Preteach Words from Spanish and French

GRAMMAR/WRITING
Preteach Adjectives and Articles

FLUENCY
Fluency Performance

Materials Needed: *Bold Moves*

Student Edition pp. 152–158

Skill Card 16

Copying Master 61

PRETEACH

Vocabulary

Copying Master 61

Lesson 16 Vocabulary   Distribute a set of Vocabulary Word Cards to each student. Hold up the card for the first word, and ask a volunteer to read it aloud. Have students repeat the word and hold up the matching card. Give the explanation for the word. Then ask students the first question below and discuss their responses. Continue for each of the Vocabulary Words.

- **What does a faucet regulate?**
- **Why should your measurements be precise when you cook something?**
- **How can you compensate if you miss practice for a team sport?**
- **Have you ever had a trial run of something? How did it turn out?**
- **If you are a perfectionist, how does your report card look?**
- **When have you counteracted something an adult asked you to do?**
- **Which animals groom themselves meticulously?**
- **What have you petitioned your teacher about?**

PRETEACH

Comprehension

Skill Card 16

Focus Skill

Point of View   Direct students' attention to side A of *Skill Card 16: Point of View*. Have a volunteer read the information at the top of the card aloud. Explain that autobiographies are written in the first-person point of view, and biographies are written in the third-person point of view. Invite students to take turns reading the passage aloud. Point to the chart and ask:

- **Is the story told from a first-person or third-person point of view?** (third-person)
- **Is this an example of an autobiography or a biography?** (biography)

Guide students to understand that words such as *he* and *his* are clues that the passage is written in third-person point of view.

Decoding/Word Attack

Decode Longer Words   Write *croissant* on the board, and have a volunteer read it aloud. Ask students how many syllables are in *croissant* and where the word should be divided. (2 syllables, crois/sant) Ask students to identify the vowels in the first syllable. (oi) Read aloud the first syllable in *croissant*. Point out that the vowels *o* and *i* combine to form one sound. These are called vowel digraphs. Repeat the procedure with *mosquito*.

Decoding/Spelling

Words from Spanish and French   Tell students that one way they can learn to spell new words is by knowing the origin of that word. Write *bouquet, campaign, adobe,* and *rodeo* on the board. Have students repeat each word after you. Point out that *bouquet* and *campaign* are French, and *rodeo* and *adobe* are Spanish. Discuss with students the sounds they hear and how each sound is spelled. Tell students that these are some of the next lesson's Spelling Words.

Grammar/Writing

Adjectives and Articles   Explain that adjectives describe nouns by telling *what kind, which one, how many,* or *how much*. Point out that articles like *a, an* and *the* act like adjectives by making a noun specific or general. Pronouns, too, can serve as adjectives to modify another noun, such as *my* or *our*. Even proper nouns can become proper adjectives when used to describe another noun (*England,* the *English* weather). Write the following sentence on the board:

> A hundred meteors crossed the night sky.

Guide students to identify the adjectives *hundred* and *night*. Point out that *hundred* tells how many meteors and *night* tells what kind of sky. Then have a volunteer circle the articles. (A, the)

VOCABULARY

Student-Friendly Explanations

regulates When someone regulates something, he or she controls its functions and workings.

precise When something is exact and accurate, it is precise.

compensate When you compensate for something, you provide something else to balance out its negative effects.

trial A trial run is a test or experiment to see whether or not something will work.

perfectionist Somebody who feels that he or she has to do everything absolutely right is a perfectionist.

counteracted When you have counteracted something, you have acted in an opposite manner to prevent or reduce its effect.

meticulously When you do something meticulously, you do it carefully, paying strict attention to details.

petition When you petition a higher authority, you formally make a request for an action or decision from someone who has more power than you have.

Fluency

pp. 152–158 **Fluency Performance** Invite students to read aloud the passages from "Raven and the Tides" that they selected and practiced earlier. Have students rate their own oral reading on the 1–4 scale. Give students the opportunity to continue practicing and then to read the passage to you again.

DAY AT A GLANCE

Day 1

30+ Minutes

LESSON 16

VOCABULARY
Reteach *regulates, precise, compensate, trial, perfectionist, counteracted, meticulously, petition*

COMPREHENSION
Reteach Point of View

DECODING/SPELLING
Reteach Words from Spanish and French

GRAMMAR/WRITING
Preteach Comparing with Adjectives

FLUENCY
Fluency Practice

Materials Needed: *Bold Moves*

Student Edition pp. 160–161 | Practice Book p. 63 | Skill Card 16 | Copying Master 62

RETEACH

Vocabulary

Lesson 16 Vocabulary   Read aloud the Vocabulary Words and the Student-Friendly Explanations. Then have students read the story on page 160 of their books. Guide them in answering the questions on page 161. Then have students read the answers along with you. If students are unable to answer the questions, refer to the story. (Answers for page 161: Possible responses: 2. Newton meticulously tested his ideas in trial cases because he wanted his findings to be precise. 3. If an experiment is not precise, your results might not be correct. 4. An object might be counteracted when another force stops it or slows it down. 5. The force of gravity between Earth and the moon regulates the ocean tides. 6. They are hoping the Society will publish their papers. 7. This means the idea can be a good one, but it isn't any good if the experiments to prove it are sloppy.)

RETEACH

Comprehension

  Point of View   Have students look at side B of *Skill Card 16: Point of View*. Ask a volunteer to read the Skill Reminder. Have a volunteer read the passage aloud as students follow along. Remind students of the passage they read on side A of *Skill Card 16*. Discuss how the two passages are different.

GUIDED PRACTICE   Guide students in copying and completing the chart. Remind them to look for clue words that hint at the point of view. (Title: Believe What You See; Genre: autobiography; Point of View: First-person; Clues: Use of *I*, *me*, and *my*)

Decoding/Spelling

Words from Spanish and French Distribute *Copying Master 62*. Model reading the Spelling Words as students repeat them. Review the Spelling Words and draw students' attention to any patterns they might see in word endings. Then have students complete the following activity which is based on the traditional Memory Game. Pairs of students make two sets of game cards using the lesson's Spelling Words with one syllable missing; a dash appears in the place of the syllable. After a student matches two cards, he or she must supply the correct missing letters of the syllable to keep the game cards. If the wrong letter is supplied, the opponent gets the game cards and the next turn.

Copying Master 62

Grammar/Writing

Comparing with Adjectives Tell students that adjectives take different forms to compare. Comparative forms compare two things or people. Superlative forms compare three or more. Explain that to make a comparative adjective, *-er* or *more* is added to the word. To make a superlative adjective, add *-est* or *most* to the word. Write *bright* and *intelligent* on the board. Guide students to write the comparative and superlative forms of each word. (brighter, brightest, more intelligent, most intelligent) Then write these sentences on the board:

> The north star is the _____ one in the night sky.
>
> This theory was _____ than his last one.

Have the students use correct comparative or superlative form of the adjectives *bright* and *intelligent* to complete each sentence. (brightest, more intelligent)

Student-Friendly Explanations

regulates When someone regulates something, he or she controls its functions and workings.

precise When something is exact and accurate, it is precise.

compensate When you compensate for something, you provide something else to balance out its negative effects.

trial A trial run is a test or experiment to see whether or not something will work.

perfectionist Somebody who feels that he or she has to do everything absolutely right is a perfectionist.

counteracted When you have counteracted something, you have acted in an opposite manner to prevent or reduce its effect.

meticulously When you do something meticulously, you do it carefully, paying strict attention to details.

petition When you petition a higher authority, you formally make a request for an action or decision from someone who has more power than you have.

Fluency

Fluency Practice Have students turn to *Practice Book* page 63. Read the words in the first column aloud. Invite students to track each word and repeat the words after you. Then have students work in pairs to read the words in the first column aloud to each other. Follow the same procedure with each of the remaining columns.

Practice Book 63

LESSON 16

DAY AT A GLANCE

Day 2

VOCABULARY
Reteach *regulates, precise, compensate, trial, perfectionist, counteracted, meticulously, petition*

COMPREHENSION
"After the Apple Fell"
Build Background
Monitor Comprehension
Answers to *Think Critically* **Questions**

DECODING/SPELLING
Reteach Words from Spanish and French

GRAMMAR/WRITING
Preteach Irregular Comparative and Superlative Adjectives

FLUENCY
Fluency Practice

Materials Needed: *Bold Moves*

| Student Edition pp. 162–169 | Practice Book pp. 63, 64 | Copying Masters 61, 62 |

RETEACH

Vocabulary

Lesson 16 Vocabulary Distribute a set of Vocabulary Word Cards for groups of three students. Have students work together to put the words in alphabetical order. Have students take turns reading a definition to their teammates, who then point to the word that matches it.

Copying Master 61

Comprehension

Build Background: "After the Apple Fell"
Ask students to tell about a time they had to learn something new in order to solve a problem. Was it an easy thing to do? Did they have a lot of problems reaching their goal? What did they have to do to help themselves succeed?

Monitor Comprehension: "After the Apple Fell"
pp. 162–163
Read the title of the story aloud. Then have students read pages 162–163 to find out who this biography is about and what he liked and didn't like to do.

After reading the pages, ask: **Who is this biography about?** (Isaac Newton) **What does the main character like to do?** (Possible responses: be alone, construct things, study the sun, stars, and planets) **What doesn't he like to do?** (Possible responses: work on the farm, grow things) **SUMMARIZE**

Discuss the Stop and Think question on page 162: **What is the point of view in this biography? How do you know?** (The point of view is third person. I know this because of the use of words like *Isaac Newton, he,* and *his;* It's a biography.) Guide students in writing the answer to this question. **POINT OF VIEW**

Ask: **Was Newton a perfectionist about farming?** (no) **How do you know?** (Possible responses: He avoided his farming responsibilities. He hid in a hedge to avoid the work.) **CHARACTERS' TRAITS**

Discuss the Stop and Think question on page 163: **How do you think Isaac felt about leaving school?** (Possible responses: I think Isaac felt disappointed, upset, and sad.) Guide students in writing the answer to this question. **CHARACTERS' EMOTIONS**

pp. 164–165

Discuss the Stop and Think question on page 164: **What did Newton do in 1665?** (In 1665, Newton had to return home for two years, but he continued to investigate gravity, light, and mathematics.) Guide students in writing the answer to this question. NOTE DETAILS

Discuss the Stop and Think question on page 165: **How did Newton change people's beliefs about light and prisms?** (Newton was able to compensate for the poor quality of prisms at that time and show that light is actually made of all different colors mixed together.) Guide students in writing the answer to this question. CAUSE AND EFFECT

 pp. 166–167

Discuss the Stop and Think question on page 166: **Do you think it was right for Newton to stop publishing his ideas? Explain.** (Possible response: I think that it was not right because he was keeping important discoveries from the public. Plus, with his meticulous notes, he could prove he was the one to uncover the new findings.) Guide students in writing the answer to this question. EXPRESS PERSONAL OPINIONS

Read aloud the first paragraph on page 167 to model how to analyze a character's traits.

(THINK ALOUD) **As I read this paragraph, it gives me an idea of the person Newton was. He worked hard and tested his ideas He worked day and night. He repeated the same experiments over and over. I can understand why people thought he was a perfectionist.** CHARACTERS' TRAITS

Discuss the Stop and Think question on page 167: **How do you think other scientists will feel about Newton's paper?** (Possible response: I think other scientists will feel either excited about the breakthrough and new form of math, or they will feel jealous of Newton's progress.) Guide students in writing the answer to this question. MAKE JUDGMENTS

 page 168

Ask: **What would happen if there was no gravity?** (Possible response: The planets would leave their orbits around the sun, objects on Earth would not fall toward the center, the Moon would leave its orbit around the Earth, and the ocean tides would be affected.) SUMMARIZE

Discuss the Stop and Think question on page 168: **What are some of the ideas Newton explained in his paper?** (Newton explained that an object will travel on the same path at the same speed until counteracted; gravity keeps planets in orbit, pulls objects on Earth towards its center, and regulates the tides.) Guide students in writing the answer to this question. MAKE CONNECTIONS

VOCABULARY

Student-Friendly Explanations

regulates When someone regulates something, he or she controls its functions and workings.

precise When something is exact and accurate, it is precise.

compensate When you compensate for something, you provide something else to balance out its negative effects.

trial A trial run is a test or experiment to see whether or not something will work.

perfectionist Somebody who feels that he or she has to do everything absolutely right is a perfectionist.

counteracted When you have counteracted something, you have acted in an opposite manner to prevent or reduce its effect.

meticulously When you do something meticulously, you do it carefully, paying strict attention to details.

petition When you petition a higher authority, you formally make a request for an action or decision from someone who has more power than you have.

Spelling Words: Lesson 16

1. adobe	11. ballet
2. barbecue	12. beret
3. barracuda	13. bouquet
4. embargo	14. campaign
5. mosquito	15. cassette
6. patio	16. croissant
7. rodeo	17. envelope
8. sombrero	18. plateau
9. tornado	19. sergeant
10. cargo	20. depot

Answers to *Think Critically* Questions   Help students read and answer the *Think Critically* questions on page 169. Then guide students in writing the answer to each question. Possible responses are provided.

1. [Next] In 1667, Hooke took credit for Newton's ideas. [Then] In 1672, Newton avoided publishing new ideas. [Finally] In 1687, Newton wrote a paper on gravity. **SEQUENCE**

2. Newton's ideas caused us to think about how gravity plays an important role in our solar system and led to math and research methods to better study the universe. **CAUSE AND EFFECT**

3. I have learned that Isaac Newton was supposed to be a farmer but became a scientist instead. **MAIN IDEA AND DETAILS**

RETEACH

Decoding/Spelling

Words from Spanish and French   Have students refer to *Copying Master 62* and work with a partner to write each Spelling Word on an index card. Have partners work together to sort the cards into groups by the number of syllables. Then ask partners to take turns displaying each card and reading and spelling the word aloud.

PRETEACH

Grammar/Writing

Practice Book 64 **Irregular Comparative and Superlative Adjectives** Explain to students that sometimes adjectives are irregular and don't follow the rule of adding the *-er* and *-est* or *more* and *most*. Write *good, bad, little* and *much* on the board. Guide students to understand that in order to compare with these adjectives, *good* becomes *better* and *best*, *bad* becomes *worse* and *worst*, *little* becomes *less* and *least*, and *much* becomes *more* and *most*.

GUIDED PRACTICE Direct students' attention to page 64 in their *Practice Books*. Invite a volunteer to read aloud the directions. Have students work in pairs to complete the page. Remind them that the articles *a, an,* and *the* are considered a type of adjective.

Fluency

Practice Book 63 **Fluency Practice** Invite students to look at the bottom half of *Practice Book* page 63. These sentences have been broken into natural phrases. Tell students to repeat each phrase after you, mirroring your expression, phrasing, and pace. After students have repeated each sentence, invite them to practice reading the sentences to a partner.

COMPREHENSION
Preteach Foreign Words in English
Reread and Summarize "After the Apple Fell"

DECODING/SPELLING
Reteach Words from Spanish and French

BUILD ROBUST VOCABULARY
Teach Words from "After the Apple Fell"

GRAMMAR/WRITING
Reteach Writing Trait: Voice

FLUENCY
Fluency Practice

Materials Needed: *Bold Moves*

  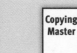

Student Edition pp. 162–168

Practice Book pp. 63, 65

Copying Master 63

PRETEACH

Comprehension

Copying Master 63

Foreign Words in English   Distribute *Copying Master 63*. Have students look at the chart and read along as you read about foreign words that have been adapted into English. Explain that some words, such as *patio* and *stove,* are so familiar that they are difficult to identify as "foreign." Tell students that when they come across an unfamiliar word, they could use a dictionary to look up its meaning and origin.

GUIDED PRACTICE   Have students work in pairs and read the chart together. Then ask them to find the foreign words in the passage, using the chart as a guide. Ask volunteers to share the words they identified.

Reread and Summarize   Have students reread and summarize "After the Apple Fell" in sections, as described below.

pp. 162–163

Let's reread pages 162–163 to recall what Isaac Newton's life was like at the beginning of the story.
Summary: Isaac Newton was born in 1642. His mother expected to him to work as a farmer, but Isaac was a quiet boy, more interested in science and building things than farming.

pp. 164–165

Now let's reread pages 164–165 to remember what Newton learned in school.
Summary: Newton studied Aristotle and Galileo's theories about the solar system. After a two-year break, Newton returned to Cambridge with his own ideas about gravity. His experiments led to the discovery that light was made of different colors mixed together.

pp. 166–168

Lastly, to find out what happens with Newton's scientific findings, let's reread pages 166–168.
Summary: Newton came up with extraordinary findings and wrote about them in 1687. His paper explained how gravity keeps the planets in orbit, keeps objects on Earth, and controls the ocean tides. We use his methods in mathematics and astronomy today.

RETEACH

Decoding/Spelling

Words from Spanish and French   Write *rodeo* on the board and have a volunteer divide it into syllables. (ro/de/o) Have students say the syllables aloud and point out the letter that stands for the long *o* sound at the end of the word. Ask students to find more Spelling Words with this end sound. (embargo, mosquito, patio, sombrero, cargo) Explain that some letter combinations in Spanish and French have sounds that may be unfamiliar.

TEACH

Build Robust Vocabulary

pp.
164–
166
Words from "After the Apple Fell" Have students locate the word *rotated* on page 164 of "After the Apple Fell." Ask a volunteer to read aloud the sentence in which this word appears. (Line 6: *Aristotle believed that the planets rotated around Earth*.) Explain that this sentence means that Aristotle believed the planets went around Earth. Continue by asking students to locate and read aloud the sentence in which the word *investigate* appears on page 164. (Last sentence: *It was then that he really started to investigate gravity, light, and mathematics*.) Explain that this sentence means that he studied these things carefully to learn the facts about how they worked. Then ask students to locate and read aloud the sentence in which the word *promoting* appears on page 166. (Line 4: *They tested new, promising ideas and assisted the inventors and scientists by promoting their work*.) Explain that this sentence means that the Royal Society helped the scientists develop or move forward with their work.

Ask each student to write the words on cards. Give an explanation of each word and have students hold up the correct word card.

RETEACH

Grammar/Writing

Practice Book 65
Writing Trait: Voice Have students turn to page 65 in their *Practice Books*. Read the information about voice. Then read the first sentence: **Jackson and Alfredo sat huddled in the cold, dark room.** Tell students the *cold, dark room* reveals the writer's voice and helps readers visualize the setting right away. If the writer had chosen to say *Jackson and Alfredo hid in the room*, this would have made the writing flat. Invite volunteers to take turns reading the passage aloud. Then direct students to work in small groups to answer the questions.

GUIDED PRACTICE Monitor students' progress and guide them in finding example phrases that show voice. Give students time to complete Part C on a separate sheet of paper. Invite volunteers to share their endings.

Fluency

Practice Book 63
Fluency Practice Tell students that today they will reread the sentences on the bottom of *Practice Book* page 63. Have students locate and point to the first sentence. Tell students that everyone is going to read the sentence together. This choral reading will give students an opportunity to hear others and listen to the natural phrasing of the sentences. Choral-read each of the sentences several times.

30+ Minutes

DAY AT A GLANCE

Day 4

COMPREHENSION
Reteach Foreign Words in English

DECODING/SPELLING
Reteach Words from Spanish and French

BUILD ROBUST VOCABULARY
Reteach Words from "After the Apple Fell"

GRAMMAR/WRITING
Reteach Writing Form: Journal Entry

FLUENCY
Fluency Practice

Materials Needed: *Bold Moves*

Student Edition pp. 162–168

Practice Book p. 66

Copying Masters 63, 64

Spelling Words: Lesson 16

1. adobe	11. ballet
2. barbecue	12. beret
3. barracuda	13. bouquet
4. embargo	14. campaign
5. mosquito	15. cassette
6. patio	16. croissant
7. rodeo	17. envelope
8. sombrero	18. plateau
9. tornado	19. sergeant
10. cargo	20. depot

Comprehension

Copying Master 63 **Foreign Words in English** Remind students that many words in English conversation and writing come from other languages. Direct students to *Copying Master 63*. Have them use the chart to help identify foreign words in this activity.

Then read this sentence aloud:

> **If Newton never studied gravity, would we have the cliché *what goes up, must come down*?**

Ask students to identify the foreign word. Explain that this word is French and point out the accent mark. Now, write these sentences on the board:

> Have you studied Newton and his ideas about our universe?
>
> Are we supposed to measure the results in degrees Fahrenheit?

Have students identify the foreign words in each question. (universe, supposed, Fahrenheit)

GUIDED PRACTICE Have students write a sentence that answers each question and contains a word of foreign origin.

Decoding/Spelling

Practice Book 66 **Words from Spanish and French** Have students number a sheet of paper 1–18. Write *adobe* on the board. Tell students that the first nine words you will say are Spanish in origin. After students write each word, display it so they can proofread their work. Then, write *ballet* on the board. Tell students that the next nine words are borrowed from French.

1. barbecue	2. barracuda	3. embargo	4. mosquito
5. patio	6. rodeo	7. sombrero	8. tornado
9. cargo	10. beret	11. bouquet	12. campaign
13. cassette	14. croissant	15. envelope	16. plateau
17. sergeant	18. depot		

Have students turn to page 66 in their *Practice Books*. Read the directions and the passage together. Once they have finished the page, have students circle the Spanish and French words in the selection.

Build Robust Vocabulary

Words from "After the Apple Fell"   Review the meanings of the words *rotated, investigate,* and *promoting.* Then say these sentences and ask which word describes each sentence. Have students explain why.

- **The horses on the carousel went around a brightly colored pole.** (rotated)

- **Eli studied the facts carefully to see if he could figure out how his dog kept getting out of the yard.** (investigate)

- **The artist's friend helped her move forward with her work by telling others about her talent.** (promoting)

Grammar/Writing

Copying Master 64

Writing Form: Journal Entry   Distribute *Copying Master 64.* Explain that a journal entry is always written in the first person. It tells of something the writer has experienced firsthand. Have volunteers read the information at the top and take turns reading the passage. Direct students' attention to the margin notes.

GUIDED PRACTICE   Have students work in small groups to discuss how voice helps readers picture the story in their minds. Allow time for students to share their completed responses.

Fluency

pp. 162–168

Fluency Practice   Have each student work with a partner to read passages from "After the Apple Fell" aloud to each other. Students may select a passage that they enjoyed or choose one of the following options:

- Read page 164. (Total: 111 words)

- Read page 168. (Total: 114 words)

Encourage students to read the selected passage aloud to their partner three times. Have the student rate his or her reading on the 1–4 scale.

1	Need more practice
2	Pretty good
3	Good
4	Great!

DAY AT A GLANCE
Day 5

VOCABULARY
Preteach *publicize, contortions, grimy, testimony, faint, foresight, distraction*

COMPREHENSION
 Preteach Point of View

DECODING/WORD ATTACK
Preteach Decode Longer Words

DECODING/SPELLING
Preteach Words with Prefixes *im-, in-, ir-, il-*

GRAMMAR/WRITING
Preteach Verbs and Verb Phrases

FLUENCY
Fluency Performance

Materials Needed: *Bold Moves*

Student Edition pp. 162–168   Copying Master 65

PRETEACH
Vocabulary

Copying Master 65 — **Lesson 17 Vocabulary** Distribute a set of Vocabulary Word Cards to each student. Hold up the first Vocabulary Word Card. And ask a volunteer to read it aloud. Have students repeat the word and hold up the matching card. Give the explanation for the word. Ask students the first question below and discuss their responses. Continue for each Vocabulary Word.

- How would you **publicize** a new after-school club you were starting?
- What kind of **contortions** have you seen people perform?
- What can you do when your backpack gets **grimy**?
- Would you be nervous if you had to give **testimony** in court?
- What do you do when someone is speaking in a voice too **faint** for you to hear?
- Who do you know that shows **foresight** in many situations?
- What is the worst **distraction** for you when you are tying to study?

PRETEACH
Comprehension

pp. 162–168 **Point of View** Tell students that point of view is the perspective from which a story is told. A story in first-person point of view is told by one of the characters and uses the pronouns *I, me,* and *we*. A story in third-person point of view is told by an outside observer or narrator. Third-person point of view uses the pronouns *he, she,* and *they*. Ask students to recall what they read in "After the Apple Fell." Then ask:

- **Who tells this story?** (an outside narrator)
- **What pronouns are used?** (he, she, they)
- **From which point of view is this story told?** (third-person)

Explain that in third-person limited point of view, the reader knows what only one character in the story knows or thinks. Third-person omniscient point of view lets the reader find out what everyone in the story knows and thinks. Ask students:

- **Whose thoughts do we know while reading "After the Apple Fell"?** (only Newton's)
- **Is this story told from third-person limited or third-person omniscient point of view?** (third-person limited)

PRETEACH
Decoding/Word Attack

Decode Longer Words   Write the word *impartial* on the board and have a volunteer read the word aloud. Model counting the syllables and identifying where the word should be divided. (3, im/par/tial) Have students identify the prefix. (im-) Then have students identify the root word. (partial) Tell students to divide words with a prefix immediately after the prefix so that the prefix forms the first syllable. Repeat the procedure with the words *inaudible, indigestion,* and *immobile.*

PRETEACH
Decoding/Spelling

Words with Prefixes *im-, in-, ir-, il-*   Tell students that a prefix is a word part added to the beginning of a word. It sometimes changes the meaning of the word. Write the words below on the board and read them aloud. Then add prefixes to form the words in parentheses. Have a volunteer read aloud each new word.

ability (inability)	mobile (immobile)	responsible (irresponsible)	secure (insecure)

Explain that these are some of the next lesson's Spelling Words. Help students notice that when you add the prefix *im-, in-, ir,* or *il-,* you do not change the root word, so you often end up with double letters (especially *mm* and *rr*) in words with these prefixes.

PRETEACH
Grammar/Writing

Verbs and Verb Phrases   Write the following sentence and read it aloud:

> Alec lifted the glass.

Remind students that verbs show an action or a state of being. Have a volunteer underline the verb. (lifted) Then write this sentence on the board:

> Gil is sleeping on the couch.

Ask: **What words tell about action in this sentence?** (is sleeping) Underline *is sleeping.* The verb phrase is a combination of a helping verb and a main verb. In this sentence, *is* is the helping verb and *sleeping* is the main verb.

VOCABULARY
Student-Friendly Explanations

publicize   When you publicize something, you make it widely known to the public.

contortions   When you put something through contortions, you twist it into unnatural shapes.

grimy   Something that is grimy is covered with dirt or soot.

testimony   When you give testimony, you give proof in support of a fact.

faint   When something is faint, it is not noticeable or intense.

foresight   People who have foresight are able to envision possible problems in the future.

distraction   A distraction takes your attention away from what you are trying to do.

Fluency

pp. 162–168   **Fluency Performance** Invite students to read aloud the passages from "After the Apple Fell" that they selected and practiced earlier. Note the number of words each student reads correctly and incorrectly. Have students rate their own oral reading on the 1–4 scale. Allow students to continue practicing and then to read the passage to you again.

DAY AT A GLANCE

Day 1

VOCABULARY
Reteach *publicize, contortions, grimy, testimony, faint, foresight, distraction*

COMPREHENSION
 Reteach Point of View

DECODING/SPELLING
Reteach Words with Prefixes *im-, in-, ir-, il-*

GRAMMAR/WRITING
Preteach Main Verbs and Helping Verbs

FLUENCY
Fluency Practice

Materials Needed: *Bold Moves*

Student Edition pp. 170–171 | Practice Book p. 67 | Skill Card 17 | Copying Master 66

Vocabulary

pp. 170–171 **Lesson 17 Vocabulary** Read aloud the Vocabulary Words and the Student-Friendly Explanations. Then have students read the diary and fill in the blanks on pages 170–171 of their books. Have a volunteer read each paragraph aloud, adding the word they inserted. If students are unable to give reasonable responses, refer to the Student-Friendly Explanations. (Answers for pages 170–171: 2. *faint*, 3. *distraction*, 4. *contortions*, 5. *testimony*, 6. *grimy*, 7. *foresight*)

Comprehension

Skill Card 17 **Point of View** Have students look at side A of *Skill Card 17: Point of View*. Have a student read the definitions at the top. Then have another volunteer read the passage aloud as students follow along. Point to the chart. Ask these questions and guide students to answer using information from the middle column of the chart:

- **What pronouns are used in this story?**
- **Who tells the story?**
- **Whose thoughts do we know from reading this story?**

GUIDED PRACTICE Now have students look at side B of *Skill Card 17: Point of View*. Read the Skill Reminder information aloud. Then have a student read the story aloud while others follow along. Guide students in copying the chart and completing it to determine the point of view. (Pronouns: he, they, them; Told by: an outside narrator; Whose thoughts I know: both Matt's and Marco's; Point of View: third-person omniscient)

Decoding/Spelling

Words with Prefixes *im-, in-, ir-, il-* Distribute *Copying Master 66*. Model reading the Spelling Words aloud and have students repeat them. Review the instructions about prefixes, and then have students complete the following activity based on the traditional Memory Game. Pairs of students make two sets of game cards using the lesson's Spelling Words, but with the prefixes missing; a dash appears in place of each prefix. After a student matches two cards, he or she must supply the correct prefix to keep the game cards. If the wrong prefix is supplied, the opponent gets the game cards and the next turn.

Grammar/Writing

Main Verbs and Helping Verbs Remind students that a verb phrase is made up of a helping verb and a main verb. Write the following sentence on the board:

> Aiesha is walking to school.

Ask a volunteer to read the sentence aloud. Then ask: **What is the verb phrase in this sentence?** (is walking) Underline *is walking*. **Which is the main verb?** (walking) Circle *walking*. **Which is the helping verb?** (is) Place a second underline under the word *is*. Tell students that they can find verb phrases in statements and questions. Write the following question on the board:

> Is Aiesha playing tennis today?

Tell students that one way to find the verb phrase in a question is to turn it into a statement. Write the following statement on the board:

> Aiesha is playing tennis today.

Ask a volunteer to underline the verb phrase in the statement. (is playing) Ask students: **What is the verb phrase in the question?** (is playing) Underline *is* and *playing* in the question.

VOCABULARY
Student-Friendly Explanations

publicize When you publicize something, you make it widely known to the public.

contortions When you put something through contortions, you twist it into unnatural shapes.

grimy Something that is grimy is covered with dirt or soot.

testimony When you give testimony, you give proof in support of a fact.

faint When something is faint, it is not noticeable or intense.

foresight People who have foresight are able to envision possible problems in the future.

distraction A distraction takes your attention away from what you are trying to do.

Fluency

Fluency Practice Have students turn to *Practice Book* page 67. Read the words in the first column aloud. Invite students to track each word and repeat the words after you. Then have students work in pairs to read the words in the first column aloud to each other. Follow the same procedure with each of the remaining columns. After partners have practiced reading aloud the words in each column, have them practice reading all of the words.

VOCABULARY
Reteach *publicize, contortions, grimy, testimony, faint, foresight, distraction*

COMPREHENSION
"The Three Little Kids"
Build Background
Monitor Comprehension
Answers to *Think Critically* **Questions**

DECODING/SPELLING
Reteach Words with Prefixes *im-, in-, ir-, il-*

GRAMMAR/WRITING
Preteach Main Verb or Helping Verb?

FLUENCY
Fluency Practice

Materials Needed: *Bold Moves*

| Student Edition pp. 172–179 | Practice Book pp. 67, 68 | Copying Masters 65, 66 |

Vocabulary

Copying Master 65

Lesson 17 Vocabulary Distribute a set of Vocabulary Word Cards to each pair of students. One holds up a card, and the other uses the word in a sentence. If the student uses the word correctly, he or she keeps the card. When the student has earned all the cards, the students trade jobs and repeat the process.

Comprehension

Build Background: "The Three Little Kids"
Ask students to share experiences they have had with skits or school plays. Have they watched plays at school? Did they act in a play or help with one? If so, what were the challenges and rewards of putting on a play?

pp. 172–173

Monitor Comprehension: "The Three Little Kids"
Read the title of the story aloud. Then have students read pages 172–173 to find the goal of the main characters and what problem they face.

Discuss the Stop and Think question on page 172: **What makes the drama contest so difficult to win?** (The contest is so difficult to win because the young judges are hard to please.) Guide students in writing the answer to this question. **DRAW CONCLUSIONS**

Ask: **What determines whether a play is a hit or a flop?** (the looks on the kids' faces) **NOTE DETAILS**

Discuss the Stop and Think question on page 173: **What problem do the characters face?** (Possible response: The problem is that the kids need to find a way to win the drama contest.) Guide students in writing the answer to the question. **CONFLICT/RESOLUTION**

Ask: **What is Tina's idea?** (to have little kids participate in the play) **What reason does she give to support her idea?** (Maybe having kids in the play will cause the critics to relax.) **CONFLICT/RESOLUTION**

pp. 174–175

Discuss the Stop and Think question on page 174: **What point of view does the author use in this story? How do you know?** (Possible response: The author uses third-person limited point of view. We know only what Lin is thinking.) Guide students in writing the answer to this question. **POINT OF VIEW**

Read aloud the second paragraph on page 174. Model a strategy for interpreting figurative language.

THINK ALOUD **What does Paul mean when he says, "I think it sounds nuts"? I don't think that Lin's question really made a sound like a bunch of nuts rolling around. I think this must be figurative language, where the words mean something other than what they seem to say. I know people sometimes use the word *nuts* to mean "wild" or "a little crazy." If I try one of those meanings here, it might work. Yes. "I think it sounds a little crazy," works in this story. I think that must be what the writer means.** FIGURATIVE LANGUAGE

Ask: **What plan do the sixth-graders come up with?** (Tina is to narrate, Paul will direct, and Dawn and Lin will whisper the kids' lines.) SUMMARIZE

Discuss the Stop and Think question on page 175: **How do you think the play will go? Why do you think so?** (Possible response: I think the play will be a flop because the little kids will goof around.) Guide students in writing the answer to this question. MAKE PREDICTIONS

 After reading the pages, discuss the Stop and Think question on page 176: **How would you describe Sarah Barnes?** (Possible response: Sarah Barnes is a serious or grumpy child.) Guide students in writing the answer to this question. CHARACTERS' TRAITS

Discuss the Stop and Think question on page 177: **What happens during the play? Summarize the events.** (Possible response: During the play, Lili is scared of the dark, Patrick acts like a dog, and Lili gets mad and spits crackers.) Guide students in writing the answer to this question. SUMMARIZE

Ask: **What would you be feeling if you were one of these sixth-graders?** (Possible response: I would be nervous.) IDENTIFY WITH CHARACTERS

 Discuss the Stop and Think question on page 178: **What does Dawn mean when she says they are "making history"?** (Possible response: Dawn means that this new strategy is a first in the history of the contest, and it's a successful one.) Guide students in writing the answer to this question. CONTEXT CLUES

Ask: **What is the result of the contest?** (Possible response: The audience loved the play; they won first prize.) DRAW CONCLUSIONS

Ask: **Do you think the students will put on another play? Explain.** (Possible response: Yes, this one was successful and fun, so they will want to do it again.) PERSONAL RESPONSE

pp. 176– 177

page 178

VOCABULARY

Student-Friendly Explanations

publicize When you publicize something, you make it widely known to the public.

contortions When you put something through contortions, you twist it into unnatural shapes.

grimy Something that is grimy is covered with dirt or soot.

testimony When you give testimony, you give proof in support of a fact.

faint When something is faint, it is not noticeable or intense.

foresight People who have foresight are able to envision possible problems in the future.

distraction A distraction takes your attention away from what you are trying to do.

Spelling Words: Lesson 17

1. inability	11. insecure
2. inaccessible	12. irresponsible
3. inadequate	13. immobile
4. inadmissible	14. immovable
5. inappropriate	15. impartial
6. inattentive	16. impassive
7. impress	17. ineffective
8. inaudible	18. illogical
9. indigestion	19. illuminate
10. irrational	20. improper

page 179 **Answers to *Think Critically* Questions** Help students read and answer the *Think Critically* questions on page 179. Possible responses are provided.

1. The kids win the drama contest. **Conflict/Resolution**
2. If the audience had not laughed, the kids would not have won the contest. **Plot**
3. The author makes me smile by describing funny events. **Author's Purpose**

RETEACH

Decoding/Spelling

Copying Master 66 **Words with Prefixes *im-, in-, ir-, il-*** Tell students that adding a prefix changes the meaning of a root word. The prefixes *im-, in-, ir-,* and *il-* all mean "not" or "unable to." Write the following on the board:

> adequate: good enough
>
> in + adequate = inadequate: not good enough

Help students see that adding the prefix changed the meaning of the root word. Ask: **How did adding *in-* change the meaning of *adequate*?** (It added not.) Have students take turns choosing a Spelling Word from *Copying Master 66* and writing it on the board. Have the student underline the root word and tell the meaning of it, then circle the prefix and tell how it changed the meaning of the root word.

Grammar/Writing

Practice Book 68

Main Verb or Helping Verb?   Write the following sentence on the board:

> The actors practice their lines for the play.

Underline *practice* and remind students that a verb shows action or a state of being. Then write these sentences on the board:

> Have you learned all of your lines?

Help students recall that a verb phrase includes a main verb and one or more helping verbs. Point out that a verb phrase can be in a question or a sentence. Have volunteers identify the main verb and helping verb in each sentence. Then write the following sentences on the board:

> He has a lot of lines to learn. His friend has helped him.

Explain that forms of *have* and *do* can be either helping verbs or main verbs. Point to the word *has* in the first sentence and point out that it is the main verb. Then point to *has* in the second sentence and explain that it is the helping verb in that sentence. Then write the following sentences on the board:

> I did wash the dog.
> I did all my homework.

Guide students' to understand that *did* is a helping verb in the first sentence, and a main verb in the second sentence.

GUIDED PRACTICE   Direct students' attention to *Practice Book* page 68. Have a volunteer read aloud the directions. Remind students that some sentences will have only a verb and others will have a verb phrase. Some of the sentences include forms of *have* and *do*—either as main verbs or as helping verbs. Have students work in pairs to identify the verb or verb phrase and then the helping verb in each sentence.

Fluency

Practice Book 67   **Fluency Practice**   Invite students to look at the bottom half of *Practice Book* page 67. These sentences have been broken into natural phrases. Tell students to repeat each phrase after you, mirroring your expression, phrasing, and pace. After students have repeated each sentence, invite them to practice reading the sentences to a partner.

DAY AT A GLANCE
Day 3

30+ Minutes

COMPREHENSION
Preteach Figurative Language

Reread and Summarize "The Three Little Kids"

DECODING/SPELLING
Reteach Words with Prefixes *im-, in-, ir-, il-*

BUILD ROBUST VOCABULARY
Teach Words from "The Three Little Kids"

GRAMMAR/WRITING
Reteach Writing Trait: Voice

FLUENCY
Fluency Practice

Materials Needed: *Bold Moves*

Student Edition pp. 172–178

Practice Book pp. 67, 69

Copying Master 67

PRETEACH
Comprehension

Figurative Language   Distribute *Copying Master* 67. Have students listen as a volunteer reads the information at the top of the page. Have a student read the passage aloud as students follow along. Then, guide students to fill in the first row of blanks in the chart, finding the simile in the passage and interpreting it. Discuss how the interpretation of figurative language is different from the actual words used.

GUIDED PRACTICE   Have students work in pairs to complete the rest of the chart. Allow time for pairs to share their responses with others.

Reread and Summarize   Have students reread and summarize "The Three Little Kids" in sections, as described below.

pp. 172–173

Let's reread pages 172–173 to remember the goal of the main characters and the problem they face.
Summary: The sixth-graders' goal is to win the drama contest, but they know the audience is hard to please. Tina has the idea to use little kids as actors.

pp. 174–175

Let's reread pages 174–175 to recall how things go when the kids first start working on the play.
Summary: Lin worries, but Paul says they can handle the toddlers. The first rehearsal is a disaster, but things get better. They publicize the play.

pp. 176–178

Let's reread pages 176–178 to find out what happened on the day of the play.
Summary: Lin worries about the difficult audience. One pig actor decides to be a dog, and another sprays cracker crumbs all over Paul. The audience laughs. They all celebrate their success at the diner.

RETEACH
Decoding/Spelling

Words with Prefixes *im-, in-, ir-, il-* Write the following items on the board:

__itate	__attentive	__ritate	__logical
__proper	__terest	__responsible	__luminate

Ask students which items are still real words without their prefixes. (inattentive/attentive, illogical/logical, improper/proper, irresponsible/responsible) Guide students to use a dictionary if they are not sure whether the remaining letters make a real word or not.

Build Robust Vocabulary

page 172 **Words from "The Three Little Kids"** Have students locate the word *light-hearted* on page 172 of "The Three Little Kids." Ask a volunteer to read aloud the sentence in which this word appears. (Line 6: *At first, the contest was a light-hearted one, with people acting out different folktales for the children's enjoyment.*) Explain that this sentence means that the contests were cheerful and just for fun. Continue by asking students to locate and read aloud the sentence in which the word *flop* appears on page 172. (Last sentence: *If they yawned, it was a flop.*) Explain that this sentence means that the play would not be a success if the audience was bored.

Have students complete the thought as you say the following sentences:

- **I would not like to participate in a flop because ___.**
- **I would feel light-hearted if someone asked me to participate in an ice cream eating contest because ___.**

Grammar/Writing

Practice Book 69 **Writing Trait: Voice** Have students turn to *Practice Book* page 69. Discuss the information in the graphic organizer. Recall how the author of "The Three Little Kids" chose words and language to make readers feel as if they were right there in the action. Then read the directions aloud. Have a volunteer read the example sentence. Point out how the underlined phrases help readers feel and see what it might be like to see something amazing or unexpected.

GUIDED PRACTICE Work with students to complete Part A. Then direct students to complete Parts B and C on their own.

Fluency

Practice Book 67 **Fluency Practice** Tell students that today they will reread the sentences on the bottom of *Practice Book* page 67. Have students locate and point to the first sentence. Tell students that everyone is going to read the sentence together. This choral reading will give students an opportunity to hear others and to listen to the natural phrasing of the sentences. Choral-read each of the sentences several times.

30+ Minutes

COMPREHENSION
Reteach Figurative Language

DECODING/SPELLING
Reteach Words with Prefixes *im-*, *in-*, *ir-*, *il-*

BUILD ROBUST VOCABULARY
Reteach Words from "The Three Little Kids"

GRAMMAR/WRITING
Reteach Writing Form: Autobiographical Narrative

FLUENCY
Fluency Practice

Materials Needed: *Bold Moves*

   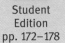

Student Edition pp. 172–178

Practice Book p. 70

Copying Master 68

Spelling Words: Lesson 17

1. inability	11. insecure
2. inaccessible	12. irresponsible
3. inadequate	13. immobile
4. inadmissible	14. immovable
5. inappropriate	15. impartial
6. inattentive	16. impassive
7. impress	17. ineffective
8. inaudible	18. illogical
9. indigestion	19. illuminate
10. irrational	20. improper

Figurative Language   Remind students that figurative language may include the following:

- **Simile:** comparison of two things using *like* or *as*
- **Metaphor:** comparison of two things without using *like* or *as*
- **Personification:** when the writer gives human qualities to things that are not human.

Write the following sentences on the board:

> The trees bowed down to please the wind.
>
> The snow sparkled in the sun, a blanket of gleaming points.

Have a volunteer read each sentence aloud and tell which type of figurative language is used. (personification; metaphor)

GUIDED PRACTICE   Write the following sentences on the board:

> The rocking chair, groaning, carried Granny's body to and fro.
>
> The smell of her perfume hit me like a wall of water.
>
> His face was a puzzle as he struggled through the test.

Have students work in pairs to identify the figurative language in each sentence. Ask volunteers to explain the image created by the figurative language. (personification; simile; metaphor)

Words with Prefixes *im-*, *in-*, *ir-*, *il-*   Have students number a sheet of paper 1–16. Write the Spelling Word *inability* on the board and point to the prefix. Tell students that the first nine words you dictate will have the prefix *in-*. After students write each word, display it so they can proofread their work. Continue with the remaining words, using these examples: *immobile* (five words), *illuminate* (one word), and *irrational* (one word).

Practice Book **70**

1. inaccessible	2. inadequate	3. inadmissible	4. inappropriate
5. inattentive	6. inaudible	7. indigestion	8. insecure
9. ineffective	10. impress	11. immovable	12. improper
13. impartial	14. impassive	15. illogical	16. irresponsible

Have students turn to *Practice Book* page 70. Have a volunteer read the passage aloud. Direct students to circle the words that begin with the prefixes *im-*, *in-*, *ir-*, and *il-*. Then have students complete the sentences, either independently or as a group. If students have difficulty, encourage them to revisit the passage.

RETEACH

Build Robust Vocabulary

Words from "The Three Little Kids" Review the meanings of the words *light-hearted* and *flop*. Then say these sentences and ask which word describes each sentence. Have students explain why.

- **On the first day of summer vacation, Nat felt cheerful.** (light-hearted)
- **The idea of making a raft out of cardboard was not a success.** (flop)

RETEACH

Grammar/Writing

Copying Master 68

Writing Form: Autobiographical Narrative Remind students that an autobiographical narrative is something written about an event that actually happened to the author. Autobiographical writing is always done in the first-person point of view. Distribute *Copying Master 68*. Have a volunteer read the information at the top of the page, and then the Student Model. Then go over the notes in the margin together. Write this sentence from the narrative on the board:

> I didn't want to do that.

Model for students how the sentence could be improved.

> No thanks. or I had no desire to go in either direction.

GUIDED PRACTICE Invite a volunteer to read the first numbered item aloud. Help students understand that *Here is the story of how I learned to ride,* tells what the narrative is about. Then have students work through the remaining exercises.

Fluency

pp. 172–178

Fluency Practice Have each student work with a partner to read passages from "The Three Little Kids" aloud to each other. Students may select a passage that they enjoyed or choose one of the following options:

- Read page 175. (Total: 125 words)
- Read page 176. (Total: 99 words)

Encourage students to read the selected passage aloud to their partner three times. Have the student rate his or her reading on the 1–4 scale.

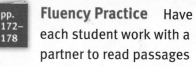

1	Need more practice
2	Pretty good
3	Good
4	Great!

VOCABULARY

Preteach *beacon, disturbances, coincidentally, enthralled, clamor, persisted, objections, marvel*

COMPREHENSION

 Preteach Make Judgments

DECODING/WORD ATTACK

Preteach Decode Longer Words

DECODING/SPELLING

Preteach Words with Suffixes *-ant, -ent, -ist*

GRAMMAR/WRITING

Preteach Action Verbs and Objects

FLUENCY

Fluency Performance

Materials Needed: *Bold Moves*

Student Edition pp. 172–178

Copying Master 69

PRETEACH

Vocabulary

Copying Master 69

Lesson 18 Vocabulary Distribute a set of Vocabulary Word Cards to each student or pair of students. Hold up the card for the first word, and ask a volunteer to read it aloud. Have students repeat the word and hold up the matching card. Give the explanation for the word. Then ask students the first question below and discuss their responses. Continue for each Vocabulary Word.

- **When was the last time you saw a beacon? Describe it.**
- **What kinds of disturbances do you cope with when you are doing homework?**
- **What has happened coincidentally that surprised you?**
- **What kinds of books have enthralled you?**
- **What kinds of events raise a clamor in your school or town?**
- **When have you persisted at a difficult task?**
- **What kinds of objections do students raise about homework?**
- **What kinds of things have made you marvel recently?**

PRETEACH

Comprehension

pp. 172–178

Make Judgments Explain that readers must often make assertions, or judgments, based on what they read. Readers must read carefully to decide whether evidence from the writer supports their assertions. Have students think back to "The Three Little Kids." Then ask:

- **What claim might we make about the play?** (It was successful.)
- **What evidence supports this assertion?** (The audience laughed. The parents of the actors were happy. The young actor, Patrick, liked Paul so much he crawled in his lap. The kids putting on the show were happy at the end.)

Explain that readers should also look for evidence that contradicts, or goes against, their assertions. Ask:

- **What evidence goes *against* our assertion?** (The rehearsals were a disaster at first.)
- **Should we change our judgment?** (No, the evidence from the performance confirms that the play was successful.)

Decoding/Word Attack

Decode Longer Words   Write *defendant, dependent,* and *panelist* on the board. Ask volunteers to read each word aloud and identify the suffix in each word. (-ant, -ent, -ist) Then, separate the suffixes from the words to find the roots. (defend, depend, panel) Guide students to divide the roots into syllables. (de/fend, de/pend, pan/el) Finally, blend all the syllables, including the suffixes.

Decoding/Spelling

Words with Suffixes *-ant, -ent, -ist*   Remind students that suffixes are added to the ends of words and that sometimes the spelling of a root word is changed when the suffix is added. Write the suffixes *-ant, -ent,* and *-ist* on the board. The write *contestant, cartoonist, confident,* and *significant* on the board. Have a volunteer underline the suffix in each word. Read each word aloud and have students repeat. Explain that students must memorize when to use *-ant* or *-ent* because these two suffixes sound alike and it is hard to know the spelling from the sound of the word.

Grammar/Writing

Action Verbs and Objects   Write the following sentence and read it aloud:

> Heather opened the door for Alissa.

Tell students that the action verb, *opened,* tells what the subject of the sentence, *Heather,* did. Action verbs work with objects, which can be direct or indirect. A direct object is the noun affected by the action. *Door* is the direct object affected by the action, *opened.* Have a student underline the action verb and circle the direct object. Tell students that an indirect object tells who or what the action is done to or for. The door is opened for Alissa; *Alissa* is the indirect object. Have a student box the indirect object. (Alissa) Erase the verb and objects in the sentence on the board and ask students to suggest other words that can work in their places. (Possible responses: Heather (baked, wrote, built) the (brownies, poem, birdhouse) for (Maggie, Aiden, Mom).

VOCABULARY
Student-Friendly Explanations

beacon   A light or fire that acts as a signal or warning is a beacon.

disturbances   Disturbances are things that disrupt or interfere with something else.

coincidentally   When two things happen coincidentally, they happen by accident at the same time, but they seem to be connected.

enthralled   When you are enthralled by something, it is completely holding your interest or attention.

clamor   When there is a clamor for something, people are asking for it noisily or angrily.

persisted   When you have continued a task for a long time even though it is difficult, you have persisted.

objections   When you make objections to something, you give reasons why you do not like or agree with it.

marvel   When you marvel at something, you feel intense surprise or amazement at it.

Fluency

Fluency Performance   pp. 172–178   Invite students to read aloud the passages from "The Three Little Kids" that they selected and practiced earlier. Note the number of words each student reads correctly and incorrectly. Have students rate their own oral reading on the 1–4 scale. Give students the opportunity to continue practicing and then to read the passage to you again.

DAY AT A GLANCE

Day 1

LESSON 18

The Big Wheel that Could

VOCABULARY

Reteach *beacon, disturbances, coincidentally, enthralled, clamor, persisted, objections, marvel*

COMPREHENSION

 Reteach Make Judgments

DECODING/SPELLING

Reteach Words with Suffixes *-ant, -ent, -ist*

GRAMMAR/WRITING

Preteach Linking Verbs and Predicates

FLUENCY

Fluency Practice

Materials Needed: *Bold Moves*

Student Edition pp. 180–181	Practice Book p. 71	Skill Card 18	Copying Master 70

Vocabulary

Lesson 18 Vocabulary Read aloud the Vocabulary Words and the Student-Friendly Explanations. The have students turn to pages 180–181 of their books. Have a volunteer read the articles aloud as students follow along. Guide students in completing the blanks in the story by selecting the correct word from the word list. Have a volunteer read each completed sentence aloud. Then have students read the completed story along with you. If students are unable to give reasonable responses, refer to the Student-Friendly Explanations. (Answers for pages 180–181: 2. *enthralled*, 3. *beacon*, 4. *persisted*, 5. *marvel*, 6. *coincidentally*, 7. *objections*, 8. *disturbance*)

pp. 180–181

Comprehension

Skill Card 18 **Make Judgments** Have students look at side A of *Skill Card 18: Make Judgments*. Have a student read aloud the introductory information. Then have another student read aloud the passage as others follow along. Point to the chart. Ask:

- **What is the assertion about this passage?**
- **What evidence supports this assertion?**
- **Does the passage include any evidence that contradicts this assertion?** (no)

GUIDED PRACTICE Now have students look at side B of *Skill Card 18: Make Judgments*. Have a volunteer read aloud the Skill Reminder. Then have students read the passage. Guide students in copying the chart and completing it with an assertion and evidence to support the assertion. (Possible assertion: Roller coaster designers need to know a lot of physics. Possible evidence: They need to know Newton's laws of motion. They need to understand gravity. They have to learn to match different forces.) Remind students they need to look for evidence against their judgments. One way to do this is to try making an opposite assertion. For example: Roller coaster designers do not need to know physics. Can students find evidence to support this assertion? (no) If not, their original assertion is likely to be accurate.

RETEACH

Decoding/Spelling

Copying Master 70

Words with Suffixes -ant, -ent, -ist Distribute *Copying Master 70*. Model reading the Spelling Words and have students repeat them. Review the instruction for adding these suffixes to words, and then have students complete the following activity. This activity is based on the traditional Memory Game. Pairs of students make two sets of game cards using the lesson's Spelling Words with the suffixes missing; a dash appears in place of each suffix. After a student matches two cards, he or she must supply the correct missing letters to keep the game cards. If the wrong letters are supplied, the opponent gets the game cards and the next turn.

PRETEACH

Grammar/Writing

Linking Verbs and Predicates Remind students that verbs are words that show action or a state of being. Write the following sentence on the board:

Peyton is a writer.

Tell students that the linking verb, *is*, links the subject, *Peyton*, to a predicate, a word that names or describes the subject. In this sentence, the predicate is *writer*. Have a volunteer underline the linking verb and circle the predicate. Then write the following two sentences on the board:

Yuri was the soloist.
Yuri felt confident.

Explain that there are two types of predicates. A predicate that names the subject is a predicate nominative. *Soloist* is a predicate nominative; it names the subject, *Yuri*. A predicate that describes the subject is a predicate adjective. *Confident* is a predicate adjective that describes Yuri. Have a volunteer underline the linking verbs (was, felt), circle the predicate nominative (soloist), and box the predicate adjective. (confident)

VOCABULARY

Student-Friendly Explanations

beacon A light or fire that acts as a signal or warning is a beacon.

disturbances Disturbances are things that disrupt or interfere with something else.

coincidentally When two things happen coincidentally, they happen by accident at the same time, but they seem to be connected.

enthralled When you are enthralled by something, it is completely holding your interest or attention.

clamor When there is a clamor for something, people are asking for it noisily or angrily.

persisted When you have continued a task for a long time even though it is difficult, you have persisted.

objections When you make objections to something, you give reasons why you do not like or agree with it.

marvel When you marvel at something, you feel intense surprise or amazement at it.

Fluency

Practice Book 71

Fluency Practice Have students turn to *Practice Book* page 71. Read the words in the first column aloud. Invite students to track each word and repeat the words after you. Then have students work in pairs to read the words in the first column aloud to each other. Follow the same procedure with each of the remaining columns. Then have partners practice reading all of the words.

LESSON 18

30+ Minutes

VOCABULARY
Reteach *beacon, disturbances, coincidentally, enthralled, clamor, persisted, objections, marvel*

COMPREHENSION
"The Big Wheel That Could"
Build Background
Monitor Comprehension
Answers to *Think Critically* **Questions**

DECODING/SPELLING
Reteach Words with Suffixes *-ant, -ent, -ist*

GRAMMAR/WRITING
Preteach Action Verb or Linking Verb?

FLUENCY
Fluency Practice

Materials Needed: *Bold Moves*

Student Edition pp. 182–189

Practice Book pp. 71, 72

Copying Masters 69, 70

Vocabulary

Copying Master 69

Lesson 18 Vocabulary Distribute a set of Vocabulary Word Cards to each student or pair of students. Read aloud the meaning of one of the Vocabulary Words, and have students display and read the matching card. Ask a volunteer to compose a sentence using the Vocabulary Word. Continue until students have matched all the words.

Comprehension

Build Background: "The Big Wheel That Could"
Invite students to share any experiences they have had with new inventions. Have they ever doubted something could work, and then been proved wrong? How did they feel after the experience?

pp. 182–183

Monitor Comprehension: "The Big Wheel That Could"
Read the title of the story aloud. Then have students read pages 182–183 to find out what George Ferris was planning to do and what problems he faced.

After reading the pages, ask: **What is George Ferris trying to do?** (He is trying to build a giant steel wheel that people can ride at the Chicago World's Fair.) Mᴀɪɴ Iᴅᴇᴀ ᴀɴᴅ Dᴇᴛᴀɪʟs

Discuss the Stop and Think question on page 182: **Why do some people think the wheel can't be made?** (Some people think it can't be made because it will be difficult to fit together all the steel pieces, especially if they are made in different factories.) Guide students in writing the answer to this question. Dʀᴀᴡ Cᴏɴᴄʟᴜsɪᴏɴs

Ask: **If people tell you something can't be done, do you keep trying to do it anyway?** (Possible response: Yes, I know what I can do.) **Do you think Ferris will persist in building his wheel? Why or why not?** (Yes, he knows more about building it than the people who say it can't be done.) Iᴅᴇɴᴛɪғʏ ᴡɪᴛʜ Cʜᴀʀᴀᴄᴛᴇʀs/Mᴀᴋᴇ Pʀᴇᴅɪᴄᴛɪᴏɴs

Discuss the Stop and Think question on page 183: **What is wrong with the ground at Jackson Park? How do the workers solve this problem?** (The ground is sandy. The workers drive wood posts deep into the ground and pour concrete around them.) Guide students in writing the answer to the question. Cᴏɴғʟɪᴄᴛ/Rᴇsᴏʟᴜᴛɪᴏɴ

pp. 184–185

Have students read page 184 to find out what else was worrying the builders of the Ferris wheel. Discuss the Stop and Think question on page 184: **Do you think the wheel will hold up? Explain your answer.** (Possible response: I think the wheel will hold up because it's made of steel.) Guide students in writing the answer to this question. **MAKE JUDGMENTS**

Read aloud the first sentence of the second paragraph on page 184. Model the strategy of combining information from the text with personal knowledge to make inferences.

(THINK ALOUD) **When I read this, I wondered why they put the boilers so far from the engines and built such long pipes. That seems like an awful lot of extra work. But then I saw that they were steam engines. I know steam is hot and can burn people. They probably put the boilers far away from the crowds to keep the fair visitors safe. MAKE INFERENCES**

Discuss the Stop and Think question on page 185: **How long does it take the wheel to make a full turn? Underline the words that tell you this.** (The wheel takes 20 minutes to make a full turn. Students should underline the last sentence on page 185.) Guide students in writing the answer to this question. **MAIN IDEA AND DETAILS**

pp. 186–187

Discuss the Stop and Think question on page 186: **Why does William Gronau feel that he can't refuse the trip?** (Possible response: He feels he can't refuse because he helped build the wheel. If he doesn't go, then everyone will think it is not safe.) Guide students in writing the answer to this question. **MAKE INFERENCES**

Ask: **What did the first ride and the first storm tell people about the wheel?** (Possible response: that the wheel was safe and very interesting to ride) **MAKE JUDGMENTS**

Discuss the Stop and Think question on page 187: **What do you think happens to the wheel after the storm?** (Possible responses: After the storm, the wheel continues to be a popular ride at the fair.) Guide students in writing the answer to this question. **MAKE PREDICTIONS**

page 188

Discuss the Stop and Think question on page 188: **How has Ferris's idea endured?** (Possible response: Ferris's idea has endured because the Ferris wheel is still a popular amusement ride.) Guide students in writing the answer to this question. **MAKE JUDGMENTS**

VOCABULARY

Student-Friendly Explanations

beacon A light or fire that acts as a signal or warning is a beacon.

disturbances Disturbances are things that disrupt or interfere with something else.

coincidentally When two things happen coincidentally, they happen by accident at the same time, but they seem to be connected.

enthralled When you are enthralled by something, it is completely holding your interest or attention.

clamor When there is a clamor for something, people are asking for it noisily or angrily.

persisted When you have continued a task for a long time even though it is difficult, you have persisted.

objections When you make objections to something, you give reasons why you do not like or agree with it.

marvel When you marvel at something, you feel intense surprise or amazement at it.

Spelling Words: Lesson 18

1. compliant	11. participant
2. contestant	12. scientist
3. immigrant	13. biologist
4. informant	14. columnist
5. inhabitant	15. medalist
6. significant	16. cartoonist
7. irritant	17. efficient
8. observant	18. pollutant
9. resident	19. obedient
10. panelist	20. confident

 page 189

Answers to *Think Critically* Questions   Help students read and answer the *Think Critically* questions on page 189. Then guide students in writing the answer to each question. Possible responses are provided.

1. George Ferris built the first Ferris wheel in Chicago in 1892. **Main Idea and Details**

2. I think he wanted to build it because he wanted to impress the people at the World's Fair. **Character**

3. I think he wants me to respect the hard work that went into building the first Ferris wheel. **Author's Purpose**

RETEACH

Decoding/Spelling

Copying Master 70

Words with Suffixes *-ant, -ent, -ist*   Write the suffixes *-ant, -ent,* and *-ist* on the board as headings for three columns. Have students look at *Copying Master 70* to find a Spelling Word that ends with the suffix *-ant*. Ask a volunteer to write the Spelling Word on the board under the *-ant* heading. Continue until students have listed all words with suffix *-ant*. (compliant, contestant, immigrant, informant, inhabitant, significant, irritant, observant, participant, pollutant) Follow the same procedure with the *-ent* and *-ist* words. (resident, efficient, obedient, confident; panelist, scientist, biologist, columnist, medalist, cartoonist)

Grammar/Writing

Practice Book 72

Action Verb or Linking Verb? Write the following sentence on the board:

> The driver delivered the pizza to Mr. White.

Guide students to identify the action verb. (delivered) Point out that a direct object is the person, place, or thing affected by the action. In this sentence, *pizza* is the direct object. An indirect object is who or what the action is done to or for. Help students understand that *Mr. White* is the indirect object.

Use the following sentence to guide students to understand linking verbs, predicate nominatives, and predicate adjectives:

> Naomi was the driver, and she was prompt.

Explain that a linking verb links the subject of the sentence to a predicate, a word that names or describes the subject. A predicate that names the subject is a predicate nominative. A predicate that describes the subject is a predicate adjective. In the example sentence, *was* and *was* are linking verbs, *driver* is a predicate nominative, and *prompt* is a predicate adjective.

GUIDED PRACTICE Direct students' attention to *Practice Book* page 72. Have a volunteer read aloud the directions, then complete the first sentence together. Have students work in pairs to complete the page as directed.

Fluency

Practice Book 71

Fluency Practice Invite students to look at the bottom half of *Practice Book* page 71. These sentences have been broken into natural phrases. Tell students to repeat each phrase after you, mirroring your expression, phrasing, and pace. After students have repeated each sentence, invite them to practice reading the sentences to a partner.

LESSON 18

DAY AT A GLANCE

Day 3

COMPREHENSION
Preteach Follow Multiple-Step Instructions

Reread and Summarize "The Big Wheel That Could"

DECODING/SPELLING
Reteach Words with Suffixes -*ant*, -*ent*, -*ist*

BUILD ROBUST VOCABULARY
Teach Words from "The Big Wheel That Could"

GRAMMAR/WRITING
Reteach Writing Trait: Sentence Fluency

FLUENCY
Fluency Practice

Materials Needed: *Bold Moves*

Student Edition pp. 182–188

Practice Book pp. 71, 73

Copying Master 71

30+ Minutes

Comprehension

 Follow Multiple-Step Instructions Distribute *Copying Master 71*, and have a volunteer read aloud the information at the top of the page. Then have a student read aloud the multiple-step instructions. Guide students as they fill in the first box on the chart, listing what students should do before building their models. Have students work in pairs or on their own to fill in the remaining boxes on the chart.

Reread and Summarize Have students reread and summarize "The Big Wheel That Could" in sections, as described below.

pp. 182–183 **Let's reread pages 182–183 to remember what George Ferris wanted to do and some of the problems he encountered.**
Summary: In 1892, George Ferris wanted to build a giant steel wheel for the Chicago's World's Fair. He had problems finding enough steel, and making sure the ground was stable.

pp. 184–185 **Now let's reread pages 184–185 to recall what happened when the wheel was finally built.**
Summary: Building the wheel was complicated. It took a year longer than planned. For such a large structure, it looked very delicate. It took 20 minutes for the huge wheel to make its first turn.

pp. 186–188 **Last, let's reread pages 186–188 to see how riders reacted to the wheel and what happened to it after the fair.**
Summary: Some riders were nervous, but many were eager to ride. After the wheel proved to be safe, lots of people rode. The wheel was moved after the fair and used until it was torn down.

Decoding/Spelling

Words with Suffixes -*ant*, -*ent*, -*ist* Remind students that, because the suffixes -*ant* and -*ent* usually make the same /uhnt/ sound, it can be difficult to know the correct spelling. Write the following word pairs on the board:

immigrant/ immigrent   inhabitent/ inhabitant   efficient/ efficiant

Have volunteers choose the correctly spelled word in each pair. (immigrant, inhabitant, efficient)

TEACH

Build Robust Vocabulary

pp. 183–187

Words from "The Big Wheel That Could" Have students locate *engineers* and *determined* on page 183 of "The Big Wheel That Could." Ask a volunteer to read aloud the sentence in which those words appear. (Line 1: *Engineers determined that the two towers that held the wheel, each 140 feet tall, should be strong and stable.*) Explain that this sentence means that people who are experts in planning buildings and machines decided that the towers needed to be strong. Then ask students to locate and read aloud the sentence in which the word *demolished* appears on page 187. (Last sentence: *Another ride was demolished, but the strong wind shook the wheel and its hundreds of riders just a little bit.*) Explain that this sentence means that one ride was blown down. *Demolish* means "to tear down or destroy."

Ask each student to choose a word and make up a sentence using it. Then have triads of students with different words share their sentences.

RETEACH

Grammar/Writing

Practice Book 73

Writing Trait: Sentence Fluency Have students turn to *Practice Book* page 73. Discuss the types of sentences described in the graphic organizer. Recall how the author of "The Big Wheel That Could" uses sentences of different lengths, structures, and purposes. Then, have a volunteer read the example sentence in Part A. Guide students to consider whether or not each of the options presented applies to the sentence. Is it short? (no) Is it an interrogative? (no) Is it a compound—a combination of two short sentences? (yes)

GUIDED PRACTICE Work with students to complete the rest of Part A. Then guide students to read aloud the sentence in Part B and choose words that describe its length, structure, and purpose. Finally, have students complete Part C with sentences of their own.

Fluency

Practice Book 71

Fluency Practice Tell students that today they will reread the sentences on the bottom of *Practice Book* page 71. Have students locate and point to the first sentence. Tell students that everyone is going to read the sentence together. This choral reading will give students an opportunity to hear others and to listen to the natural phrasing of the sentences. Choral-read each of the sentences several times.

COMPREHENSION
Reteach Follow Multiple-Step Instructions

DECODING/SPELLING
Reteach Words with Suffixes *-ant, -ent, -ist*

BUILD ROBUST VOCABULARY
Reteach Words from "The Big Wheel That Could"

GRAMMAR/WRITING
Reteach Writing Form: Letter of Request

FLUENCY
Fluency Practice

Materials Needed: *Bold Moves*

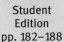

Student Edition pp. 182–188

Practice Book p. 74

Copying Master 72

Spelling Words: Lesson 18

1. compliant	11. participant
2. contestant	12. scientist
3. immigrant	13. biologist
4. informant	14. columnist
5. inhabitant	15. medalist
6. significant	16. cartoonist
7. irritant	17. efficient
8. observant	18. pollutant
9. resident	19. obedient
10. panelist	20. confident

RETEACH

Comprehension

Follow Multiple-Step Instructions   Remind students to do all of the following when they follow multiple-step instructions:

- **Read all instructions before you begin.**
- **Understand all the steps.**
- **Gather all the materials you need before you begin.**
- **Follow the steps in order.**
- **Do not skip any steps.**

Write the following instructions on the board: *Draw a circle on a piece of paper. Put two dots inside the upper half of the circle, and, finally, draw a curving line below the two dots.*

Ask students:

- **What is the first thing you should do with these instructions?** (Read them all.)
- **What materials do you need to follow these instructions?** (paper and a writing tool)

RETEACH

Decoding/Spelling

Practice Book 74

Words with Suffixes *-ant, -ent, -ist*   Have students number a sheet of paper 1–17. Write *compliant* on the board and tell students that the suffix *-ant* is at the end of the first nine words you will dictate. After students write each word, display it so they can proofread their work. Repeat this activity for the other suffixes using *resident* as an example for *-ent* (three words) and *panelist* as the example for *-ist* (five words).

1. contestant	2. immigrant	3. informant	4. inhabitant
5. significant	6. irritant	7. observant	8. participant
9. pollutant	10. efficient	11. obedient	12. confident
13. scientist	14. biologist	15. columnist	16. medalist
17. cartoonist			

Have students turn to *Practice Book* page 74. Have a student read aloud the passage. Then read the first sentence together. Invite the group to choose the word that correctly completes the sentence. If students have difficulty, encourage them to revisit the passage for the answer. Have students complete the remaining sentences.

RETEACH
Build Robust Vocabulary

Words from "The Big Wheel That Could" Review the meanings of the words *engineers, determined*, and *demolished*. Then say these sentences and ask which word each sentence describes. Have students explain why.

- **My aunt's job is to plan buildings and roads.** (engineer)
- **Luis decided for sure that he had all the materials he needed for his project.** (determined)
- **The city tore down the old library to make a bigger, better one.** (demolished)

RETEACH
Grammar/Writing

Copying Master 72

Writing Form: Letter of Request Distribute *Copying Master 72* and have a student read aloud the first paragraph. Then have volunteers read each paragraph in the body of the letter and the notes in the margin.

GUIDED PRACTICE Have students work independently or in pairs to complete the page. Allow time for students to share their answers with the group.

Fluency

pp. 182–188

Fluency Practice Have each student work with a partner to read passages from "The Big Wheel That Could" aloud to each other. Students may select a passage that they enjoyed or choose one of the following options:

- Read page 184. (Total: 119 words)
- Read page 186. (Total: 128 words)

Encourage students to read the selected passage aloud to their partner three times. Have the student rate his or her reading on the 1–4 scale.

1	Need more practice
2	Pretty good
3	Good
4	Great!

VOCABULARY
Preteach *eager, neglected, severe, beloved, demolished, humongous, abandoned*

COMPREHENSION
 Preteach Make Judgments

DECODING/WORD ATTACK
Preteach Decode Longer Words

DECODING/SPELLING
Preteach Word Parts *over, under, sub*

GRAMMAR/WRITING
Preteach Simple Tenses: Present Tense

FLUENCY
Fluency Performance

Materials Needed: *Bold Moves*

Student Edition pp. 182–188

Copying Master 73

Vocabulary

Copying Master 73

Lesson 19 Vocabulary Distribute a set of Vocabulary Word Cards to each student. Hold up the Word Card for the first Vocabulary Word and ask a volunteer to read the word aloud. Have students repeat the word and hold up the matching card. Give the explanation for the word. Then ask students the first question below and discuss their responses. Continue for each Vocabulary Word.

- **What are you most eager to do every morning?**
- **What activities get neglected when you have a lot of homework to do?**
- **Have you been in any severe storms?**
- **What is your most beloved possession?**
- **Can you think of a building that should be demolished? What is it?**
- **What is the most humongous animal you've ever seen in person?**
- **Are there any abandoned buildings near where you live?**

Comprehension

pp. 182–188

Make Judgments Explain that readers often make assertions, or judgments, based on what they read. Readers must read carefully to decide whether evidence from the writer supports their assertions. Have students think back to "The Big Wheel That Could." Then ask:

- **What assertion can we make about the success of the Ferris wheel?** (The Ferris wheel was very successful.)

- **What evidence supports this assertion?** (People lined up to ride it again and again. Instead of being torn down after the fair, it was moved. People still ride Ferris wheels today.)

Explain that readers should also look for evidence that contradicts, or goes against, their assertions. Ask:

- **Is there any evidence *against* our assertion?** (It was hard to build the first Ferris wheel. Some people were very nervous about riding it.)

- **Should we change our judgment?** (No. After the wheel was built and proved to be safe, it became very popular and successful.)

GUIDED PRACTICE Ask students what other judgments they can make about building the first Ferris wheel. Have partners look for evidence that supports or contradicts the assertion, and change the assertion if their original one is not supported. Allow pairs time to share their assertions and evidence.

PRETEACH

Decoding/Word Attack

Decode Longer Words Remind students they can use familiar word parts, such as prefixes, to help them decode longer words. Tell students to separate the prefix from the root, and try pronouncing the root. Write *overhaul* on the board. Ask students to identify the prefix in the word. (over) Then have them identify the root word they see. (haul) Then ask students how many syllables there are in *overhaul* and where it should be divided. (3; o/ver/haul) Guide students to decode each syllable and then blend them to read the word. Repeat the procedure with the words *submarine* and *undersea*.

PRETEACH

Decoding/Spelling

Word Parts *over, under, sub* Remind students that a word part can be added to the beginning of word. It sometimes changes the meaning of the word. Write *over, under* and *sub* on the board. Then write *power, take, title, confident, rated*, and *standard* on the board and read them aloud. Then add the word parts to form Spelling Words. Help students notice that they do not need to change the root word when they add these word parts, so they may sometimes end up with double letters, as in *underrated*.

PRETEACH

Grammar/Writing

Simple Tenses: Present Tense Write the following sentence on the board:

> Darla carries a backpack.

Read the sentence aloud. Tell students that a verb tense tells the reader when an action takes place. Verbs in the present tense show that the action is happening right now. Have a volunteer underline the verb in this sentence. (carries) This verb tells us that Darla is carrying the backpack right now. Erase the verb and ask students to help you think of some other present tense verbs that work in this sentence. (Possible responses: hauls, has, wants)

Student-Friendly Explanations

eager When you are eager to do something, you are enthusiastic and very interested about it.

neglected When something has not been given proper care or attention, it has been neglected.

severe If something is very serious, very harsh, or very strict, it is severe.

beloved You feel great love and affection for someone or something that is beloved.

demolished When a building has been torn or knocked down, it has been demolished, usually because it is old and dangerous.

humongous Something that is extremely large in size or amount is humongous.

abandoned Buildings that have been abandoned have been left vacant and uncared for.

Fluency

pp. 182–188 **Fluency Performance** Invite students to read aloud the passages from "The Big Wheel That Could" that they selected and practiced earlier. Note the number of words each student reads correctly and incorrectly. Have students rate their own oral reading on the 1–4 scale. Give students the opportunity to continue practicing and then to read the passage to you again.

LESSON 19

VOCABULARY

Reteach *eager, neglected, severe, beloved, demolished, humongous, abandoned*

COMPREHENSION

 Reteach Make Judgments

DECODING/SPELLING

Reteach Word Parts *over, under, sub*

GRAMMAR/WRITING

Preteach Subject-Verb Agreement

FLUENCY

Fluency Practice

Materials Needed: *Bold Moves*

Student Edition pp. 190–191	Practice Book p. 75	Skill Card 19	Copying Master 74

RETEACH

Vocabulary

pp. 190–191

Lesson 19 Vocabulary Read aloud the Vocabulary Words and the Student-Friendly Explanations. Then have students turn to the selection on page 190 of their books. Have volunteers read the selection aloud as other students follow along. Guide students as they answer the questions on page 191. Invite volunteers to read their answers aloud. If students are unable to give reasonable responses, refer to the Student-Friendly Explanations. (Possible responses for page 191: 2. They are very heavy; a lot of rain falls in a short time. 3. The logging companies were eager to cut down the redwood forests. 4. It is cut down for lumber. 5. It means the person did not take care of or attend to the duty. 6. It is the "beloved redwood" because it is much loved. 7. Julia stayed in the tree; she did not leave it.)

RETEACH

Comprehension

 Skill Card 19

Make Judgments Have students look at side A of *Skill Card 19: Make Judgments*. Have a student read the definitions in the first paragraph. Then have a volunteer read aloud the passage as students follow along. Point to the chart. Ask:

- **What assertion has been made based on this passage?**

- **What evidence supports this assertion?**

- **Does the passage include any evidence that contradicts this assertion?** (no)

GUIDED PRACTICE Now have students look at side B of *Skill Card 19: Make Judgments*. Have a volunteer read aloud the Skill Reminder. Then have a student read aloud the passage while others follow along. Guide students in copying the chart and completing it with an assertion and evidence to support their judgment. (Possible assertion: There are many ways to remember your travels. Evidence: Some travelers keep journals. Many travelers remember through pictures. A few travelers create collections.) Remind students that they need to look for evidence against their judgments. Remind them that one way to do this is to try making an opposite assertion.

Decoding/Spelling

Copying Master 74

Word Parts *over, under, sub* Distribute *Copying Master 74.* Model reading the Spelling Words and have students repeat them. Review the instruction for adding these word parts to words, and then have students complete the following activity: This activity is based on the traditional Memory Game. Pairs of students make two sets of game cards using the lesson's Spelling Words with the prefixes missing; a dash appears in place of each prefix. After a student matches two cards, he or she must supply the correct prefix to keep the game cards. If the wrong letters are supplied, the opponent gets the game cards and the next turn.

Grammar/Writing

Subject-Verb Agreement Remind students that the verb tense tells readers when the action takes place, and that verbs in the present tense show action taking place right now. Then write the following two sentences on the board:

> Kelly walks down the street.
> They walk down the street.

Explain that verbs must agree with their subjects. A singular subject needs a singular verb, and plural subjects need plural verbs. Ask volunteers to circle the subject of each sentence and tell whether the subject is singular or plural. (Kelly, singular; They, plural) Have a volunteer underline the verb in each sentence. (walks, walk) Discuss why each verb is singular or plural, and why each matches its subject.

Erase the verb in each sentence and ask students to suggest other present-tense words that can work in place of these verbs. (Possible responses: Kelly (looks, runs, saunters, strolls, drives) down the street. They (look, run, saunter, stroll, drive) down the street.) Write students' suggestions and have volunteers read aloud the new sentences.

GUIDED PRACTICE Have students work in pairs to underline the verb in each sentence and decide whether it is singular or plural. Invite students to take turns explaining their choices.

Student-Friendly Explanations

eager When you are eager to do something, you are enthusiastic and very interested about it.

neglected When something has not been given proper care or attention, it has been neglected.

severe If something is very serious, very harsh, or very strict, it is severe.

beloved You feel great love and affection for someone or something that is beloved.

demolished When a building has been torn or knocked down, it has been demolished, usually because it is old and dangerous.

humongous Something that is extremely large in size or amount is humongous.

abandoned Buildings that have been abandoned have been left vacant and uncared for.

Fluency

Practice Book 75

Fluency Practice Have students turn to *Practice Book* page 75. Read the words in the first column aloud. Invite students to track each word and repeat the words after you. Then have students work in pairs to read the words in the first column aloud to each other. Follow the same procedure with each of the remaining columns. After partners have practiced reading aloud the words in each of the columns, have them practice reading all of the words.

LESSON 19

VOCABULARY

Reteach *eager, neglected, severe, beloved, demolished, humongous, abandoned*

COMPREHENSION

"Redwoods: Up Close and Personal!"

Build Background

Monitor Comprehension

Answers to *Think Critically* Questions

DECODING/SPELLING

Reteach Word Parts *over, under, sub*

GRAMMAR/WRITING

Preteach Easily Confused Verbs

FLUENCY

Fluency Practice

Materials Needed: *Bold Moves*

Student Edition pp. 192–199

Practice Book pp. 75, 76

Copying Masters 73, 74

Vocabulary

Lesson 19 Vocabulary Distribute a set of Word Cards to each pair of students. One student should say the meaning of one of the Vocabulary Words, without showing the word to his or her partner. The other partner displays and reads the corresponding Word Card, and uses the Vocabulary Word in an original sentence. Continue until one partner has matched all the words, and then switch roles.

Copying Master 73

Comprehension

Build Background: "Redwoods: Up Close and Personal!"
Talk about trees. Have any students visited the redwoods? What were their impressions? Have students noticed large or unusual trees in their own neighborhoods? Where? What were they like? Do students like climbing trees? Would they ever want to live in a tree?

Monitor Comprehension: "Redwoods: Up Close and Personal!"
Read the title of the story aloud. Then have students read pages 192–193 to find out where they would have to go to see a live redwood tree.

pp. 192–193

After reading the pages, ask: **Where would you have to go to see a live redwood tree?** (Possible response: Redwood trees grow in a few forests in California.) **MAIN IDEA AND DETAILS**

Discuss the Stop and Think question on page 192: **What do you learn about redwood trees?** (Possible response: Some redwood trees are at least 3,000 years old and grow as tall as 385 feet.) Guide students in writing the answer to this question. **NOTE DETAILS**

Direct students' attention to the pictures of redwoods on page 193. Ask: **What do these pictures add to the facts we learn about redwoods?** (Possible response: They show comparisons with familiar objects to give an idea of how huge redwoods are.) **CONTEXT CLUES**

Discuss the Stop and Think question on page 193: **Do you think that these tourist stops are a good idea? Explain your answer.** (Possible responses: I think that these tourist stops are a good idea because they help people get close to and understand the trees.) Guide students in writing the answer to the question. **MAKE JUDGMENTS**

Have students read page 194 to find out about two other redwood tourist stops. Discuss the Stop and Think question on page 194: **How are these two tourist stops alike? How are they different?** (Possible responses: Here is how they are alike: Both are made from old redwood trees. Here is how they are different: World Famous Tree House is a hollow tree trunk with a light bulb, while Famous One Log House is a cozy bedroom in a tree trunk, held together by metal loops.) Guide students in writing the answer to this question. **COMPARE AND CONTRAST**

Reread aloud pages 193–194. Model the strategy of evaluating evidence to make assertions.

(THINK ALOUD) **After reading these pages, I think we might assert that people have made several interesting tourist attractions out of old redwood trees. Now we need to look for evidence. There is a tree you can drive through. That's interesting. And another tree trunk you can drive right onto. There are several interesting houses made in tree trunks. Those all support my judgment. Does anything here go against my assertion? No. Then I'll stick with the statement, "People have made several interesting tourist attractions out of old redwoods."** MAKE JUDGMENTS

Discuss the Stop and Think question on page 195: **Which would you most like to visit: a redwood tourist stop or a redwood forest? Explain your answer.** (Possible response: I would most like to visit a redwood forest because I could see huge, old trees that are still growing.) Guide students in writing the answer to this question. **EXPRESS PERSONAL OPINIONS**

Discuss the Stop and Think question on page 196: **Why does Julia decide to live in the tree?** (Julia decides to live in the tree because she doesn't think the logging company will cut it down if she's in it.) Guide students in writing the answer to this question. **DRAW CONCLUSIONS**

Discuss the Stop and Think question on page 197: **What do you think will happen to Luna? Explain your answer.** (Possible response: I think Luna will survive because of the attention Julia got.) Guide students in writing the answer to this question. **MAKE PREDICTIONS**

Discuss the Stop and Think question on page 198: **Do you think you could live in a tree like Julia did? Explain your answer.** (Possible response: I think that I could live in a tree because I am not afraid of heights and I would want to save the tree.) Guide students in writing the answer to this question. **PERSONAL RESPONSE**

Spelling Words: Lesson 19

1. overbearing	11. underdone
2. overcast	12. underestimate
3. overconfident	13. underrated
4. overdevelop	14. undertake
5. overdraft	15. underwent
6. overhang	16. submerge
7. overindulge	17. substandard
8. overlay	18. underground
9. overpower	19. subcontract
10. undercarriage	20. subtitle

Answers to *Think Critically* Questions Help students read and answer the *Think Critically* questions on page 199. Then guide students in writing the answer to each question. Possible responses are provided.

1. Giant redwoods are so awe-inspiring because they are so tall and old; they can survive for thousands of years. **GENERALIZE**

2. [Main Idea] Julia Hill saved Luna by living in the tree for two years. **MAIN IDEA AND DETAILS**

3. I think the author feels that protecting the redwoods is important. **AUTHOR'S VIEWPOINT**

RETEACH

Decoding/Spelling

Word Parts *over, under, sub* Have students work in pairs or small groups. Each group should copy the Spelling Words from *Copying Master 74* onto cards or slips of paper, with one Spelling Word written correctly on each card. As a group, sort the cards into three piles, according to their word parts. Finally, a student chooses a card from one of the piles, and reads the word. The other students try to write the word correctly. The first student then spells the word aloud. Continue by having the next student choose a card and read it, and so on, until all the cards have been used.

Grammar/Writing

Practice Book 76

Simple Tenses: Subject-Verb Agreement and Easily Confused Verbs Review the forms of singular and plural present-tense verbs, and the fact that they must agree in number with their subjects. Write the following sentences on the board:

> Hai reads a book.
>
> Hai and Tina read a book.

Ask students to help you identify the verb in each sentence. (reads, read)
Ask: **When is the action happening in these sentences?** (now, in the present)
Why are these verbs different? (*Reads* is singular to match, or agree with, its singular subject; *read* is plural to agree with its plural subject.)

Tell students that some verbs are easily confused. Distinguish the meanings of *lie* (to rest or recline) and *lay* (to put or place), *sit* (to be seated) and *set* (to put something down), and *rise* (to get up) and *raise* (to move to a higher place, to grow). Use each word in a sentence, then have some volunteers make their own sentences using the words.

GUIDED PRACTICE Direct students' attention to *Practice Book* page 76. Read aloud the directions for the activity together. Remind students that verbs must match subjects, singular verbs for singular subjects and plural verbs for plural subjects.

Fluency

Practice Book 75

Fluency Practice Invite students to look at the bottom half of *Practice Book* page 75. These sentences have been broken into natural phrases. Tell students to repeat each phrase after you, mirroring your expression, phrasing, and pace. After students have repeated each sentence, invite them to practice reading the sentences to a partner.

DAY AT A GLANCE

Day 3

30+ Minutes

COMPREHENSION
Preteach Foreign Words in English
Reread and Summarize "Redwoods: Up Close and Personal!"

DECODING/SPELLING
Reteach Word Parts *over, under, sub*

BUILD ROBUST VOCABULARY
Teach Words from "Redwoods: Up Close and Personal!"

GRAMMAR/WRITING
Reteach Writing Trait: Sentence Fluency

FLUENCY
Fluency Practice

Materials Needed: *Bold Moves*

Student Edition
pp. 192–198

Practice Book
pp. 75, 77

Copying Master 75

Comprehension

Copying Master 75

Foreign Words in English   Distribute *Copying Master 75*, and have a student read aloud the information at the top of the page. Have a volunteer read aloud the passage. Talk through the first row in the chart. Then guide students to use their own knowledge or a dictionary to complete the remaining rows of the chart.

Reread and Summarize   Have students reread and summarize "Redwoods: Up Close and Personal!" in sections, as described below.

pp. 192–193

Let's reread pages 192–193 to remember some facts about redwoods and how they are of interest to tourists.
Summary: Giant redwoods can grow 385 feet tall, and some are 3,000 years old. They grow in only a few California forests. Thick bark helps protect them from disease and fire.

pp. 194–195

Now let's reread pages 194–195 to recall more redwood tourist stops.
Summary: Some giant redwoods have been converted into rooms or "houses." Live redwoods are even more impressive. They support habitats in their branches. Due to logging, however, few old redwoods remain.

pp. 196–198

Last, let's reread pages 196–198 to recall what happened when Julia Hill decided to live in a redwood tree.
Summary: Julia climbed the redwood to save it from loggers. Finally, the loggers agreed to keep the tree safe. Now it is illegal to cut giant redwoods.

Decoding/Spelling

Word Parts *over, under, sub*   Write the following pairs of words on the board:

overdraft / overdaft   subtitle / subtile

Have volunteers read each word as written, and guide students to notice the spelling errors. Tell students that a common mistake is to leave out a letter. Ask students to rewrite each word correctly. Point out that spellings can be verified by using a dictionary.

TEACH

Build Robust Vocabulary

pp. 192–194

Words from "Redwoods: Up Close and Personal!" Have students locate *towering* on page 192 of "Redwoods Up Close and Personal!" Ask a volunteer to read aloud the sentence in which this word appears. (Line 1: *When you see your first towering redwood tree, it's hard to believe that anything can grow that tall and that gigantic.*) Explain that *towering* means much taller than anything else around it. Continue by asking students to locate and read aloud the sentence in which *suspended* appears on page 194. (Line 5: *World Famous Tree House is a hollow redwood with a light bulb suspended way up in the trunk of the tree.*) Explain that this sentence means that there is a light bulb hanging from something.

Have partners make flashcards for the two words. They should write the word on one side and the meaning on the other. Ask students to take turns using the flashcards to quiz each other about the meanings.

RETEACH

Grammar/Writing

Practice Book 77

Writing Trait: Sentence Fluency Have students turn to *Practice Book* page 77. Explain that good writers keep their readers interested by using a variety of sentence types. Discuss the sentence-structure categories presented in the graphic organizer. Recall how the author of "Redwoods: Up Close and Personal!" uses simple, complex, and compound sentences. Then, have a volunteer read the example sentence. Ask: **How many clauses, or parts, does it have?** (two) **Could each clause work as a sentence on its own?** (yes) **What is the sentence structure?** (compound)

GUIDED PRACTICE Work with students to complete the rest of Part A. Then have students complete Parts B and C on their own.

Fluency

Practice Book 75

Fluency Practice Tell students that today they will reread the sentences on the bottom of *Practice Book* page 75. Have students locate and point to the first sentence. Tell students that everyone is going to read the sentence together. This choral reading will give students an opportunity to hear others and to listen to the natural phrasing of the sentences. Choral-read each of the sentences several times.

LESSON 19

DAY AT A GLANCE

Day 4

COMPREHENSION
Reteach Foreign Words in English

DECODING/SPELLING
Reteach Word Parts *over, under, sub*

BUILD ROBUST VOCABULARY
Reteach Words from "Redwoods: Up Close and Personal!"

GRAMMAR/WRITING
Reteach Writing Form: Essay of Explanation

FLUENCY
Fluency Practice

Materials Needed: *Bold Moves*

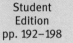

Student Edition pp. 192–198 | Practice Book p. 78 | Copying Master 76

Spelling Words: Lesson 19

1. overbearing	11. underdone
2. overcast	12. underestimate
3. overconfident	13. underrated
4. overdevelop	14. undertake
5. overdraft	15. underwent
6. overhang	16. submerge
7. overindulge	17. substandard
8. overlay	18. underground
9. overpower	19. subcontract
10. undercarriage	20. subtitle

30+ Minutes

RETEACH

Comprehension

Foreign Words in English Remind students that when people from different cultures mix, they share their languages with one another. English writers and speakers often use words from other languages, especially names of foods, greetings, and common expressions. Remind students that they can look up the origins of words in the dictionary to better understand the meanings. Write the following sentence on the board:

> The rays of the afternoon sun slanted through the open walls of the loggia as we hurried along the covered walkway.

Ask: What word in this sentence is borrowed from a language other than English? (loggia) **What does *loggia* seem to mean from this sentence?** (a covered walkway with open walls) **Let's look *loggia* up in the dictionary. What language does it comes from?** (Italian)

GUIDED PRACTICE Have students work in pairs to look up the meaning and the country of origin of these words: *portico, debut, fiasco.* (portico: a covered walkway at the entrance of a building, Italian; debut: a first appearance, French; fiasco: a complete failure, Italian) Allow time for students to share their findings and to use each word in a sentence.

RETEACH

Decoding/Spelling

Practice Book 78

Word Parts *over, under, sub* Have students number a sheet of paper 1–17. Write the *overbearing* on the board and tell students the first eight words you will dictate begin with *over*. After students write each word, display it so they can proofread their work. Repeat, using *undercarriage* (six words) and *submerge* (three words) as the examples.

1. overcast	2. overconfident	3. overdevelop
4. overdraft	5. overhang	6. overindulge
7. overlay	8. overpower	9. underdone
10. underestimate	11. underrated	12. undertake
13. underwent	14. underground	15. substandard
16. subcontract	17. subtitle	

Have students turn to *Practice Book* page 78. Invite a volunteer to read aloud the passage, then the first sentence. Have students work together to complete the activities.

Build Robust Vocabulary

Words from "Redwoods: Up Close and Personal!" Review the meanings of *towering* and *suspended*. Then say these sentences and ask which word each sentence describes. Have students explain why.

- **A wind chime hangs from a branch of the tree.** (suspended)

- **The star basketball player was much taller than the other players on the team.** (towering)

Grammar/Writing

Copying Master 76

Writing Form: Essay of Explanation Explain that an essay of explanation is a paper in which the writer describes or introduces something. Note that an essay of explanation should be logically organized. Organizing information by categories is one good way to help readers understand. Each category can go in a separate paragraph. Distribute *Copying Master 76*. Have volunteers read aloud each paragraph, then the margin notes.

GUIDED PRACTICE Have a volunteer read the first direction aloud. Guide the students in finding the two sentences in which the writer states the topic of the essay. Have students work independently or in pairs to follow the rest of the directions. Allow time for students to share their answers with others.

Fluency

pp. 192–198 **Fluency Practice** Have each student work with a partner to read passages from "Redwoods: Up Close and Personal!" aloud to each other. Students may select a passage that they enjoyed or choose one of the following options:

- Read page 195. (Total: 122 words)

- Read page 197. (Total: 95 words)

Encourage students to read the selected passage aloud to their partner three times. Have the student rate his or her reading on the 1–4 scale.

1	Need more practice
2	Pretty good
3	Good
4	Great!

DAY AT A GLANCE
Day 5

VOCABULARY
Preteach *aficionados, brainchild, astute, conventional, utilitarian, wage, commemorate, traction, unison, avid*

COMPREHENSION
 Reteach Point of View

DECODING/WORD ATTACK
Reteach Decode Longer Words

DECODING/SPELLING
Reteach Words from Spanish and French

GRAMMAR/WRITING
Reteach Adjectives and Verbs

FLUENCY
Fluency Performance

Materials Needed: *Bold Moves*

| Student Edition pp. 192–198 | Copying Master 77 | Skill Card 20 |

Vocabulary

Copying Master 77

Lesson 20 Vocabulary Distribute a set of Vocabulary Word Cards to each student. Hold up the card for the first word, and ask a volunteer to read it aloud. Have students repeat the word and hold up the matching card. Give the explanation for the word. Then ask students the first question below and discuss their responses. Continue for each of the Vocabulary Words.

- If you wanted to know about a subject, why would you ask an **aficionado**?
- What is an example of a **brainchild** that an inventor might have?
- Would an **astute** person allow someone to trick them into giving away a secret?
- What would you eat for a **conventional** breakfast?
- What is an example of a **utilitarian** piece of furniture in your house?
- What is a good reason to **wage** an argument?
- What does your community do to **commemorate** the Fourth of July?
- What is something you need to use **traction** to move?
- What kinds of performers usually move in **unison**?
- Would an **avid** sports fan ever miss his team's games? Explain.

Comprehension

Skill Card 20

Point of View Have students look at side A of *Skill Card 20: Review: Point of View*. Have a volunteer read aloud the Skill Reminder at the top of the page. Have students examine the illustration on the page and then read aloud the three statements. Discuss with students the clues in each passage that help them determine the point of view. Have students copy the chart onto a separate sheet of paper. Guide students to complete the chart by matching the correct statements to the points of view. (1. B, 2. C, 3. A)

Decoding/Word Attack

Decode Longer Words   Write *mosquito* and *bouquet* on the board. Ask students how many syllables are in each word and where the words should be divided. (3, mo/squi/to; 2, bou/quet) Point out to students that the letters *ui* in *mosquito* combine to make the long *e* sound. Then have students identify the letters in *bouquet* that combine to form the long *o* sound. Remind students that vowel digraphs are two vowels that combine to make one sound.

Decoding/Spelling

Words from Spanish and French   Remind students that one way they can learn and remember a new word is by finding its origin in a dictionary. Explain that a dictionary shows not only the pronunciation and meaning of a word, but also where that word came from before it entered the English language. Then write *adobe, mosquito, tornado*, and *envelope* on the board. Have students or pairs of students use a dictionary to find the origin of each word. (envelope is French, the rest are Spanish)

Grammar/Writing

Adjectives and Verbs   Remind students that adjectives modify or describe nouns or pronouns. Proper adjectives begin with a capital letter. Have students recall that comparative adjectives compare two things using *more* or *-er*. Superlative adjectives compare three or more things using *most* or *-est*. Then review that a verb phrase contains a main verb and one or more helping verbs. Then write the following sentences on the board:

> We will read a Spanish folktale in our literature class.
>
> The woman is writing a better book this year.

Have students identify the verb phrases in each sentence. (will read, is writing) Then ask volunteers to circle the adjectives. (Spanish, our, literature, better, this)

VOCABULARY

Student-Friendly Explanations

aficionados Aficionados are people who are enthusiastic and knowledgeable about a particular subject.

brainchild A brainchild is someone's original thought or idea.

astute If you are astute, you are shrewd and clever about situations and behavior.

conventional When something is conventional, it conforms to the usual and accepted standards.

utilitarian Objects that are utilitarian are designed and built to be useful rather than attractive.

wage When you wage something, you begin an action and carry it out for a period of time.

commemorate When you commemorate an event, you perform an action to honor its memory.

traction Traction is the force exerted by the act of pulling an object.

unison When objects or people move in unison, they move at the same time.

avid If you are avid about something, you are very enthusiastic and dedicated about it.

Fluency

Fluency Performance pp. 192–198 Invite students to read aloud the passages from "Redwoods: Up Close and Personal!" that they selected and practiced earlier. Note the number of words each student reads correctly and incorrectly. Have students rate their own oral reading on the 1–4 scale.

VOCABULARY
Reteach *aficionados, brainchild, astute, conventional, utilitarian, wage, commemorate, traction, unison, avid*

COMPREHENSION
 Reteach Make Judgments

DECODING/WORD ATTACK
Reteach Decode Longer Words

DECODING/SPELLING
Reteach Words with Prefixes *im-, in-, ir-, il-*

GRAMMAR/WRITING
Reteach Adjectives and Verbs

FLUENCY
Fluency Practice

Materials Needed: *Bold Moves*

| Student Edition pp. 200–201 | Practice Book pp. 79, 80 | Skill Card 20 | Copying Master 78 |

RETEACH
Vocabulary

Lesson 20 Vocabulary Read aloud the Vocabulary Words and the Student-Friendly Explanations. Then have students turn to pages 200–201 in their books. Ask a volunteer to read the directions aloud. Remind students that they should read each sentence to themselves with the word they choose to be sure it makes sense. If students have difficulty choosing the correct word, refer to the Student-Friendly Explanations. (Answers for pages 200–201: 2. *brainchild*, 3. *wage*, 4. *utilitarian*, 5. *commemorate*, 6. *avid*, 7. *traction*, 8. *conventional*, 9. *unison*, 10. *astute*, 11. A puppet aficionado is a person who knows a lot about puppets. 12. They were used to commemorate the gods in ancient Egypt and Greece.)

RETEACH
Comprehension

Make Judgments Have students look at side B of *Skill Card 20: Review: Make Judgments*. Ask a volunteer to read the Skill Reminder aloud. Have another volunteer read the passage aloud as the other students follow along. Then ask:

- **What type of person was Raul's grandmother?** (Possible response: Raul's grandmother was an honest person.)

- **What evidence supports the judgment that Raul respected his grandmother?** (Possible response: Raul often thought about what she said and he followed her advice to be honest.)

Ask students what judgment they can make about Raul. Discuss their ideas as a group.

GUIDED PRACTICE Have a volunteer read the instructions for the activity aloud. Guide students in copying the chart and completing it with a judgment and evidence from the passage. Invite students to discuss their judgments and supporting evidence. (Evidence: Raul did not cheat on the test; Evidence: Raul did not keep the extra change; Evidence: Raul did not take the man's wallet; Judgment/Assertion: Raul is honest.)

RETEACH

Decoding/Word Attack

Decode Longer Words Write *illuminate* on the board. Circle the prefix for the word. (*il-*) Underline the root word. (*luminate*) Then guide students to divide the word into syllables. (*il/lu/mi/nate*) Remind students that when they see prefixes, they should divide the word immediately after the prefix so that the prefix forms the first syllable. Ask students to repeat the process for *immobile, inability*, and *irrational*. (im/mo/bile, in/a/bil/i/ty, ir/ra/tion/al)

RETEACH

Decoding/Spelling

Copying Master 78

Words with Prefixes *im-, in-, ir-, il-* Distribute *Copying Master 78*. Echo-read the Spelling Words with students. Then ask students to identify the words that have the prefixes *im-* and *in-*. (inability, immobile, indigestion, informant) Write the words on the board, and have a volunteer draw a slash between the prefix and the root word in each word. (*in/ability, im/mobile, in/digestion, in/formant*) Remind students that the prefixes *im-* and *in-* change the meaning of a word to "not" or "unable to."

RETEACH

Grammar/Writing

Practice Book 80

Adjectives and Verbs Have students recall that adjectives describe nouns or pronouns and review the types of adjectives. Remind them that proper adjectives are capitalized. Then remind students that a verb phrase contains a main verb and one or more helping verbs. The verb forms need to match the nouns and pronouns for a sentence to be correct.

GUIDED PRACTICE Have students turn to page 80 in their *Practice Books*. Ask a volunteer to read the activity directions aloud. Have students work in pairs to identify the correct words and make corrections. Allow time for pairs to share their responses.

VOCABULARY

Student-Friendly Explanations

aficionados Aficionados are people who are enthusiastic and knowledgeable about a particular subject.

brainchild A brainchild is someone's original thought or idea.

astute If you are astute, you are shrewd and clever about situations and behavior.

conventional When something is conventional, it conforms to the usual and accepted standards.

utilitarian Objects that are utilitarian are designed and built to be useful rather than attractive.

wage When you wage something, you begin an action and carry it out for a period of time.

commemorate When you commemorate an event, you perform an action to honor its memory.

traction Traction is the force exerted by the act of pulling an object.

unison When objects or people move in unison, they move at the same time.

avid If you are avid about something, you are very enthusiastic and dedicated about it.

Fluency

Practice Book 79

Fluency Practice Have students turn to *Practice Book* page 79. Read the words in the first column aloud. Invite students to track each word and repeat the words after you. Then have students work in pairs to read the words in the remaining columns.

30+ Minutes

VOCABULARY
Reteach *aficionados, brainchild, astute, conventional, utilitarian, wage, commemorate, traction, unison, avid*

COMPREHENSION
"Puppets Around the World"
Build Background
Monitor Comprehension
Answers to *Think Critically* **Questions**

DECODING/WORD ATTACK
Reteach Decode Longer Words

DECODING/SPELLING
Reteach Words with Suffixes *-ant, -ent, -ist*

GRAMMAR/WRITING
Reteach Verbs

FLUENCY
Fluency Practice

Materials Needed: *Bold Moves*

   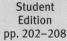

Student Edition
pp. 202–208

Practice Book
p. 79

Copying Masters
77, 78

Vocabulary

Copying Master 77

Lesson 20 Vocabulary   Distribute a set of Vocabulary Word Cards for each student or pair of students. Read aloud the Student-Friendly Explanation for one of the words. Have students display and read the matching Word Card. Ask a volunteer to use the word in a sentence. Continue until students have used all of the words.

Comprehension

Build Background: "Puppets Around the World"
Ask students to share stories about performances they have seen. Have they ever seen a puppet show? Have they ever made a puppet or created a puppet show themselves? If so, what type of puppet did they make? How did it move?

pp. 202–203

Monitor Comprehension: "Puppets Around the World"
Read the title of the story aloud. Then have students read pages 202–203 to find out what the *Kid News* report is about and who Manfred Cooper is.

After reading the pages, ask: **What is the *Kid News* report about?** (Possible response: They are reporting on the tenth annual Festival of Puppets.) Then ask: **Who is Manfred Cooper?** (Manfred Cooper is the well-known puppeteer that started the festival.) **MAIN IDEA AND DETAILS**

Ask: **Why do you think Manfred Cooper started the festival?** (Possible response: He wanted to share the world of puppetry with others.) **CHARACTERS' MOTIVATIONS**

Discuss the Stop and Think question on page 202: **What information do you think Manfred Cooper will share?** (Possible response: I think Manfred Cooper will share information about puppetry and the puppet festival.) Guide students in writing the answer to this question. **MAKE PREDICTIONS**

Discuss the Stop and Think question on page 203: **How does Manfred Cooper feel about puppetry?** (Possible response: Manfred Cooper feels that puppetry is an important art form.) Guide students in writing the answer to the question. **POINT OF VIEW**

pp. 204–205

Discuss the Stop and Think question on page 204: **How do flat rod puppets work?** (Flat rod puppets are held up behind a screen to make shadows. Light, such as that provided by candles or torches, is placed behind the screen to create shadows.) Guide students in writing the answer to this question. **SUMMARIZE**

After students read page 205 aloud, model the skill of making judgments.

(THINK ALOUD) **As I read the selection, I remember that I can make judgments based on the text. I think that Japanese Bunraku puppets are probably much more difficult to move than flat rod puppets. I found evidence in the text that Japanese Bunraku puppets are large, lifelike puppets that have strings attached at the top, the arms, and the legs. The text also says that the Bunraku puppets are mega-puppets that require a lot of traction to move. But flat rod puppets are smaller, lighter puppets that make shadows.**

 Make Judgments

Discuss the Stop and Think question on page 205: **What can you tell about Bunraku puppets?** (Possible responses: I can tell that Bunraku puppets are much larger and more lifelike than puppets I have seen; they are operated with strings like some puppets I have seen.) **Guide students in writing the answer to this question. Make Connections**

pp. 206–207

Discuss the Stop and Think question on page 206: **How are the Japanese puppet theaters and today's TV shows alike?** (Possible response: They are alike because they both tell stories about regular people and their lives.) **Guide students in writing the answer to this question. Compare and Contrast**

Discuss the Stop and Think question on page 207: **Why are hand puppets more conventional?** (Possible response: They are more conventional because many children around the world have seen them and they are easy to move.) **Guide students in writing the answer to this question. Vocabulary**

page 208

Have students read page 208 to find out about the marionette and the Hopi puppet ceremony. Ask: **How does a puppeteer move a marionette?** (A puppeteer uses his hands and wrists to pull the strings to move the marionette.) **Note Details**

Discuss the Stop and Think question on page 208: **Do you think puppets are an important part of history and culture? Explain.** (Possible response: I think that puppets are an important part of history and culture because they were used in ancient ceremonies and to celebrate different cultures.) **Guide students in writing the answer to this question.** **Make Judgments**

Student-Friendly Explanations

aficionados Aficionados are people who are enthusiastic and knowledgeable about a particular subject.

brainchild A brainchild is someone's original thought or idea.

astute If you are astute, you are shrewd and clever about situations and behavior.

conventional When something is conventional, it conforms to the usual and accepted standards.

utilitarian Objects that are utilitarian are designed and built to be useful rather than attractive.

wage When you wage something, you begin an action and carry it out for a period of time.

commemorate When you commemorate an event, you perform an action to honor its memory.

traction Traction is the force exerted by the act of pulling an object.

unison When objects or people move in unison, they move at the same time.

avid If you are avid about something, you are very enthusiastic and dedicated about it.

Spelling Words: Lesson 20

1. adobe	11. informant
2. mosquito	12. significant
3. tornado	13. participant
4. bouquet	14. medalist
5. envelope	15. columnist
6. inability	16. overdraft
7. irrational	17. overdevelop
8. immobile	18. underwent
9. illuminate	19. submerge
10. indigestion	20. subtitle

page 209

Answers to *Think Critically* Questions   Help students read and answer the *Think Critically* questions on page 209. Then guide students in writing the answer to each question. Possible responses are provided.

1. Here is how they are alike: They all help to tell a story; they are important parts of culture. Here is how they are different: Some are made with strings and some are made with rods; some are small while others are very large; they come from different cultures. **COMPARE AND CONTRAST**

2. I have learned that puppets have been an important part of many cultures around the word for centuries. **MAIN IDEA AND DETAILS**

3. I think the author feels that puppets are important and not just for children. **AUTHOR'S PURPOSE**

RETEACH

Decoding/Word Attack

Decode Longer Words   Remind students that many English words end with suffixes, and that the suffixes *-ant, -ent,* and *-ist* are very common. Write *biologist, assistant,* and *resident* on the board. Have volunteers tell how the words should be divided into syllables. (*bi/ol/o/gist, as/sist/ant, res/i/dent*) Then remind students that the suffixes *-ant* and *-ent* are pronounced the same, and that the suffix *-ist* usually refers to a person. Have them recall that looking for suffixes can help them break longer words into syllables.

Copying
Master
78

RETEACH
Decoding/Spelling

Words with Suffixes *-ant, -ent, -ist* Have students review the Spelling Words and identify the words that have the suffixes *-ant, -ent,* and *-ist.* Write the words on the board. (informant, significant, participant, medalist, columnist) Have students read each word aloud as you circle the suffix. Remind students that the suffixes *-ant* and *-ent* are pronounced the same, and they must memorize which suffix goes with a particular root or root word. Then guide students to count the number of syllables in *informant,* and have a volunteer write the number. (3) Continue the process with the remaining words.

RETEACH
Grammar/Writing

Verbs Remind students that an action verb describes an action or activity. The noun or pronoun that receives the action is the direct object. The noun or pronoun that receives the action indirectly is the indirect object. Then have students recall that a linking verb joins the subject of the sentence to words in the predicate. These words in the predicate are predicate nominatives (nouns or pronouns) or predicate adjectives. Also point out that verbs have past, present, and future tenses to tell when something happened. Write the following sentences on the board:

> The rollercoaster is exciting.
>
> They will see the movie this weekend.
>
> She made her sister a sweater.

Guide students to identify the verb tense in each sentence. (present, future, past) Underline *exciting,* and ask students to identify it as a predicate adjective or a predicate nominative. (predicate adjective) Then ask them to name the direct object (sweater) and indirect object (sister) in the last sentence.

Fluency

Practice
Book
79

Fluency Practice Invite students to look at the bottom half of *Practice Book* page 79. These sentences have been broken into natural phrases. Tell students to repeat each phrase after you, mirroring your expression, phrasing, and pace. After students have repeated each sentence, invite them to practice reading the sentences to a partner.

COMPREHENSION
Reteach Foreign Words in English
Reread and Summarize "Puppets Around the World"

DECODING/WORD ATTACK
Reteach Decode Longer Words

DECODING/SPELLING
Reteach Word Parts *over, under, sub*

BUILD ROBUST VOCABULARY
Teach Words from "Puppets Around the World"

GRAMMAR/WRITING
Reteach Verbs

FLUENCY
Fluency Practice

Materials Needed: *Bold Moves*

Student Edition pp. 202–208

Practice Book pp. 79, 81

Copying Master 78

30+ Minutes

RETEACH
Comprehension

Foreign Words In English Remind students that many words used in English originally come from other languages. Ask: **What foreign words do you know that are used in English?** Discuss that some foreign words come into the English language as different cultures come into contact with each other. Foreign words are added as cultures interact and communication among nations grows.

GUIDED PRACTICE Have students work in groups to find and list foreign words in "Puppets Around the World."

Reread and Summarize Have students reread and summarize "Puppets Around the World" in sections, as described below.

 pp. 202–203
Let's reread pages 202–203 to recall what *Kid News* **is reporting about and how some of the first puppets were used.**
Summary: The reporters from *Kid News* are reporting about the tenth annual Festival of Puppets. Some of the first puppets were used for ceremonies and storytelling.

 pp. 204–205
Now let's reread pages 204–205 to remember what we learned about flat rod puppets and Japanese Bunraku puppets.
Summary: Flat rod puppets are held up in front of candles or torches to create shadows on a silk screen. Japanese Bunraku puppets are large, lifelike puppets with strings attached to the arms and legs.

 pp. 206–208
Last, let's reread pages 206–208 to recall what we learned about other kinds of puppets.
Summary: Conventional hand puppets are probably the oldest kinds of puppets. Marionette puppets are moved by strings. Marionettes, or Kachina dolls, are used to perform the puppet corn ceremony.

RETEACH
Decoding/Word Attack

Decode Longer Words Remind students that they can use word parts to help them decode longer words. For example, *sub* has one syllable and follows the CVC pattern. Review how to divide *under* between the two consonants and *over* between the first vowel and the consonant. (*un/der, o/ver*) Then write *overactive, subordinate,* and *undervalue* on the board. Guide students to decode and pronounce the words.

Decoding/Spelling

Copying Master 78

Word Parts *over, under, sub*   Discuss the meanings of the word parts *over*, *under*, and *sub* and how they change the meaning of words to which they are added. Remind students that the spelling of a word does not change when *over*, *under*, or *sub* is added to the beginning of it. Distribute *Copying Master 78*. Have pairs of students work together to complete the activity.

TEACH

Build Robust Vocabulary

pp. 203–207

Words from "Puppets Around the World"   Have students locate the word *complex* on page 203 of "Puppets Around the World." Ask a volunteer to read aloud the sentence in which this word appears. (Line 4: *But some puppets can be quite complex and require the work of skilled artists.*) Explain that this sentence means that some puppets can be hard to understand or have many parts. Then ask students to locate and read aloud the sentence in which the word *evidence* appears on page 207. (Line 10: *Early paintings in China show evidence of hand puppets, so we do know they have been around a long time.*) Explain that this sentence means that early paintings show proof of puppets.

Hold up several items, such as a piece of chalk, a dictionary, and so on, one at a time. For each ask: **Is this complex?** If students say it is, ask: **What is the evidence that it is complex?**

Grammar/Writing

Practice Book 81

Verbs   Review with students the differences between linking verbs and action verbs. Then remind students that verbs have past, present, and future tenses that tell when something happened.

GUIDED PRACTICE   Have students turn to page 81 in their *Practice Books*. Ask a volunteer read the activity directions aloud. Have students work in pairs to identify the words and make corrections. Allow time for pairs to share their responses.

Fluency

Practice Book 79

Fluency Practice   Tell students that today they will reread the sentences on the bottom of *Practice Book* page 79. Have students locate and point to the first sentence. Tell students that everyone is going to read the sentence together. This choral reading will give students an opportunity to hear others and listen to the natural phrasing of the sentences. Choral-read each of the sentences several times.

DAY AT A GLANCE

Day 4

30+ Minutes

COMPREHENSION
Reteach Follow Multiple-Step Instructions

DECODING/SPELLING
Cumulative Review

BUILD ROBUST VOCABULARY
Reteach Words from "Puppets Around the World"

GRAMMAR/WRITING
Cumulative Review

FLUENCY
Fluency Practice

Materials Needed: *Bold Moves*

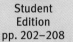

Student Edition pp. 202–208

Practice Book p. 82

Copying Masters 79, 80

Spelling Words: Lesson 20

1. adobe	11. informant
2. mosquito	12. significant
3. tornado	13. participant
4. bouquet	14. medalist
5. envelope	15. columnist
6. inability	16. overdraft
7. irrational	17. overdevelop
8. immobile	18. underwent
9. illuminate	19. submerge
10. indigestion	20. subtitle

Comprehension

Copying Master 79

Follow Multiple-Step Instructions Have students recall that they will often have to follow instructions with multiple steps. Distribute *Copying Master 79* and have a volunteer read aloud the information at the top of the page. Read aloud and discuss each step for following instructions with students. Then have a volunteer read the passage aloud as the other students follow along.

GUIDED PRACTICE Have a volunteer read aloud the instructions for the activity on *Copying Master 79*. Provide pencils and crayons and allow students time to answer the questions and complete the page. Then have students compare and discuss their pictures.

Decoding/Spelling

Practice Book 82

Cumulative Review Have students number a sheet of paper 1–16. Write *envelope* on the board, and point out that this word is French in origin. Explain that first four words you will dictate have French or Spanish origins. After students write each word, display it so they can proofread their work. Repeat the activity using *illuminate* for the prefixes *im-, in-, ir-*, and *il-* (five words), *significant* for the suffixes *-ant, -ent*, and *-ist* (three words), and *submerge* for the word parts *over, under*, and *sub* (four words).

1. bouquet	2. tornado	3. adobe	4. mosquito
5. inability	6. irrational	7. immobile	8. indigestion
9. informant	10. participant	11. medalist	12. columnist
13. overdraft	14. overdevelop	15. underwent	16. subtitle

Have students turn to page 82 in their *Practice Books*. Read the instructions aloud. Then have a volunteer read the passage aloud while the other students follow along. Ask students to complete *Practice Book* page 82 on their own.

RETEACH
Build Robust Vocabulary

Words from "Puppets Around the World" Review the meanings of the words *complex* and *evidence*. Then say these sentences and ask which word describes each sentence. Have students explain why.

- **Jon's puzzle had 1,000 pieces and was hard to put together.** (complex)

- **The crumbs on the table were proof that Jen had eaten a piece of cake after school.** (evidence)

RETEACH
Grammar/Writing

Copying Master 80

Cumulative Review Have students recall the grammar skills they reviewed in this lesson. Discuss examples for each of these skills:

- proper, comparative, and superlative adjectives
- verbs, verb phrases, main verbs, and helping verbs
- action verbs, direct objects, and indirect objects
- linking verbs, predicate nominatives, and predicate adjectives
- verb tenses and plural and singular verbs

GUIDED PRACTICE Distribute *Copying Master 80* to each student. Have a volunteer read the directions. Then guide students as they proofread for errors and rewrite the sentences. Allow time for students to discuss their answers.

Fluency

pp. 202–208 **Fluency Practice** Have each student work with a partner to read passages from "Puppets Around the World" aloud to each other. Remind students that they should

- vary their pace to match the complexity of the text.

- read smoothly and evenly and pause at appropriate punctuation.

Encourage students to read the selected passage aloud to their partner three times. Have the student rate his or her reading on the 1–4 scale.

1	Need more practice
2	Pretty good
3	Good
4	Great!

DAY AT A GLANCE

Day 5

VOCABULARY
Preteach *urges, modern, logic, ethics, influenced, pursuit, promote, banned*

COMPREHENSION
 Preteach Compare and Contrast

DECODING/WORD ATTACK
Preteach Decode Longer Words

DECODING/SPELLING
Preteach Words with Greek and Latin Word Parts—Body Language

GRAMMAR/WRITING
Preteach Past Tense (Regular Verbs)

FLUENCY
Fluency Performance

Materials Needed: *Bold Moves*

Student Edition pp. 202–208	Copying Master 81

PRETEACH

Vocabulary

Copying Master 81

Lesson 21 Vocabulary Distribute a set of Vocabulary Word Cards to each student. Hold up the first Vocabulary Word Card, and ask a volunteer to read it aloud. Have students repeat the word and hold up the matching card. Give the explanation for the word. Ask students the first question below and discuss their responses. Continue for each Vocabulary Word.

- Who **urges** you to do your homework?
- What is an example of a **modern** appliance in your kitchen?
- Who is more likely to use **logic** at work, a singer, a driver, or a mathematician?
- What kind of **ethics** does a good leader have?
- What experiences **influenced** who you are today?
- What would a sprinter in **pursuit** of first place in a race have to do?
- How might you **promote** physical fitness at your school?
- Why might swimming be **banned** in certain places?

PRETEACH

Comprehension

 pp. 202–208

Compare and Contrast Explain that when we compare, we identify how objects or ideas are the same. When we contrast, we look at how they are different. Ask students to recall what they read in "Puppets Around the World." Then ask:

- How do Akina Yoshida's Japanese Bunraku puppets and Tom Baxter's marionettes compare? (Possible response: Puppeteers pull strings to move both kinds of puppets.)
- How do flat rod puppets and hand puppets contrast? (Possible response: The audience sees only the shadows from flat rod puppets, but they see the actual puppets when hand puppets perform.)

GUIDED PRACTICE Explain that a Venn diagram can help organize ideas when comparing and contrasting. Draw a blank Venn diagram on the board and explain its parts. Have the class choose two types of puppets discussed in "Puppets Around the World" to compare and contrast. Help students use information from the selection to complete the Venn diagram.

PRETEACH

Decoding/Word Attack

Decode Longer Words   Write *manuscript* on the board and say it aloud. Have students repeat the word after you, and then challenge students to determine how many syllables it contains. (3) Remind them that every syllable must include a vowel. Help students recognize that the *u* in the middle of the word forms a syllable and is pronounced like *you*. Draw lines to show the syllable divisions. Have students pronounce the word, pointing out how the accent falls on the first syllable. (MAN/u/script)

PRETEACH

Decoding/Spelling

Words with Greek and Latin Word Parts—Body Language   Explain to students that some words have roots that stem from Greek or Latin words for parts of the human body: *ped/pod* = foot, *dent* = tooth, *voc* = voice, *man* = hand, and *mem* = mind. Then write these words on the board:

| pedal | tripod | dentures | memoir |
| vocalist | dentist | manual | maneuver |

Have volunteers underline the Greek or Latin part of each word. (<u>ped</u>al, tri<u>pod</u>, <u>dent</u>ures, <u>mem</u>oir, <u>voc</u>alist, <u>dent</u>ist, <u>man</u>ual, <u>man</u>euver) Discuss with students how these roots contribute to the meaning of the Spelling Words.

PRETEACH

Grammar/Writing

Past Tense (Regular Verbs)   Explain that past tense verbs describe actions started and completed in the past. Many past tense verbs end in *-ed*. Explain that some verbs change their spelling when you add *-ed* to form the past tense. Then write the following sentences on the board:

1. The students tried very hard to pass the test.
2. Taylor tripped over a bump in the sidewalk.
3. Mrs. Hall lived to be 100 years old.

For each sentence, point to the past tense verb and explain the spelling rule. (1.) When a verb ends in a consonant followed by a *y*, change the *y* to *i* and add *-ed*. (2.) When a single-syllable verb ends in one vowel followed by one consonant (but not *w* or *y*), double the consonant and add *-ed*. (3.) When a verb ends in *e*, drop the *e* and add *-ed*.

VOCABULARY

Student-Friendly Explanations

urges   When someone urges you to do something, he or she is encouraging you to perform that action.

modern   Something that is modern is characteristic of the present time.

logic   Logic is the science of reasoning, which decides the truth of a statement by using a set of rules.

ethics   Your ethics are your beliefs and rules about what is right and wrong.

influenced   When something has influenced you, it has had an impact on your development or decisions.

pursuit   Your pursuit of a goal involves the actions you perform and the attempts you make to achieve it.

promote   When you promote something, you contribute to its growth and help to make it happen.

banned   When it is officially stated that something cannot be done, shown, or used, it has been banned.

Fluency

pp. 202–208   **Fluency Performance**   Invite students to read aloud the passages from "Puppets Around the World" that they selected and practiced earlier. Have students rate their own oral reading on the 1–4 scale. Give students the opportunity to continue practicing and then to read the passage to you again.

VOCABULARY
Reteach *urges, modern, logic, ethics, influenced, pursuit, promote, banned*

COMPREHENSION
 Reteach Compare and Contrast

DECODING/SPELLING
Reteach Words with Greek and Latin Word Parts—Body Language

GRAMMAR/WRITING
Preteach Future Tense

FLUENCY
Fluency Practice

Materials Needed: *Bold Moves*

Student Edition pp. 210–211 | Practice Book p. 83 | Skill Card 21 | Copying Master 82

RETEACH

Vocabulary

pp. 210–211 **Lesson 21 Vocabulary** Read aloud the Vocabulary Words and the Student-Friendly Explanations. Then have volunteers read aloud the passage on pages 210 and 211 as other students follow along. Guide students to complete each sentence with a Vocabulary Word. Then have students complete the synonym web on page 211 and discuss their responses. If students are unable to give reasonable responses, refer to the Student-Friendly Explanations. . (Answers for page 210–211: 2. *ethics*, 3. *banned*, 4. *logic*, 5. *modern*, 6. *pursuit*, 7. *urges*, 8. *influenced*, 9. *modern*)

RETEACH

Comprehension

  Compare and Contrast Have students look at side A of *Skill Card 21: Compare and Contrast.* Have a volunteer read the information at the top of the page. Then ask a student to read the passage aloud as other students follow along. Refer to the diagram and ask:

- **How are the sisters the same?**
- **How are the sisters different?**

Discuss how the Venn diagram organizes information from the passage.

GUIDED PRACTICE Now have students look at side B of *Skill Card 21: Compare and Contrast.* Have a student read aloud the skill reminder and then the passage. Guide students in copying the Venn diagram and completing it. (Camping: long drive, slept in tents, cool weather, warm clothes, hiked, took pictures, built campfires. Both: family trip, talked and listened to music in car, cooked hot dogs and hamburgers, read and sang at night. Beach: short drive, slept in a cottage, warm weather, swam in ocean, played games on the sand, built sand castles.)

RETEACH

Decoding/Spelling

Copying Master 82

Words with Greek and Latin Word Parts—Body Language
Distribute *Copying Master 82*. Have students repeat the Spelling Words as you read them. Review the instruction for Greek and Latin roots related to the human body. Then have pairs of students write the Spelling Words on index cards. Have one student draw a card and read the word aloud; the other student writes the word. Then have partners switch roles. When a student spells a word correctly, he or she initials the card and returns it to the pile. Students should work through the pile twice or until each student has had the opportunity to spell each of the words. Have students write down each word they do not spell correctly to study later.

PRETEACH

Grammar/Writing

Future Tense Explain that future tense verbs describe actions that will occur in the future. To form the future tense, add the helping verb *will* to the main verb. Write the following sentence on the board:

> We will play kickball this afternoon.

Note that the verb has two words—*will play*. Point out that the future tense is formed in the same way for all verbs. Then write the following sentence on the board:

> I will go to a new school next year.

Explain that the verb tense often depends on information in the sentence or paragraph. Words such as *next year* give context clues to indicate future tense.

GUIDED PRACTICE Write the following sentence frames on the board. Guide students in copying the frames and completing them with future tense verbs of their choice. (Students' answers will vary, but should all include *will*.)

> This afternoon, I _____ _____.
> Next week, I _____ _____.
> I _____ _____ tomorrow.
> Next year, I _____ _____.

VOCABULARY

Student-Friendly Explanations

urges When someone urges you to do something, he or she is encouraging you to perform that action.

modern Something that is modern is characteristic of the present time.

logic Logic is the science of reasoning, which decides the truth of a statement by using a set of rules.

ethics Your ethics are your beliefs and rules about what is right and wrong.

influenced When something has influenced you, it has had an impact on your development or decisions.

pursuit Your pursuit of a goal involves the actions you perform and the attempts you make to achieve it.

promote When you promote something, you contribute to its growth and help to make it happen.

banned When it is officially stated that something cannot be done, shown, or used, it has been banned.

Fluency

Practice Book 83

Fluency Practice Have students turn to *Practice Book* page 83. Read the words in the first column aloud. Invite students to track each word and repeat the words after you. Then have students work in pairs to read the words in the first column aloud to each other. Follow the same procedure with each of the remaining columns.

LESSON 21

DAY AT A GLANCE

Day 2

30+ Minutes

VOCABULARY
Reteach *urges, modern, logic, ethics, influenced, pursuit, promote, banned*

COMPREHENSION
"The Olympics: Yesterday and Today"

Build Background

Monitor Comprehension

Answers to *Think Critically* Questions

DECODING/SPELLING
Reteach Words with Greek and Latin Word Parts—Body Language

GRAMMAR/WRITING
Preteach Simple Tenses: Present, Past, Future

FLUENCY
Fluency Practice

Materials Needed: *Bold Moves*

| Student Edition pp. 212–219 | Practice Book pp. 83, 84 | Copying Masters 81, 82 |

RETEACH

Vocabulary

Lesson 21 Vocabulary Distribute a set of Vocabulary Word Cards to each student. Display the definition of one of the Vocabulary Words and have a volunteer read it aloud. Have students display and read the matching card. Then ask a volunteer to use the word in an example sentence. Continue until students match and give an example for each word.

Copying Master 81

Comprehension

Build Background: "The Olympics: Yesterday and Today"
Ask students to share what they know about the Olympics. Have they been to an Olympic event or watched Olympic events on television? What are some of their favorite Olympic sports and events?

 Monitor Comprehension: "The Olympics: Yesterday and Today"
pp. 212–213

Read the title of the story aloud. Then have students read pages 212–213 to find out the topic of the selection.

After reading the pages, ask: **What is the topic of this selection?** (the modern and ancient Olympic games) **What is happening at the beginning of the selection?** (Possible response: A woman is taking her turn in the shot put event.) **MAIN IDEA AND DETAILS**

Discuss the Stop and Think question on page 212: **What can you tell about this selection from its title?** (Possible response: I can tell that this selection will be about how the Olympics of the past compare and contrast to the Olympics today.) Guide students in writing the answer to this question. **MAKE INFERENCES**

Ask: **What does the author think about the ancient Greeks' decision to ban women from the Olympics? How do you know?** (Possible response: The author thinks it was a poor decision. The author says that the ancient Greeks used faulty logic.) **AUTHORS' VIEWPOINT**

Discuss the Stop and Think question on page 213: **How are the ancient Olympics different from today's Olympics?** (Possible responses: In the ancient Olympics, only Greek men competed in the athletic events; women were not allowed to participate or to watch. OR: ...athletes were from Greece; modern athletes come from around the world.) Guide students in writing the answer to the question.
 COMPARE AND CONTRAST

---

pp. 214–215

Discuss the Stop and Think question on page 214: **How might the Olympics have begun?** (Possible response: The Olympics might have begun when Greeks started competing in small games, and the games grew to become more formal.) Guide students in writing the answer to this question. Sᴜᴍᴍᴀʀɪᴢᴇ

Draw a Venn diagram on the board. Model the strategy of using the graphic organizer to compare and contrast the ancient Olympics and today's games. Use details found on pages 214 and 215.

(THINK ALOUD) **I want to draw a Venn diagram comparing and contrasting ancient and modern Olympics. I'll label the left oval "Ancient Olympics" and the right "Modern Olympics." The text says that the first Olympics had just one event. I'll list that fact in the left oval. Today's Olympics have many events. I'll list that fact in the right oval. Sportsmanship was valued in the ancient Olympics and it's valued in the modern Olympics. I'll write that fact in the middle of the diagram.** Cᴏᴍᴘᴀʀᴇ ᴀɴᴅ Cᴏɴᴛʀᴀꜱᴛ/Uꜱᴇ Gʀᴀᴘʜɪᴄ Oʀɢᴀɴɪᴢᴇʀꜱ

Discuss the Stop and Think question on page 215: **Do you think the chariot race was fair? Explain your answer.** (Possible response: I think the chariot race was not fair because Nero should not have won the race. He only won because the others were afraid of him.) Guide students in writing the answer to this question. Mᴀᴋᴇ Jᴜᴅɢᴍᴇɴᴛꜱ

pp. 216–217

Discuss the Stop and Think question on page 216: **Do you think the founders' dream will come true? Explain your answer.** (Possible response: I think that the founders' dream will come true because when people come together to participate in an event, they learn how to get along with each other.) Guide students in writing the answer to this question. Mᴀᴋᴇ Pʀᴇᴅɪᴄᴛɪᴏɴꜱ

Discuss the Stop and Think question on page 217: **How were the first modern games like a track meet?** (Possible response: They were like a track meet because there was little ceremony and they included track-and-field events.) Guide students in writing the answer to this question. Mᴀᴋᴇ Cᴏɴɴᴇᴄᴛɪᴏɴꜱ

page 218

Discuss the Stop and Think question on page 218: **Why might the ancient Greeks not like seeing female athletes?** (Possible response: They might not like seeing female athletes because they didn't think females had the right body type for athletic games and banned them from competing.) Guide students in writing the answer to this question. Mᴀᴋᴇ Iɴꜰᴇʀᴇɴᴄᴇꜱ

VOCABULARY

Student-Friendly Explanations

urges When someone urges you to do something, he or she is encouraging you to perform that action.

modern Something that is modern is characteristic of the present time.

logic Logic is the science of reasoning, which decides the truth of a statement by using a set of rules.

ethics Your ethics are your beliefs and rules about what is right and wrong.

influenced When something has influenced you, it has had an impact on your development or decisions.

pursuit Your pursuit of a goal involves the actions you perform and the attempts you make to achieve it.

promote When you promote something, you contribute to its growth and help to make it happen.

banned When it is officially stated that something cannot be done, shown, or used, it has been banned.

Spelling Words: Lesson 21

1. pedal	11. manipulate
2. peddler	12. manufacture
3. pedestrian	13. vocalist
4. pedestal	14. memoir
5. dental	15. memorial
6. dentist	16. memorize
7. dentures	17. tripod
8. vocalize	18. podium
9. manual	19. memorable
10. manuscript	20. maneuver

 page 219

Answers to *Think Critically* Questions   Help students read and answer the *Think Critically* questions on page 219. Possible responses are provided.

1. The modern Olympics promote Greek values by letting all citizens compete; promoting fairness and sportsmanship in the events. **MAIN IDEA AND DETAILS**

2. athletes compete in events; promote fairness and unity
    COMPARE AND CONTRAST

3. The author compares the two because she wants to show how the games began and how they have changed over time. **AUTHOR'S PURPOSE**

RETEACH

Decoding/Spelling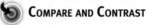

Copying Master 82

Words with Greek and Latin Word Parts—Body Language
Distribute five index cards to each small group of students. Have students write one Greek or Latin root on each card. (ped/pod, dent, voc, man, mem) Then ask students to look at the chart on *Copying Master 82*. Have them copy the chart on another sheet of paper and add a third column on the right.

Root	Meaning	Spelling Word
ped/pod	foot	(pedal, peddler, pedestrian, pedestal, tripod, podium)
dent	tooth	(dental, dentist, dentures)
voc	voice	(vocalize, vocalist)
man	hand	(manual, manuscript, manipulate, manufacture, maneuver)
mem	mind	(memoir, memorial, memorize, memorable)

Tell groups to place the cards face down in front of them. Have one student at a time choose a card. The student says and spells one of the Spelling Words that has the root named on the card. Groups members can refer to *Copying Master 82* to check spelling. Continue until all the Spelling Words have been spelled correctly.

PRETEACH

Grammar/Writing

 Practice Book 84 **Simple Tenses: Present, Past, Future**   Write the sentences below on the board to remind students that present tense verbs refer either to actions happening at the moment or to actions that happen regularly.

> She bakes cookies.
>
> She bakes cookies every Saturday.

Using the sentences below as examples, discuss the following rules for forming past tense verbs:

- A past tense verb describes an action that was started and completed in the past. Many past tense verbs end in -ed.
- When a verb ends in a consonant followed by y, change the y to i and add -ed.
- When a single-syllable verb ends in one vowel followed by one consonant (but not w or y), double the consonant and add -ed.
- When a verb ends in e, drop the e and add -ed.

> Tom walked to school yesterday.
>
> Jane cried at the end of the movie.
>
> Mom stopped at the red light.
>
> Gary believed he won the contest.

Review with students that future tense verbs describe actions that will occur in the future. To form the future tense, add the helping word will to the main verb.

> Tomorrow I will start piano lessons.

GUIDED PRACTICE   Direct students' attention to page 84 in their *Practice Books*. Read the first sentence in the activity together. Guide students to complete the sentence with the correct form of the verb. Then have students complete the rest of the activity on their own.

Fluency

Practice Book 83 **Fluency Practice**   Invite students to look at the bottom half of *Practice Book* page 83. These sentences have been broken into natural phrases. Tell students to repeat each phrase after you, imitating your expression, phrasing, and pace. After students have repeated each sentence, invite them to practice reading the sentences to a partner.

LESSON 21

DAY AT A GLANCE

Day 3

COMPREHENSION
Preteach Study Techniques

Reread and Summarize "The Olympics: Yesterday and Today"

DECODING/SPELLING
Reteach Words wtih Greek and Latin Word Parts—Body Language

BUILD ROBUST VOCABULARY
Teach Words from "The Olympics: Yesterday and Today"

GRAMMAR/WRITING
Reteach Writing Trait: Ideas

FLUENCY
Fluency Practice

Materials Needed: *Bold Moves*

Student Edition pp. 212–218

Practice Book pp. 83, 85

PRETEACH

Comprehension

Study Techniques   Explain that study techniques are special strategies to help readers clarify and understand nonfiction readings. A K-W-L chart helps determine a purpose for reading by asking what you know, what you want to find out, and what you learned after reading.

GUIDED PRACTICE   Draw a K-W-L chart like this on the board and have students copy it on their own paper.

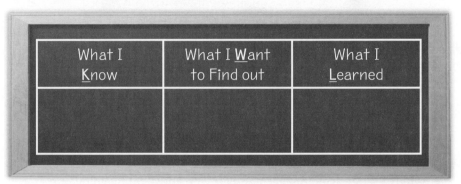

What I **K**now	What I **W**ant to Find out	What I **L**earned

Guide students to complete the chart for "The Olympics: Yesterday and Today."

Reread amd Summarize   Have students reread and summarize "The Olympics: Yesterday and Today" in sections, as described below.

 pp. 212–213   **Let's reread pages 212–213 to recall how the ancient Olympics are different from today's Olympics.**
Summary: The shot put event at the 2004 Olympics was held where the ancient Olympic games were held. At the ancient games, women were banned from competing or watching. Today, both men and women compete.

 pp. 214–215   **Now let's reread pages 214–215 to remember what the ancient Greek Olympics were like.**
Summary: The first Olympics we know about were in 776 B.C., and there was just one race. Later, more events were added. Athletes followed Greek ideals and ethics, until the Romans changed the games into entertainment.

 pp. 216–218   **Last, let's reread pages 216–218 to review what the modern Olympics are like.**
Summary: The founders of the modern Olympics believed the games could promote peace. Now the summer and winter Olympics are worldwide events. In spite of differences, the games still uphold ancient Greek ideals.

Decoding/Spelling

Words with Greek and Latin Word Parts—Body Language Explain that sometimes word parts do not sound the way they are spelled. Write the following Spelling Words on the board:

peddler	podium	maneuver	pedestal
memoir	manual	memorize	dentures

Discuss which part of each word is difficult to spell, and underline it. Then have students copy the words on a sheet of paper and underline the points of difficulty.

Build Robust Vocabulary

pp. 212–215 **Words from "The Olympics: Yesterday and Today"** Have students locate the word *hurl* on page 212 of "The Olympics: Yesterday and Today." Ask a volunteer to read aloud the sentence in which this word appears. (Line 7: *The first athlete prepares to hurl the ball as far as she can, and then she lets go of it.*) Explain that this sentence means that the athlete throws the ball very hard. Then ask students to locate and read aloud the sentence in which the word *venue* appears on page 213. *(Line 7: Each Olympic event has its own site, or venue.)* Explain that a venue is a place where something happens.

Have partners take turns saying one of the words and having the other student tell its meaning.

Grammar/Writing

Practice Book 85 **Writing Trait: Ideas** Explain that a good essay includes only ideas and details that support the main idea of the essay. Ask students to turn to page 85 in their *Practice Books*.

GUIDED PRACTICE Complete Parts A and B together. Then have students write their essays for Part C on another sheet of paper.

Fluency

Practice Book 83 **Fluency Practice** Tell students that today they will reread the sentences on the bottom of *Practice Book* page 83. Have students locate and point to the first sentence. Tell students that everyone is going to read the sentence together. This choral reading will give students an opportunity to hear others and to listen to the natural phrasing of the sentences. Choral-read each of the sentences several times.

DAY AT A GLANCE
Day 4

COMPREHENSION
Reteach Study Techniques

DECODING/SPELLING
Reteach Words with Greek and Latin Word Parts—Body Language

BUILD ROBUST VOCABULARY
Reteach Words from "The Olympics: Yesterday and Today"

GRAMMAR/WRITING
Reteach Writing Form: Compare-and-Contrast Composition

FLUENCY
Fluency Practice

Materials Needed: *Bold Moves*

Student Edition pp. 212–218

Practice Book p. 86

Copying Masters 83, 84

Spelling Words: Lesson 21

1. pedal	11. manipulate
2. peddler	12. manufacture
3. pedestrian	13. vocalist
4. pedestal	14. memoir
5. dental	15. memorial
6. dentist	16. memorize
7. dentures	17. tripod
8. vocalize	18. podium
9. manual	19. memorable
10. manuscript	20. maneuver

Comprehension

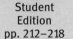 Copying Master 83

Study Techniques Remind students that study techniques are special strategies that readers use to understand what they have read. The SQ3R technique takes the reader through the study process from beginning to end. List the steps on the board:

- **S:** Survey—Look at headings and captions; skim text.
- **Q:** Ask questions about the selection to get a purpose for reading.
- **3R:** Read the selection, recite what you learned, and review answers to questions to clarify understanding.

Discuss with students how they might use each step to study the selection "The Olympics: Yesterday and Today." Ask:

- **How might you survey the selection?** (Possible response: I might look at illustrations, skim the paragraphs, and read the captions.)
- **What questions might you ask to set a purpose for reading?** (Possible response: How are the ancient and modern Olympics different? How are they the same?)
- **What would you do next to understand what you have read?** (Possible response: I would read the selection, recite the information I learned in my own words, and answer the questions.)

GUIDED PRACTICE Direct students' attention to *Copying Master 83*. Have volunteers read the information at the top of the page. Then tell students that they will create an outline for the passage on the page. Have a volunteer read the passage aloud. Then complete the outline together.

Decoding/Spelling

Practice Book 86

Words with Greek and Latin Word Parts—Body Language Have students number a sheet of paper 1–14. Write the Spelling Word *peddler* on the board and point to the root, *ped*. Tell students that the root *ped* is found in the first three words you will dictate. After students write each word, display it so they can proofread their work. Repeat this activity for the other Greek and Latin roots using these example words: *podium* (*pod*—one word), *dentist* (*dent*—2 words), *vocalize* (*voc*—one word), *manufacture* (*man*—four words), and *memorable* (*mem*—three words).

1. pedal	2. pedestrian	3. pedestal	4. tripod
5. dental	6. dentures	7. vocalist	8. manual
9. manuscript	10. manipulate	11. maneuver	12. memoir
13. memorial	14. memorize		

Have students turn to page 86 in their *Practice Books*. Have a volunteer read the instructions aloud. Then complete the first item together. Remind students to examine each picture carefully before selecting the best sentence. Then have students complete *Practice Book* page 86 on their own.

RETEACH
Build Robust Vocabulary

Words from "The Olympics: Yesterday and Today"   Review the meanings of the words *hurl* and *venue*. Then say these sentences and ask which word describes each sentence. Have students explain why.

- **The rock made a big splash when I threw it hard into the lake.** (hurl)
- **The setting for our class picnic will be Logan Park.** (venue)

RETEACH
Grammar/Writing

Copying Master 84

Writing Form: Compare-and-Contrast Composition   Tell students that in a compare-and-contrast composition, a writer identifies the similarities and differences between two things. When you write a compare-and-contrast composition, it is important to focus only on details that help compare the two chosen things or topics. Distribute *Copying Master 84*. Have a volunteer read the description of a compare-and-contrast composition. Then read the Student Model together. Write the following sentence from the passage on the board:

> My country hosted the summer Olympics last year.

Model for students how you came to the conclusion that the sentence does not support the main topic or subtopic and should be removed.

GUIDED PRACTICE   Have students follow the instructions at the bottom of *Copying Master 84*. Discuss students' responses. Then ask them to find a detail sentence in the second paragraph that does not support the topic and draw a line through it. (Many people say that their favorite event is figure skating.)

Fluency

pp. 212– 218   **Fluency Practice**   Have each student work with a partner to read passages from "The Olympics: Yesterday and Today" aloud to each other. Students may select a passage that they enjoyed or choose one of the following options:

- Read page 213. (Total: 117 words)
- Read page 215. (Total: 128 words)

Encourage students to read the selected passage aloud to their partner three times. Have the student rate his or her reading on the 1–4 scale.

1	Need more practice
2	Pretty good
3	Good
4	Great!

DAY AT A GLANCE

Day 5

30+ Minutes

VOCABULARY
Preteach *restored, prolong, precede, trespass, strategically, temperaments, resigned, lustrous*

COMPREHENSION
 Preteach Text Structure: Compare and Contrast

DECODING/WORD ATTACK
Preteach Decode Longer Words

DECODING/SPELLING
Preteach Words with Greek and Latin Word Parts

GRAMMAR/WRITING
Preteach Present and Present Participle

FLUENCY
Fluency Performance

Materials Needed: *Bold Moves*

Student Edition pp. 212–218

Copying Master 85

PRETEACH

Vocabulary

Copying Master 85

Lesson 22 Vocabulary Distribute a set of Vocabulary Word Cards to pairs of students. Hold up the card for the first word, and ask a volunteer to read it aloud. Have students repeat the word and hold up the matching card. Give the explanation for the word. Then ask students the first question below and discuss their responses. Continue for each Vocabulary Word.

- **What kind of object would need to be restored?**
- **If you could, what activity would you choose to prolong?**
- **What might precede a visit to the doctor?**
- **Why is it wrong to trespass on someone else's property?**
- **Where might you strategically place your shoes so you don't lose them?**
- **Can you think of people who have very different temperaments? Describe them.**
- **What sorts of things are you resigned to?**
- **What types of materials are good for making lustrous jewelry?**

PRETEACH

Comprehension

pp. 212–218

 Focus Skill

Text Structure: Compare and Contrast Explain that compare and contrast is a common text structure that authors of nonfiction use to point out how two or more things are alike and how they are different. Note that comparing is telling how things are alike. Contrasting is telling how things are different. Ask students to recall what they read in "The Olympics: Yesterday and Today." Then ask:

- **How do the ancient Olympics and modern Olympics compare?**
  (Possible response: Both Olympics promoted the ideals and ethics of the ancient Greeks.)
- **How do the ancient Olympics and today's Olympics contrast?**
  (Possible response: The ancient Olympics had few events and included only male athletes.)

Point out that the selection follows a compare and contrast text structure. Then explain that authors use clue words such as *like, similar, both, too, unlike, different, but*, and *on the other hand* to alert readers to upcoming comparisons and contrasts.

PRETEACH

Decoding/Word Attack

Decode Longer Words   Tell students that many words in English have Greek or Latin word parts. Write the word *biology* on the board and read it aloud. Discuss with students how many syllables are in *biology* and where it should be divided. (4; bi/ol/o/gy) Tell students to say longer words slowly and clearly to help distinguish the syllables and divide the word correctly. Repeat the procedure with the words *geology, cosmopolitan, metropolis,* and *democracy.*

PRETEACH

Decoding/Spelling

Words with Greek and Latin Word Parts   Write these word parts and their meanings on the board: *bio* = life, *ology* = knowledge or study of, *graphy* = writing, and *geo* = earth. Then write the following words on the board:

biome	geology
geometry	biography

Have volunteers underline the Greek or Latin word part or parts in each word. (biome; geology; geometry; biography) Discuss how the Greek and Latin meanings contribute to understanding the Spelling Words.

PRETEACH

Grammar/Writing

Present and Present Participle   Write this sentence on the board:

> They smile for the camera.

Underline the verb *smile.* Explain that a verb in the present tense describes something that is happening now. The verb *smile* is in the present tense. Then write the following sentence on the board:

> She is smiling for the camera.

Explain that the verb phrase *is smiling* is a present participle; it describes an action that is ongoing. To form the present participle, use the helping verbs *am, is,* or *are* and add *-ing* to the end of the main verb.

VOCABULARY

Student-Friendly Explanations

restored   When you have restored something, you put it back to its earlier and better condition.

prolong   When you prolong something, you make it last longer or go on longer.

precede   When something occurs or goes before something else, it precedes it.

trespass   When you trespass, you walk on someone's property without permission.

strategically   When you place something strategically, you put it in the place that will be the most useful or have the most effect.

temperaments   People's temperaments are how they react to situations and their basic qualities of mind.

resigned   When you are resigned to something, you accept it as it is because you know you cannot change it.

lustrous   Something that shines or glows is lustrous.

Fluency

pp. 212–218   **Fluency Performance**   Invite students to read aloud the passages from "The Olympics: Yesterday and Today" that they selected and practiced earlier. Note the number of words each student reads correctly and incorrectly. Have students rate their own oral reading on the 1–4 scale. Give students the opportunity to continue practicing and then to read the passage to you again.

DAY AT A GLANCE

Day 1

VOCABULARY
Reteach *restored, prolong, precede, trespass, strategically, temperaments, resigned, lustrous*

COMPREHENSION
 Reteach Text Structure: Compare and Contrast

DECODING/SPELLING
Reteach Words with Greek and Latin Word Parts

GRAMMAR/WRITING
Preteach Past and Past Participle

FLUENCY
Fluency Practice

Materials Needed: *Bold Moves*

Practice Book	Skill Card	Copying Master	
Student Edition pp. 220–221	Practice Book p. 87	Skill Card 22	Copying Master 86

RETEACH

Vocabulary

Lesson 22 Vocabulary Read aloud the Vocabulary Words and the Student-Friendly Explanations. Then direct students' attention to the passage on pages 220 and 221. Have students read the passage aloud and guide them to complete each sentence with a Vocabulary Word from the box. If students are unable to give reasonable responses, refer to the Student-Friendly Explanations. Then have students complete the synonym web on page 221 and discuss their responses. (Answers for pages 220–221: 2. *resigned*, 3. *strategically*, 4. *precede*, 5. *lustrous*, 6. *restored*, 7. *prolong*, 8. *trespass*, 9. *lustrous*)

RETEACH

Comprehension

Text Structure: Compare and Contrast Have students look at side A of *Skill Card 22: Text Structure: Compare and Contrast*. Have a volunteer read aloud the information at the top of the card. Then direct students' attention to the pictures on the card. Ask:

- **How are the stores the same?** (Possible response: same size; both are advertising sales)

- **How are the stores different?** (Possible response: The women's clothing store is disorganized and the store hours are not clear. The hardware store is organized and the store hours are clearly printed on the door.)

Have a volunteer read the description of a Venn diagram on the *Skill Card* and review the parts of the diagram. Discuss how the diagram organizes information about how the stores compare and contrast.

GUIDED PRACTICE Now have students look at side B of *Skill Card 22: Text Structure: Compare and Contrast*. Have a volunteer read the Skill Reminder aloud. Then have another student read the paragraph aloud. Guide students in completing the Venn diagram. (Emma: paints big shapes, paints with bold colors, experiments with new shapes, likes to work inside; Both: enjoy painting, art is favorite class, asked for art supplies for birthday, enjoy painting at school; Alan: paints detailed landscapes and portraits, uses pastels and muted colors, creates precise paintings, likes to paint outside.)

RETEACH

Decoding/Spelling

Words with Greek and Latin Word Parts Distribute *Copying Master 86*. Model reading the Spelling Words, and have students repeat them. Review the instruction for word parts with Greek and Latin meanings. Then have students complete the following activity: Have students work in pairs. Each student writes a sentence for each Spelling Word but leaves a blank for the actual word. The partners then switch papers and fill in the blanks in each other's sentences. Students should give themselves one point for each correctly spelled word.

Copying Master 86

PRETEACH

Grammar/Writing

Past and Past Participle Write the following sentence on the board:

> The coach praised the team after the game.

Underline the verb *praised*. Explain that a verb in the past tense describes an action that was started and completed in the past. The verb *praised* is in the past tense. Then write the following sentence on the board:

> The coach has praised each player on the team.

Underline the verb phrase *has praised*. Explain that a past participle describes an action that was started in the past but is ongoing or continuous. The verb *has praised* is a past participle. To form the past participle of regular verbs, use the helping verb *has* or *have* and add *-ed* to the end of the main verb. Note that for irregular verbs, the past and past participle may use different forms of the verb. For example, the past tense of *go* is *went*, and the past participle is *has* or *have gone*.

GUIDED PRACTICE Write the following verbs on the board: *paint, explore, study, play*. Model writing the past and past participle forms of *paint*. (painted, has/have painted) Then guide students to repeat the process for the other words. (explored, has/have explored; studied, has/have studied; played, has/have played)

Student-Friendly Explanations

restored When you have restored something, you put it back to its earlier and better condition.

prolong When you prolong something, you make it last longer or go on longer.

precede When something occurs or goes before something else, it precedes it.

trespass When you trespass, you walk on someone's property without permission.

strategically When you place something strategically, you put it in the place that will be the most useful or have the most effect.

temperaments People's temperaments are how they react to situations and their basic qualities of mind.

resigned When you are resigned to something, you accept it as it is because you know you cannot change it.

lustrous Something that shines or glows is lustrous.

Fluency

Fluency Practice Have students turn to *Practice Book* page 87. Read the words in the first column aloud. Invite students to track each word and repeat the words after you. Then have students work in pairs to read the words in the first column aloud to each other. Follow the same procedure with each of the remaining columns. After partners have practiced reading aloud the words in each column, have them practice reading all of the words.

Practice Book 87

30+ Minutes

VOCABULARY
Reteach *restored, prolong, precede, trespass, strategically, temperaments, resigned, lustrous*

COMPREHENSION
"The Caves Where Art Was Born"
Build Background
Monitor Comprehension
Answers to *Think Critically* **Questions**

DECODING/SPELLING
Reteach Words with Greek and Latin Word Parts

GRAMMAR/WRITING
Preteach Principal Parts of Verbs

FLUENCY
Fluency Practice

Materials Needed: *Bold Moves*

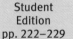

| Student Edition pp. 222–229 | Practice Book pp. 87, 88 | Copying Masters 85, 86 |

RETEACH

Vocabulary

Copying Master 85

Lesson 22 Vocabulary Distribute a set of Vocabulary Word Cards to each student or pair of students. Use the Student-Friendly Explanations to give students clues, such as: **I am thinking of a word that means I have just put something back to its earlier or better condition. What word am I thinking of?** (restored) Have students display and read the matching word. Continue until students match each clue with a Vocabulary Word.

Comprehension

Build Background: "The Caves Where Art Was Born"
Ask students to share experiences they have had visiting a museum or gallery. Or, ask what kind of museum they would like to visit. What kind of art or other objects did they see or would they want to see? What did they learn, or what might they learn?

pp. 222–223

Monitor Comprehension: "The Caves Where Art Was Born"
Read the title of the selection aloud. Then have students read pages 222–223 to find out what teenagers found near Lascaux, France, and how it changed the way we think about Stone Age cave dwellers.

After reading the pages, ask: **What did the four teenagers find near Lascaux, France, in 1940?** (The teenagers found a cave filled with paintings by Stone Age cave dwellers.) **How did the discovery of the cave paintings change the way we think about Stone Age cave dwellers?** (Possible response: We no longer believe they were resigned to a life of just trying to stay alive. The paintings give insight to their temperaments, interests, and artistic skills.) **MAIN IDEA AND DETAILS**

Discuss the Stop and Think question on page 222: **What do you think you will learn from this selection?** (Possible response: I think I will learn about Stone Age artists and how they created cave art.) **Guide** students in writing the answer to this question. **MAKE PREDICTIONS**

Discuss the Stop and Think question on page 223: **How can you tell that the artists were skillful?** (Possible response: I can tell that they were skillful because their paintings are placed on parts of the cave that make them dramatic, and they show depth.) **Guide** students in writing the answer to this question. **MAKE INFERENCES**

pp. 224–225

Discuss the Stop and Think question on page 224: **Why does the author explain three tricks used by Stone Age artists?** (Possible response: The author explains the three tricks because he wants us to understand how clever the Stone Age artists were.) **Guide** students in writing the answer to this question. **AUTHOR'S PURPOSE**

Direct students' attention to pages 224–225. Draw a main idea and details chart on the board and model the strategy of using the graphic organizer to list details that support the main idea.

(THINK ALOUD) **As I read this selection, I can tell that the author wants us to understand that the Stone Age cave dwellers were clever and skillful artists. The author provides many details to support this main idea. I can use a main idea and details chart to organize this information. The main idea is "Stone Age artists were clever and skillful." Now let's add details that support the main idea. For example, "The artists created depth in the paintings by setting one animal in front of another." What other details support the main idea?** Continue modeling the strategy until students have listed several details that support the main idea. **USE GRAPHIC ORGANIZERS/MAIN IDEA AND DETAILS**

Discuss the Stop and Think question on page 225: **What do you learn about tools used by Stone Age artists?** (I learn that the artists ground rocks for paint, made brushes, and used reeds to blow paint.) Guide students in writing the answer to this question. **NOTE DETAILS**

 pp. 226–227

Discuss the Stop and Think question on page 226: **How are the two caves alike? How are they different?** (Possible responses: Here is how they are alike: Both caves are in France. Here is how they are different: Chauvet is older than Lascaux and shows different animals.) Guide students in writing the answer to this question. 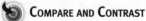 **COMPARE AND CONTRAST**

Discuss the Stop and Think question on page 227: **Why do you think Stone Age artists made these pictures?** (Possible response: I think that they made the pictures because they wanted to remember things that happened.) Guide students in writing the answer to this question. **EXPRESS PERSONAL OPINIONS**

page 228

Discuss the Stop and Think question on page 228: **Why were the Lascaux caves closed to the public?** (They were closed to the public because the paintings were damaged from the carbon dioxide in people's breath.) Guide students in writing the answer to this question. **CAUSE AND EFFECT**

Ask: **How do experts protect the art at Lascaux and Chauvet now?** (Possible response: Experts make sure the air inside the caves is strictly regulated and that no one can trespass on the important sites.) **NOTE DETAILS**

Student-Friendly Explanations

restored When you have restored something, you put it back to its earlier and better condition.

prolong When you prolong something, you make it last longer or go on longer.

precede When something occurs or goes before something else, it precedes it.

trespass When you trespass, you walk on someone's property without permission.

strategically When you place something strategically, you put it in the place that will be the most useful or have the most effect.

temperaments People's temperaments are how they react to situations and their basic qualities of mind.

resigned When you are resigned to something, you accept it as it is because you know you cannot change it.

lustrous Something that shines or glows is lustrous.

Spelling Words: Lesson 22

1. biology	11. microwave
2. biography	12. psychology
3. biome	13. archaeology
4. democracy	14. microscopic
5. demonstrate	15. political
6. epidemic	16. metropolis
7. geology	17. police
8. geography	18. cosmopolitan
9. geometry	19. policy
10. archaic	20. politician

 page 229 **Answers to *Think Critically* Questions** Help students read and answer the *Think Critically* questions on page 229. Possible responses are provided.

1. I have learned that Stone Age artists were skilled and knew how to make their own supplies. **MAIN IDEA AND DETAILS**

2. Both: know perspective, paint pictures of their lives, value artwork **COMPARE AND CONTRAST**

3. The author compares them to "buried treasure" because he feels the paintings are valuable. They can help us learn more about the first artists. **AUTHOR'S PURPOSE**

RETEACH

Decoding/Spelling

Copying Master 86 **Words with Greek and Latin Word Parts** Have students work in small groups to create descriptive definitions for each Spelling Word. Guide students to refer to the chart of the meanings for the Greek and Latin word parts on *Copying Master 86* for ideas for their definitions. Write these sample definitions on the board:

> geo + graphy = "earth" + "write" = writing about Earth
>
> archae + ology = "beginning" + "study of" = study of the beginning

Then have group spokespersons read their definitions and challenge other groups to come up with the word being defined. For example, students might say:

I mean writing about Earth. What word am I? (geography)
I am the study of the beginning. What word am I? (archaeology)

PRETEACH

Grammar/Writing

Principal Parts of Verbs Remind students that the principal parts of verbs include the present, present participle, past, and past participle tenses. Review that a present tense verb describes something happening right now, a present participle describes an action that is ongoing and continuous, a past tense verb describes an action started and completed in the past, and a past participle describes an action that was started in the past but is ongoing or continuous. Then write the following sentence on the board:

> The team jogs around the track.

Underline the verb *jogs* and ask students to tell what tense the verb is. (present) Continue the procedure for the present participle, past, and past participle tenses using the following sentences:

> The team is jogging this afternoon.
> The team jogged two miles yesterday.
> The team has jogged six laps so far.

Review with students how to form the present and past participle. To form the present participle, use one of the helping verbs *is, am,* or *are* and add *-ing* to the the end of the main verb. To form the past participle of regular verbs, use the helping verb *has* or *have* and add *-ed* to the end of the main verb. Also remind students that irregular verbs usually change completely in the past and past participle tenses. They have different forms, which students will have to memorize. For example: *come* becomes *came, has/have come.*

GUIDED PRACTICE Read the directions for the activity on *Practice Book* page 88 together. Point out to students that in some sentences they will underline only a verb. In other sentences they will underline a verb and its helping verb. Have students work in pairs to complete the activity.

Practice Book **88**

Fluency

Practice Book **87**

Fluency Practice Invite students to look at the bottom half of *Practice Book* page 87. These sentences have been broken into natural phrases. Tell students to repeat each phrase after you, mirroring your expression, phrasing, and pace. After students have repeated each sentence, invite them to practice reading the sentences to a partner.

COMPREHENSION
Reteach Graphic Aids

Reread and Summarize "The Caves Where Art Was Born"

DECODING/SPELLING
Reteach Words with Greek and Latin Word Parts

BUILD ROBUST VOCABULARY
Teach Words from "The Caves Where Art Was Born"

GRAMMAR/WRITING
Reteach Writing Trait: Ideas

FLUENCY
Fluency Practice

Materials Needed: *Bold Moves*

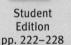

| Student Edition pp. 222–228 | Practice Book pp. 87, 89 | Copying Master 87 |

RETEACH

Comprehension

Graphic Aids Distribute *Copying Master 87* to each student. Have a volunteer read the information at the top of the page. Discuss what a diagram is, how it makes information easier to understand, and where readers might see diagrams. If one is available, show students a diagram in your classroom.

GUIDED PRACTICE Guide students to read the passage on *Copying Master 87* and to interpret its information. After students label the parts of the diagram, talk about how much easier it is to understand the boat parts from the diagram than it is to search them out in the paragraph.

Reread and Summarize Have students reread and summarize "The Caves Where Art Was Born" in sections, as described below.

 pp. 222–223

Let's reread pages 222–223 to recall the discovery made in Lascaux, France.
Summary: In 1940, four French teenagers discovered a cave filled with Stone Age paintings in Lascaux, France. The cave paintings showed that Stone Age artists were skilled painters.

 pp. 224–225

Now let's reread pages 224–225 to recall the painting techniques and tools Stone Age artists used.
Summary: Stone Age artists used three tricks to create depth in the cave paintings. The artists also mixed their own paint, made brushes, and came up with other clever methods for painting in the caves.

pp. 226–228

Last, let's reread pages 226–228 to recall the cave paintings in the Chauvet cave, why Stone Age artists might have made the paintings, and how and why the caves are protected today.
Summary: Even older paintings were found in another French cave called Chauvet. Stone Age artists may have created the paintings for a ceremony, to capture a memory, or to tell a story. Today the air in the caves is regulated to prevent damage to the paintings.

Decoding/Spelling

Words with Greek and Latin Word Parts   Have students examine the Spelling Words *biography* and *geography*. Guide students to see that *graph* comes at the end of each word. Also, each word is spelled with the letter *y* at the end. Then write the following word parts on the board:

ology	demo	micro	geo
epi	archae	poli	bio

Have students note and discuss the patterns in words that include those word parts. Point out spelling tips, such as dropping one *o* when a word part ending in *o* is combined with a word part beginning in *o* (bio + ology = biology, geo + ology = geology).

TEACH

Build Robust Vocabulary

Words from "The Caves Where Art Was Born"   Have students locate the word *confirm* on page 225 of the selection. Ask a volunteer to read aloud the sentence in which this word appears. (Line 5: *Holes found in some of the upper parts of the cave walls confirm this*.) Explain that *confirm* means to check or to prove that something is true. Continue by asking students to locate and read aloud the sentence in which *masterpieces* appears on page 225. (Line 11: *How could these artists create masterpieces in such dark caves?*) Explain that this sentence means that the cave dwellers created art that is considered valuable.

Play a guessing game with students. Give clues such as: **I am thinking of a word for a valuable piece of art or music. What am I thinking of?** (masterpiece)

Grammar/Writing

Writing Trait: Ideas   Have a volunteer read aloud the information at the top of *Practice Book* page 89. Discuss the information in the graphic organizer. Then have a volunteer read aloud the directions for Part A. Guide students to complete the activity.

GUIDED PRACTICE   Have a volunteer read the instructions for Part B. Ask another volunteer to read the passage, and complete the activity together. Then have students work in pairs to complete Part C. Invite volunteers to share their responses.

Fluency

Fluency Practice   Tell students that today they will reread the sentences at the bottom of *Practice Book* page 87. Have students locate and point to the first sentence. Tell students that everyone is going to read the sentence together. This choral reading will give students an opportunity to hear others and to listen to the natural phrasing of the sentences. Choral-read each sentence several times.

30+ Minutes

COMPREHENSION
Reteach Graphic Aids

DECODING/SPELLING
Reteach Words with Greek and Latin Word Parts

BUILD ROBUST VOCABULARY
Reteach Words from "The Caves Where Art Was Born"

GRAMMAR/WRITING
Reteach Writing Form: Compare-and-Contrast Composition

FLUENCY
Fluency Practice

Materials Needed: *Bold Moves*

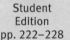

Student Edition pp. 222–228

Practice Book p. 90

Copying Master 88

Spelling Words: Lesson 22

1. biology	11. microwave
2. biography	12. psychology
3. biome	13. archaeology
4. democracy	14. microscopic
5. demonstrate	15. political
6. epidemic	16. metropolis
7. geology	17. police
8. geography	18. cosmopolitan
9. geometry	19. policy
10. archaic	20. politician

Graphic Aids   Remind students that graphic aids are diagrams, maps, charts or tables, time lines, and graphs that make information easy to understand. Graphic aids are usually found in nonfiction books and articles. Then ask the following questions:

- **In what kind of book or article might you find a map?** (Possible response: in a book or article about history or about a certain place)

- **Where might you find a time line?** (Possible response: in a book or article about a series of events or about a person's life)

- **Why might a newspaper article include a graph?** (Possible response: It might show information more easily than having to put the information in words.)

GUIDED PRACTICE   Explain that writers include graphic aids to support their own work. Note that choosing the right kind of graphic aid is important. Ask these questions:

- **I need to organize some informative words and numbers. What type of graphic aid should I use?** (chart or table)

- **I'm writing a biography. What graphic aid should I use?** (time line)

- **I'm writing instructions for assembling a bookshelf. What type of graphic aid should I use?** (diagram)

Practice Book 90

Words with Greek and Latin Word Parts   Have students number a sheet of paper 1–13. Write the Spelling Word *biome* on the board, and point to the word part *bio*. Tell students that the word part *bio* is found in the next word you will dictate. After students write each word, display it so they can proofread their work. Repeat this activity for other Greek and Latin word parts using these examples: *biology* (1 word), *epidemic* (2 words), *archaeology* (1 word), *microscopic* (1 word), *police* (5 words), and *geology* (2 words).

1. biography	2. psychology	3. democracy	4. demonstrate
5. archaic	6. microwave	7. political	8. cosmopolitan
9. metropolis	10. policy	11. politician	12. geography
13. geometry			

Have students turn to *Practice Book* page 90. Read the instructions aloud. Then have a volunteer read the passage aloud while other students follow along. Guide students as they circle words with Greek and Latin word parts. Then read the instructions for the activity and complete the first item together. Remind students to refer to the passage for answers. Then have students complete the page on their own.

RETEACH

Build Robust Vocabulary

Words from "The Caves Where Art Was Born" Review the meanings of the words *confirm* and *masterpieces*. Then say these sentences and ask which word describes each sentence.

- **I think the party starts at 7:00, but I want to check to be sure this is true.** (confirm)

- **The cakes from Shaw's Bakery are decorated with more artistic skill than cakes from any other bakery.** (masterpieces)

RETEACH

Grammar/Writing

Copying Master 88

Writing Form: Compare-and-Contrast Composition Distribute *Copying Master 88*. Have a volunteer read the information at the top of the page. Then read the Student Model together. Write the following sentence from the passage on the board:

> Also, preservatives are now used to keep food fresh.

Discuss whether or not the sentence is in logical order. Does the idea support the comparison or the contrast? (contrast) Where should the detail appear? (in the second paragraph, after the second sentence)

GUIDED PRACTICE Have students answer the questions on *Copying Master 88*. Complete the activity by having students identify details or think of additional ideas that help support how cooking today and long ago compare and contrast.

Fluency

pp. 222–228

Fluency Practice Have each student work with a partner to read passages from "The Caves Where Art Was Born" aloud to each other. Students may select a passage that they enjoyed or choose one of the following options:

- Read page 222. (Total: 132 words)
- Read page 225. (Total: 130 words)

Encourage students to read the selected passage aloud to their partner three times. Have the student rate his or her reading on the 1–4 scale.

1	Need more practice
2	Pretty good
3	Good
4	Great!

DAY AT A GLANCE

Day 5

30+ Minutes

VOCABULARY
Preteach *unsettling, befitting, tolerated, dispute, savory, vigilantly, revered, disposition*

COMPREHENSION
 Preteach Literary Devices

DECODING/WORD ATTACK
Preteach Decode Longer Words

DECODING/SPELLING
Preteach Words with Greek and Latin Word Parts—Science

GRAMMAR/WRITING
Preteach Regular and Irregular Verbs

FLUENCY
Fluency Performance

Materials Needed: *Bold Moves*

| Student Edition pp. 222–228 | Skill Card 23 | Copying Master 89 |

PRETEACH

Vocabulary

Copying Master 89

Lesson 23 Vocabulary Distribute a set of Vocabulary Word Cards to each student or pair of students. Hold up the card for the first word, and ask a volunteer to read it aloud. Have students repeat the word and hold up the matching card. Give the explanation for the word. Then ask students the first question below and discuss their responses. Continue for each Vocabulary Word.

- **How does something unsettling make you feel?**
- **What kinds of clothes are befitting a party?**
- **What is an example of something you have tolerated?**
- **What is a good way to settle a dispute?**
- **What is an example of a savory meal?**
- **In what type of situation would you act vigilantly?**
- **How do people usually treat someone who is revered?**
- **What is the disposition of your best friend?**

PRETEACH

Comprehension

Skill Card 23

Literary Devices Have students look at side A of *Skill Card 23: Literary Devices*. Have a volunteer read aloud the information at the top of the card. Then guide students to examine the picture on the card. Have a volunteer read the passage while the other students follow along. Direct students' attention to the chart and talk about the information entered there.

GUIDED PRACTICE Create a three-column chart on the board like the one at the bottom of side A of *Skill Card 23: Literary Devices*. Guide students to make additional observations about the passage's dialogue, symbols, and tone. Record their ideas in the chart.

PRETEACH

Decoding/Word Attack

Decode Longer Words Write the word *triangle* on the board. Model breaking the word into syllables. Then underline the first syllable (tri) and point out that it is the accented syllable. Explain that the accented syllable may fall in different places in different words. Then explain that in two-syllable words, such as *monarch*, the first syllable is usually the one that is stressed. In words with prefixes or suffixes, students should first try pronouncing the word with the accent on the root or root word.

PRETEACH

Decoding/Spelling

Words with Greek and Latin Word Parts—Science Explain that many English words contain parts that come from Greek and Latin number words. Write these word parts and their meanings on the board: *mono* = one, *tri* = three, and *cent* = hundred. Then write these words on the board and say each one:

> monarch   tricycle   centipede   monotone

Have volunteers underline the Greek and Latin number word parts in each word. (<u>mon</u>arch, <u>tri</u>cycle, <u>cent</u>ipede, <u>mono</u>tone) Note that some of the word parts drop a letter when joined with a root word.

PRETEACH

Grammar/Writing

Regular and Irregular Verbs Write these sentences on the board:

> The children walked home from practice yesterday.
> The children raced home for dinner last night.

Read the sentences aloud. Then underline *walked* and explain that it is a regular, past tense verb. To form the past tense and past participle of most regular verbs, add *-ed* to the end of the verb.

Underline *raced* and tell students that because *race* ends with *e*, simply add *-d* to the end of the verb. Point out that past tense and past participle irregular verbs do not follow this pattern.

Student-Friendly Explanations

unsettling Something that is unsettling causes you to feel uncertain or insecure.

befitting When something is befitting, it is suitable or appropriate for a person.

tolerated When you have let something that you did not agree with continue, you have tolerated it.

dispute If you have a dispute with someone, you have a serious disagreement or quarrel.

savory Something savory has an appetizing taste or smell and tastes salty or spicy, not sweet.

vigilantly When you have been watchful and alert to a problem or a danger, you have acted vigilantly.

revered If you are revered, you are highly respected and admired.

disposition Your disposition is your typical mood or temperament, especially, the way you act, behave, or feel.

Fluency

pp. 222–228

Fluency Performance Invite students to read aloud the passages from "The Caves Where Art Was Born" that they selected and practiced earlier. Note the number of words each student reads correctly and incorrectly. Have students rate their own oral reading on the 1–4 scale. Give students the opportunity to continue practicing and then to read the passage to you again.

LESSON 23

DAY AT A GLANCE

Day 1

VOCABULARY
Reteach *unsettling, befitting, tolerated, savory, vigilantly, dispute, revered, disposition*

COMPREHENSION
 Reteach Literary Devices

DECODING/SPELLING
Reteach Words with Greek and Latin Word Parts—Science

GRAMMAR/WRITING
Preteach Common Irregular Verbs

FLUENCY
Fluency Practice

Materials Needed: *Bold Moves*

| Student Edition pp. 230–231 | Practice Book p. 91 | Skill Card 23 | Copying Master 90 |

pp. 230–231 **Lesson 23 Vocabulary** Have volunteers read aloud the Vocabulary Words. Then give the Student-Friendly Explanation for each word. Direct students' attention to the passage on page 230. Have students read the passage aloud, pausing to discuss each Vocabulary Word in dark type. Then have students work in pairs to answer the questions on page 231 in complete sentences. If students are unable to give reasonable responses, refer to the Student-Friendly Explanations. (Students' responses on page 231 will vary.)

Skill Card 23 **Literary Devices** Have students look at side B of *Skill Card 23: Literary Devices*. Have a volunteer read aloud the Skill Reminder at the top of the page. Then have another volunteer read the passage while other students follow along. Ask:

- **How do you know how Tim feels about Jason playing basketball?** (Tim says it.)

- **How do you think the author feels about basketball? Why do you think so?** (Possible response: I think the author likes basketball because he has the character join the team.)

Remind students not to confuse a character's beliefs or ideas with those of the author.

GUIDED PRACTICE Have a volunteer read aloud the instructions for the activity at the bottom of side B of *Skill Card 23: Literary Devices*. Have students work in pairs to complete the chart based on the passage. (Possible responses: *Dialogue*—Example: "How can you give up the great days we have in the park?" argued his friend Tim. Analysis: Tim does not think Jason should join the team. *Symbol*—Example: "He joined the basketball team..." Analysis: Jason's decision to join the team symbolizes him growing up and changing. *Tone*—Example: "But Jason's father made a stronger point:" Analysis: The author believes that people should try new things.)

Decoding/Spelling

Copying Master 90

Words with Greek and Latin Word Parts—Science Distribute *Copying Master* 90. Model reading the Spelling Words and have students repeat them. Have students examine the chart. Then have students complete the following activity based on the Memory Game. Each student makes a set of game cards by writing the lesson's Spelling Words with prefixes missing; a dash appears in place of each prefix. Partners then shuffle their cards and place them face down. After a student matches two cards, he or she must supply the correct prefix to keep the game cards. If the wrong prefix is supplied, the opponent gets the game cards.

Grammar/Writing

Common Irregular Verbs Write the following words on the board:

> walk   walked   (has, have, had) walked

Point out that *walk* is a regular verb because its past and past participle forms end in *-ed*. Then write these irregular verbs on the board:

> have   had   (has, have, had) had
>
> do   did   (has, have, had) done

Point to *have* and explain that it is an irregular verb. Its past form is *had*. Like all verbs, it joins with the helping verb *has, have,* or *had* in the past participle. Repeat the process with the irregular verb *do.*

Then lead students to understand that the past forms of *be* change, depending on the noun or pronoun that does the action: *I was, you were, he/she/it was, we were, they were.* Say sentences that include the past forms of *be* so that students can hear the correct forms.

GUIDED PRACTICE Write the following sentences on the board:

> Trish _____ a coat over her arm. (have)
>
> We _____ the first ones to finish. (be)
>
> Jude _____ _____ all of the raking. (do)

Have volunteers complete each sentence with the correct past or past participle form of the verb in parentheses. (*had, were, had done*)

Student-Friendly Explanations

unsettling Something that is unsettling causes you to feel uncertain or insecure.

befitting When something is befitting, it is suitable or appropriate for a person.

tolerated When you have let something that you did not agree with continue, you have tolerated it.

dispute If you have a dispute with someone, you have a serious disagreement or quarrel.

savory Something savory has an appetizing taste or smell and tastes salty or spicy, not sweet.

vigilantly When you have been watchful and alert to a problem or a danger, you have acted vigilantly.

revered If you are revered, you are highly respected and admired.

disposition Your disposition is your typical mood or temperament, especially, the way you act, behave, or feel.

Fluency

Practice Book 91

Fluency Practice Have students turn to *Practice Book* page 91. Read the words in the first column aloud. Invite students to track each word and repeat the words after you. Then have students work in pairs to read the words in the first column aloud to each other. Follow the same procedure with the remaining columns. After partners have practiced reading aloud the words in each column, have them practice reading all of the words.

DAY AT A GLANCE

Day 2

30+ Minutes

VOCABULARY
Reteach *unsettling, befitting, tolerated, dispute, savory, vigilantly, revered, disposition*

COMPREHENSION
"The Eight Children of Inti"
Build Background
Monitor Comprehension
Answers to *Think Critically* **Questions**

DECODING/SPELLING
Reteach Words with Greek and Latin Word Parts—Science

GRAMMAR/WRITING
Preteach More Irregular Verbs

FLUENCY
Fluency Practice

Materials Needed: *Bold Moves*

 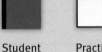

| Student Edition pp. 232–239 | Practice Book pp. 91, 92 | Copying Masters 89, 90 |

Vocabulary

Copying Master 89

Lesson 23 Vocabulary Review the Student-Friendly Explanations. Distribute a set of Vocabulary Word Cards to each pair of students. One partner should choose a card, read the word aloud, and use the word in a sentence. Then the other partner takes a turn. Partners continue until all the words have been used.

Comprehension

Build Background: "The Eight Children of Inti"
Ask children to share experiences they have had with their families. What is their family's favorite thing to do together? Have they traveled together? Has a family member ever taught them how to do something that they will remember forever?

pp. 232–233

Monitor Comprehension: "The Eight Children of Inti"
Read the title of the story aloud. Then have students read pages 232–233 to find out about Inti and some of his children.

Ask: **Where do Inti and his children live?** (on a lake high in the Andes Mountains) **How many children does Inti have?** (eight) Note Details

Discuss the Stop and Think question on page 232: **Why is Inti's family so revered?** (Possible responses: Inti's family is so revered because they have great knowledge and skills.) Guide students in writing the answer to this question. Characters' Traits

Ask: **What does Inti want to do? Why?** (Possible response: Inti wants to help people learn survival skills so that they will not go hungry and suffer.) Characters' Motivations

Discuss the Stop and Think question on page 233: **What can Inti's sons teach the people beyond the lake?** (Possible response: Inti's sons can teach the people how to grow crops, how to build homes, and how to make tools.) Guide students in writing the answer to this question. Summarize

pp. 234–235

Discuss the Stop and Think question on page 234: **How are Inti's two youngest children different from their brothers and sisters?** (Possible response: Inti's two youngest children are not as skilled as their brothers and sisters.) Guide students in writing the answer to this question. Make Comparisons

Read page 235 aloud. Model identifying literary devices.

(THINK ALOUD) **As I read this selection, I notice that the author uses literary devices. On this page, the author uses dialogue to tell the story. From what Inti says, I learn what he wants his children to do. His instructions help me to understand what will happen next in the story. Also, the formal tone of Inti's speech helps me to understand that Inti is powerful.** LITERARY DEVICES: DIALOGUE, TONE

Discuss the Stop and Think question on page 235: **How might the rod be a symbol?** (Possible response: The rod might be a symbol for the power of a ruler.) Guide students in writing the answer to this question. LITERARY DEVICES: SYMBOL

pp. 236–237

Ask: **Why do you think failing to break the ground was unsettling for Inti's children?** (Possible response: Inti's children were probably worried that they might never find their new home.) IDENTIFY WITH CHARACTERS

Discuss the Stop and Think question on page 236: **What do you think will happen next?** (Possible response: I think that some of the children of Inti will give up.) Guide students in writing the answer to this question. MAKE PREDICTIONS

Ask: **What do Manco and Mamak do?** (Possible response: Manco and Mamak decide to continue the journey. They search for many more years until they find a valley where the rod sinks into the ground.) **How are they rewarded?** (Possible response: They find the spot for the great city of Cusco.) CONFLICT/RESOLUTION

Discuss the Stop and Think question on page 237: **How can you tell that this is a legend?** (Possible response: I can tell that this is a legend because it includes events that can't be true, such as the leaders searching for 180 years.) Guide students in writing the answer to this question. CONNECTING TEXTS

page 238

Have students read page 238 to find out what skills Manco and Mamak had. Then ask: **Where did Manco and Mamak learn the skills that they taught the members of the Inca Empire?** (Possible response: They learned the skills by watching their brothers and sisters.) NOTE DETAILS

Discuss the Stop and Think question on page 238: **According to the legend, why is the Andes known for its cloth and pottery?** (Possible response: It's known for cloth and pottery because Mamak had taught the people how to spin, weave, and make pottery.) Guide students in writing the answer to this question. MAKE INFERENCES

Spelling Words: Lesson 23

1. polygon	11. dialogue
2. monopoly	12. diagram
3. century	13. diagonal
4. centimeter	14. biannual
5. quadruple	15. bicoastal
6. centennial	16. bifocals
7. centipede	17. monochromatic
8. tricycle	18. monarch
9. triangle	19. monologue
10. diameter	20. monotone

page 239 **Answers to *Think Critically* Questions** Help students read and answer the *Think Critically* questions on page 239. Possible responses are provided.

1. The turning point is when the six older children give up, and Manco and Mamak decide to continue the search. **Plot**

2. strong-willed; obedient; fast learners **Characters' Traits**

3. This legend tries to explain how the Inca Empire was founded; how the Inca learned to make cloth and pottery, cook, farm, and build stone shelters. **Author's Purpose**

RETEACH

Decoding/Spelling

Copying Master 90 **Words with Greek and Latin Word Parts—Science** Arrange students in small groups. Have each group create a chart like the one below. Say a Spelling Word. The first member in each group should write the word in the appropriate column on his or her group's chart. Continue with the entire spelling list, making sure that all group members take turns. Refer students to *Copying Master 90* to check their spelling. Groups earn 1 point for each correctly spelled word. A perfect score is 19.

mono	bi-/di-	tri-	quadri-	centi-
monopoly	diameter	tricycle	quadruple	century
monochromatic	dialogue	triangle		centimeter
monarch	diagram			centennial
monologue	diagonal			centipede
monotone	biannual			
	bicoastal			
	bifocals			
(5 points)	(7 points)	(2 points)	(1 points)	(4 points)

PRETEACH

Grammar/Writing

Practice Book 92

More Irregular Verbs Explain that the past tense and past participle of irregular verbs, such as *be, have, do,* and *see,* are formed in several ways. The past tense is often different from the past participle form. Write the following sentences on the board and discuss how the past tense and past participle are different.

> She saw many animals.
>
> She had seen many animals that day.

GUIDED PRACTICE Read the directions for the activity on *Practice Book* page 92. Work through the first exercise together. Guide children to write *swum* in the blank and point out that the word is an irregular verb. Then have students complete the activity.

Fluency

Practice Book 91

Fluency Practice Invite students to look at the bottom half of *Practice Book* page 91. These sentences have been broken into natural phrases. Tell students to repeat each phrase after you, mirroring your expression, phrasing, and pace. After students have repeated each sentence, invite them to practice reading the sentences to a partner.

COMPREHENSION
Preteach Theme

Reread and Summarize "The Eight Children of Inti"

DECODING/SPELLING
Reteach Words with Greek and Latin Word Parts—Science

BUILD ROBUST VOCABULARY
Teach Words from "The Eight Children of Inti"

GRAMMAR/WRITING
Reteach Writing Trait: Conventions

FLUENCY
Fluency Practice

Materials Needed: *Bold Moves*

| Student Edition pp. 232–238 | Practice Book pp. 91, 93 | Copying Master 91 |

PRETEACH

Comprehension

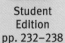 **Copying Master 91**

Theme Distribute *Copying Master 91* and have volunteers read aloud the information about theme and the passage. Remind students that a theme is a lesson or message of a story. Ask students what the theme of the passage might be. Point out that the passage describes Manco and Mamak's determination to do many things, and that their hard work paid off. Then direct students' attention to the web on the bottom of the page. Have a volunteer read the theme in the center of the web. Then ask students how Manco and Mamak's hard work was rewarded. Guide students to see that Manco and Mamak became rulers of the new empire. Students should write this clue to the theme in one of the circles.

GUIDED PRACTICE Have students work in small groups to complete the web with clues from the passage. Ask students to explain how each clue helps them understand the theme of the passage.

Reread and Summarize Have students reread and summarize "The Eight Children of Inti" in sections, as described below.

 pp. 232–233
Let's reread pages 232–233 to recall what problem Inti sees with the world and what Inti's sons can teach people.
Summary: Inti and his family were revered for their wisdom, knowledge, and skills. Inti sees that other people have no skills and realizes his children can help. His sons can teach people how to farm, build homes, and make tools.

 pp. 234–235
Now let's reread pages 234–235 to recall what skills Inti's daughters have, how two of his children are different, and what Inti's plan is.
Summary: Inti's daughters can cook, save and store food, weave wool, and make pottery. The two youngest children are not as skilled as the others. Inti wants his children to teach people skills and to find the place for a great city.

 pp. 236–238
Last, let's reread pages 236–238 to recall what happened on the children's journey and what Manco and Mamak did.
Summary: The children traveled for many years teaching and looking for a place for the city. The six oldest children gave up, but Manco and Mamak kept searching. They founded a great city and ruled over the Inca Empire.

Decoding/Spelling

Words with Greek and Latin Word Parts—Science   Write the word pairs *poligon/polygon* and *diagonal/dyeagonal* on the board. Explain to students that when proofreading, they should compare possible spellings of a word to see which one looks right. They can also use a dictionary to check the word. Model selecting the correct spellings. (polygon, diagonal) Remind students to use their knowledge of Greek and Latin word parts to choose the correct spelling.

TEACH

Build Robust Vocabulary

pp. 235–238

Words from "The Eight Children of Inti"   Have students locate and read aloud the sentence that includes the word *summoned* on page 235 of "The Eight Children of Inti." Ask a volunteer to read aloud the sentence in which this word appears. (First sentence: *Inti summoned his eight children and placed his challenge before them*.) Explain that this sentence means that Inti told his children to come to him for a certain reason. Continue by asking students to locate and read aloud the sentence in which the word *establish* appears on page 235. (Line 4: *Then you must establish a great city in which you, and your children after you, will reign*.) Explain that this sentence means that Inti told them to set up or start a city. Then ask students to locate and read aloud the sentence in which the word *architect* appears on page 238. (Line 3: *Manco became a master farmer, architect, and toolmaker*.) Explain that an architect is a person who designs buildings. Work with students to make a small crossword puzzle using the words *summoned, established,* and *architect*.

RETEACH

Grammar/Writing

Practice Book 93   **Writing Trait: Conventions**   Have students turn to *Practice Book* page 93. Have a volunteer read aloud the information at the top of the page and discuss the information in the graphic organizer. Recall how the author of "The Eight Children of Inti" followed writing conventions for grammar, spelling, punctuation, and capitalization. Then have a volunteer read the activity directions and the first sentence in Part A. Guide students to understand the answers given. Complete the sentences with students.

GUIDED PRACTICE   Work with students to complete Parts B and C on *Practice Book* page 93.

Fluency

Practice Book 91   **Fluency Practice**   Tell students that today they will reread the sentences on the bottom of *Practice Book* page 91. Have students locate and point to the first sentence. Tell students that everyone is going to read the sentence together. This choral reading will give students an opportunity to hear others and to listen to the natural phrasing of the sentences. Choral-read each of the sentences several times.

COMPREHENSION
Reteach Theme

DECODING/SPELLING
Reteach Words with Greek and Latin Word Parts—Science

BUILD ROBUST VOCABULARY
Reteach Words from "The Eight Children of Inti"

GRAMMAR/WRITING
Reteach Writing Form: Essay of Explanation

FLUENCY
Fluency Practice

Materials Needed: *Bold Moves*

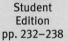

Student Edition pp. 232–238

Practice Book p. 94

Copying Master 92

Spelling Words: Lesson 23

1. polygon	11. dialogue
2. monopoly	12. diagram
3. century	13. diagonal
4. centimeter	14. biannual
5. quadruple	15. bicoastal
6. centennial	16. bifocals
7. centipede	17. monochromatic
8. tricycle	18. monarch
9. triangle	19. monologue
10. diameter	20. monotone

Comprehension

Theme Remind students that the theme of a story is the author's main message. The theme is usually not stated directly, but the author includes clues to the theme in the story. Remind students that they can find clues to the theme by thinking about what characters say, do, and feel. Discuss with students how they might identify the theme of the story "The Eight Children of Inti." Ask:

- **How did Inti feel about helping people learn survival skills?** (Possible response: Inti wanted people to know survival skills so that they would not go hungry and suffer.)

- **What did Inti do?** (Possible response: Inti asked his children to travel around and teach their skills to the people.)

- **What is the theme of the story?** (Possible response: It is important to share knowledge and skills for survival.)

GUIDED PRACTICE Ask pairs of students to identify more clues in the story that support the theme. Have pairs share the clues they find and discuss them as a group.

Decoding/Spelling

Practice Book **94** **Words with Greek and Latin Word Parts—Science** Have students number a sheet of paper 1–15. Write the Spelling Word *monotone* on the board, and point to the word part *mono*. Tell students that the next four words you dictate will begin with the same word part. After students write each word, display it so they can proofread their work. Repeat this activity for other Greek and Latin word parts using these examples: *diagonal* (three words), *bicoastal* (two words), *tricycle* (one word), and *centimeter* (three words). Finally, dictate the words *quadruple* and *polygon* for students to spell.

1. monopoly	2. monochromatic	3. monarch	4. monologue
5. diameter	6. dialogue	7. diagram	8. biannual
9. bifocals	10. triangle	11. century	12. centennial
13. centipede	14. quadruple	15. polygon	

Have students turn to page 94 in their *Practice Books*. Have a volunteer read the instructions and the first item aloud while other students follow along. Then complete the first item together. Remind students to examine each picture carefully and to read all three sentences before selecting the best sentence. Then have students complete *Practice Book* page 94 on their own.

Build Robust Vocabulary

Words from "The Eight Children of Inti" Review the meanings of the words *summoned, establish,* and *architect*. Then say these sentences and ask which word describes each sentence. Have students explain their answers.

- **The teacher asked the children to come in from the playground so they could get back to work.** (summoned)

- **"I want you to set up a area of your room where you can study," Dad told Marty.** (establish)

- **Uncle Scott's job is designing how the new school will look.** (architect)

Grammar/Writing

Copying Master 92

Writing Form: Essay of Explanation Distribute *Copying Master 92* to students. Have a volunteer read the information at the top of the page. Talk with students about a time when they might need to write an essay to explain *how, why* or *what*. Have students read the passage aloud, pausing to discuss the steps in the margin and to help students identify the mistakes in the essay.

GUIDED PRACTICE Have students answer the questions on *Copying Master 92*. Complete the activity by reviewing the corrections students made to the grammar, spelling, punctuation, and capitalization in the essay.

Fluency

pp. 232–238 **Fluency Practice** Have each student work with a partner to read passages from "The Eight Children of Inti" aloud to each other. Students may select a passage that they enjoyed or choose one of the following options:

- Read page 233. (Total: 95 words)
- Read page 236. (Total: 111 words)

Encourage students to read the selected passage aloud to their partner three times. Have the student rate his or her reading on the 1–4 scale.

1	Need more practice
2	Pretty good
3	Good
4	Great!

DAY AT A GLANCE
Day
5

VOCABULARY
Preteach *primitive, fertile, flourishing, descendants, rituals, intact, immortalized, reinforces*

COMPREHENSION
 Preteach Literary Devices

DECODING/WORD ATTACK
Preteach Decode Longer Words

DECODING/SPELLING
Preteach Word Parts *-ation, -ition, -ion*

GRAMMAR/WRITING
Preteach Present Perfect

FLUENCY
Fluency Performance

Materials Needed: *Bold Moves*

Student
Edition
pp. 232–238

Copying
Master
93

30+ Minutes

PRETEACH

Vocabulary

Copying Master 93

Lesson 24 Vocabulary Distribute a set of Vocabulary Word Cards to each student. Hold up the card for the first word, and ask a volunteer to read it aloud. Have students repeat the word and hold up the matching card. Give the explanation for the word. Then ask students the first question below and discuss their responses. Continue for each Vocabulary Word.

- **What is an example of a primitive object you have seen?**
- **Is land in a desert fertile? Why or why not?**
- **What types of things flourish in the spring?**
- **Your parents are the descendants of what other family members?**
- **What is an example of a ritual performed in your community?**
- **Why would you hope for something sent by mail to arrive intact?**
- **What might a community create to immortalize a person?**
- **How can you reinforce what you learn at school?**

PRETEACH

Comprehension

pp. 232–238

Literary Devices Remind students that literary devices help an author tell a story. Explain that imagery is a type of literary device. It helps to set a mood and create a tone in a story. Imagery includes descriptive words and phrases that help readers understand how things look, sound, smell, taste, and feel. Ask students to recall what they read in "The Eight Children of Inti." Then ask:

- **What imagery helps you imagine how you might feel inside one of Cachi's stone shelters?** (Possible response: The phrase "strong shelters" helps me imagine that I would feel safe, and the phrase "homes that would keep them warm and dry" helps me imagine that I would be warm and comfortable.)
- **What imagery helps you imagine what Cora's food might taste like?** (Possible response: The phrase "savory dishes" helps me imagine that Cora's food tastes good.)

Decoding/Word Attack

Decode Longer Words   Write the words *animation* and *opposition* on the board and ask a volunteer to read them aloud. Then underline *-ation* and *-ition* and explain that these are suffixes—word parts added to the end of root words. Ask a volunteer to identify each root word. (animate, oppose) Repeat the procedure with the word *rejection*. Explain to students that looking for suffixes such as *-ation, -ition,* and *-ion* can help them break longer words into syllables. When they see the suffixes they should break the words after *a* or *i* in the suffix and then use other strategies they have learned to break the root or root word into syllables.

Decoding/Spelling

Word Parts *-ation, -ition, -ion*   Write *recognition* and *destination* on the board. Have a volunteer read the words aloud. Underline the last syllable in each word. (-tion) Tell students that a suffix with the sound /shən/ is usually spelled *-tion* or *-sion*.

Grammar/Writing

Present Perfect   Explain that the present perfect tense is formed by using *has/have* with the past participle of a verb. Present perfect tense verbs describe an action that happened some indefinite time in the past, an action that began in the past and continues into the present, or an action that has happened recently. Write these sentences on the board.

> Kurt has traveled in Peru before.
>
> I have just started my project.
>
> They have practiced every day since last month.

Guide students to identify the present perfect tense in each sentence. (has traveled, have started, have practiced) Help them identify what the present perfect tense shows in each case. (an action that happened at an indefinite time, an action that happened recently, an action that happened in the past and continues into the present)

Student-Friendly Explanations

descendants Your relatives in future generations are your descendants.

fertile Land that is fertile is full of nutrients that are good for growing crops.

flourishing Something that is flourishing is successful and growing rapidly.

immortalized When someone is immortalized, something has been created to keep the memory of that person living on.

intact When something is intact, it is whole and undamaged.

primitive Something that is primitive is crude, simple, and not technologically advanced.

reinforces When something reinforces something else, it is giving it additional strength and support.

rituals A culture's rituals are its ceremonies, which involve a series of actions performed according to a set order.

Fluency

Fluency Performance
pp. 232–238
Invite students to read aloud the passages from "The Eight Children of Inti" that they selected and practiced earlier. Note the number of words each student reads correctly and incorrectly. Have students rate their own oral reading on the 1–4 scale. Give students the opportunity to continue practicing and then to read the passage to you again.

VOCABULARY
Reteach *primitive, fertile, flourishing, descendants, rituals, intact, immortalized, reinforces*

COMPREHENSION
Reteach Literary Devices

DECODING/SPELLING
Reteach Word Parts *-ation, -ition, -ion*

GRAMMAR/WRITING
Preteach Past Perfect

FLUENCY
Fluency Practice

Materials Needed: *Bold Moves*

Student Edition pp. 240–241

Practice Book p. 95

Skill Card 24

Copying Master 94

Vocabulary

 pp. 240–241 **Lesson 24 Vocabulary** Read aloud the Vocabulary Words and the Student-Friendly Explanations. Then direct students' attention to the passage on pages 240–241. Have students read the passage aloud and guide them to complete each sentence with a Vocabulary Word from the list. If students are unable to give reasonable responses, refer to the Student-Friendly Explanations. (Answers for pp. 240–241: 2. *fertile*, 3. *intact*, 4. *immortalized*, 5. *reinforces*, 6. *rituals*, 7. *primitive*, 8. *descendants*)

Comprehension

 Skill Card 24 Focus Skill **Literary Devices** Have students look at side A of *Skill Card 24: Literary Devices.* Invite a volunteer to read aloud the introductory information. Then have a student read the passage aloud as the group follows along. Discuss how certain details appeal to the senses, such as the brilliant blue of the sky or the paddles splashing in the water. Point out that the mood of the passage is peaceful and the author's tone is pleasant. Using the web, guide students to understand how each example of imagery supports the peaceful mood of the passage.

GUIDED PRACTICE Now have students look at side B of *Skill Card 24: Literary Devices.* Ask volunteers to read the Skill Reminder and the passage aloud. Guide students in copying the web and completing it with information from the passage. (The mood is scary and suspenseful; rode slowly, grasping the handles; steered through dark, unexpected puddles; His clothes were heavy with water and plastered to his arms and legs; Only walking would be safe.)

RETEACH

Decoding/Spelling

Copying Master 94

Word Parts *-ation, -ition, -ion* Distribute *Copying Master 94*. Model reading the Spelling Words and have students repeat them. Then have students complete the following activity. Have pairs of students write the Spelling Words on index cards. Have one student draw a card and read its word aloud and the other student write the word; then have partners switch roles. When a student spells a word correctly, he or she initials the card and returns it to the pile. Students should work through the pile twice or until each student has had the opportunity to spell each of the words. Have students write down each word they do not spell correctly to study later.

PRETEACH

Grammar/Writing

Past Perfect Tell students that the past perfect is formed by using *have/had* and the past participle form of a verb. The past perfect is used to show which of two events happened first. Write the following sentence on the board:

> Jesse had watched most of the movie when her friend arrived.
>
> When her friend arrived, Jesse had watched most of the movie.

Underline the verb *had watched* in each sentence. Point out that no matter where that sentence part appears, you still know that the event happened first. Both sentences have the same meaning.

VOCABULARY

Student-Friendly Explanations

descendants Your relatives in future generations are your descendants.

fertile Land that is fertile is full of nutrients that are good for growing crops.

flourishing Something that is flourishing is successful and growing rapidly.

immortalized When someone is immortalized, something has been created to keep the memory of that person living on.

intact When something is intact, it is whole and undamaged.

primitive Something that is primitive is crude, simple, and not technologically advanced.

reinforces When something reinforces something else, it is giving it additional strength and support.

rituals A culture's rituals are its ceremonies, which involve a series of actions performed according to a set order.

Fluency

Practice Book 95

Fluency Practice Have students turn to *Practice Book* page 95. Read the words in the first column aloud. Invite students to track each word and repeat the words after you. Then have students work in pairs to read the words in the first column aloud to each other. Follow the same procedure with each of the remaining columns. Then have partners practice reading all of the words.

LESSON 24

30+ Minutes

DAY AT A GLANCE

Day 2

VOCABULARY
Reteach *primitive, fertile, flourishing, descendants, rituals, intact, immortalized, reinforces*

COMPREHENSION
"Stone Puzzle"

Build Background

Monitor Comprehension

Answers to *Think Critically* Questions

DECODING/SPELLING
Reteach Word Parts *-ation, -ition, -ion*

GRAMMAR/WRITING
Preteach Future Perfect

FLUENCY
Fluency Practice

Materials Needed: *Bold Moves*

| Student Edition pp. 242–249 | Practice Book pp. 95, 96 | Copying Masters 93, 94 |

Vocabulary

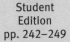
Copying Master 93

Lesson 24 Vocabulary Distribute a set of Vocabulary Word Cards to each student or pair of students. Use the Student-Friendly Explanations to give students clues, such as "I am thinking of a word that means something is whole and undamaged. What word am I thinking of?" (intact) Have students display and read the matching word. Continue for each Vocabulary Word.

Comprehension

Build Background: "Stone Puzzle"
Ask students to share their recollections of very tall buildings or other impressive landmarks they have seen. How were the structures built? How long do they think the construction took?

Monitor Comprehension: "Stone Puzzle"
pp. 242–243
Read the title of the story aloud. Then have students read pages 242–243 to find out why Machu Picchu is one of the eight wonders of the world and what we know about the stone walls of the city.

After reading the pages, ask: **Why do you think that people consider Machu Picchu one of the eight wonders of the world?** (Possible response: I think that people consider Machu Picchu one of the eight wonders because it looks impressive and no one is exactly sure how it was constructed.) **MAKE CONNECTIONS**

Discuss the Stop and Think question on page 242: **Why was building Machu Picchu a "real feat"?** (Possible response: It was a "real feat" because it was built with heavy stones hundreds of years ago on a high mountaintop, with no modern equipment.) Guide students in writing the answer to this question. **DRAW CONCLUSIONS**

Point out that the author describes the walls at Machu Picchu on page 243. Then ask: **What imagery does the author use to help you visualize how well the stones in the wall fit together?** (Possible response: The author explains that the stones were placed so that you couldn't slip even a knife between the joints.) **LITERARY DEVICES**

Ask: **What does the author compare the stone wall to?** (The author compares the stone wall to a puzzle.) **MAKE COMPARISONS**

Discuss the Stop and Think question on page 243: **What do you want to know about the stone walls?** (Possible response: I want to know how the stone walls were built.) Guide students in writing the answer to this question. **PERSONAL RESPONSE**

pp. 244–245

Discuss the Stop and Think question on page 244: **Why does the author describe Machu Picchu as if you are there?** (Possible response: The author describes it this way because it is more interesting to feel as if you are there.) Guide students in writing the answer to this question. **AUTHOR'S CRAFT**

Have students read page 244 aloud. Model the strategy of identifying imagery that an author uses to bring a story to life.

THINK ALOUD **As I read this page, I notice that the author uses imagery to help me visualize Machu Picchu. The description of a tropical climate with rainy summers and mild winters appeals to my sense of touch. There are many images on this page that appeal to my sense of sight. Images such as ruins of a stone city, high in the clouds, a ridge between two mountain peaks, the green, fertile jungle, and a winding river help me visualize the location of Machu Picchu.** **LITERARY DEVICES**

Discuss the Stop and Think question on page 245: **Do you think the Inca king was successful? Explain your answer.** (Possible response: I think that the Inca king was not successful because the task was too challenging.) Guide students in writing the answer to this question. **MAKE PREDICTIONS**

pp. 246–247

Ask: **Was the king's attempt successful?** (No; the rock rolled away and crushed many people.) **SUMMARIZE**

Discuss the Stop and Think question on page 246: **Why can't we call the Inca's work primitive?** (Possible response: We can't call it primitive because it was a complex task that required a lot of skill.) Guide students in writing the answer to this question. **VOCABULARY**

Discuss the Stop and Think question on page 247: **How did the Inca supply their city with water?** (The Inca got their water by enlarging a natural spring and then building a stone trench to carry the water to fountains throughout the city.) Guide students in writing the answer to this question. **SUMMARIZE**

page 248

Discuss the Stop and Think question on page 248: **How do we know that the Inca built good roads?** (Possible response: We know they built good roads because they are still in use today.) Guide students in writing the answer to this question. **MAKE INFERENCES**

Spelling Words: Lesson 24

1. accusation	11. definition
2. adaptation	12. rejection
3. animation	13. ignition
4. application	14. opposition
5. conversation	15. recognition
6. dehydration	16. observation
7. destination	17. emotion
8. preparation	18. duplication
9. specialization	19. celebration
10. variation	20. transportation

Answers to *Think Critically* Questions

Help students read and answer the *Think Critically* questions on page 249. Then guide students in writing the answer to each question. Possible responses are provided.

1. [Third column] built by skilled stone cutters; has complex water system; no one knows how the stones were moved. **MAIN IDEA AND DETAILS**

2. Machu Picchu was so difficult to build because it was on top of a high mountain, and modern equipment was not available to help build it. **CAUSE AND EFFECT**

3. The title "Stone Puzzle" could mean that Machu Picchu is fitted together like a puzzle, and it is also puzzling because no one knows how it was built. **AUTHOR'S CRAFT**

RETEACH

Decoding/Spelling

Copying Master 94

Word Parts *-ation, ition, -ion* Write the following root words on the board: *accuse, ignite, dehydrate,* and *converse.* Have students identify each Spelling Word that contains one of these root words. Guide students to understand that *-ition* is added to some words while *-ation* is added to others. Have them identify which suffix is added to each root word. (-tion: ignition; -ation: accusation, dehydration, conversation)

PRETEACH

Grammar/Writing

Practice Book 96

Future Perfect   The future perfect tense is formed by using *will have* with the past participle. The future perfect tense shows an action that will be completed before some other action. Write these sentences on the board, underlining the future perfect tense:

> <u>I will have finished</u> the puzzle before tomorrow.
>
> <u>I will have read</u> the chapter before the test.

Ask students to name the action that will happen before another in each example.

GUIDED PRACTICE   Direct students' attention to *Practice Book* page 96. Have a volunteer read aloud the instruction. Remind students that the present perfect is formed by using *has/have* with the past participle of a verb. The past perfect is formed by using *have/had* and the past participle form of a verb. Then guide students through the activity.

Fluency

Practice Book 95

Fluency Practice   Invite students to look at the bottom half of *Practice Book* page 95. These sentences have been broken into natural phrases. Tell students to repeat each phrase after you, mirroring your expression, phrasing, and pace. After students have repeated each sentence, invite them to practice reading the sentences to a partner.

LESSON 24

DAY AT A GLANCE

Day 3

COMPREHENSION
Preteach Make Judgments
Reread and Summarize "Stone Puzzle"

DECODING/SPELLING
Reteach Word Parts -ation, -ition, -ion

BUILD ROBUST VOCABULARY
Teach Words from "Stone Puzzle"

GRAMMAR/WRITING
Reteach Writing Trait: Conventions

FLUENCY
Fluency Practice

Materials Needed: *Bold Moves*

Student Edition pp. 242–248

Practice Book pp. 95, 97

Copying Masters 94, 95

PRETEACH

Comprehension

 Make Judgments Distribute *Copying Master 95,* and have a volunteer read aloud the information at the top of the page. Then have another volunteer read the passage as the other students follow along. Ask students what judgment, or assertion, you might make based on the evidence in the passage. Point out that the passage gives many examples of the sophisticated discoveries made or things created by ancient people.

GUIDED PRACTICE Have students work in pairs to complete the graphic organizer on *Copying Master 95.* Students should complete the chart with evidence from the passage that supports the judgment. Ask students to explain how the evidence they select supports the judgment.

Reread and Summarize Have students reread and summarize "Stone Puzzle" in sections, as described below.

 Let's reread pages 242-243 to recall what the stone city and walls at Machu Picchu are like.
Summary: Machu Picchu is an ancient Inca city in Peru and one of the eight wonders of the world. The stones in the strong walls at Machu Picchu fit together like a puzzle.

 Now let's reread pages 244-245 to recall what it's like to be at Machu Picchu and the mystery of how the Inca moved massive stones.
Summary: Machu Picchu, high in the mountain jungle, has ruins of homes and structures used for rituals. Not even their descendants know how the Inca moved huge stones up the mountain.

Last, let's reread pages 246-248 to recall the other puzzles that are found at this site.
Summary: The Inca got their water from a natural spring and trenches and fountains throughout the city. The Inca also built highway systems through rough land. However, they had no system of writing.

Decoding/Spelling

Word Parts *-ation, -ition, -ion*   Distribute *Copying Master 94*. Tell students it is easier to spell a word if they break it into syllables. Remind students that a syllable is the smallest part of a word that can be said separately. Write the words *preparation* and *recognition* on the board. Have students repeat them slowly after you, sounding out the syllables.

GUIDED PRACTICE   Have students work in pairs. Ask one student to choose a Spelling Word, sound out the syllables in the word to his or her partner, and spell the word aloud. Have the partner check the spelling.

Build Robust Vocabulary

Words from "Stone Puzzle"   Have students locate the word *feat* on page 242 of "Stone Puzzle." Ask a volunteer to read aloud the sentence in which this word appears. (Last sentence: *This may be possible today, but hundreds of years ago it was a real feat.*) Explain that this sentence means that bringing stones up the mountain at that time was an amazing act. The people who did it were very strong and smart. Then ask students to locate and read aloud the sentence in which the word *trench* appears on page 247. (Line 13: *Then they made a stone trench to carry the water to the city's sixteen fountains.*) Explain that this sentence means that the Inca made a long, deep hole or ditch to carry water.

Ask yes-or-no questions. Have students explain their responses. Examples: **Is eating lunch a feat? Could you use a shovel to make a trench?**

Grammar/Writing

Writing Trait: Conventions   Have students turn to page 97 of their *Practice Books*. Have a volunteer read aloud the information at the top of the page. Discuss the information in the graphic organizer. Recall how the author of "Stone Puzzle" followed writing conventions for grammar, verb tenses, spelling, punctuation, and capitalization. Then work through the exercises in Part A with students.

GUIDED PRACTICE   Work with students to complete Parts B and C on page 97 of their *Practice Books*.

Fluency

Fluency Practice   Tell students that today they will reread the sentences on the bottom of *Practice Book* page 95. Have students locate and point to the first sentence. Tell students that everyone is going to read the sentence together. This choral reading will give students an opportunity to hear others and listen to the natural phrasing of the sentences. Choral-read each of the sentences several times.

DAY AT A GLANCE

Day 4

COMPREHENSION
Reteach Make Judgments

DECODING/SPELLING
Reteach Word Parts *-ation, -ition, -ion*

BUILD ROBUST VOCABULARY
Reteach Words from "Stone Puzzle"

GRAMMAR/WRITING
Reteach Writing Form: Descriptive Composition

FLUENCY
Fluency Practice

Materials Needed: *Bold Moves*

Student Edition pp. 242–248

Practice Book p. 98

Copying Master 96

Spelling Words: Lesson 24

1. accusation	11. definition
2. adaptation	12. rejection
3. animation	13. ignition
4. application	14. opposition
5. conversation	15. recognition
6. dehydration	16. observation
7. destination	17. emotion
8. preparation	18. duplication
9. specialization	19. celebration
10. variation	20. transportation

Comprehension

Make Judgments   Remind students that as they read a text, they should look for evidence that supports the author's conclusions. Then they can make judgments, or assertions, about the information in the text. Have students recall that an assertion is a statement or claim that is supported by evidence. Point out that readers can make several judgments based on the information in "Stone Puzzle." Ask:

- **What evidence supports the judgment that the walls at Machu Picchu were created by skilled experts?** (Possible responses: The stones were fitted together like a puzzle; some blocks were cut in unusual ways.)

- **What evidence supports the judgment that tourists are not likely to discover the Inca's secrets?** (Possible responses: The Inca did not record their secrets for others; even descendants of the Inca don't know the secrets.)

GUIDED PRACTICE   Ask students to make up their own judgments based on information in "Stone Puzzle." Then have students share and discuss their assertions and supporting evidence.

Decoding/Spelling

Practice Book
98

Word Parts *-ation, -ition, -ion*   Have students number a sheet of paper 1–18. Write *accusation* on the board, and point to the word part *-ation*. Explain that the word part *-ation* is found in the first thirteen words you will dictate. After students write each word, display it so they can proofread their work. Repeat this process for the Spelling Words with the suffix *-tion,* using *definition* as an example.

1. adaptation	2. animation	3. application	4. conversation
5. dehydration	6. destination	7. preparation	8. specialization
9. variation	10. observation	11. duplication	12. celebration
13. transportation	14. rejection	15. ignition	16. opposition
17. recognition	18. emotion		

Have students turn to page 98 in their *Practice Books*. Have a volunteer read the instructions aloud. Then have students read the passage. Work with students to complete the first multiple-choice item. Then have students complete *Practice Book* page 98 on their own.

RETEACH
Build Robust Vocabulary

Words from "Stone Puzzle" Review the meanings of the words *feat* and *trench*. Then say these sentences and ask which word each sentence describes. Have students explain why.

- **The gymnast performed an amazing somersault.** (feat)
- **The workers dug a long, deep line in the ground to bury the water pipe.** (trench)

RETEACH
Grammar/Writing

Copying Master 96

Writing Form: Descriptive Composition Distribute *Copying Master 96* to students. Have a volunteer read the information. Then ask students to read the passage aloud, pausing to discuss the steps in the margin. Remind students that they should follow the conventions of writing and look for errors. Have students locate the sentence with errors. (Grandfather keeps a collecshun of Art, in the library.) **Have them** rewrite the sentence correctly: Grandfather keeps a collection of art in the library.

GUIDED PRACTICE Have students answer the questions on *Copying Master 96*. Invite them to share their responses.

Fluency

pp. 242– 248

Fluency Practice Have each student work with a partner to read passages from "Stone Puzzle" aloud to each other. Students may select a passage that they enjoyed or choose one of the following options:

- Read page 244. (Total: 146 words)
- Read page 247. (Total: 142 words)

Encourage students to read the selected passage aloud to their partner three times. Have the student rate his or her reading on the 1–4 scale.

1	Need more practice
2	Pretty good
3	Good
4	Great!

DAY AT A GLANCE
Day 5

VOCABULARY
Preteach *overwhelming, ornery, aggravated, sophisticated, imposing, notable, prosperous, unassuming, conspicuous, pillaged*

COMPREHENSION
 Reteach Compare and Contrast

DECODING/WORD ATTACK
Reteach Decode Longer Words

DECODING/SPELLING
Reteach Words with Greek and Latin Word Parts—Body Language

GRAMMAR/WRITING
Reteach Simple Past and Future Tenses, Principal Parts of Verbs

FLUENCY
Fluency Performance

Materials Needed: *Bold Moves*

Student Edition pp. 242–248 | Skill Card 25 | Copying Master 97

PRETEACH

Vocabulary

Copying Master 97 **Lesson 25 Vocabulary** Distribute a set of Vocabulary Word Cards to each student. Hold up the word card for the first Vocabulary Word, and ask a volunteer to read it aloud. Have students repeat the word and hold up the matching card. Give the explanation for the word. Then ask students the first question below and discuss their responses. Continue for each of the Vocabulary Words.

- What is something that happened to you that felt **overwhelming**?
- What might make you act **ornery**?
- What kind of injury could be **aggravated** by walking?
- What kinds of things are part of a **sophisticated** culture?
- What traits make a person **imposing**?
- What is something **notable** that you would like to achieve?
- How could you tell if a family was **prosperous**?
- How might an **unassuming** person react to praise?
- What would you wear to make yourself **conspicuous**?
- How would someone feel if his or her town was **pillaged**?

RETEACH

Comprehension

Skill Card 25 **Compare and Contrast** Have students look at side A of *Skill Card 25: Review: Compare and Contrast.* Ask a volunteer to read the Skill Reminder. Ask students to read the passage. Remind students that clue words and phrases, such as *both, similar, like, on the other hand,* and *unlike,* hint at upcoming comparisons and contrasts.

GUIDED PRACTICE Ask students to copy the Venn diagram onto a separate sheet of paper. Be sure they understand that the overlapping parts of the circles are for similarities and the parts that do not overlap are for differences. Guide students to fill in the diagram. (Possible responses: Egyptian Pyramids: built much earlier, were larger, had smooth sides and pointed tips; Mayan Pyramids: built later, were smaller, built in steps or tiers, had flat tops; Same: used as burial places, had temples for worship, had square bases and four sides.)

RETEACH
Decoding/Word Attack

Decode Longer Words Write the word *pedal* on the board. Underline the word part *ped.* Remind students that *ped* is a Latin root that means "foot." Explain that recognizing Greek and Latin words for body parts can help in decoding longer words. Then review these roots: *man* (hand), *voc* (voice), *dent* (tooth).

RETEACH
Decoding/Spelling

Words with Greek and Latin Word Parts—Body Language Write *manuscript* on the board. Ask students to identify the Latin root in *manuscript.* (man) Then explain that *man* means "hand." Repeat this activity for the word *dentures.* Ask: **What Latin root is in *dentures*?** (dent) **What does it mean?** (tooth)

RETEACH
Grammar/Writing

Simple Past and Future Tenses, Principal Parts of Verbs Review simple tenses and principal parts of verbs with students. Remind them that many past tense verbs end in *-ed.* Verbs in the future tense take the helping verb *will.* Verbs in the present participle tense describe an action that is ongoing or continuous. Verbs in the past participle tense describe an action that started in the past but is ongoing or continuous. Write these sentences on the board:

> Josh walks his dog every day.
>
> He walked the dog yesterday.
>
> He will walk the dog tomorrow.
>
> Josh is throwing the ball for his dog.
>
> The dog has dropped the ball.

Invite volunteers to underline each verb or verb phrase. Then guide students to identify the verb tense. (present, past, future, present participle, past participle)

VOCABULARY
Student-Friendly Explanations

overwhelming Something overwhelming has such a great effect that you do not know how to handle it.

ornery An ornery person or animal is usually uncooperative and irritable.

aggravated When a situation has been aggravated, it was already bad and has been made even worse.

sophisticated Cultures that are sophisticated are more advanced and modern than other cultures.

imposing Things that are imposing are very impressive in their appearance.

notable Notable people and events are important or interesting.

prosperous People and places that are successful and rich are prosperous.

unassuming People and things that are unassuming are quiet and without an air of superiority.

conspicuous Something that stands out is conspicuous.

pillaged Places that have been pillaged have had artifacts and possessions stolen or taken by others.

Fluency

pp. 242–248 **Fluency Performance** Invite students to read aloud the passages from "Stone Puzzle" that they selected and practiced earlier. Note the number of words each student reads correctly and incorrectly. Have students rate their own oral reading on the 1–4 scale. Allow students to read the passage to you again.

DAY AT A GLANCE

Day 1

LESSON 25

VOCABULARY

Reteach *overwhelming, ornery, aggravated, sophisticated, imposing, notable, prosperous, unassuming, conspicuous, pillaged*

COMPREHENSION

 Reteach Literary Devices

DECODING/WORD ATTACK

Reteach Decode Longer Words

DECODING/SPELLING

Reteach Words with Greek and Latin Word Parts—Social Studies

GRAMMAR/WRITING

Reteach Simple Past and Future Tenses, Principal Parts of Verbs

FLUENCY

Fluency Practice

Materials Needed: *Bold Moves*

| Student Edition pp. 250–251 | Practice Book pp. 99, 100 | Skill Card 25 | Copying Master 98 |

RETEACH

Vocabulary

 pp. 250–251

Lesson 25 Vocabulary   Read aloud the Vocabulary Words and the Student-Friendly Explanations. Then ask students to turn to pages 250–251 in their books. Have them read the directions, and remind them that they should read each sentence to themselves with the word they have chosen to be sure it makes sense. If students have difficulty choosing the correct word to complete the sentence, refer to the Student-Friendly definitions. After students have completed the pages, ask volunteers to read aloud each sentence. (Answers for pages 250–251: 2. *notable*, 3. *ornery*, 4. *aggravated*, 5. *prosperous*, 6. *unassuming*, 7. *sophisticated*, 8. *pillaged*, 9. *overwhelming*, 10. *conspicuous*)

RETEACH

Comprehension

 Skill Card 25

Literary Devices   Have students look at side B of *Skill Card 25: Review: Literary Devices.* Ask students to read the Skill Reminder. Then have a volunteer read the passage aloud as students read along. Remind students that identifying literary devices can help them better understand a text. Discuss the literary devices in the passage. Ask:

- **To what senses do the descriptions appeal?** (sight and hearing)
- **What general mood does the imagery of the passage create?** (Possible response: a slightly scary or ominous mood)

GUIDED PRACTICE   Guide students in copying the chart and completing it with imagery from the passage and the mood it creates. Invite students to think of details that would appeal to other senses and strengthen the mood. (Imagery: ruins "loomed over us," the "slap-slap of our boots on the stones," "roars of a crowd dead for centuries faded to an eerie quiet;" Appeals to what sense?: sight, hearing, hearing; Creates what mood?: threatening, lonely, scary)

RETEACH
Decoding/Word Attack

Decode Longer Words   Write *geography* on the board. Ask a volunteer to underline the word part that is Greek. (geo-) Tell students that it means "earth." Then point out that the word part -*graphy* is Greek and means "to write." Remind students that recognizing Greek and Latin words used in Social Studies words can help them decode longer words. Point out that other Greek and Latin word parts are *psych* (mind), *demo* (people), *poli* (government), *bio* (life), and *ology* (study of).

RETEACH
Decoding/Spelling

Copying Master 98

Words with Greek and Latin Word Parts—Social Studies
Distribute *Copying Master 98*. Have students read the Spelling Words aloud. Then ask students to identify the words with Greek and Latin word parts. Write the words on the board: *biology, democracy, geography, archaeology*. Work with students to define each word part. (*bio-*, life; -*ology*, the study of; *demo-*, people; *geo-*, earth; -*graphy*, write; *archaeo-*, ancient)

RETEACH
Grammar/Writing

Practice Book 100

Simple Past and Future Tenses, Principal Parts of Verbs
Review the simple tenses and principal parts of verbs with students. Then write this sentence on the board:

> Mattie jump off the high board yesterday.

Underline the verb *jump*. Ask: **Is this the correct tense to use in the sentence?** (no) Ask a volunteer to suggest the correct verb tense. (past) Point out that the word *yesterday* suggests that the action happened in the past.

GUIDED PRACTICE   Have students turn to page 100 in their *Practice Books*. Ask a volunteer to read the activity directions aloud. Then have students work in pairs to proofread and correct each sentence.

VOCABULARY
Student-Friendly Explanations

overwhelming Something overwhelming has such a great effect that you do not know how to handle it.

ornery An ornery person or animal is usually uncooperative and irritable.

aggravated When a situation has been aggravated, it was already bad and has been made even worse.

sophisticated Cultures that are sophisticated are more advanced and modern than other cultures.

imposing Things that are imposing are very impressive in their appearance.

notable Notable people and events are important or interesting.

prosperous People and places that are successful and rich are prosperous.

unassuming People and things that are unassuming are quiet and without an air of superiority.

conspicuous Something that stands out is conspicuous.

pillaged Places that have been pillaged have had artifacts and possessions stolen or taken by others.

Fluency

Practice Book 99

Fluency Practice   Have students turn to *Practice Book* page 99. Read the words in the first column aloud. Invite students to track each word and repeat the words after you. Then have students work in pairs to read the words in each column aloud to each other.

LESSON 25

30+ Minutes

DAY AT A GLANCE

Day 2

VOCABULARY
Reteach *overwhelming, ornery, aggravated, sophisticated, imposing, notable, prosperous, unassuming, conspicuous, pillaged*

COMPREHENSION
"Visiting the Stone Circles"
Build Background
Monitor Comprehension
Answers to *Think Critically* **Questions**

DECODING/WORD ATTACK
Reteach Decode Longer Words

DECODING/SPELLING
Reteach Words with Greek and Latin Word Parts—Science

GRAMMAR/WRITING
Reteach Regular and Irregular Verbs, Perfect Tenses

FLUENCY
Fluency Practice

Materials Needed: *Bold Moves*

Student Edition pp. 252–259

Practice Book p. 99

Copying Masters 97, 98

RETEACH

Vocabulary

Copying Master 97

Lesson 25 Vocabulary Distribute a set of Vocabulary Word Cards to each student. Read aloud the Student-Friendly Explanations for one of the words, leaving out the word. Have students display and read the matching Word Card. Continue until students have matched all the words.

Comprehension

Build Background: "Visiting the Stone Circles"
Ask students if they can name any large monuments built by civilizations in the past. Some possibilities include the Colosseum, the Parthenon, and the pyramids. List their responses on the board. Discuss the reasons why each monument was built.

pp. 252–253

Monitor Comprehension: "Visiting the Stone Circles"
Read the title of the story aloud. Then have students read pages 252–253 to find out where the characters are going and why.

After reading the pages, ask: **Where are the characters going, and why?** (They are going to Europe to see stone circles.) NOTE DETAILS

Discuss the Stop and Think question on page 252: **What do you learn about stone circles?** (Possible response: I learn that stone circles are found throughout the world and some are thousands of years old.) Guide students in writing the answer to this question. NOTE DETAILS

Ask: **How do Lily and Rocky feel?** (Possible response: Lily and Rocky feel excited about the trip, but hungry and tired, too.)

Discuss the Stop and Think question on page 253: **How do you think Uncle Ted feels?** (Possible response: I think Uncle Ted feels excited but also a little aggravated with Lily and Rocky.) Guide students in writing the answer to this question. CHARACTERS' EMOTIONS

pp. 254–255

Discuss the Stop and Think question on page 254: **How are the pyramids and Newgrange alike? How are they different?** (Possible response: Here is how they are alike: both are large burial places. Here is how they are different: Newgrange may be older than the pyramids, Newgrange is more unassuming than the pyramids.) Guide students in writing the answer to this question.

 COMPARE AND CONTRAST

292 Lesson 25 • Bold Moves

Ask: **Why does Lily find Newgrange overwhelming?** (Possible response: because it was created so long ago) **Draw Conclusions**

Discuss the Stop and Think question on page 255: **What do you think they will do next?** (Possible responses: I think they will visit the gift shop; visit another stone circle.) **Guide students in writing the answer to this question. Make Predictions**

pp. 256–257

Ask students to read pages 256–257 to find out about the stone circle Callanish.

Ask: **Why is Callanish conspicuous?** (Possible response: It sits on a high hill and can be seen from far away.) **Vocabulary**

Read aloud the dialogue about Callanish on page 256. Model the strategy of compare and contrast.

(THINK ALOUD) **When I read about Callanish, I can understand it better by comparing and contrasting it to Newgrange. It is similar in that both have stone columns that are huge and old. It is different because it seems sadder, is more isolated and less prosperous, and does not have a gift shop or guards.** Compare and Contrast

Discuss the Stop and Think question on page 256: **How are the stone columns like a line of humans?** (Possible response: The stone columns are tall and narrow and standing still on top of a hill.) Guide students in writing the answer to this question. **Literary Devices**

Discuss the Stop and Think question on page 257: **Why is there a fence around Stonehenge?** (Possible response: There's a fence around Stonehenge because too many people were stealing stones and damaging the site.) Guide students in writing the answer to this question. **Draw Conclusions**

page 258

Discuss the Stop and Think question on page 258: **Why do you think people built stone circles?** (Possible response: I think people built stone circles because they wanted to use the sky to keep track of time.) Guide students in writing the answer to this question. **Express Personal Opinions**

VOCABULARY

Student-Friendly Explanations

overwhelming Something overwhelming has such a great effect that you do not know how to handle it.

ornery An ornery person or animal is usually uncooperative and irritable.

aggravated When a situation has been aggravated, it was already bad and has been made even worse.

sophisticated Cultures that are sophisticated are more advanced and modern than other cultures.

imposing Things that are imposing are very impressive in their appearance.

notable Notable people and events are important or interesting.

prosperous People and places that are successful and rich are prosperous.

unassuming People and things that are unassuming are quiet and without an air of superiority.

conspicuous Something that stands out is conspicuous.

pillaged Places that have been pillaged have had artifacts and possessions stolen or taken by others.

Spelling Words: Lesson 25

1. pedal	11. cosmopolitan
2. dentures	12. century
3. manuscript	13. tricycle
4. memorial	14. diagram
5. tripod	15. bifocals
6. memorable	16. monotone
7. biology	17. conversation
8. democracy	18. rejection
9. geography	19. celebration
10. archaeology	20. definition

page 259

Answers to *Think Critically* Questions Help students read and answer the *Think Critically* questions on page 259. Then guide students in writing the answer to each question. Possible responses are provided.

1. Here is how they are alike: they all are made of stone columns and arranged in a circle. Here is how they are different: some are more well-known than others; Stonehenge has a fence around it, while the others don't; Newgrange was created around an earth mound, while Callanish was created on top of a hill. **COMPARE AND CONTRAST**

2. I have learned that stone circles are very old; stone circles are all over the world; no one knows for certain why stone circles were built. **MAIN IDEA AND DETAILS**

3. I think the author feels that the stone circles should be protected because they are very important clues about people who lived long ago. **AUTHOR'S VIEWPOINT**

RETEACH

Decoding/Word Attack

Decode Longer Words Write *democracy* and *cosmopolitan* on the board. Have students identify the number of syllables in each word. (4, 5) Remind students that in longer words, one syllable is usually pronounced with more stress. It is called the accented syllable. Remind students to first try pronouncing the word with the accent on the root or root word. Then have students identify the accented syllables in the words on the board. (moc, pol)

RETEACH

Decoding/Spelling

Copying Master 98

Words with Greek and Latin Word Parts—Science   Have students review *Copying Master 98* to identify the Spelling Words that have Greek and Latin roots for numbers. Write *tripod, century, tricycle, bifocals,* and *monotone* on the board. Have students read each word aloud as you circle the Greek or Latin root in each. Tell students that *mono* means *one, bi* and *di* mean *two, tri* means *three,* and *cent* means *hundred* or *hundredth.* Then have students work in pairs to play the game described on the bottom of *Copying Master 98.*

RETEACH

Grammar/Writing

Regular and Irregular Verbs, Perfect Tenses   Remind students that the past tense and the past participle of some verbs are irregular. Then have students recall the present perfect tense is formed by using *has/have* with the past participle of a verb, and the past perfect tense is formed by using the past tense of *have* or *had* and the past participle form of a verb. The future perfect is formed by using *will have* with the past participle. Then draw this chart on the board:

Present tense	Past tense	Past participle
eat	ate	eaten
see	saw	seen
go	went	gone

Review perfect tenses. Remind students that the present perfect shows an action that happened at some indefinite time in the past, an action that began in the past and continues in the present, or an action that happened recently. The past perfect is used to show which of two events happened first. The future perfect tense shows an action that will be completed before some other action.

GUIDED PRACTICE   Write these sentences on the board.

> I ate a cracker.
> I have eaten my snack.
> I had eaten lunch by noon.

Ask students to identify the verb tense in each sentence. (past; present perfect; past perfect)

Fluency

Practice Book 99

Fluency Practice   Invite students to look at the bottom half of *Practice Book* page 99. These sentences have been broken into natural phrases. Tell students to repeat each phrase after you, imitating your expression, phrasing, and pace. After students have repeated each sentence, invite them to practice reading the sentences to a partner.

COMPREHENSION
Reteach Study Techniques
Reread and Summarize "Visiting the Stone Circles"

DECODING/WORD ATTACK
Reteach Decode Longer Words

DECODING/SPELLING
Reteach Word Parts -ation, -ition, -ion

BUILD ROBUST VOCABULARY
Teach Words from "Visiting the Stone Circles"

GRAMMAR/WRITING
Reteach Regular and Irregular Verbs, Perfect Tenses

FLUENCY
Fluency Practice

Materials Needed: *Bold Moves*

Student Edition
pp. 252–258

Practice Book
pp. 99, 101

30+ Minutes

RETEACH

Comprehension

Study Techniques Remind students that study techniques can help them understand the nonfiction they read. The SQ3R technique takes the reader through the study process from beginning to end. Surveying gives a reader an idea of what the selection will be about. Asking questions provides a purpose for reading. Then reading, reciting what was learned, and reviewing the answers helps clarify a reader's understanding. The K-W-L chart helps determine a purpose for reading by asking what you know, what you want to find out, and then what you learned after reading. A main idea and details organizer is a great way to organize ideas after reading. It helps the reader remember the main topics or ideas and the important details.

Reread and Summarize Have students reread and summarize "Visiting the Stone Circles" in sections, as described below.

pp. 252–253

Let's reread pages 252–253 to recall how the characters got to their first stone circle.
Summary: Uncle Ted, Lily, and Rocky fly from Boston to Ireland. Then they drive to Newgrange to see the stone circle there.

pp. 254–255

Now let's read pages 254–255 to find out about the Newgrange stone circles.
Summary: The characters see the Newgrange stone circle. They learn about the people who built it and why it may have been built.

pp. 256–258

Last, let's read pages 256–258 to recall what happened at the other stone circles.
Summary: The characters visit Callanish, which is a Scottish stone circle. Finally, they visit Stonehenge, the most famous stone circle.

RETEACH

Decoding/Word Attack

Decode Longer Words Write *conversation, definition,* and *rejection* on the board. Ask volunteers to underline the suffix in each word. Then explain that the suffixes are similar because they all end in *-ion*. Remind students that looking for suffixes such as *-ation, -ition,* and *-ion* can help them break longer words into syllables. Tell them that when they see the suffixes *-ation* and *-ition,* break the words after the *a* or *i* in the suffix. Then use other strategies to break the rest of the word into syllables.

RETEACH

Decoding/Spellling

Word Parts *-ation, -ition, -ion*   Remind students that the verb form of an English word can sometimes be changed into a noun by adding *-ation, -ition,* or *-ion.* Stress that the spelling of the root word may change. Have students write the noun form of each of these words by adding *-ation, -ition,* or *-ion.*

duplicate (duplication)   oppose (opposition)   accuse (accusation)

TEACH

Build Robust Vocabulary

 pp. 252-254   **Words from "Visiting the Stone Circles"**   Have students locate the word *pillars* on page 252 of "Visiting the Stone Circles." Ask a volunteer to read aloud the sentence in which this word appears. (Line 3: *Circles made of stone pillars are found throughout the world, and some of them are thousands of years old.*) Explain that this sentence means that the circles were made with poles or columns of stone. Then ask students to locate and read aloud the sentence in which the word *glistens* appears on page 254. (Last sentence: *A moment later, the stone at the end of the passage tomb glistens in the morning light.*) Explain that this sentence means that the stone shines or sparkles in the light.

Have students sit in a circle. Go around the circle asking each student to tell where he or she might see a pillar. Then go around the circle and have each tell something that glistens. Give students the option of passing and having you come back to them if they don't have an immediate idea.

RETEACH

Grammar/Writing

Practice Book 101   **Regular and Irregular Verbs, Perfect Tenses**   Review irregular verbs and perfect tenses with students. Write *sing, sang,* and *sung* on the board. Ask students to name the tense of each. (present, past, past participle) Remind them that the perfect tenses use the past participle verb form.

GUIDED PRACTICE   Ask students to turn to page 101 in their *Practice Books.* Have students read the activity directions. Then direct them to work in pairs to complete the activity. Encourage students to take turns identifying the verb tense.

Fluency

Practice Book 99   **Fluency Practice**   Tell students that today they will reread the sentences on the bottom of *Practice Book* page 99. Have students locate and point to the first sentence. Tell students that everyone is going to read the sentence together. This choral reading will give students an opportunity to hear others and listen to the natural phrasing of the sentences. Choral-read each of the sentences several times.

LESSON 25

30+ Minutes

DAY AT A GLANCE
Day 4

COMPREHENSION
Reteach Graphic Aids

DECODING/SPELLING
Cumulative Review

BUILD ROBUST VOCABULARY
Reteach Words from "Visiting the Stone Circles"

GRAMMAR/WRITING
Cumulative Review

FLUENCY
Fluency Practice

Materials Needed: *Bold Moves*

Student Edition pp. 252–258

Practice Book p. 102

Copying Masters 99, 100

Spelling Words: Lesson 25

1. pedal	11. cosmopolitan
2. dentures	12. century
3. manuscript	13. tricycle
4. memorial	14. diagram
5. tripod	15. bifocals
6. memorable	16. monotone
7. biology	17. conversation
8. democracy	18. rejection
9. geography	19. celebration
10. archaeology	20. definition

RETEACH

Comprehension

Copying Master 99

Graphic Aids   Review with students that graphic aids are often used in nonfiction to provide additional information and to help the reader better visualize the information. Graphic aids include illustrations, photos, diagrams, maps, graphs, and charts. Ask students: **What kind of graphic aid can show you how a population changes over time?** (a chart or graph) **What kind of graphic aid can show you how many miles long the Mississippi River is?** (a map)

GUIDED PRACTICE   Distribute *Copying Master* 99 to students. Guide them to choose the correct graphic aid to help them answer each question.

RETEACH

Decoding/Spelling

Practice Book 102

Cumulative Review   Have students number a sheet of paper 1–16. Write *pedal* on the board and circle *ped*. Tell students that the first four words you will dictate come from Greek and Latin words for body parts. After students write each word, display it so they can proofread their work. Repeat this activity using *biology* for Greek and Latin Social Studies words (four words). Repeat again with *century* for Greek and Latin Science words (five words). Finally, use *conversation* for suffixes *-ation, -ition,* and *-ion*.

1. dentures	2. manuscript	3. memorial	4. memorable
5. democracy	6. geography	7. archaeology	8. cosmopolitan
9. tripod	10. tricycle	11. diagram	12. bifocals
13. monotone	14. rejection	15. celebration	16. definition

Have students turn to page 102 in their *Practice Books*. Ask a volunteer to read the story aloud. Point out that students should choose the answer that best tells about the story. Once students have completed the page, invite them to identify the Spelling Words in the story.

RETEACH
Build Robust Vocabulary

Words from "Visiting the Stone Circles" Review the meanings of the words *pillars* and *glistens*. Then say these sentences and ask which word describes each sentence. Have students explain why.

- **Two wooden columns hold up our front porch.** (pillars)
- **Leah's hair shines in the light after she washes it.** (glistens)

RETEACH
Grammar/Writing

Copying Master 100

Cumulative Review Have students recall the grammar skills they have learned in this lesson. Discuss examples for each skill:

- simple past and future tenses
- principal parts of verbs
- irregular verbs
- perfect tenses

GUIDED PRACTICE Distribute *Copying Master 100* to each student. Invite a volunteer to read the directions. Then have students proofread each sentence, underline the mistakes, and write the sentence correctly.

Fluency

pp. 252–258 **Fluency Practice** Have each student work with a partner to read passages from "Visiting the Stone Circles" aloud to each other. Remind students to:

- organize words into phrases that make sense.
- use punctuation to help them organize their words.

Encourage partners to read the selected passage aloud three times. Have the students rate their own reading on the 1–4 scale.

1	Need more practice
2	Pretty good
3	Good
4	Great!

DAY AT A GLANCE
Day 5

VOCABULARY
Preteach *scale, impact, barren, warped, mottled, chasm, prominent, distinctive*

COMPREHENSION
 Preteach Draw and Evaluate Conclusions

DECODING/WORD ATTACK
Preteach Decode Longer Words

DECODING/SPELLING
Preteach Words with Prefix + Root + Suffix; Words with Root + Root

GRAMMAR/WRITING
Preteach Present Progressive

FLUENCY
Fluency Performance

Materials Needed: *Bold Moves*

Student Edition pp. 252–258

Copying Master 101

Skill Card 26

Vocabulary

Copying Master 101

Lesson 26 Vocabulary Distribute a set of Vocabulary Word Cards to each student or pair of students. Hold up the Word Card for the first word and ask a volunteer to read it aloud. Have students repeat the word and hold up the matching card. Give the explanation for the word. Then ask students the first question below and discuss their responses. Continue for each Vocabulary Word.

- **Why might it be helpful to see a model showing the scale of distance between planets?**
- **What could be the effect of an asteroid's impact on Earth?**
- **Have you been someplace that looked barren? What did it look like?**
- **If you left a CD in the hot sun, would it be warped? Why or why not?**
- **Why might a person's skin look mottled?**
- **Would you want to jump across a chasm? Why or why not?**
- **What is the most prominent landmark in your area?**
- **What is something about yourself that is distinctive?**

Comprehension

Skill Card 26

Draw and Evaluate Conclusions Ask students to look at side A of *Skill Card 26: Draw and Evaluate Conclusions* and have a volunteer read the first paragraph. Tell students that at times readers must draw their own conclusions based on facts or data that they have been given. They must evaluate whether an author's conclusions are valid, based on the evidence provided. Use these points to summarize:

- Conclusions are based on facts given in a text or on prior knowledge gained from personal experiences or reading.
- Conclusions should proceed logically from the facts.
- Authors should give enough reasonable evidence to support their conclusions.

Have a student read aloud the text model on *Skill Card 26*. Then refer to the chart and ask:

- **What are some facts about border collies?** (They herd sheep; they learn commands easily and well; they can learn tricks.)
- **What conclusion did the reader draw from these facts?** (Border collies are smart.)

PRETEACH

Decoding/Word Attack

Decode Longer Words Tell students that some words consist of a root word with both a prefix and a suffix. Write *misinformation* on the board. Have volunteers identify the prefix, root word, and suffix. (mis-, inform, -ation) Explain that other words consist of two roots joined together. Write *microscope* on the board. Have volunteers identify the two root words. (micro, scope)

PRETEACH

Decoding/Spelling

Words with Prefix + Root + Suffix; Words with Root + Root Tell students that some of the next lesson's Spelling Words combine two roots. Others combine a prefix, root, and suffix. Write the following root words on the board and read them aloud. Then add the prefixes, suffixes, and roots to make the words in parentheses. Have volunteers read each word and underline the prefix, suffix, and root.

> certain   prove   meter
> (uncertainly)   (improvement)   (thermometer)

PRETEACH

Grammar/Writing

Present Progressive Tell students that progressive forms of verbs express action that is ongoing. Explain that the present progressive uses a form of the verb *to be—is, are,* or *am*—depending on the subject. Then *-ing* is added to the end of the main verb. Write this sentence on the board:

> Lily is watching the game.

Underline *is watching.* Explain that *is* is a form of the verb *to be.* The subject, Lily, is singular, so the verb form is singular. The *-ing* at the end of *watch* tells us the action is ongoing. Now write this sentence on the board:

> Her brothers are batting well.

Read the sentence aloud. Note that the subject of the sentence, *brothers,* is plural, so the form of *to be* used is plural, *are.* Point out that the final consonant in *bat* is doubled before adding *-ing.*

VOCABULARY

Student-Friendly Explanations

scale You refer to the scale of something when you want to represent and compare size and distances, but the real measurements are too enormous to be shown.

impact When one object smashes into another, it is called an impact.

barren Land that does not have trees and other plant life is barren.

warped When something is warped, it is twisted out of shape, usually by heat or water, so that it does not function in a normal manner.

mottled A surface that is mottled has irregular shapes, patterns, and colors on it.

chasm A deep split or crack in rock or ice is a chasm.

prominent When a feature is prominent, it noticeably sticks out from a surface.

distinctive When something is distinctive, it has special characteristics that make it easily recognizable.

Fluency

pp. 252–258 **Fluency Performance** Invite students to read aloud the passages from "Stone Circles" that they selected and practiced earlier. Note the number of words each student reads correctly and incorrectly. Have students rate their own oral reading on the 1–4 scale. Give students the opportunity to continue practicing and then to read the passage to you again.

DAY AT A GLANCE

Day 1

30+ Minutes

LESSON 26

VOCABULARY
Reteach *scale, impact, barren, warped, mottled, chasm, prominent, distinctive*

COMPREHENSION
 Reteach Draw and Evaluate Conclusions

DECODING/SPELLING
Reteach Words with Prefix + Root + Suffix; Words with Root + Root

GRAMMAR/WRITING
Preteach Past Progressive

FLUENCY
Fluency Practice

Materials Needed: *Bold Moves*

| Student Edition pp. 260–261 | Practice Book p. 103 | Skill Card 26 | Copying Master 102 |

RETEACH

Vocabulary

 Lesson 26 Vocabulary Read aloud the Vocabulary Words and the Student-Friendly Explanations. Have a volunteer read the article on page 260 aloud while other students follow along. Ask students to complete the sentences on page 260 by choosing the correct word from the box. Ask a volunteer to read each completed sentence aloud. Then have students read the article on page 261 and ask them to complete the sentences by choosing the correct word from the box. If students are unable to give reasonable responses, refer to the Student-Friendly Explanations. (Answers for pages 260–261: 2. *mottled*, 3. *prominent*, 4. *warped*, 5. *scale*, 6. *impact*, 7. *barren*, 8. *chasm*)

RETEACH

Comprehension

 Draw and Evaluate Conclusions Have students look at side B of *Skill Card 26: Draw and Evaluate Conclusions*. Remind students how to draw and evaluate conclusions. Then have a volunteer read the passage aloud as the other students follow along. Ask:

- **What are some facts you learned about lava?** (It flows from volcanoes; it is reddish-orange, it burns things in its path; it dries to black.)

GUIDED PRACTICE Ask students to think of possible conclusions they can draw about lava. (Possible response: It is very hot.) Have them name facts that support their conclusions. (It is reddish-orange; it burns things in its path.) Discuss other conclusions students draw and ask them to name the facts that support their conclusions.

Decoding/Spelling

Copying Master 102

Words with Prefix + Root + Suffix; Words with Root + Root Distribute *Copying Master 102*. Read aloud the Spelling Words and have students repeat them. Review the instructions for adding prefixes, suffixes, and roots to root words. Then have students complete the activity. Have students work in pairs. Each student writes a sentence for each Spelling Word, but leaves a blank for the actual word. The partners then switch papers and fill in the blanks in each other's sentences. Students should give themselves one point for each correctly spelled word.

PRETEACH

Grammar/Writing

Past Progressive Explain to students that the past progressive uses the same verb form as the present progressive: *watching* or *batting*, for example. The difference between past and present progressive is the form of the verb *to be*. Write this sentence on the board:

> My dog was barking wildly.

Underline the verb phrase *was barking*, and have a volunteer identify the form of the verb *to be*. (was) Point out that the verb form is singular and in the past tense. Then write this sentence on the board:

> Soon other dogs were joining in.

Have a volunteer identify the form of *to be* in the sentence. (were) Point out that it is plural and in the past tense.

GUIDED PRACTICE Write these sentences on the board:

> Sandy _____ (finish) her homework.
> Her friends _____ (wait) for her.

Help students determine the correct past progressive form of each verb in parentheses. (was finishing; were waiting)

VOCABULARY

Student-Friendly Explanations

scale You refer to the scale of something when you want to represent and compare size and distances, but the real measurements are too enormous to be shown.

impact When one object smashes into another, it is called an impact.

barren Land that does not have trees and other plant life is barren.

warped When something is warped, it is twisted out of shape, usually by heat or water, so that it does not function in a normal manner.

mottled A surface that is mottled has irregular shapes, patterns, and colors on it.

chasm A deep split or crack in rock or ice is a chasm.

prominent When a feature is prominent, it noticeably sticks out from a surface.

distinctive When something is distinctive, it has special characteristics that make it easily recognizable.

Fluency

Practice Book 103

Fluency Practice Have students turn to *Practice Book* page 103. Read the words in the first column aloud. Invite students to track each word and repeat it after you. Then have students work in pairs to read the words in the first column aloud to each other. Follow the same procedure with the remaining columns. After partners have practiced reading aloud the words in each column, have them practice reading all of the words.

30+ Minutes

VOCABULARY
Reteach *scale, impact, barren, warped, mottled, chasm, prominent, distinctive*

COMPREHENSION
"The Asteroid Belt"
Build Background
Monitor Comprehension
Answers to *Think Critically* Questions

DECODING/SPELLING
Reteach Words with Prefix + Root + Suffix; Words with Root + Root

GRAMMAR/WRITING
Preteach Future Progressive

FLUENCY
Fluency Practice

Materials Needed: *Bold Moves*

| Student Edition pp. 262–269 | Practice Book pp. 103, 104 | Copying Masters 101, 102 |

Vocabulary

Copying Master 101

Lesson 26 Vocabulary Distribute a set of Vocabulary Word Cards to each pair of students. Have one student in a pair make up and say aloud a sentence using one of the words, but saying *blank* for the word itself. The other student should say the Vocabulary Word that correctly completes the sentence. Have students reverse roles and continue until they have used all the words.

Comprehension

Build Background: "The Asteroid Belt"
Ask students if they have ever seen a shooting star. Have volunteers describe the experience. What did they think it was?

pp. 262–263

Monitor Comprehension: "The Asteroid Belt"
Read the title of the story aloud. Then have students read pages 262–263 to find out what the astronomer Piazzi discovered in the night sky.

After reading the pages, ask: **What did Plazzi discover?** (He discovered an asteroid.) MAIN IDEA AND SUPPORTING DETAILS

Discuss the Stop and Think question on page 262: **How is an asteroid like a small planet?** (Possible response: An asteroid is like a small planet because they both follow a certain path.) Guide students in writing the answer to this question. COMPARE AND CONTRAST

Ask: **What did scientists once think about asteroids?** (Possible response: They thought they were parts of an old planet that had exploded.) NOTE DETAILS

Discuss the Stop and Think question on page 263: **What did scientists learn from studying asteroids?** (Possible response: Scientists learned that asteroids are likely what was left over when the planets formed.) Guide students in writing the answer to this question. SUMMARIZE

Ask: What problems did Galileo's and Kepler's telescopes have? (Possible response: Galileo's telescope produced distorted images; Kepler's telescope produced upside-down images.) **SUMMARIZE**

Discuss the Stop and Think question on page 264: **Why does the author include facts about telescopes?** (Possible response: The author includes these facts because telescopes are important tools in the study of asteroids.) **Guide students in writing the answer to the question. AUTHOR'S PURPOSE**

Read aloud the second paragraph on page 265. Model the strategy of drawing and evaluating conclusions.

(THINK ALOUD) **This paragraph tells me some facts: space probes have sent back images, samples, and data about asteroids. It tells me that one probe landed on an asteroid. From these facts, I can conclude that we have learned a lot about asteroids from space probes.** DRAW AND EVALUATE CONCLUSIONS

Discuss the Stop and Think question on page 265: **What do you learn about space probes?** (Possible response: I learn that space probes send images and samples back to Earth for scientists to research.) **Guide students in writing the answer to the question. NOTE DETAILS**

 Ask: How is Jupiter like a solar system? (Possible response: Its many moons are like small planets orbiting it.) **MAKE COMPARISONS**

Discuss the Stop and Think question on page 266: **How does Jupiter's large mass help the other planets?** (Possible response: Jupiter's large mass keeps the asteroids orbiting around Jupiter so they don't hit the other planets.) **Guide students in writing the answer to this question.** DRAW AND EVALUATE CONCLUSIONS

Discuss the Stop and Think question on page 267: **What do you think you will learn about next?** (Possible response: I think I will learn about asteroids that actually hit Earth.) **Guide students in writing the answer to the question. MAKE PREDICTIONS**

 After students have read the page, ask: **Are meteors a danger to Earth?** (Possible response: Not really, because they only hit once every million years or so.) **DRAW CONCLUSIONS**

Discuss the Stop and Think question on page 268: **What would you do if you found a meteorite?** (Possible responses: I would show it to my friends; take it to a museum; take it to school.) **Guide students in writing the answer to this question. PERSONAL RESPONSE**

Spelling Words: Lesson 26

1. postponement	11. telescope
2. misinformation	12. thermometer
3. uncertainly	13. microscope
4. improvement	14. mischievous
5. indestructible	15. prescription
6. uncomfortable	16. telephone
7. unbeatable	17. octopus
8. unexpectedly	18. process
9. reexamination	19. transport
10. unmistakable	20. aquatic

page 269 **Answers to *Think Critically* Questions**   Help students read and answer the *Think Critically* questions on page 269. Have students copy the graphic organizer in question 1 on a separate sheet of paper. Then guide students in writing the answer to each question. Possible responses are provided.

1. Asteroids are space objects that are like rocks. Most orbit between Mars and Jupiter along the Asteroid Belt. **Main Idea and Details**

2. When asteroids enter our atmosphere, they either burn up or land on Earth. **Cause and Effect**

3. Scientists study asteroids because they may give clues about the origins of the planets. **Draw Conclusions**

RETEACH

Decoding/Spelling

Copying Master 102 **Words with Prefix + Root + Suffix; Words with Root + Root**   Remind students that they can decode a new word by identifying its parts. Some words combine two roots. Others combine a prefix, root, and suffix. Play "The Match Game" by writing root words, prefixes, and suffixes that create Spelling Words on individual index cards. Pass out one card to each student. Then ask students to find classmates with cards that combine with theirs to make up one of the Spelling Words. Conclude the activity with groups of students spelling their completed words aloud.

PRETEACH

Grammar/Writing

 Practice Book 104

Future Progressive Explain to students that the progressive forms of verbs express action that is continuous or ongoing. Write the following sentence on the board:

> We will be laughing about these
> pictures for years to come.

Have a volunteer underline the verb phrase, and point out that the future progressive form of a verb uses the future tense of *to be*. Like all progressive forms, the present tense verb with an *-ing* ending follows.

GUIDED PRACTICE Have students read the instructions for the exercise on page 104 of their *Practice Books*. Then invite students to read the first sentence. Ask a volunteer to identify the progressive verb. Then ask students to identify the form. Follow the same procedure for the rest of the sentences.

Fluency

 Practice Book 103

Fluency Practice Invite students to look at the bottom half of *Practice Book* page 103. These sentences have been broken into natural phrases. Tell students to repeat each phrase after you, mirroring your expression, phrasing, and pace. After students have repeated each sentence, invite them to practice reading the sentences to a partner.

30+ Minutes

COMPREHENSION
Preteach Fact and Opinion

Reread and Summarize "The Asteroid Belt"

DECODING/SPELLING
Reteach Words with Prefix + Root + Suffix; Words with Root + Root

BUILD ROBUST VOCABULARY
Teach Words from "The Asteroid Belt"

GRAMMAR/WRITING
Reteach Writing Trait: Organization

FLUENCY
Fluency Practice

Materials Needed: *Bold Moves*

| Student Edition pp. 262–268 | Practice Book pp. 103, 105 | Copying Masters 102, 103 |

Comprehension

Copying Master 103
Fact and Opinion Distribute *Copying Master 103* and have volunteers read aloud the information at the top of the page.

GUIDED PRACTICE Have students read the passage. Ask volunteers to identify each fact. For each fact, ask: **How do you know this is a fact?** (Possible response: It can be proven.) Then have them identify the opinions in the passage. For each opinion, ask: **How do you know this is an opinion?** (Possible response: It expresses feelings or beliefs.)

Reread and Summarize Have students reread and summarize "The Asteroid Belt" in sections, as described below.

pp. 262–263

Let's reread pages 262–263 to recall how asteroids were first discovered.
Summary: An astronomer named Piazzi discovered the first asteroid in 1801. Asteroids can look very different. They are probably what was left over when planets were formed.

pp. 264–265

Let's look back at pages 264–265 to recall how asteroids have been observed and studied.
Summary: Telescopes were invented by Galileo and perfected by others. They allowed astronomers to view and study asteroids. Now space probes provide images and samples of asteroids for research.

pp. 266–268

Last, let's look at pages 266–268 to find out about asteroids and the planets.
Summary: Jupiter's gravity keeps asteroids in orbit. Sometimes asteroids cross paths with Earth or enter Earth's atmosphere. When they enter the atmosphere, they are called meteors. When they land on Earth, they are called meteorites and can cause great damage.

Decoding/Spelling

Copying Master 102
Words with Prefix + Root + Suffix; Words with Root + Root *Copying Master 102.* Write *prove* and *examine* on the board. Ask students what the words have in common. (They end in silent *e.*) Have volunteers write the Spelling Words that contain these words on the board and underline the root word in each. (improvement, reexamination) Point out that the final *e* is dropped when the suffix begins with a vowel. When the suffix begins with a consonant, the final *e* stays. Write *mistake* on the board. Ask a volunteer to find the Spelling Word that contains that root and to write it on the board. (unmistakable) Talk about how the silent *e* was dropped before the suffix was added.

TEACH

Build Robust Vocabulary

Words from "The Asteroid Belt" Have students locate the word *revolve* on page 262 of "The Asteroid Belt." Ask a volunteer to read aloud the sentence in which this word appears. (Last sentence: *Piazzi had discovered the first asteroid, a space object that orbits, or revolves around, the sun.*) Explain that this sentence means that an asteroid moves in a circle around the sun. Continue by asking students to locate and read aloud the sentence in which the word *impressed* appears on page 264. (Line 15: *Newton was not impressed and continued his own design.*) Explain that this sentence means that Newton did not think Cassegrain's telescope was great. *Impress* means to make people admire or like something. Then ask students to locate and read aloud the sentence in which the word *disaster* appears on page 267. (Line 10: *If a city had been hit, the result could have been a major disaster.*) Explain that this sentence means that if an asteroid hit a city, many buildings could have been destroyed and people hurt or killed. Help students look up each word in a dictionary. Discuss what else they learn about each word's meaning from this resource.

RETEACH

Grammar/Writing

Writing Trait: Organization Have students turn to page 105 in their *Practice Books*. Explain that when writers write nonfiction, it is important to organize ideas logically so readers understand the information being presented. Have students read the information in the box. Tell students that when they describe, they may use spatial order. They can describe a place from farthest to nearest or from nearest to farthest. Clue words or phrases such as *before, in front of, behind, above,* and *below* indicate spatial order. When they are writing to persuade, they may use order of importance. They can write their reasons from least important to most important. Clue words or phrases such as *first, next, then, most important,* and *last* can indicate order of importance.

GUIDED PRACTICE Complete *Practice Book* page 105 together. In Part C, be sure students include clue words or phrases to indicate spatial order in their descriptions.

Fluency

Fluency Practice Tell students that today they will reread the sentences on the bottom of *Practice Book* page 103. Have students point to the first sentence. Tell students that everyone is going to read the sentence together. This choral reading will give students an opportunity to hear others and to listen to the natural phrasing of the sentences. Choral-read each of the sentences several times.

LESSON 26

DAY AT A GLANCE

Day 4

COMPREHENSION
Reteach Fact and Opinion

DECODING/SPELLING
Reteach Words with Prefix + Root + Suffix; Words with Root + Root

BUILD ROBUST VOCABULARY
Reteach Words from "The Asteroid Belt"

GRAMMAR/WRITING
Reteach Writing Form: Persuasive Paragraph

FLUENCY
Fluency Practice

Materials Needed: *Bold Moves*

Student Edition pp. 262–268

Practice Book p. 106

Copying Master 104

Spelling Words: Lesson 26

1. postponement	11. telescope
2. misinformation	12. thermometer
3. uncertainly	13. microscope
4. improvement	14. mischievous
5. indestructible	15. prescription
6. uncomfortable	16. telephone
7. unbeatable	17. octopus
8. unexpectedly	18. process
9. reexamination	19. transport
10. unmistakable	20. aquatic

30+ Minutes

RETEACH

Comprehension

Fact and Opinion   Remind students of the following:

- A **fact** can be checked and proved to find out whether it is true. Verifiable **numbers** can be clues to facts.

- An **opinion** is a personal belief and cannot be proved true or false. **Clue words,** such as *probably* and *should*, are often found in statements of opinion.

- Judge the **truth of a fact** by confirming it through another resource, such as a reference book.

- Judge the **logic of an opinion** by thinking about the reasons, evidence, and examples given to back it up.

GUIDED PRACTICE   Write these sentences from "The Asteroid Belt" on the board. Ask volunteers to identify them as facts or opinions. (fact; opinion; fact)

> Galileo made the first refracting telescope.
>
> So asteroids are likely what was left over when the planets formed.
>
> On March 23, 1989, a fifty-million-ton asteroid passed by Earth.

RETEACH

Decoding/Spelling

Practice Book 106

Words with Prefix + Root +Suffix; Words with Root + Root   Have students number a sheet of paper 1–18. Write the Spelling Word *postponement* on the board. Point to the prefix and the suffix. Tell students that the first eleven words you will dictate have a prefix, a root, and a suffix. After students write each word, display it so they can proofread their work. Repeat this process with *telephone*, telling students that the next four words have a root plus a root. Then tell students that the last three words you will dictate do not have a set root-affix pattern.

1. misinformation	2. uncertainly	3. improvement
4. indestructible	5. uncomfortable	6. unbeatable
7. unexpectedly	8. reexamination	9. unmistakable
10. prescription	11. mischievous	12. telescope
13. thermometer	14. microscope	15. transport
16. octopus	17. aquatic	18. process

---

310 Lesson 26 • Bold Moves

Have students turn to page 106 in their *Practice Books*. Have a volunteer read aloud the passage. Then ask students to circle the words with prefix + root + suffix and underline the root + root words. Have students complete the bottom half of the page independently. Then ask volunteers to share their answers and discuss the choices students made.

RETEACH

Build Robust Vocabulary

Words from "The Asteroid Belt"   Review the meanings of the words *revolve, impressed,* and *disaster*. Then say these sentences and ask which word describes each sentence. Have students explain why.

- **The baby watched the red ball move in circles around the clown on his wind-up mobile.** (revolve)
- **The teacher liked and admired Tom's story because the student had put a lot of care into writing it.** (impressed)
- **A hurricane is a storm that can cause many buildings to be destroyed and people to be hurt or killed.** (disaster)

RETEACH

Grammar/Writing

Copying Master 104

Writing Form: Persuasive Paragraph   Remind students that the purpose of a persuasive paragraph is to persuade people to think or act in a certain way. It is important to state an opinion strongly and to organize ideas logically, using signal words to indicate the order. Distribute *Copying Master 104*. Have students read the description of a persuasive paragraph. Then read the student model together. Write the following sentence from the paragraph on the board.

> Space exploration allows us to imagine.

Model for students how the sentence can be improved to show the order of importance.

> Finally, and most important, space exploration allows us to imagine.

GUIDED PRACTICE   Complete the activity by having students rewrite the introduction to the paragraph, putting the opinion statement first. Talk about how stating the opinion in the first sentence engages readers and prepares them for what is coming.

Fluency

pp. 262– 268

Fluency Practice   Have each student work with a partner to read passages from "The Asteroid Belt" aloud to each other. Students may select a passage that they enjoyed or choose one of the following options:

- Read page 263. (Total: 127 words)
- Read page 265. (Total: 131 words)

Encourage students to read the selected passage aloud to their partner three times. Have the student rate his or her reading on the 1–4 scale.

1	Need more practice
2	Pretty good
3	Good
4	Great!

DAY AT A GLANCE

Day 5

VOCABULARY
Preteach *lavish, doomed, dreaded, murky, ascent, remains*

COMPREHENSION
 Preteach Draw and Evaluate Conclusions

DECODING/WORD ATTACK
Preteach Decode Longer Words

DECODING/SPELLING
Preteach Words with Silent Letters

GRAMMAR/WRITING
Preteach Contractions with Pronouns

FLUENCY
Fluency Performance

Materials Needed: *Bold Moves*

Student Edition 262–268

Copying Master 105

PRETEACH

Vocabulary

Copying Master 105

Lesson 27 Vocabulary Distribute a set of Vocabulary Word Cards to each student. Hold up the card for the first word, and ask a volunteer to read it aloud. Have students repeat the word and hold up the matching card. Give the explanation for the word. Ask students the first question below and discuss their responses. Continue for each Vocabulary Word.

- **What kind of meal would you think of as lavish?**
- **What movie or story do you know in which a character was doomed?**
- **Have you ever had a task to do that you dreaded?**
- **Would you enjoy swimming in murky water? Why or why not?**
- **Which is harder in mountain climbing, the ascent or the return? Why?**
- **What might the remains of a birthday dinner look like?**

PRETEACH

Comprehension

pp. 262–268

Focus Skill

Draw and Evaluate Conclusions Tell students that good readers draw logical conclusions about what they read and can evaluate an author's conclusions by judging the evidence provided. Stress these points to summarize:

- Conclusions are only valid if they are based on facts or general knowledge that can be proven.
- To draw valid conclusions, readers (and writers) must have enough reasonable evidence that points toward that conclusion.

Ask students to think back to the selection "The Asteroid Belt." Then ask:

- **What facts did you learn about asteroids and Earth?** (Possible responses: Asteroids have hit Earth in the past. They have done a lot of damage. A really big one hits about once every million years.)
- **What conclusion can you draw from these facts?** (Possible response: A large asteroid will hit Earth again someday.)

GUIDED PRACTICE Have students work in small groups to talk about other conclusions they can draw about asteroids and Earth. (Possible response: If an asteroid hits, it will probably do a lot of damage.) Point out that their conclusions should be supported by evidence in the selection. Encourage them to state the evidence that supports their conclusions. (Possible response: Asteroids have done a lot of damage in the past.)

PRETEACH
Decoding/Word Attack

Decode Longer Words   Write the word *fasten* on the board and have a volunteer read it aloud. Divide the word into syllables and point out that it ends with the pattern consonant + *en*. Ask students what letters stand for the sound /fas/. (fas) Then have them identify the letters that stand for the sound /en/. (ten) Point out that the letter *t* is silent in the word *fasten*.

Repeat the decoding process above for the word *thistle,* pointing out the silent *t* in its second syllable. Then tell students the following:

- Divide the word into syllables before the *-tle* or *-ten*. The *t* in these endings is silent. The vowel sound is *schwa*.

- The previous syllable ends in a consonant, so the vowel sound is short.

PRETEACH
Decoding/Spelling

Words with Silent Letters   Write each of the Spelling Words below on the board and read them aloud. Underline the silent letter in *fasten*. Have students identify the silent letters in the remaining words.

fasten	wrinkled	knuckle	align
yolk	crumbs	shepherd	aisle

PRETEACH
Grammar/Writing

Contractions with Pronouns   Tell students that a contraction is a word made by combining two words and omitting some letters. An apostrophe takes the place of the letters that are omitted. Write this sentence on the board:

> He's going to the park.

Explain that the word *he's* is a contraction. It is made from the words *he* and *is*. An apostrophe takes the place of the *i* in *is*. Then write this sentence on the board:

> We'll meet you at the park.

Ask: **What is the contraction in this sentence?** (We'll) **What words make the contraction?** (We, will) **What letters does the apostrophe replace?** (wi)

Student-Friendly Explanations

lavish   When something is lavish, it is richly decorated and looks impressive.

doomed   If something is doomed, it is predestined to have something terrible happen to it.

dreaded   If you have dreaded something, you have greatly feared it happening.

murky   If something is murky, it is dark and difficult to see through.

ascent   When you make a steep upward climb, you make an ascent.

remains   The parts that are left of something that has died, grown old, or been destroyed are its remains.

Fluency

pp. 262–268   **Fluency Performance** Invite students to read aloud the passages from "The Asteroid Belt" that they selected and practiced earlier. Note the number of words each student reads correctly and incorrectly. Have students rate their own oral reading on the 1–4 scale. Give students the opportunity to continue practicing and then to read the passage to you again.

LESSON 27

DAY AT A GLANCE

Day 1

VOCABULARY
Reteach *lavish, doomed, dreaded, murky, ascent, remains*

COMPREHENSION
 Reteach Draw and Evaluate Conclusions

DECODING/SPELLING
Reteach Words with Silent Letters

GRAMMAR/WRITING
Preteach Common Errors: Contraction or Possessive Pronoun?

FLUENCY
Fluency Practice

Materials Needed: *Bold Moves*

| Student Edition pp. 270–271 | Practice Book p. 107 | Skill Card 27 | Copying Master 106 |

Vocabulary

pp. 270–271 **Lesson 27 Vocabulary** Read aloud the Vocabulary Words and the Student-Friendly Explanations. Then ask students to read the passage on pages 270–271 of their books. Guide students in completing the sentences on both pages by selecting the correct Vocabulary Word. Ask a volunteer to read each completed sentence aloud. Then have students write the Vocabulary Word that best completes the synonym web. If students have trouble giving correct responses, refer to the Student-Friendly Explanations. (Answers for pages 270–271: 2. *remains*, 3. *lavish*, 4. *doomed*, 5. *ascent*, 6. *dreaded*, 7. *murky*)

Comprehension

Skill Card 27 **Draw and Evaluate Conclusions** Have students look at side A of *Skill Card 27: Draw and Evaluate Conclusions*. Ask students to read the explanation of how to draw and evaluate a conclusion. Then have a volunteer read the paragraph aloud. Ask:

- **What conclusion can you draw about Spain?** (Possible response: Spain got very rich from the treasure fleet.)

- **What evidence in the passage supports this conclusion?** (The ships brought back gold, silver, jewels, and other valuable goods.)

Have students examine the chart at the bottom of the card. Remind students that a valid conclusion must be supported by facts and data.

GUIDED PRACTICE Now have students look at side B of *Skill Card 27: Draw and Evaluate Conclusions*. Have a volunteer read the information about drawing and evaluating conclusions aloud. Then have students read the passage. Guide them in copying the chart, and have them work in pairs to draw and evaluate conclusions about the passage. (Possible response: Conclusion: It was easy to get sick on a Spanish galleon. Evidence: There were animals carrying disease, the food and water were often bad, and it was impossible to get clean.)

Decoding/Spelling

Copying Master 106

Words with Silent Letters   Distribute *Copying Master 106*. Review the explanation of silent letters. Then have students complete the following activity. This activity is based on the traditional Memory Game. Pairs of students make two sets of game cards using the lesson's Spelling Words with silent letters missing; a dash appears in place of each silent letter. After a student matches two cards, he or she must supply the missing letters to keep the game cards. If the wrong letter is supplied, the opponent gets the game cards and the next turn.

Grammar/Writing

Common Errors: Contraction or Possessive Pronoun?   Explain to students that *it's* and *who's* (with apostrophes) are always contractions, not possessive pronouns. Then write these sentences on the board:

> The dog wags its tail.
>
> It's waiting to go for a walk.

Ask a volunteer to read each sentence aloud. Ask: **Which sentence has a possessive pronoun?** (the first sentence) **Which sentence has a contraction?** (the second sentence) **How can you tell?** (It's has an apostrophe.)

GUIDED PRACTICE   Write these sentences on the board:

> Who's going to the park?
>
> I know whose gloves these are.
>
> The twins asked us to their party.
>
> They're very good swimmers.

Ask students to identify the contraction or possessive pronoun in each sentence (contraction—who's; possessive pronoun—whose; possessive pronoun—their; contraction—they're)

Student-Friendly Explanations

lavish   When something is lavish, it is richly decorated and looks impressive.

doomed   If something is doomed, it is predestined to have something terrible happen to it.

dreaded   If you have dreaded something, you have greatly feared it happening.

murky   If something is murky, it is dark and difficult to see through.

ascent   When you make a steep upward climb, you make an ascent.

remains   The parts that are left of something that has died, grown old, or been destroyed are its remains.

Fluency

Practice Book 107

Fluency Practice   Have students turn to *Practice Book* page 107. Read the words in the first column aloud. Invite students to track each word and repeat the words after you. Then have students work in pairs to read the words in the first column aloud to each other. Follow the same procedure with each of the remaining columns. After partners have practiced reading aloud the words in each of the columns, have them practice reading all of the words.

30+ Minutes

VOCABULARY
Reteach *lavish, doomed, dreaded, murky, ascent, remains*

COMPREHENSION
"Gold Beneath the Sea"

Build Background

Monitor Comprehension

Answers to *Think Critically* Questions

DECODING/SPELLING
Reteach Words with Silent Letters

GRAMMAR/WRITING
Preteach Contractions with *Not*

FLUENCY
Fluency Practice

Materials Needed: *Bold Moves*

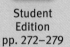

Student Edition pp. 272–279

Practice Book pp. 107, 108

Copying Masters 105, 106

Vocabulary

Copying Master 105

Lesson 27 Vocabulary Distribute a set of Vocabulary Word Cards to each student. Tell students that the Vocabulary Words can be classified into three groups: adjectives (words that describe), nouns (words that name a person, place, thing, or idea), and verbs (words that name an action or state of being). Have students classify their cards. Then ask volunteers to tell which words are in which group and why. (adjectives: lavish, doomed, murky—they describe; nouns: ascent, remains—they name things; verb: dreaded—it names an action)

Comprehension

Build Background: "Gold Beneath the Sea"
Ask students if they have ever dreamed of finding buried treasure. Have volunteers describe what they would do with such a find.

pp. 272–273

Monitor Comprehension: "Gold Beneath the Sea"
Read the title of the story aloud. Then have students read pages 272–273 to find out what kind of treasure the selection describes.

After reading the pages, ask: **What kind of treasure does the selection describe?** (gold, silver, and colorful gems) NOTE DETAILS

Discuss the Stop and Think question on page 272: **Why was 1622 an exciting time for adventurers?** (Possible response: It was an exciting time because adventurers could travel on the many ships sailing between North America and Spain.) DRAW AND EVALUATE CONCLUSIONS

Discuss the Stop and Think question on page 273: **What dangers did the ships face? Underline the words that tell you this.** (The ships faced the dangers of pirate attacks, bad weather, and sinking caused by badly balanced cargo. Students should underline *pirate attack, hurricane,* and *badly balanced cargo*, or other similar phrases.) Guide students in writing the answer to this question. NOTE DETAILS

Ask: **What do you think happened to the *Atocha*?** (Possible response: I think it sank in a hurricane.) MAKE PREDICTIONS

pp. 274–275

Ask students what is happening to the ship in the illustration. Then discuss the Stop and Think question on page 274: **Why was the ship doomed from the start?** (Possible response: The ship was doomed from the start because its heavy cargo dragged it down in the storm.) Guide students in writing the answer to this question. CAUSE AND EFFECT

Have students read the first two paragraphs on page 275. Model the strategy of drawing conclusions.

THINK ALOUD **When I read the subheading "A Modern-Day Treasure Hunter," I wonder what kind of person would want to hunt for treasure. Then I read that Mel Fisher grew up far from the sea. He read many books about shipwrecks and treasure. He loves to dive deep in the ocean. I conclude that his imagination and his love of adventure made him want to hunt for treasure.** DRAW CONCLUSIONS

Discuss the Stop and Think question on page 275: **How does the mailbox help divers find treasure?** (The mailbox sweeps away sand and mud, making it easier to see treasure on the sea floor.) Guide students in writing the answer to this question. MAKE PREDICTIONS

pp. 276– 277

Have students read pages 276–277. Ask: **What was the first clue that led to the discovery of the *Atocha*?** (They found gold coins.) NOTE DETAILS

Discuss the Stop and Think question on page 276: **Do you think Mel Fisher will find the treasure? Explain.** (Possible response: I think that Mel Fisher and his crew will find the treasure because they are very determined.) Guide students in writing the answer to this question. MAKE PREDICTIONS

Discuss the Stop and Think question on page 277: **How could everyone tell that something exciting had occurred?** (Possible response: They could tell because the diver was very excited when he came back up to the surface.) Guide students in writing the answer to this question. MAKE INFERENCES

page 278

Have students read page 278. Ask: **What problem did Mel Fisher face? How was the problem solved?** (Possible response: Florida and the U.S. government wanted the treasure he had found, but the Supreme Court decided that Fisher could keep the treasure.) PLOT: CONFLICT AND RESOLUTION

Discuss the Stop and Think question on page 278: **Do you think the United States should get a share of the treasure? Explain.** (Possible response: I think that the United States should not get a share of the treasure because Mel Fisher and his team did all the work to find it.) Guide students in writing the answer to this question. MAKE JUDGMENTS

VOCABULARY

Student-Friendly Explanations

lavish When something is lavish, it is richly decorated and looks impressive.

doomed If something is doomed, it is predestined to have something terrible happen to it.

dreaded If you have dreaded something, you have greatly feared it happening.

murky If something is murky, it is dark and difficult to see through.

ascent When you make a steep upward climb, you make an ascent.

remains The parts that are left of something that has died, grown old, or been destroyed are its remains.

Spelling Words: Lesson 27

1.	aisle	11.	reign
2.	align	12.	bustle
3.	rhythm	13.	shepherd
4.	crumbs	14.	soften
5.	fasten	15.	sword
6.	glistened	16.	thistle
7.	knotty	17.	knock
8.	knuckle	18.	wrestle
9.	often	19.	wrinkled
10.	plumber	20.	yolk

page 279 **Answers to *Think Critically* Questions** Help students read and answer the Think Critically questions on page 279. Then guide students in writing the answer to each question. Possible responses are provided.

1. Mel Fisher found the *Atocha* in 1985 after searching for many years and inventing his own equipment along the way. **MAIN IDEA AND DETAILS**

2. I can tell that Mel Fisher was a very determined and persistent person because he searched for the treasure from the Atocha for more than twenty years. He didn't give up even when his son died. **CHARACTER**

3. This selection makes me feel excited because Mel Fisher actually found a fortune of gold under the sea that no one else had been able to find. **AUTHOR'S PURPOSE**

RETEACH

Decoding/Spelling

Copying Master 106 **Words with Silent Letters** Write each Spelling Word on a card, and hand out a card to each student. Across the board, write these headings: *silent t, silent w, silent k, silent g, silent l, silent b, silent h, silent t+e, silent k+e, silent e+s, silent t+w+e.*

Have students line up as quickly as possible in front of the heading that names the spelling rule for their word. (silent *t*: fasten, glistened, often, soften; silent *w*: sword, wrinkled; silent *k*: knotty, knock; silent *g*: align, reign; silent *l*: yolk; silent *h*: shepherd, rhythm; silent *t+e*: bustle, thistle; silent *k+e*: knuckle; silent *e+s*: aisle; silent *t+w+e*: wrestle)

PRETEACH

Grammar/Writing

Practice Book 108 **Contractions with *Not*** Remind students that a contraction is a word made by combining two words and omitting some letters. Explain that an apostrophe takes the place of the letters that are omitted. Then write the following sentence on the board:

> Our families haven't seen each other all year.

Underline the word *haven't* and explain that it is a contraction formed from a verb and the adverb *not*. *Haven't* is formed from the words *have* and *not*. Point out that the apostrophe replaces the *o* in *not*.

GUIDED PRACTICE Have students turn to page 108 in their *Practice Books* and read the instruction for the activity. Have a volunteer read the first example sentence aloud. Guide students to choose the correct word to complete the sentence. Ask students to choose the correct word to complete each of the remaining example sentences. Discuss with students the words from which each contraction is formed.

Fluency

Practice Book 107 **Fluency Practice** Invite students to look at the bottom half of *Practice Book* page 107. These sentences have been broken into natural phrases. Tell students to repeat each phrase after you, mirroring your expression, phrasing, and pace. After students have repeated each sentence, invite them to practice reading the sentences to a partner.

LESSON 27

DAY AT A GLANCE

Day 3

COMPREHENSION
Preteach Connotation/Denotation

Reread and Summarize "Gold Beneath the Sea"

DECODING/SPELLING
Reteach Words with Silent Letters

BUILD ROBUST VOCABULARY
Teach Words from "Gold Beneath the Sea

GRAMMAR/WRITING
Reteach Writing Trait: Organization

FLUENCY
Fluency Practice

Materials Needed: *Bold Moves*

| Student Edition pp. 272–278 | Practice Book pp. 107, 109 | Copying Master 107 |

PRETEACH

Comprehension

Connotation/Denotation Distribute *Copying Master 107*, and have students read the information at the top of the page.

GUIDED PRACTICE Ask students to read each underlined word in the passage. Have a volunteer give a denotation for each. Then ask students whether each word's connotation is positive or negative. Discuss any differences in opinion, and have students give reasons to support their answers. Then have students complete the activity.

Reread and Summarize Have students reread and summarize "Gold Beneath the Sea" in sections, as described below.

 Let's reread pages 272–273 to recall the treasure and the ship the *Atocha*.
Summary: In 1622, ships sailed for Spain from the Americas carrying gold, silver, and jewels. The Atocha was one of these ships. It left late in the season.

 Now let's reread pages 274–275 to recall what happened to the Atocha and who Mel Fisher is.
Summary: Three hundred years ago, a hurricane hit the Atocha and sank it. Mel Fisher grew up determined to find sunken treasure.

Last, let's reread pages 276–278 to remember what happened to the treasure.
Summary: Mel Fisher and his workers finally found the treasure. The state of Florida and the U.S. government tried to claim the treasure, but the Supreme Court decided that it belonged to Mel Fisher.

RETEACH

Decoding/Spelling

Words with Silent Letters Tell students that when writing a word with silent letters, they should write all the possible spellings for the word to see which one looks right. If they are still unsure, they should check the dictionary. Say these words aloud to students: *shepherd, knotty, often, bustle, yolk.*

Have students write all the possible spellings they can think of for each word. Ask them to circle the spelling that looks right. Have students who are unsure of the correct spelling to look up the word in a dictionary.

TEACH

Build Robust Vocabulary

pp. 273– 278 **Words from "Gold Beneath the Sea"** Have students locate the word *cargo* on page 273 of "Gold Beneath the Sea." Ask a volunteer to read aloud the sentence in which this word appears. (Line 9: *Once the cargo arrived, it had to be loaded on the ships carefully.*) Explain that *cargo* means goods carried by a plane, ship, truck, or other vehicle. Continue by asking students to locate and read aloud the sentence in which the word *tragically* appears on page 276. (Line 13: *Tragically, the boat sank and all three aboard it died.*) Explain that this sentence means that it was horribly sad that the boat sank and the people died. Then ask students to locate and read aloud the sentence in which the word *proclaimed* appears on page 278. (Line 4: *Finally, the Supreme Court proclaimed that Fisher owned what he and his crew found.*) Explain that this sentence means that the court announced to the public that Fisher was the owner.

Give each student a folded slip of paper with one of the words on it. Have students pass the papers to each other as you play or sing a song. Stop the music. Have each student open his or her slip of paper, read the word, and use it in a sentence. Repeat a few times.

RETEACH

Grammar/Writing

Practice Book 109 **Writing Trait: Organization** Have students turn to page 109 in their *Practice Books*. Explain that one kind of organization to use in writing is main ideas and details. Have a student read the information in the box. Point out that the author of "Gold Beneath the Sea" used main ideas and details in each paragraph.

GUIDED PRACTICE Guide students in completing *Practice Book* page 109. Remind them that all the sentences in a paragraph should support the main idea.

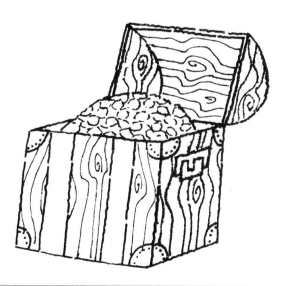

Fluency

Practice Book 107 **Fluency Practice** Tell students that today they will reread the sentences on the bottom of *Practice Book* page 107. Have students locate and point to the first sentence. Tell students that everyone is going to read the sentence together. This choral reading will give students an opportunity to hear others and listen to the natural phrasing of the sentences. Choral-read each of the sentences several times.

COMPREHENSION
Reteach Connotation/Denotation

DECODING/SPELLING
Reteach Words with Silent Letters

BUILD ROBUST VOCABULARY
Reteach Words from "Gold Beneath the Sea"

GRAMMAR/WRITING
Reteach Writing Form: A Review

FLUENCY
Fluency Practice

Materials Needed: *Bold Moves*

| Student Edition pp. 272–278 | Practice Book p. 110 | Copying Master 108 |

Spelling Words: Lesson 27

1. aisle	11. reign
2. align	12. bustle
3. rhythm	13. shepherd
4. crumbs	14. soften
5. fasten	15. sword
6. glistened	16. thistle
7. knotty	17. knock
8. knuckle	18. wrestle
9. often	19. wrinkled
10. plumber	20. yolk

RETEACH

Comprehension

Connotation/Denotation Remind students that many words have connotations as well as denotations. Point out that a writer often chooses a certain word because of its connotation. Write these sentences on the board. Ask volunteers to read each sentence aloud and define the underlined word. Then ask whether each underlined word has a positive or negative connotation. (*negative; negative*)

> As the ships passed by what is now the state of Florida, a <u>frightful</u> storm began.
>
> The crew fought back, but it was <u>hopeless</u>.

GUIDED PRACTICE Ask students to look through "Gold Beneath the Sea" to find another example of a sentence containing a word with negative connotations and an example of a sentence containing a word with positive connotations. Volunteers can read their sentences aloud and discuss the connotations of the words.

RETEACH

Decoding/Spelling

Practice Book 110 **Words with Silent Letters** Have students number a sheet of paper 1–19. Write the Spelling Word *wrestle* on the board and circle the *w,* the *t,* and the *e.* Remind students that these are silent letters, and explain that there will be either one or two silent letters in the words you dictate. After students write each word, display it so they can proofread their work.

1. fasten	2. glistened	3. often	4. bustle
5. soften	6. thistle	7. sword	8. align
9. reign	10. yolk	11. crumbs	12. plumber
13. shepherd	14. rhythm	15. knotty	16. knock
17. wrinkled	18. knuckle	19. aisle	

Have students turn to page 110 in their *Practice Books*. Ask students to identify the eight words with silent letters in the sentences. Then ask volunteers to describe and show the changes they made to the picture.

Build Robust Vocabulary

Words from "Gold Beneath the Sea" Review the meanings of the words *cargo, tragically,* and *proclaimed.* Then say these sentences and ask which word describes each sentence. Have students explain why.

- **The workers loaded goods onto the truck that would take them across the country.** (cargo)

- **Very sadly, the fire burned down the oldest building in town.** (tragically)

- **The judge announced to the public that Burke had won the art contest.** (proclaimed)

Grammar/Writing

Copying Master 108

Writing Form: A Review Remind students that a review gives an opinion about a book. Tell them that it is important to organize a review logically. Each paragraph should have a main idea expressed in a topic sentence. The other sentences in the paragraph should support the main idea. Distribute *Copying Master 108.* Ask students to read the description of a review and the Student Model. Then ask a volunteer to identify the sentence in the second paragraph that does not support the main idea. (Jean Craighead George has written a lot of other books about nature, too.)

GUIDED PRACTICE Guide students through the activities on *Copying Master 108.* Be sure they can identify the topic sentence and supporting sentences in each paragraph. Ask volunteers to read aloud their rewritten final sentences.

Fluency

pp. 272–278

Fluency Practice Have each student work with a partner to read passages from "Gold Beneath the Sea" aloud to each other. Students may select a passage that they enjoyed or choose one of the following options:

- Read page 273. (Total: 138 words)

- Read page 276. (Total: 153 words)

Encourage students to read the selected passage aloud to their partner three times. Have the student rate his or her reading on the 1–4 scale.

1	Need more practice
2	Pretty good
3	Good
4	Great!

DAY AT A GLANCE

Day 5

VOCABULARY
Preteach *qualm, contentedly, intolerable, officious, torrent, contrary, endanger, contemplate*

COMPREHENSION
 Preteach Characterization

DECODING/WORD ATTACK
Preteach Decode Longer Words

DECODING/SPELLING
Preteach Related Words

GRAMMAR/WRITING
Preteach Adverbs

FLUENCY
Fluency Performance

Materials Needed: *Bold Moves*

Student Edition pp. 272–278

Skill Card 28

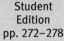
Copying Master 109

PRETEACH

Vocabulary

Copying Master 109

Lesson 28 Vocabulary   Distribute a set of Vocabulary Word Cards to each student or pair of students. Hold up the card for the first word, and ask a volunteer to read it aloud. Have students repeat the word and hold up the matching card. Give the explanation for the word. Then ask students the first question below and discuss their responses. Continue for each Vocabulary Word.

- **What is something you might feel a qualm about doing?**
- **What could you eat that would make you smile contentedly?**
- **What music do you find intolerable?**
- **Whom have you heard speak in an officious tone?**
- **What would a torrent of rain sound and look like?**
- **When did something happen to you that was contrary to your expectations?**
- **What is something a movie character has done to endanger another character?**
- **What is a place that you like to contemplate?**

PRETEACH

Comprehension

Skill Card 28 **Focus Skill**

Characterization   Tell students that authors do not give everything away about a character at once. Readers often must slowly piece together clues to figure out what a character is like. Have students look at side A of *Skill Card 28: Characterization* and read the information. Have a student read the passage aloud. Ask:

- **Who are the characters in the passage?** (Will, Raul, and Mr. Forster)
- **What does Mr. Forster look like?** (He is very tall and wears a long black coat.)
- **What does Will think of Mr. Forster?** (He thinks he is very strange.)
- **What does Raul say about Mr. Forster?** (Mr. Forster is a musical genius.)

Explain that by noting how characters look and act and how others relate to them, students can gain a more complete understanding of them. Then ask: **How would you describe Mr. Forster?** (Possible response: He may be unusual in appearance, but he is a man with an amazing talent.)

GUIDED PRACTICE   Ask students to work in small groups to think of one other character trait for Mr. Forster. Encourage them to think of ways this character trait could be revealed in the story. (Possible response: Mr. Forster is really nice. He reveals this when he offers to teach Raul and Will to play the piano.)

PRETEACH

Decoding/Word Attack

Decode Longer Words   Tell students that many English words end in suffixes. Common suffixes they should learn to recognize are *-ity, -ty, -ic,* and *-ive.* Then explain that root words often change their pronunciations when followed by a suffix. Have students say *relate* and *relative* and discuss the differences in their pronunciations. Point out that a different syllable is stressed in each word. Continue the process with the word pairs *offense/offensive, meter/metric,* and *similar/similarity.*

PRETEACH

Decoding/Spelling

Related Words   Explain to students that many words in English are related to other words. These words usually have the same root. Write each pair of words below on the board and read them aloud. Then ask a volunteer to explain how the spellings of each pair are related. (both have *ab* and *l;* both have *famil;* both have *offens*)

> able/ability
> family/familiar
> offense/offensive

PRETEACH

Grammar/Writing

Adverbs   Tell students that an adverb is a word that modifies a verb, an adjective, or another adverb. Adverbs tell *how, when, where, how much, how often,* and *to what extent.* Many adverbs—but not all—end with the suffix *-ly.* Then write this sentence on the board:

> Paul walked slowly to the door.

Explain that the word *slowly* is an adverb. It modifies the verb *walked.* It tells how Paul walked. Then write this sentence on the board:

> Paul knocked twice.

Have a volunteer read the sentence. Then ask: **What is the adverb?** (twice) **What verb does it modify?** (knocked) **What does it tell?** (how much)

VOCABULARY
Student-Friendly Explanations

qualm   When you have a qualm about something, you feel uneasy about whether it is right or wrong.

contentedly   When you act contentedly, you are pleased or satisfied with the way things are.

intolerable   Something intolerable is so awful that you cannot accept it.

officious   Someone who acts officious is very bossy and talks like they are in charge of everything.

torrent   A torrent is a large amount of water that falls or rushes forward violently.

contrary   Statements that are contrary go against accepted beliefs or understanding.

endanger   When you endanger something, you have put it in a situation where it could be hurt or damaged.

contemplate   When you contemplate an event, you think about the possibility of it.

Fluency

pp. 272–278   **Fluency Performance**   Invite students to read aloud the passages from "Gold Beneath the Sea" that they selected and practiced earlier. Note the number of words each student reads correctly and incorrectly. Have students rate their own oral reading on the 1–4 scale. Give students the opportunity to continue practicing and then to read the passage to you again.

LESSON 28

DAY AT A GLANCE

Day 1

VOCABULARY

Reteach *qualm, contentedly, intolerable, officious, torrent, contrary, endanger, contemplate*

COMPREHENSION

 Reteach Characterization

DECODING/SPELLING

Reteach Related Words

GRAMMAR/WRITING

Preteach Comparing with Adverbs

FLUENCY

Fluency Practice

Materials Needed: *Bold Moves*

| Student Edition pp. 280–281 | Practice Book p. 111 | Skill Card 28 | Copying Master 110 |

RETEACH

Vocabulary

pp. 280–281

Lesson 28 Vocabulary Read aloud the Vocabulary Words and the Student-Friendly Explanations. Then ask students to read the story on page 280 of their books. Have a volunteer read each question on page 281 aloud and ask students to write answers. (Answers for page 281: 2. Mr. Wu used to be in the driver's seat, not the box. 3. It sounds bossy and demanding. 4. It is a lot of yelling that is impossible to stand. 5. Responses will vary. 6. It means that she felt uneasy about the robot driving. 7. He was trying to figure out why the box was there.)

RETEACH

Comprehension

Skill Card 28

  Characterization Have students look at side B of *Skill Card 28: Characterization.* Ask them to read the information about characterization. Then have students read the passage. Ask them these questions.

- **Who are the characters in the passage?** (Sammi and Margot)
- **What does Sammi look like?** (She has long brown hair.)
- **How does Sammi act?** (She is thoughtful and nice.)

GUIDED PRACTICE Now have students copy the chart from side B of *Skill Card 28: Characterization.* Guide them in filling out the chart with character traits of Sammi and clues to the traits. (Character Trait: Sammi is very nice. Clues from the story: She wants to invite the new girl. She remembers how hard it was to be the new girl. Margot is fond of her. Character Trait: Sammi does the right thing. Clues: Her best friend says she is usually right.)

Then ask students how they think Sammi might act in these situations and why they think so:

- **She is asked to sing a song in public to raise money for charity.** (Possible response: She would do it because she seems very kind and generous.)
- **Somebody in her class asks her to help him cheat on a test.** (Possible response: She would not do it because she always does the right thing.)

RETEACH

Decoding/Spelling

Copying Master 110

Related Words Distribute *Copying Master 110*. Read the Spelling Words aloud and have students repeat them. Ask students to read the information about related words, and then have them complete the following activity. Have students work in pairs. Each student writes a sentence for each Spelling Word but leaves a blank for the actual word. The partners then switch papers and fill in the blanks in each other's sentences. Students should give themselves one point for each correctly spelled word.

PRETEACH

Grammar/Writing

Comparing with Adverbs Explain that making comparisons with adverbs is similar to making comparisons with adjectives. You can add *-er* or *-est* to some adverbs. Other adverbs need to follow the words *more* or *most*. Use either *-er* or *more* when comparing two actions or descriptions. Use either *-est* or *most* to say that one action or description has more of its quality than any other. Write this sentence on the board:

> Ellen runs (faster, fastest) than Kari does.

Ask a volunteer to read the sentence aloud. Ask students to identify the correct adverb and the word the adverb modifies. (faster, runs) Point out that because the sentence compares two things, the correct adverb is *faster*. Write this sentence on the board:

> Sam sings (more beautifully, most beautifully) of all of us.

Ask a volunteer to tell the correct adverb and the verb the adverb modifies. (most beautifully, sings) Point out that because Sam sings better than any other, *most beautifully* is correct.

GUIDED PRACTICE Write these sentences on the board:

> Matt plays soccer _____ than his teammates.
>
> My dog barks _____ than Shayna's dog.
>
> The person who dives _____ will win the medal.

Ask students to suggest adverbs that compare to complete each sentence. (Possible responses: more skillfully, louder, most gracefully)

VOCABULARY

Student-Friendly Explanations

qualm When you have a qualm about something, you feel uneasy about whether it is right or wrong.

contentedly When you act contentedly, you are pleased or satisfied with the way things are.

intolerable Something intolerable is so awful that you cannot accept it.

officious Someone who acts officious is very bossy and talks like they are in charge of everything.

torrent A torrent is a large amount of water that falls or rushes forward violently.

contrary Statements that are contrary go against accepted beliefs or understanding.

endanger When you endanger something, you have put it in a situation where it could be hurt or damaged.

contemplate When you contemplate an event, you think about the possibility of it.

Fluency

Practice Book 111

Fluency Practice Have students turn to *Practice Book* page 111. Read the words in the first column aloud. Invite students to track each word and repeat the words after you. Then have students work in pairs to read the words in the first column aloud to each other. Follow the same procedure with each of the remaining columns and then have partners practice reading aloud all of the words.

DAY AT A GLANCE
Day 2

VOCABULARY
Reteach *qualm, contentedly, intolerable, officious, torrent, contrary, endanger, contemplate*

COMPREHENSION
"Box Driver"
Build Background
Monitor Comprehension
Answers to *Think Critically* **Questions**

DECODING/SPELLING
Reteach Related Words

GRAMMAR/WRITING
Preteach Common Errors: Negatives (Avoiding Double Negatives)

FLUENCY
Fluency Practice

Materials Needed: *Bold Moves*

Student Edition pp. 282–289

Practice Book pp. 111, 112

Copying Masters 109, 110

30+ Minutes

Vocabulary

Copying Master 109

Lesson 28 Vocabulary   Distribute a Vocabulary Word Card to each student. Students can work in pairs. One student can ask yes or no questions to try to guess the other student's word. Urge students to keep track of how many questions it takes to guess the Vocabulary Word. When one partner has guessed correctly, the other partner can take a turn.

Comprehension

Build Background: "Box Driver"
Ask students how they feel about riding a school bus. List their positive and negative reactions. Then ask if there is any way the experience could be better. Could it be worse? If so, how could it be better or worse?

pp. 282–283
Monitor Comprehension: "Box Driver"
Read the title of the story aloud. Then have students read pages 282–283 to find out what a box driver is.

After reading the pages, ask: **What is a box driver?** (It is a robot that drives the bus.) **NOTE DETAILS**

Discuss the Stop and Think question on page 282: **Why do the students on the bus look terrified?** (Possible response: They look terrified because a metal box appears to be driving their school bus.) Guide students in writing the answer to this question. **MAKE INFERENCES**

Ask: **What does Alicia think about the new driver?** (She thinks it is a joke.) **CHARACTERS' EMOTIONS**

Discuss the Stop and Think question on page 283: **What do you learn about Santha? Underline the words that tell you about her.** (Santha is afraid of computers. Students should underline *scowl, qualm,* and *didn't like computers*.) Guide students in writing the answer to this question. **CHARACTERIZATION**

pp. 284–285
Have students look at the illustration on page 284. Then ask: **What question does this picture make you want to ask? How can you find the answer?** (Possible response: What are the students looking at? I can look at the text to find out what happens on the bus between Scott and the robot.) **ANSWER QUESTIONS**

Read aloud the first three paragraphs on page 284. Model how to evaluate a character's actions and learn about the character.

(THINK ALOUD)   **I can learn some things about Alicia's character from this passage. She shrugs as she gets on the bus. This shows me that she is not afraid. She makes a joke about the robot. This shows me that she has a good sense of humor and does not fear the box.** **CHARACTERIZATION**

Discuss the Stop and Think question on page 284: **What do you think will happen next?** (Possible response: I think the robot will report Scott to Principal Menendez.) Guide students in writing the answer to this question. **MAKE PREDICTIONS**

Discuss the Stop and Think question on page 285: **What can you tell about Scott?** (Possible response: I can tell that Scott is stubborn, doesn't like robots, and won't give up on his goal.) Guide students in writing the answer to this question. **CHARACTERS' TRAITS**

pp. 286–287 Ask students to read pages 286–287. Ask: **What happens when the principal talks to the robot?** (The robot orders him around, and Principal Menendez gets angry.) **SUMMARIZE**

Discuss the Stop and Think question on page 286: **Why is the robot imperfect?** (Possible response: The robot is imperfect because it is taking charge and showing emotions such as anger.) Guide students in writing the answer to this question. **DRAW CONCLUSIONS**

Discuss the Stop and Think question on page 287: **How are the students freed from the bus?** (The students are freed when Tony pulls the emergency lever and the doors open.) Guide students in writing the answer to this question. **NOTE DETAILS**

page 288 Ask: **Why do you think Mr. Menendez gets rid of the box driver?** (Possible response: Because it wasn't perfect and made him angry.) **CHARACTERS' MOTIVATIONS**

Ask: **Why do you think Mr. Menendez advises the students to tell Mr. Wu that they missed him?** (Possible response: He does this so Mr. Wu will feel appreciated and will like his job more.) **CHARACTERS' MOTIVATIONS**

Discuss the Stop and Think question on page 288: **What effect does the bus ride have on Santha?** (The bus ride causes Santha to want to learn more about computers.) Guide students in writing the answer to this question. **CAUSE AND EFFECT**

(VOCABULARY)

Student-Friendly Explanations

qualm When you have a qualm about something, you feel uneasy about whether it is right or wrong.

contentedly When you act contentedly, you are pleased or satisfied with the way things are.

intolerable Something intolerable is so awful that you cannot accept it.

officious Someone who acts officious is very bossy and talks like they are in charge of everything.

torrent A torrent is a large amount of water that falls or rushes forward violently.

contrary Statements that are contrary go against accepted beliefs or understanding.

endanger When you endanger something, you have put it in a situation where it could be hurt or damaged.

contemplate When you contemplate an event, you think about the possibility of it.

Spelling Words: Lesson 28

1. ability	11. precise
2. able	12. precision
3. decompose	13. relate
4. decomposition	14. relative
5. familiar	15. commerce
6. family	16. commercial
7. muscle	17. similar
8. muscular	18. similarity
9. meter	19. offense
10. metric	20. offensive

 **Answers to *Think Critically* Questions**   Help students read and answer the *Think Critically* questions on page 289. Then guide students in writing the answer to each question. Possible responses are provided.

1. Tony is good at solving problems. Tony knows about computers. **CHARACTERIZATION**

2. After the bus ride, the students walk to school and Mr. Menendez tells them that Mr. Wu will be back the next day. **PLOT**

3. I think the author feels that technology can sometimes be less reliable than real people. **AUTHOR'S PURPOSE**

RETEACH

Decoding/Spelling

Copying Master 110 **Related Words**   Have students work in pairs. One student in each pair can choose a Spelling Word and write it, passing the paper to the other student. Partners must then write a related word next to the first word. Then they can write a new Spelling Word and pass the paper back. Pairs can continue until all the related words have been spelled. The first pair to complete all the words and spell them correctly is the winner.

Grammar/Writing

Practice Book 112 **Common Errors: Negatives (Avoiding Double Negatives)** Point out that in English only one negative is used at a time. Explain that double negatives are incorrect and should not be used. Certain adverbs such as *scarcely*, *hardly*, and *barely* negate a statement. Tell students that they should not use another negative word with them. Write this sentence on the board:

> Sara has not finished none of her homework.

Read the sentence aloud. Underline the word *not* and explain that it is a negative word. Ask a volunteer to identify the other negative word in the sentence. (none) Then tell students that the word *any* can be used instead of *none* to correct the sentence.

GUIDED PRACTICE Have students look at page 112 in their *Practice Books* and read the directions for the activity. Then ask students to complete the sentences by choosing the correct word.

Fluency

Practice Book 111 **Fluency Practice** Invite students to look at the bottom half of *Practice Book* page 111. These sentences have been broken into natural phrases. Tell students to repeat each phrase after you, mirroring your expression, phrasing, and pace. After students have repeated each sentence, invite them to practice reading the sentences to a partner.

30+ Minutes

DAY AT A GLANCE
Day 3

COMPREHENSION
Preteach Connotation/Denotation
Reread and Summarize "Box Driver"

DECODING/SPELLING
Reteach Related Words

BUILD ROBUST VOCABULARY
Teach Words from "Box Driver"

GRAMMAR/WRITING
Reteach Writing Trait: Word Choice

FLUENCY
Fluency Practice

Materials Needed: *Bold Moves*

Student
Edition
pp. 282–288

Practice
Book
pp. 111, 113

Copying
Master
111

PRETEACH

Comprehension

Copying Master 111

Denotation/Connotation Distribute *Copying Master 111* and ask students to read the information about denotation and connotation. Have them read the passage. Then discuss the first underlined word (thrilled). Be sure students can correctly define the word, and discuss its possible connotations.

GUIDED PRACTICE Ask students to define the other words from the passage and write the words' connotations. Discuss students' choices of connotations, and ask them to explain their answers. Then have students complete the activity.

Reread and Summarize Have students reread and summarize "Box Driver" in sections, as described below.

 Let's reread pages 282–283 to recall what happens when the bus ride begins.
pp. 282–283
Summary: Students on a school bus find their driver has been replaced by a robot. They learn that the robot was chosen because students had been so loud and unruly on the bus the year before.

 Now let's reread pages 284–285 to find out how the students react to the new driver.
pp. 284–285
Summary: The students are uneasy about the robot driver. Scott wants to get off the bus. The robot gets angry and calls the principal.

 Finally, let's reread pages 286–288 to recall how the students get off the bus.
pp. 286–288
Summary: The robot refuses to let the students off the bus, so the principal comes to help. Finally, the students are freed from the bus when Tony pulls the emergency lever.

RETEACH

Decoding/Spelling

Related Words Point out to students that identifying the root words of related words can help them remember how to spell longer words that are related to shorter ones. Write the words *precise* and *precision* on the board. Explain that the word *precise* is the root word for both words. Point out that the letters *p, r, e, c, i,* and *s* are in both words. Then write the word pairs *relate/relative* and *able/ability* on the board. Ask students to identify the root word for each pair. (relate, able) Then ask which letters are in both words of each pair. (relat, abl)

TEACH

Build Robust Vocabulary

pp. 282–285 **Words from "Box Driver"** Have students locate the word *huddled* on page 282 of "Box Driver." Ask a volunteer to read aloud the sentence in which this word appears. (Last sentence: *The rest of the riders huddled in the back of the bus, peering out of the windows and looking slightly terrified.*) Explain that this sentence means that the riders sat close together. Continue by asking students to locate and read aloud the sentence in which the word *scowl* appears on page 283 (Line 9: *"Yikes!" Santha said with a scowl.*) Explain that this sentence means that Santha looked displeased or angry. Then ask students to locate and read aloud the sentence in which the word *droned* appears on page 285. (First sentence: *"Take your seat," the box droned.*) Explain that this sentence means that the voice coming from the box was low and boring.

Review the meanings and then ask students to act out each word.

RETEACH

Grammar/Writing

Practice Book 113 **Writing Trait: Word Choice** Have students turn to page 113 in their *Practice Books*. Explain that when writers write, using precise, vivid words can help to make descriptions, opinions, and reasons stronger. Have students read the directions and the first sentence in Part A. Ask a volunteer to name the vivid sensory words in the sentence. Point out that the vivid words make the description much stronger.

GUIDED PRACTICE Guide students to complete the activity in Part A. Then have them read the passage in Part B and find the vivid words. Finally, invite students to complete Part C by writing descriptions using vivid and precise words. Volunteers can read their descriptions aloud to the class.

Fluency

Practice Book 111 **Fluency Practice** Tell students that today they will reread the sentences on the bottom of *Practice Book* page 111. Have students locate and point to the first sentence. Tell students that everyone is going to read the sentence together. This choral reading will give students an opportunity to hear others and listen to the natural phrasing of the sentences. Choral-read each of the sentences several times.

DAY AT A GLANCE

Day 4

COMPREHENSION
Reteach Connotation/Denotation

DECODING/SPELLING
Reteach Related Words

BUILD ROBUST VOCABULARY
Reteach Words from "Box Driver"

GRAMMAR/WRITING
Reteach Writing Form: Persuasive Letter

FLUENCY
Fluency Practice

Materials Needed: *Bold Moves*

Student Edition pp. 282–288

Practice Book p. 114

Copying Master 112

Spelling Words: Lesson 28

1. ability	11. precise
2. able	12. precision
3. decompose	13. relate
4. decomposition	14. relative
5. familiar	15. commerce
6. family	16. commercial
7. muscle	17. similar
8. muscular	18. similarity
9. meter	19. offense
10. metric	20. offensive

RETEACH

Comprehension

Connotation/Denotation Remind students that words may have connotations, or associations of feelings, that influence their denotations, or dictionary meanings. Write this sentence from "Box Driver" on the board:

> Meanwhile, the rest of the students on the bus began to fidget uneasily.

Underline the word *fidget*. Explain that the denotation of *fidget* is "to move around or twitch." Ask students to explain the connotation of *fidget*. (It connotes anxiety or nervousness.)

GUIDED PRACTICE Write these sentences on the board:

> Some checked the windows to see if they would <u>budge</u>.
>
> "Oh my," the principal said, as the students <u>gasped</u>.

Ask volunteers to give each underlined word's denotation. (budge: to move; gasped: to breathe in quickly) Then discuss each word's connotation with students. (*Budge* connotes something stuck that requires force; *gasped* connotes shock or fear.) Lead them to see that the words' connotations help give the sentences meaning.

RETEACH

Decoding/Spelling

Practice Book 114

Related Words Have students number a sheet of paper 1–18. Write the Spelling Words *decompose* and *decomposition* on the board. Circle the letters *decompos* in each word and explain that the words are related. They share the same root and many of the same letters. Tell students that in each pair of words you will dictate, the words are related and share the same root. After students write each word, display it so they can proofread their work.

1. ability	2. able	3. familiar	4. family
5. muscle	6. muscular	7. meter	8. metric
9. precise	10. precision	11. relate	12. relative
13. commerce	14. commercial	15. similar	16. similarity
17. offense	18. offensive		

Have students turn to page 114 in their *Practice Books*. Ask them to read the story and circle all the words that are related. Then invite students to choose the word that correctly completes the first sentence. If students have trouble with the exercise, encourage them to look back at the passage for the answer. Have students complete the remaining sentences in the same way.

RETEACH

Build Robust Vocabulary

Words from "Box Driver" Review the meanings of the words *huddled, scowl,* and *droned.* Then say these sentences and ask which word describes each sentence. Have students explain why.

- **The sisters stood close together at the bus stop trying to keep warm.** (huddled)

- **I could tell from the displeased look on her face that Mia was not happy that her brother was using her colored pencil set.** (scowl)

- **Evan had trouble staying awake as he listened to the speaker talk in a low, boring voice.** (droned)

RETEACH

Grammar/Writing

Copying Master 112

Writing Form: Persuasive Letter Tell students that a persuasive letter is a letter that tries to make the reader think or act in a certain way. Explain that writers choose the words in a persuasive letter carefully by using specific, vivid words. This helps the reader understand what the writer is trying to say. Distribute *Copying Master 112,* and ask a student to read the letter aloud. Read the notes in the margin together.

GUIDED PRACTICE Have students indicate the sentence that states an opinion in the letter. Then ask them for examples of vivid words that appeal to the senses in the letter. (bend, ruffle, destroy, bleak, terrible) Work through the rest of the questions on the page.

Fluency

pp. 282–288

Fluency Practice Have each student work with a partner to read passages from "Box Driver" aloud to each other. Students may select a passage that they enjoyed or choose one of the following options:

- Read page 282. (Total: 111 words)

- Read page 284. (Total: 130 words)

Encourage students to read the selected passage aloud to their partner three times. Have the student rate his or her reading on the 1–4 scale.

1	Need more practice
2	Pretty good
3	Good
4	Great!

DAY AT A GLANCE

Day 5

VOCABULARY
Preteach *dejectedly, doldrums, linger, strenuous, abide, banished, misapprehension, imposter*

COMPREHENSION
 Preteach Characterization

DECODING/WORD ATTACK
Preteach Decode Longer Words

DECODING/SPELLING
Preteach Words with Unusual Plurals

GRAMMAR/WRITING
Preteach Direct Quotations

FLUENCY
Fluency Performance

Materials Needed: *Bold Moves*

Student Edition pp. 282–288

Skill Card 29

Copying Master 113

PRETEACH

Vocabulary

Copying Master 113

Lesson 29 Vocabulary Distribute a set of Vocabulary Word Cards to each student. Hold up the card for the first Vocabulary Word, and ask a volunteer to read it aloud. Have students repeat the word and hold up the matching card. Give the explanation for the word. Then ask students the first question below and discuss their responses. Continue for each of the Vocabulary Words.

- **Why would you act dejectedly if a friend went away for the summer?**
- **How would a person behave if he were in the doldrums?**
- **Why would you want to linger with your friends after the movie?**
- **What would be a strenuous activity? Why?**
- **Do you abide by your parent's wishes? Explain.**
- **What would cause someone to get banished from a club?**
- **Why would you have misapprehension about a new math formula?**
- **How could you tell someone is an imposter?**

PRETEACH

Comprehension

Skill Card 29

Characterization Tell students that characters' actions show what kind of people they are. What characters say, think, and feel gives readers clues to their traits. Have students look at side A of *Skill Card 29: Characterization*, and ask a volunteer to read the information. Have a volunteer read the passage aloud. Then ask:

- **How does Jeremy feel about looking at stars?** (excited and curious)
- **What actions does Jeremy take that show his interest?** (Jeremy prepares his telescope; He tries to get his friend interested in watching for Mars.)

Tell students the actions of characters should be believable and represent who they are. Guide students to examine the chart and the information from the passage. Remind students that a character's words as well as actions can serve as clues.

Decoding/Word Attack

Decode Longer Words   Write the words *vetoes, carefully, mosquitoes,* and *moderate* on the board and have a volunteer read each word aloud. Explain that a syllable you pronounce with greater stress is accented. In two-syllable words, such as *vetoes,* the first syllable is usually accented. In words with prefixes or suffixes, such as *carefully,* the stress usually falls on the root word. Then explain that in a long word, such as *mosquitoes,* the syllable with the strongest stress has the primary accent. The other stressed syllable has the secondary accent. Tell students that in homographs, such as the noun *produce* and the verb *produce,* the part of speech usually determines the stress. If the word is used as a noun or adjective, the first syllable usually gets the accent. If the word is used as a verb, the second syllable usually gets the accent.

Decoding/Spelling

Words with Unusual Plurals   Write *allergy, yourself, potato,* and *crisis* on the board. Model how to write the plural form of each word. (allergies, yourselves, potatoes, crises) Explain how you changed each of these words into its unusual plural form. Then guide students to change *battery, loaf, quiz,* and *piano* into their plural forms. (batteries, loaves, quizzes, pianos)

Grammar/Writing

Direct Quotations   Tell students a direct quotation is a person's exact words just as they are spoken. Write the following sentence on the board:

> The teacher asked, "How is
> everyone doing today?"

Explain to students that a direct quotation is set off from the rest of the sentence by quotation marks. Show students how the first word of the sentence and the first word in the direct quotation are capitalized. Then show students how the periods, question marks, and exclamation points in a direct quotation are placed inside the quotation marks.

Student-Friendly Explanations

dejectedly People act dejectedly when they are disheartened or in low spirits.

doldrums When you feel dull and lacking in energy, you are in the doldrums.

linger When you linger someplace, you are slow in leaving it.

strenuous A strenuous activity requires you to use a lot of energy and effort to complete it.

abide If you abide by a decision, you agree to it.

banished People who are banished from a place are sent away and cannot return.

misapprehension When you have a misapprehension, you have misunderstood something.

imposter A person who pretends to be someone else is an imposter.

Fluency

pp. 282–288 **Fluency Performance** Invite students to read aloud the passages from "Box Driver" that they selected and practiced earlier. Note the number of words each student reads correctly and incorrectly. Have students rate their own oral reading on the 1–4 scale. Give students the opportunity to continue practicing and then to read the passage to you again.

LESSON 29

30+ Minutes

VOCABULARY
Reteach *dejectedly, doldrums, linger, strenuous, abide, banished, misapprehension, imposter*

COMPREHENSION
 Reteach Characterization

DECODING/SPELLING
Reteach Words with Unusual Plurals

GRAMMAR/WRITING
Preteach Divided Quotations

FLUENCY
Fluency Practice

Materials Needed: *Bold Moves*

| Student Edition pp. 290–291 | Practice Book p. 115 | Skill Card 29 | Copying Master 114 |

RETEACH

Vocabulary

pp. 290–291

Lesson 29 Vocabulary   Read aloud the Vocabulary Words and the Student-Friendly Explanations. Then have students read the letters on pages 290–291 of their books. Guide students in completing the sentences with the Vocabulary Words. Have a volunteer reread the completed letters. If students are unable to give reasonable responses, refer to the Student-Friendly Explanations. (Answers for pp. 290–291: 2. *strenuous*, 3. *imposter*, 4. *misapprehension*, 5. *dejectedly*, 6. *banished*, 7. *linger*, 8. *abide*)

RETEACH

Comprehension

Skill Card 29

Characterization   Have students look at side B of *Skill Card 29: Characterization*. Remind students that characters must be believable. Have students recall that authors give clues about characters' traits through:

- interaction with other characters
- interaction with the character's environment, or setting
- internal thoughts
- past events
- dialogue

Have a volunteer read aloud the Skill Reminder. Then have another volunteer read aloud the passage.

GUIDED PRACTICE   Guide students as they copy and complete the chart with details from the passage. Allow time for students to share the character's traits and the clues they found. (Possible responses: Character Trait: feels for others; Clues: understands what a hospital stay feels like, knows his parents have to be home with the family; Character Trait: outgoing; Clues: collects toys and encourages others to do so, hands out toys to children in the hospital)

RETEACH
Decoding/Spelling

Words with Unusual Plurals Distribute *Copying Master 114.*
Ask a volunteer to read the information about writing these unusual
plurals. Then have students work in pairs. Each student writes a
sentence for each Spelling Word but leaves a blank for the actual word. The
partners then switch papers and fill in the blanks in each other's sentences.
Students should give themselves one point for each correctly spelled word.

Copying Master 114

PRETEACH
Grammar/Writing

Divided Quotations Tell students that a divided quotation is when a
speaker tag interrupts a direct quotation. Show students that when the
speaker tag interrupts the direct quotation, the speaker tag and quotation
should be set off by commas. Write the following sentences on the board:

> "We left early," said Bruce, "so we could be on time!"
>
> "Look over there," exclaimed Jed, "at those beautiful
> waterfalls!"

Point out how the beginning of the continued quotation is not capitalized
because it is not a new sentence. All other rules for direct quotations still
apply.

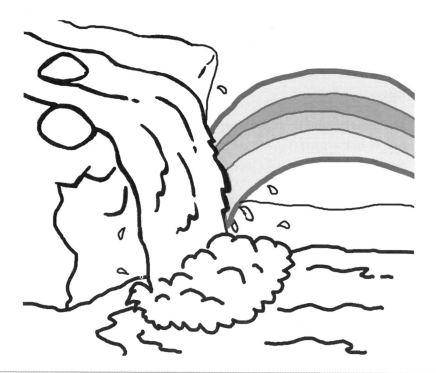

VOCABULARY
Student-Friendly Explanations

dejectedly People act dejectedly when they are disheartened or in low spirits.

doldrums When you feel dull and lacking in energy, you are in the doldrums.

linger When you linger someplace, you are slow in leaving it.

strenuous A strenuous activity requires you to use a lot of energy and effort to complete it.

abide If you abide by a decision, you agree to it.

banished People who are banished from a place are sent away and cannot return.

misapprehension When you have a misapprehension, you have misunderstood something.

imposter A person who pretends to be someone else is an imposter.

Fluency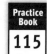

Fluency Practice Have students turn to *Practice Book* page 115. Read the words in the first column aloud. Invite students to track each word and repeat the words after you. Then have students work in pairs to read the words in the first column aloud to each other. Follow the same procedure with each of the remaining columns. After partners have practiced reading aloud the words in each of the columns, have them practice reading all of the words.

Practice Book 115

30+ Minutes

VOCABULARY
Reteach *dejectedly, doldrums, linger, strenuous, abide, banished, misapprehension, imposter*

COMPREHENSION
"In the Land of Language"
Build Background
Monitor Comprehension
Answers to *Think Critically* **Questions**

DECODING/SPELLING
Reteach Words with Unusual Plurals

GRAMMAR/WRITING
Preteach Colons

FLUENCY
Fluency Practice

Materials Needed: *Bold Moves*

Student Edition
pp. 292–299

Practice Book
pp. 115, 116

Copying Master
113

Vocabulary

Copying Master 113

Lesson 29 Vocabulary Distribute a set of Vocabulary Word Cards to each student or pair of students. Read aloud the meaning of one of the Vocabulary Words, and have students display and read the matching card. Continue until students have matched all the words.

Comprehension

Build Background: "In the Land of Language"
Ask students to share experiences they may have had with idioms. Have they ever heard that it's *raining cats and dogs*? What does it mean when someone is a *back seat driver*? Why do we use these idioms instead of just saying what we mean?

pp. 292–293

Monitor Comprehension: "In the Land of Language"
Read the title of the story aloud. Then have students read pages 292–293 to find out who the main characters are in the story and where the Land of Language is.

After reading the pages, ask: **Who are the main characters in the story?** (The main characters are Maxwell and his dog, Roger.) **Where is the Land of Language?** (It is an imaginary place at the end of a railroad line.) NOTE DETAILS

Discuss the Stop and Think question on page 292: **How can you tell that this is a fantasy?** (Possible response: I can tell this is a fantasy because the dog talks.) Guide students in writing the answer to this question. DRAW CONCLUSIONS

Ask: **How do you think people will react to a talking dog?** (Possible response: I think people will think a talking dog is funny.) PERSONAL RESPONSE

Ask: **How do you think Maxwell feels when Lady Rhyme welcomes him to her world?** (Possible response: I think Maxwell may feel like he is in a strange place.) IDENTIFY WITH CHARACTERS

Discuss the Stop and Think question on page 293: **Why is Lady Rhyme excited?** (Possible response: Lady Rhyme is excited because "Roger dog" has a lovely ring to it.) Guide students in writing the answer to this question. CHARACTERS' EMOTIONS

pp.
294–
295

Discuss the Stop and Think question on page 294: **What can you tell about Master Fact?** (Possible response: I can tell that Master Fact only talks about facts and does not like idioms.) Guide students in writing the answer to this question. **CHARACTERIZATION**

Use the details on page 295 to model the strategy of using what characters say to identify character traits.

THINK ALOUD   **When I read the page, I can see that Sir Idiom likes to play with words and that Master Fact just wants to use words for what they mean. I think Sir Idiom's character is someone who is clever and witty, while Master Fact is logical and precise.** **CHARACTERS' TRAITS**

Discuss the Stop and Think question on page 295: **Why are Sir Idiom and Master Fact arguing?** (Possible response: They are arguing because Sir Idiom likes to play with words and Master Fact only likes the words used correctly.) Guide students in writing the answer to this question. **DRAW CONCLUSIONS**

pp.
296–
297

Ask: **What character trait do both Sir Idiom and Master Fact have? Explain.** (Possible response: They are both stubborn. Neither one will try to understand the other's argument.) **CHARACTERIZATION**

Discuss the Stop and Think question on page 296: **Do you think Maxwell's advice is good? Explain your answer.** (Possible response: I think that Maxwell's advice is good because it always helps to try to understand each other when you can't agree.) Guide students in writing the answer to this question. **MAKE JUDGMENTS**

Discuss the Stop and Think question on page 297: **What do you think will happen next?** (Possible response: I think that Sir Idiom and Master Fact will come to understand each other better.) Guide students in writing the answer to this question. **MAKE PREDICTIONS**

page
298

Discuss the Stop and Think question on page 298: **What do Sir Idiom and Master Fact discover?** (Possible response: They discover that each of them can use a mix of idioms and facts.) Guide students in writing the answer to this question. **DRAW CONCLUSIONS**

Ask: **What do you suppose the author is trying to teach us in this play?** (Possible response: I think the author wants us to learn that with understanding, people can work things out.) **AUTHOR'S PURPOSE**

Ask: **When you disagree with someone, why is it important to listen to what he or she has to say?** (Possible response: It is important because I might understand why they feel a certain way.) **MAKE JUDGMENTS**

VOCABULARY
Student-Friendly Explanations

dejectedly People act dejectedly when they are disheartened or in low spirits.

doldrums When you feel dull and lacking in energy, you are in the doldrums.

linger When you linger someplace, you are slow in leaving it.

strenuous A strenuous activity requires you to use a lot of energy and effort to complete it.

abide If you abide by a decision, you agree to it.

banished People who are banished from a place are sent away and cannot return.

misapprehension When you have a misapprehension, you have misunderstood something.

imposter A person who pretends to be someone else is an imposter.

Spelling Words: Lesson 29

1.	allergies	11.	chiefs
2.	data	12.	lenses
3.	bacteria	13.	quizzes
4.	yourselves	14.	heroes
5.	potatoes	15.	oxen
6.	pianos	16.	batteries
7.	loaves	17.	mosquitoes
8.	canoes	18.	spacecraft
9.	thieves	19.	crises
10.	scarves	20.	vetoes

page 299

Answers to *Think Critically* Questions

Help students read and answer the *Think Critically* questions on page 299. Then guide students in writing the answer to each question. Possible responses are provided.

1. Maxwell and Roger help to resolve the conflict when they help the others see that both facts and idioms are important. **PLOT**

2. [Character Trait] Smart and witty; [Clues from the Story] He's a talking dog, and Lady Rhyme calls him clever. **CHARACTER**

3. I think that the author uses a dream because it makes ideas as idioms and rhymes easier to understand. **AUTHOR'S CRAFT**

RETEACH

Decoding/Spelling

Words with Unusual Plurals Have students work in pairs. Write the following word pairs on the board: *loafs/loaves, pianos/pianoes, oxes/oxen,* and *chiefs/chieves.* Have partners decide the correct spelling of the plural for each pair of words. Ask them to take turns naming the rule that helps them remember how to spell each plural.

PRETEACH

Grammar/Writing

Practice Book 116

Colons Write the following sentences on the board:

> Bring these things to class: paper, a pencil, and an eraser.
>
> When you come to class, bring paper, a pencil, and an eraser.

Tell students that in the first sentence, a colon is used after a statement to introduce a list of items. Point out that in the second sentence, the list follows the verb *bring*. When a list follows directly after a verb or proposition, a colon should not be used. Tell students a colon is also used after the greeting in a formal or business letter. Write the following greetings on the board:

> Dear Mr. President:
>
> To Mrs. Randolph Montgomery:

Have a volunteer circle the colon at the end of each greeting.

GUIDED PRACTICE Have students turn to page 116 of their *Practice Books*. Remind students that direct quotations are set off from the rest of a sentence by quotation marks. Have them recall that the first word in a quotation is capitalized and punctuation in the quotation is placed inside the quotation marks. Then remind them that when a speaker tag interrupts the direct quotation, it should be set off by commas. Guide students as they complete the activities.

Fluency

Practice Book 115

Fluency Practice Invite students to look at the bottom half of *Practice Book* page 115. These sentences have been broken into natural phrases. Tell students to repeat each phrase after you, mirroring your expression, phrasing, and pace. After students have repeated each sentence, invite them to practice reading the sentences to a partner.

LESSON 29

30+ Minutes

DAY AT A GLANCE
Day 3

COMPREHENSION
Preteach Forms of Fiction

Reread and Summarize "In the Land of Language"

DECODING/SPELLING
Reteach Words with Unusual Plurals

BUILD ROBUST VOCABULARY
Teach Words from "In the Land of Language"

GRAMMAR/WRITING
Reteach Writing Trait: Word Choice

FLUENCY
Fluency Practice

Materials Needed: *Bold Moves*

Student Edition pp. 292–298 · Practice Book pp. 115, 117 · Copying Masters 114, 115

PRETEACH

Comprehension

Copying Master 115

Forms of Fiction Distribute *Copying Master 115*. Tell students that fictional stories come in many forms, or genres. Have students brainstorm different forms of fiction, such as realistic fiction and historical fiction. Write their responses on the board. Ask students to identify characteristics of their forms of fiction. Tell students that when they read a story or play they should pay attention to the characters' actions, setting, and dialogue to help them identify the form of fiction.

GUIDED PRACTICE Have a volunteer read aloud the instruction on *Copying Master 115*. Then have volunteers share reading the passage. Guide students in following the directions below the passage.

Reread and Summarize Have students reread and summarize "In the Land of Language" in sections, as described below.

 pp. 292–293 **Let's reread pages 292–293 to recall who the main characters are, what the setting is, and where the characters end up.**
Summary: Maxwell and Roger are the main characters who end up in a strange place by train, but find out they are in the Land of Language.

 pp. 294–295 **Now let's reread pages 294–295 to remember what happens as they meet Sir Idiom and Master Fact.**
Summary: When they meet Sir Idiom and Master Fact, they find out Sir Idiom speaks with creative expressions and Master Fact doesn't understand why Sir Idiom can't use the words correctly.

 pp. 296–298 **Last, let's reread pages 296–298 to find out what Sir Idiom and Master Fact learn about the use of language.**
Summary: With the help of Maxwell, Roger, and Lady Rhyme, Sir Idiom and Master Fact learn that language would be dull and lack information without using idioms and facts.

RETEACH

Decoding/Spelling

Copying Master 114

Words with Unusual Plurals Have students review the spelling pattern rules on *Copying Master 114*. Write the singular form of the Spelling Words on the board. Have volunteers write the plural forms. Then ask them to identify the rules they followed to write each plural. Challenge students to identify the words that do not fit the rules. (chiefs, pianos, crises)

TEACH

Build Robust Vocabulary

pp. 293–296

Words from "In the Land of Language" Have students locate the word *fantastic* on page 293 in their books. Ask a volunteer to read aloud the speaking part in which this word appears. (Line 12: *Roger dog! Roger dog! Fantastic! It has a lovely ring to it.*) Explain that "fantastic" means very good, very creative, and excellent. Continue by asking students to locate and read aloud the sentence in which the word *canine* appears on page 294. (Line 12: *Oh, and you're a clever canine, too!*) Explain that "canine" is another word for dog. Then ask students to locate and read aloud the sentence in which the word *conclusion* appears on page 296. (Line 6: *This argument never reaches a conclusion.*) Explain that this sentence means that there was not an end to the argument. There was no decision about which side was right.

Divide the students into three groups. Write the words on slips of paper, and give each group one word. One member in each group should tell the meaning of the word, and each of the remaining group members should say the word in a sentence.

RETEACH

Grammar/Writing

Practice Book 117

Writing Trait: Word Choice   Write the following on the board:

> **Vivid words and phrases:** strong, energetic, appeal to emotions
>
> **Precise words and phrases:** exact meaning, state writer's views
>
> **Sensory words:** how things look, sound, feel, taste, smell

Tell students that authors use these types of word choices to help readers understand, and be persuaded by, the writer's thoughts and ideas. Have students turn to page 117 of their *Practice Books*. Ask a volunteer to read aloud the information about word choice. Discuss the three categories with students and review the examples. Have students give other examples of each type.

GUIDED PRACTICE   Guide students in completing the activities on page 117 of their *Practice Books*. When writing for Part C, students should present their story in the order of importance.

Fluency

Practice Book 115

Fluency Practice   Tell students that today they will reread the sentences on the bottom of *Practice Book* page 115. Have students locate and point to the first sentence. Tell students that everyone is going to read the sentence together. This choral reading will give students an opportunity to hear others and listen to the natural phrasing of the sentences. Choral-read each of the sentences several times.

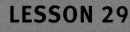

LESSON 29

30+ Minutes

COMPREHENSION
Reteach   Forms of Fiction

DECODING/SPELLING
Reteach   Words with Unusual Plurals

BUILD ROBUST VOCABULARY
Reteach   Words from "In the Land of Language"

GRAMMAR/WRITING
Reteach   Writing Form: Persuasive Composition

FLUENCY
Fluency Practice

Materials Needed: *Bold Moves*

Student Edition pp. 292–298	Practice Book p. 118	Copying Master 116

Spelling Words: Lesson 29

1. allergies	11. chiefs
2. data	12. lenses
3. bacteria	13. quizzes
4. yourselves	14. heroes
5. potatoes	15. oxen
6. pianos	16. batteries
7. loaves	17. mosquitoes
8. canoes	18. spacecraft
9. thieves	19. crises
10. scarves	20. vetoes

Comprehension

Forms of Fiction   Remind students there are many forms of fictional stories. The author makes up the story using one form or a combination of forms. Draw a three-column, three-row chart on the board with the column titles: *Genre, Characteristics,* and *Examples*. Ask students to recall the play "In the Land of Language." Ask them to identify the characteristics of the play and to identify the genre. (unrealistic events, fantasy) Write their response in the chart. Remind students that when reading a story, they should pay attention to the setting, the characters' actions, the dialogue, and the plot to help them identify the form of fiction.

GUIDED PRACTICE   Have students recall other forms of fiction. Add their ideas to the chart. Have them give examples of stories they have read that represent each of those forms.

Decoding/Spelling

 Words with Unusual Plurals   Have students number a piece of paper from 1–16. Write *loaves* on the board and underline the *-ves*. Tell students the first three words you will dictate have a similar plural spelling. After students write each word, display it so they can proofread their work. Repeat this activity using these examples: *allergies,* (one word), *potatoes* (four words), *and chiefs* (two words). Then tell students that the last six words you will dictate have their own special plural forms.

1. yourselves	2. thieves	3. scarves	4. batteries
5. lenses	6. heroes	7. vetoes	8. mosquitoes
9. canoes	10. pianos	11. oxen	12. quizzes
13. crises	14. data	15. bacteria	16. spacecraft

Have students turn to page 118 in their *Practice Books*. Guide students in matching the correct sentence with the picture.

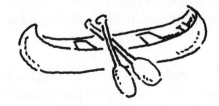

RETEACH
Build Robust Vocabulary

Words from "In the Land of Language"   Review the meanings of the words *fantastic, canine,* and *conclusion*. Then say these sentences and ask which word describes each sentence. Have students explain why.

- **Tom's project won first prize at the science fair because it was so creative and so good.** (fantastic)
- **We signed Ruffy up to go to dog school because we want her to learn how to behave.** (canine)
- **Our family is trying to come to a decision about where to go for summer vacation.** (conclusion)

RETEACH
Grammar/Writing

Copying Master 116

Writing Form: Persuasive Composition   Tell students that in addition to using sensory, vivid, and precise words and phrases, writers put their ideas in order of importance. They do this to help persuade the reader of their position. Some try to catch the reader's attention by stating the most important reason first, while others build up to the most important reason, placing it at the end.

GUIDED PRACTICE   Distribute *Copying Master 116* and have a volunteer read the instruction. Then have a student read aloud the Student Model. Discuss the margin notes and how each strengthens a persuasive composition. Have students complete the activities following the Student Model.

Fluency

pp. 292–298

Fluency Practice   Have each student work with a partner to read passages from "In the Land of Language" aloud to each other. Students may select a passage that they enjoyed or choose one of the following options:

- Read page 294. (Total: 122 words)
- Read page 296. (Total: 106 words)

Encourage students to read the selected passage aloud to their partner three times. Have the student rate his or her reading on the 1–4 scale.

1	Need more practice
2	Pretty good
3	Good
4	Great!

DAY AT A GLANCE

Day 5

VOCABULARY
Preteach *entrust, critical, understatement, emanates, erratic, elusive, unprecedented, cacophony, implode, acute*

COMPREHENSION
 Reteach Draw and Evaluate Conclusions

DECODING/WORD ATTACK
Reteach Decode Longer Words

DECODING/SPELLING
Reteach Words with Prefix + Root + Suffix, Root + Root

GRAMMAR/WRITING
Reteach Progressive Forms, Contractions

FLUENCY
Fluency Performance

Materials Needed: *Bold Moves*

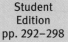

| Student Edition pp. 292–298 | Skill Card 30 | Copying Master 117 |

Vocabulary

Lesson 30 Vocabulary   Distribute a set of Vocabulary Word Cards to each student. Hold up the card for the first word, and ask a volunteer to read it aloud. Have students repeat the word and hold up the matching card. Give the explanation for the word. Then ask students the first question below and discuss their responses. Continue for each of the Vocabulary Words.

Copying Master 117

- **Whom would you entrust with an important secret?**
- **What skill do you think is most critical when performing a play?**
- **Why might someone use understatement when complimenting a friend?**
- **What smell emanates from the kitchen on Thanksgiving?**
- **What is something an erratic driver might do?**
- **What animal might be considered elusive?**
- **What is something you have done that was unprecedented in your family?**
- **What does a cacophony sound like?**
- **What would happen if a building were to implode?**
- **What would you do if you felt acute pain?**

Comprehension

Skill Card 30

 Draw and Evaluate Conclusions   Have students look at side A of *Skill Card 30: Review: Draw and Evaluate Conclusions*. Ask a volunteer to restate how to draw and evaluate a conclusion. Have students read the passage. Then ask:

- **What facts are known about giant squids now?** (Possible response: They can grow to 100 feet long; they are eaten by sperm whales.)
- **How do scientists know these facts about giant squids?** (Possible response: Remains of giant squids have been found in the stomachs of sperm whales.)

GUIDED PRACTICE   Ask students to copy the chart onto a separate sheet of paper. Then ask students to suggest a conclusion that can be drawn. Lead students to see that the facts about giant squids support the conclusion. (Conclusion: The giant squid does exist; Evidence: People have reported seeing giant squids for centuries; Giant squid remains have been found in the stomachs of sperm whales.)

Decoding/Word Attack

Decode Longer Words   Write *reusable* on the board. Remind students that a prefix is a word that begins a word, a root or a root word is the main part of a word, and a suffix is the word part at the end of the word. Explain that some long English words are made by combining some or all of these parts. Ask students to find the prefix, root, and suffix in *reusable*. (re/us/able) Explain that finding these words parts can help them read a word. Then write *biography* on the board. Remind students that sometimes a long word uses two Greek or Latin roots. Have them identify the roots in *biography*. (bio, graphy)

Decoding/Spelling

Words with Prefix + Root + Suffix, Root + Root   Write *postponement* on the board. Have a volunteer draw a line between the prefix and root and between the root and suffix. (post/pone/ment) Remind students that some words are formed with a prefix + root + suffix. Repeat with *uncertainly* and *unexpectedly*. (un/certain/ly, un/expected/ly) Write *microscope* on the board. Have students recall that some words are formed using two Greek or Latin roots. Have a volunteer draw a line between the roots. (micro/scope)

Grammar/Writing

Progressive Forms and Contractions   Remind students that progressive forms of verbs express action that is continuous or ongoing. Then have them recall that a contraction is a word made by combining two words and omitting some letters. An apostrophe replaces the omitted letters. Write these sentences on the board:

> The dog was barking wildly.
>
> I'll be having a party next week.

Ask volunteers to circle the contraction and write the words that it is made from. (I'll, I will) Then have them underline the progressive verb form in each sentence. (was barking, (wi)ll be having)

Student-Friendly Explanations

entrust When you entrust someone with something, you give him or her the responsibility to care for it.

critical When something is critical, it is extremely important and essential.

understatement When you make an understatement, you say something that does not fully express the extent to which something is true.

emanates When a sound emanates from an object, it comes from that object.

erratic Something that is erratic acts in an unpredictable way.

elusive When something is hard to understand, find, or achieve, it is elusive.

unprecedented When something occurs that has never happened before, it is unprecedented.

cacophony A cacophony is a collection of harsh sounds that all happen at once.

implode When something collapses in on itself, it implodes.

acute When something, like a problem, is acute, it is intense and severe.

Fluency

Fluency Performance
pp. 292–298
Invite students to read aloud the passages from "In the Land of Language" that they selected and practiced earlier. Note the number of words each student reads correctly and incorrectly. Have students rate their own oral reading on the 1–4 scale. Allow students to read the passage to you again.

LESSON 30

VOCABULARY
Reteach *entrust, critical, understatement, emanates, erratic, elusive, unprecedented, cacophony, implode, acute*

COMPREHENSION
 Reteach Characterization

DECODING/WORD ATTACK
Reteach Decode Longer Words

DECODING/SPELLING
Reteach Words with Silent Letters

GRAMMAR/WRITING
Reteach Progressive Forms, Contractions

FLUENCY
Fluency Practice

Materials Needed: *Bold Moves*

| Student Edition pp. 300–301 | Practice Book pp. 119, 120 | Skill Card 30 | Copying Master 118 |

RETEACH

Vocabulary

 pp. 300–301

Lesson 30 Vocabulary Read aloud the Vocabulary Words and the Student-Friendly Explanations. Then ask students to turn to pages 300–301 in their books. Have them read the directions, and remind them that they should read each sentence to themselves with the word they have chosen to be sure it makes sense. If students have difficulty choosing the correct word to complete the sentence, refer to the Student-Friendly Explanations. Invite students to share their answers to the questions. (Answers for pages 300–301: 2. *entrust*, 3. *unprecedented*, 4. *critical*, 5. *implode*, 6. *understatement*, 7. *elusive*, 8. *emanates*, 9. *erratic*, 10. *acute*, She dives alone and walks on the sea floor. 12. The Jim Suit is critical to Dr. Earle.)

RETEACH

Comprehension

 Skill Card 30

Characterization Have students look at side B of *Skill Card 30: Review: Characterization*. Ask students to read the Skill Reminder. Then have a volunteer read the passage aloud. Remind students to look at the things the characters say and do in order to make inferences about the characters' traits.

GUIDED PRACTICE Guide students as they copy the chart and complete it with information from the passage. Ask them to point out the clues that help them determine each trait. (Trait: fearful: Elena shivers and speaks shakily; it's her first dive; Trait: determined: Says she is ready, says she promised herself; Trait: stubborn: Says she will dive when Jim says she doesn't have to.)

RETEACH

Decoding/Word Attack

Decode Longer Words Write *glistened* on the board. Divide the word into syllables. (glis/tened) Point out that the letter *t* is silent in the second syllable. Repeat with *shepherd* and *wrestle*. Say each word aloud and have students repeat after you. Then ask students to identify the silent letters. (h, w, e) Tell students that many English words have silent letters. Explain that the spelling of words with silent letters must be memorized.

RETEACH

Decoding/Spelling

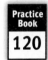 **Words with Silent Letters** Distribute *Copying Master 118*. Remind students that some words in English contain silent letters. For example, the letter *w* is often silent when it begins a word and is followed immediately by the letter *r*. Have students read the Spelling Words aloud. Then ask students to identify the words with silent letters. (reign, rhythm, wrinkled, plumber, muscle, softened)

RETEACH

Grammar/Writing

Practice Book 120 **Progressive Forms and Contractions** Review progressive forms and forming contractions. Then write this sentence on the board:

> Ill be take the train.

Guide students as they proofread the sentence for errors. Invite a volunteer to write the sentence correctly on the board. (I'll be taking the train.)

GUIDED PRACTICE Have students turn to page 120 in their *Practice Books*. Ask a volunteer to read the activity directions aloud. Then have students work individually to proofread each sentence and make corrections. Volunteers can share their responses.

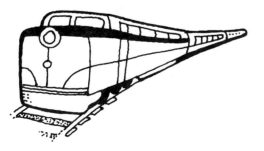

VOCABULARY

Student-Friendly Explanations

entrust When you entrust someone with something, you give him or her the responsibility to care for it.

critical When something is critical, it is extremely important and essential.

understatement When you make an understatement, you say something that does not fully express the extent to which something is true.

emanates When a sound emanates from an object, it comes from that object.

erratic Something that is erratic acts in an unpredictable way.

elusive When something is hard to understand, find, or achieve, it is elusive.

unprecedented When something occurs that has never happened before, it is unprecedented.

cacophony A cacophony is a collection of harsh sounds that all happen at once.

implode When something collapses in on itself, it implodes.

acute When something, like a problem, is acute, it is intense and severe.

Fluency

Practice Book 119 **Fluency Practice** Have students turn to *Practice Book* page 119. Read the words in the first column aloud. Invite students to track each word and repeat the words after you. Then have students work in pairs to read the words in the first column aloud to each other. Follow the same procedure with each of the remaining columns. Then have them practice reading all of the words.

VOCABULARY

Reteach *entrust, critical, understatement, emanates, erratic, elusive, unprecedented, cacophony, implode, acute*

COMPREHENSION
"A Daring Dive"
Build Background
Monitor Comprehension
Answers to *Think Critically* Questions

DECODING/WORD ATTACK
Reteach Decode Longer Words

DECODING/SPELLING
Reteach Related Words

GRAMMAR/WRITING
Reteach Adverbs, Quotation Marks, and Colons

FLUENCY
Fluency Practice

Materials Needed: *Bold Moves*

Student Edition
pp. 302–309

Practice Book
p. 119

Copying Masters
117, 118

Vocabulary

Copying Master 117

Lesson 30 Vocabulary   Distribute a set of Vocabulary Word Cards to each student. Read aloud the Student-Friendly Explanation for one of the words, leaving out the word. Have students display and read the matching Word Card. Continue until students have matched all the words.

Comprehension

Build Background: "A Daring Dive"
Ask students if any of them have ever gone snorkeling or seen a show about snorkeling or scuba diving. Have them share their impressions. What amazing things can people see in the ocean? What dangers do they face?

pp. 302–303

Monitor Comprehension: "A Daring Dive"
Read the title of the selection aloud. Then have students read pages 302–303 to find out what the Jim Suit is and why it is used.

After reading the pages, ask: **What is the Jim Suit? Why is it used?** (Possible response: It is a deep-sea diving suit. It is used by divers to get to greater depths.) **SUMMARIZE**

Discuss the Stop and Think question on page 302: **Why do you think the diving suit is named the "Jim Suit"?** (Possible response: I think that it's named the "Jim Suit" because it was originally used by a man named Jim Jarrett.) **Guide students in writing the answer to this question.** **DRAW AND EVALUATE CONCLUSIONS**

Discuss the Stop and Think question on page 303: **What can you tell about Dr. Earle? How can you tell?** (Possible response: I can tell that Dr. Earle is brave and confident because she says driving on the freeway is more dangerous than a deep-sea dive.) **Guide students in writing the answer to this question.** **CHARACTERIZATION**

Ask: **What would the effect be if the air pressure inside the suit changed?** (Possible response: The suit could implode.) **CAUSE AND EFFECT**

pp. 304–305

Discuss the Stop and Think question on page 304: **How does Dr. Earle feel?** (Possible response: She feels like a walking refrigerator.) **Guide students in writing the answer to this question.** **CHARACTERS' EMOTIONS**

Discuss the Stop and Think question on page 305: **What causes the coral to blink?** (The coral blinks because Dr. Earle is brushing against it, and the coral gives off light when predators come too close.) Guide students in writing the answer to this question. **CAUSE AND EFFECT**

Model for students how to draw and evaluate conclusions. Point out Dr. Earle's and Al Giddings's words at the bottom of page 305.

(THINK ALOUD) **As I read these words about the crab, I think about what they tell me and what I already know. Dr. Earle and Al Giddings say the crab has never seen a human before. I know the Jim Suit is a new invention. I can conclude that few people have ever gone so deep in the sea before. DRAW AND EVALUATE CONCLUSIONS**

Ask students to read pages 306–307 to find out more about Dr. Earle's dive. Ask: **To what does Dr. Earle compare the lantern fish?** (She compares them to ocean liners with lighted windows.) **FIGURATIVE LANGUAGE**

Discuss the Stop and Think question on page 306: **How might walking on the ocean floor feel like walking on the moon?** (Possible response: Walking on the ocean floor might feel as if there is very little gravity because water is all around you.) Guide students in writing the answer to this question. **MAKE INFERENCES**

Ask: **Would you, like Dr. Earle, want to explore even deeper into the sea? Why or why not?** (Possible response: Yes, because I'd want to see places and things no one had ever seen before.) **IDENTIFY WITH CHARACTERS**

Discuss the Stop and Think question on page 307: **Do you think Dr. Earle will continue to make deep-sea dives? How can you tell?** (Possible response: I think Dr. Earle will continue to make deep-sea dives because she wants to find a way to go even deeper into the sea.) Guide students in writing the answer to this question. **MAKE PREDICTIONS**

Discuss the Stop and Think question on page 308: **Do you think "Her Deepness" is a good nickname for Dr. Earle? Why or why not?** (Possible response: I think "Her Deepness" is a good nickname because she dived to great depths and walked on the sea floor alone.) Guide students in writing the answer to this question. **MAKE JUDGMENTS**

Ask: **What does Dr. Earle's determination to go further into the deep tell you about her character?** (Possible response: She is courageous and determined.) **CHARACTERIZATION**

VOCABULARY

Student-Friendly Explanations

entrust When you entrust someone with something, you give him or her the responsibility to care for it.

critical When something is critical, it is extremely important and essential.

understatement When you make an understatement, you say something that does not fully express the extent to which something is true.

emanates When a sound emanates from an object, it comes from that object.

erratic Something that is erratic acts in an unpredictable way.

elusive When something is hard to understand, find, or achieve, it is elusive.

unprecedented When something occurs that has never happened before, it is unprecedented.

cacophony A cacophony is a collection of harsh sounds that all happen at once.

implode When something collapses in on itself, it implodes.

acute When something, like a problem, is acute, it is intense and severe.

Spelling Words: Lesson 30

1. postponement
2. uncertainly
3. unexpectedly
4. microscope
5. aquatic
6. rhythm
7. plumber
8. reign
9. softened
10. wrinkled
11. muscle
12. muscular
13. precise
14. precision
15. offense
16. offensive
17. pianos
18. canoes
19. chiefs
20. oxen

page 309

Answers to *Think Critically* Questions

Help students read and answer the *Think Critically* questions on page 309. Then guide students in writing the answer to each question. Possible responses are provided.

1. Dr. Earle dove to the sea floor because she wanted to test out the Jim Suit and she also wanted to walk on the ocean floor alone. **MAIN IDEA AND DETAILS**

2. This selection makes me feel excited about exploring the ocean. **AUTHOR'S PURPOSE**

3. I think the sea floor should be explored because there could be new animals down there that no one has discovered yet. **MAKE JUDGMENTS**

RETEACH

Decoding/Word Attack

Decode Longer Words Write *similarity, metric, royalty,* and *offensive* on the board. Ask students to find the suffix in each word. (-ity, -ic, -ty, -ive) Tell students that a root before the suffix *-ity, -ic,* or *-ive* is often pronounced differently than when it stands alone. Say *meter* and *metric* to demonstrate this. Usually, the syllable before the suffix is stressed. This is not true when the suffix is *-ty,* however.

Decoding/Spelling

Copying Master 118

Related Words Remind students that many words in English are related, usually because they have the same root. Have students review *Copying Master 118* to identify the related Spelling Words. (muscle/muscular, precise/precision, offense/offensive) Point out that the root may not be spelled exactly the same way in the related words. Often, when a suffix is added, a root that ends in *e* drops that letter before the suffix. Other roots change in different ways.

Grammar/Writing

Adverbs, Quotation Marks, and Colons Remind students that adverbs modify verbs and tell *how, where, when, how often,* and *to what extent*. Then remind students of the rules for using quotation marks and colons.

Write these sentences on the board:

> The crowd clapped wildly.
>
> The band had these instruments: a violin, a flute, and a guitar.
>
> "I play the piano," said June.

Point out the adverb *wildly*. Ask students what word it modifies and what it tells. (clapped; how) Then have students explain why a colon is used in the second sentence. (It comes before a list.) Then ask why quotation marks are used in the third sentence. (They set off the speaker's words.)

Fluency

Practice Book 119

Fluency Practice Invite students to look at the bottom half of *Practice Book* page 119. These sentences have been broken into natural phrases. Tell students to repeat each phrase after you, mirroring your expression, phrasing, and pace. After students have repeated each sentence, invite them to practice reading the sentences to a partner.

30+ Minutes

COMPREHENSION
Reteach Fact and Opinion

Reread and Summarize
"A Daring Dive"

DECODING/WORD ATTACK
Reteach Decode Longer Words

DECODING/SPELLING
Reteach Unusual Plurals

BUILD ROBUST VOCABULARY
Teach Words from "A Daring Dive"

GRAMMAR/WRITING
Reteach Adverbs, Quotation Marks, and Colons

FLUENCY
Fluency Practice

Materials Needed: *Bold Moves*

| Student Edition pp. 302–308 | Practice Book pp. 119, 121 | Copying Masters 118, 119 |

RETEACH

Comprehension

Copying Master 119

Fact and Opinion Have students recall that nonfiction can include both facts and opinions. Distribute *Copying Master 119,* and have a volunteer read aloud the information at the top of the page. Remind students to consider whether a statement can be verified, or proven true, when they are thinking about facts and opinions.

GUIDED PRACTICE Have students complete the page individually. Invite volunteers to state the facts and opinions they found in the passage.

Reread and Summarize

Have students reread and summarize "A Daring Dive" in sections, as described below.

pp. 302–303

Let's reread pages 302–303 to recall how Dr. Earle begins her dive.
Summary: Dr. Earle puts on the Jim Suit that will allow her to dive far beneath the sea. Tethered to a ship, she begins her descent.

pp. 304–306

Now let's read pages 304–306 to find out what Dr. Earle sees below the sea.
Summary: Dr. Earle sees the plants and animals of a coral reef. She walks on the sea floor and sees bioluminescent coral, lantern fish, and crabs.

pp. 307–308

Last, let's read pages 307–308 to recall what happened at the end of Dr. Earle's sea exploration.
Summary: After a two-hour dive, Dr. Earle ascends to the surface. She is determined to find a way to go deeper still. With Graham Hawkes, she develops the Deep Rover, a deep-sea submersible.

RETEACH

Decoding/Word Attack

Decode Longer Words Remind students that in words with more than one syllable, one of the syllables is usually pronounced with more stress. It is called an accented syllable. Remind students that the first syllable is usually accented in two-syllable words. The root word is usually accented in words with prefixes or suffixes. Also have students recall that some words have a primary and secondary accent. The primary accent is pronounced with greater stress than the secondary.

RETEACH

Decoding/Spelling

Copying Master 118

Unusual Plurals Remind students that some English words have unusual plurals that must be memorized. Have students review *Copying Master 118* and identify the Spelling Words that are unusual plurals. (pianos, canoes, chiefs, oxen) Then ask students to complete this activity. Have students work in pairs. Each student writes a sentence for each Spelling Word but leaves a blank for the actual word. The partners then switch papers and fill in the blanks in each other's sentences. Students should give themselves one point for each correctly spelled word.

TEACH

Build Robust Vocabulary

pp. 303–305

Words from "A Daring Dive" Have students locate the word *tethered* on page 303 of "A Daring Dive." Ask a volunteer to read aloud the sentence in which this word appears. (Line 12: *Dr. Earle will be tethered by strap to a small submarine.*) Explain that this means that Dr. Earle will be tied to the submarine so she can't float away. Then ask students to locate and read aloud the sentence in which the word *lumbering* appears on page 305. (Line 17: *I doubt it's seen a strange jointed creature like me lumbering around on the sea floor before!*) Explain that *lumbering* means moving in a heavy, ungraceful way.

Give each student a card with the letters of one of the words scrambled on it. Have students unscramble their words and prepare a sentence that includes the word. Have students take turns sharing their sentences with the group.

RETEACH

Grammar/Writing

Practice Book 121

Adverbs, Quotation Marks, and Colons Review adverbs and the use of colons with students. Then write this sentence on the board:

> She quick counted the fish tuna, groupers, and eels.

Ask a volunteer to read the sentence aloud and circle the errors. (quick, space after fish) Invite another volunteer to make corrections to the sentence. (She quickly counted the fish: tuna, groupers, and eels.)

GUIDED PRACTICE Have students turn to *Practice Book* page 121. Have a student read the directions aloud. Have students work in pairs to complete the activity. Allow time for pairs to share their responses.

Fluency

Practice Book 119

Fluency Practice Tell students that today they will reread the sentences on the bottom of *Practice Book* page 119. Have students locate and point to the first sentence. Tell students that everyone is going to read the sentence together. This choral reading will give students an opportunity to hear others and listen to the natural phrasing of the sentences. Choral-read each of the sentences several times.

LESSON 30

COMPREHENSION
Reteach Connotation/Denotation

DECODING/SPELLING
Cumulative Review

BUILD ROBUST VOCABULARY
Reteach Words from "A Daring Dive"

GRAMMAR/WRITING
Cumulative Review

FLUENCY
Fluency Practice

Materials Needed: *Bold Moves*

Student
Edition
pp. 302–308

Practice
Book
p. 122

Copying
Master
120

Spelling Words: Lesson 30

1. postponement		11. muscle	
2. uncertainly		12. muscular	
3. unexpectedly		13. precise	
4. microscope		14. precision	
5. aquatic		15. offense	
6. rhythm		16. offensive	
7. plumber		17. pianos	
8. reign		18. canoes	
9. softened		19. chiefs	
10. wrinkled		20. oxen	

RETEACH
Comprehension

Connotation/Denotation   Remind students that a denotation is an exact dictionary definition. A connotation is the feeling a word gives the reader—its shade of meaning. Write this sentence from "A Daring Dive" on the board:

> I doubt it's seen a <u>strange</u> jointed <u>creature</u> like me <u>lumbering</u> around on the sea floor before!

Ask a volunteer to read the sentence aloud. Then have a student offer a definition of the word *strange*. (Possible response: unusual) Point out that the connotation of *strange* includes the idea of being different or foreign. Lead students to see that the speaker is saying that humans have never been seen by the deep sea animals before. Repeat the activity with the words *creature* and *lumbering*. (Possible responses: Denotations: creature—living being; lumbering—moving; Connotations: creature—scary, strange; lumbering—heavy, clumsy)

RETEACH
Decoding/Spelling

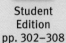 **Cumulative Review**   Have students number a sheet of paper 1–16. Write *uncertainly* on the board. Tell students that the first three words you will dictate can be divided into prefixes, suffixes, or roots. After students write each word, display it so they can proofread their work. Repeat this activity using the word *softened* for words with silent letters, *precision* for related words, and *pianos* for unusual plurals.

1. postponement	2. unexpectedly	3. microscope	4. microscope
5. rhythm	6. plumber	7. reign	8. wrinkled
9. precise	10. muscle	11. muscular	12. offense
13. offensive	14. canoes	15. chiefs	16. oxen

Have students turn to page 122 in their *Practice Books*. When students have completed the page, invite them to identify the Spelling Words in the sentences.

RETEACH

Build Robust Vocabulary

Words from "A Daring Dive"   Review the meanings of the words *tethered* and *lumbering*. Then say these sentences and ask which word describes each sentence. Have students explain why.

- **We tied Ruff to a tree with his leash so he wouldn't run into the street.**
  (tethered)

- **The big brown bear walked heavily and clumsily through the forest.**
  (lumbered)

RETEACH

Grammar/Writing

Copying Master 120

Cumulative Review   Have students recall the grammar skills they learned in this lesson. Discuss examples for each skill:

- progressive verb forms

- contractions

- adverbs

- quotation marks

- colons

GUIDED PRACTICE   Distribute *Copying Master 120* to each student. Invite a student to read the directions. Then have students proofread each sentence to find the errors. Next, they should write the sentence correctly. Allow time for students to share their corrected sentences with the group.

Fluency

pp. 302–308   **Fluency Practice**   Have each student work with a partner to read passages from "A Daring Dive" aloud to each other. Remind students to:

- use their voice to express emotions.

- emphasize important words and phrases.

Encourage students to read the selected passage aloud to their partner three times. Have the student rate his or her reading on the 1–4 scale.

1	Need more practice
2	Pretty good
3	Good
4	Great!

30+ Minutes

VOCABULARY

Reteach *entrust, critical, understatement, emanates, erratic, elusive, unprecedented, cacophony, implode, acute*

COMPREHENSION

 Reteach Draw and Evaluate Conclusions, Characterization

DECODING/ SPELLING

Cumulative Review

GRAMMAR/WRITING

Cumulative Review

FLUENCY

Fluency Performance

Materials Needed: *Bold Moves*

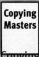

Student Edition
pp. 302–308

Copying Masters

Copying Masters
117, 118

RETEACH

Vocabulary

Copying Master 117

Lesson 30 Vocabulary   Have students work in pairs, and distribute a set of Vocabulary Word Cards to each pair. Have partners take turns selecting a card from the pile and acting out the word for the other partner to guess. If students have trouble acting out a word using phrases and gestures, guide them with performance ideas.

RETEACH

Comprehension

pp. 302–308

 Focus Skill

Draw and Evaluate Conclusions, Characterization
Review with students that they can use a character's actions, words, and what others say about them to determine what a character is like. Point out that readers can draw a conclusion about a character's traits, and then evaluate this conclusion based on evidence in a passage. Reread "A Daring Dive" with students. Discuss what each character in the play is like.

GUIDED PRACTICE   Have students work in small groups. Assign each group a character from the play: Graham Hawkes, Al Giddings, Phil Newton, or Dr. Sylvia Earle. Ask each group to draw conclusions about the character's traits, based on his or her words, actions, and interactions with the other characters. Remind students to record evidence for each trait. Invite groups to share their conclusions with the class.

Decoding/Spelling

Copying Master 118

Cumulative Review Review with students the rules that apply to this lesson's Spelling Words. Then have students work in small groups. Ask groups to write each Spelling Word on an index card, and then cut the word into syllables. Tell them to mix up the cards and then work together to join the word parts to form words.

Grammar/Writing

Cumulative Review Review with students what they have learned about the progressive forms of verbs, contractions, adverbs, quotation marks, and the use of colons. Then, make grammar cards by writing each of these phrases or words individually on index cards: *progressive form, contraction, adverb, quotation marks,* and *colon.* Have the group form two teams. Shuffle the grammar cards and hand a card to each team. Students work together to write an example sentence for the grammar word or phrase on their card. For example, if a team had the card *colon*, they might write *I have three things in my pocket: a coin, a key, and a marble.* If a team shows the correct example and writes the sentence correctly, they get a point. Continue until all of the grammar cards have been used.

VOCABULARY

Student-Friendly Explanations

entrust When you entrust someone with something, you give him or her the responsibility to care for it.

critical When something is critical, it is extremely important and essential.

understatement When you make an understatement, you say something that does not fully express the extent to which something is true.

emanates When a sound emanates from an object, it comes from that object.

erratic Something that is erratic acts in an unpredictable way.

elusive When something is hard to understand, find, or achieve, it is elusive.

unprecedented When something occurs that has never happened before, it is unprecedented.

cacophony A cacophony is a collection of harsh sounds that all happen at once.

implode When something collapses in on itself, it implodes.

acute When something, like a problem, is acute, it is intense and severe.

Fluency

pp. 302–308

Fluency Performance Invite partners to read aloud the passages from "A Daring Dive" that they selected and practiced earlier. Give partners the opportunity to continue practicing and then to read the passage to you again.